Credit Suisse Group Banks in the Second World War

Credit Suisse Group Banks in the Second World War

A critical review

Edited by Joseph Jung

Neue Zürcher Zeitung Publishing

This volume contains translations of studies
taken from 'Zwischen Bundeshaus und
Paradeplatz. Die Banken der Credit Suisse Group im
Zweiten Weltkrieg. Studien und Materialien',
which was published in German in 2001.

© 2002, Credit Suisse Group, Zurich
Neue Zürcher Zeitung Publishing, Zurich
Translated by James Knight (Leamington Spa, England)

Additional translation: V. Elizabeth Powell (Washington, USA)
Proof reading: Edgar Haberthür, Alfred Schaufelberger, Nicole Schenker
Design: Heinz Egli, Schlieren
Charts: Roger Turin, Nassenwil ZH
Printing: NZZ Fretz AG, Schlieren
Binding: Buchbinderei Burkhardt AG, Mönchaltorf
ISBN 3-85823-985-2
Printed in Switzerland

Contents

Preface to the original edition

The Second World War left many unhealed wounds, and in recent years unresolved issues that were suppressed for a long time during the Cold War have, rightly, been revisited. In particular, the plight of Holocaust victims and their survivors has been
pushed to the forefront of the world's consciousness. Their treatment by the 'victorious' powers and the neutrals has been subjected to critical re-examination; and since
the mid-1990s Switzerland, too, has been confronted with the darker side of the survival strategy that served it so well during the war. After initial hesitation, our country
is now undergoing a sometimes painful, but necessary, process of reappraisal. The
worlds of politics, business and academia have been called upon not only to disclose
historical facts, but also to judge these facts in context according to the knowledge we
have today.

Credit Suisse Group has approached this task with all the seriousness it demands.
As far back as the bank's 1997 general meeting of shareholders, Rainer E. Gut, Chairman of the Board of Directors of Credit Suisse Group from 1983 to 2000, who also
proposed that this book be produced, addressed the issue very clearly: 'For a long time
we failed to acknowledge the importance of the unresolved issues. This makes us, and
it makes me personally, all the more committed to sorting things out as best we can using all the documents available today. We are not responsible for the things that our
predecessors did or omitted to do. But we are responsible for the way we now deal with
our history. I give my personal assurance that we are ready to thoroughly investigate
our past and to lay open the results for all to see.'

It is important to me that by publishing the studies contained in this book we are
making a further contribution to our Group's openness about these crucial matters.
Though we have to understand the emotions and subjective views involved, the experience of recent years shows that the reappraisal of our history always produces the
most valuable insights when the debate centers on facts and context. And this, it seems
to me, is where the real value of this book lies. The historian Joseph Jung and a team of
authors and researchers – using numerous sources, intensive examination of archives,
and interviews with contemporary eye-witnesses – turn the spotlight on hitherto
largely overlooked aspects of Credit Suisse Group companies' business operations during the Second World War. They have done this with great objectivity and without the
censoriousness that has hindered, rather than helped, some discussions of the subject.
I would like to thank all those involved for their valuable work.

We cannot change history, we cannot change our past. But we can, and we want to, learn the vital lessons that history teaches us. With the 1998 Settlement Agreement between the major Swiss banks and the plaintiffs in the USA, we proved that we take the issue very seriously. The settlement attracted both praise and criticism, but in my view neither of these reactions absolves us from continuing the debate – a debate to which this book can, I believe, make an important contribution.

Zurich, September 2001

Lukas Mühlemann
Chairman and Chief Executive Officer
of Credit Suisse Group

Credit Suisse Group banks during the Second World War: an overview

By Joseph Jung

Research subject

During the 1990s, the subject of Switzerland in the Second World War once again found its way to the center of public interest. From fall 1996, following complaints to the Swiss commercial banks about their handling of dormant accounts, and in the wake of subsequent efforts to find a political solution to this problem, a great deal of attention was focused on gold transactions, particularly those carried out by the Swiss National Bank (SNB). The debate then broadened out to encompass the entire Swiss economy before ultimately taking on international dimensions. The range of topics under scrutiny expanded to include such issues as forced labor, looted assets and 'aryanization'. In Switzerland itself, many aspects of the country's role during the Second World War had already been uncovered by previous research, though not all of this information was widely known among the general population. More than anything else, accusations from the USA quickly made it clear that key chapters of Switzerland's economic history were yet to be written. Today, businesses in many European countries are examining their history during the time of the National Socialist regime in Germany; some have already published the results of their investigations into individual areas.

The original German edition of this book, 'Zwischen Bundeshaus und Paradeplatz. Die Banken der Credit Suisse Group im Zweiten Weltkrieg', selections from which make up this volume, presents the results of several years of research into the most important Swiss institutions that were eventually incorporated into today's Credit Suisse Group (CSG). The aim is to contribute to a new history of the Swiss financial center in the Second World War.

Taking care to establish the economic and historical context, the original edition focuses on the three Swiss major banks that have since been incorporated into CSG: Schweizerische Kreditanstalt (SKA, known internationally as Credit Suisse), Schweizerische Volksbank (SVB) and Bank Leu. When reviewing certain topics, it also refers to other formerly autonomous institutions, such as Schweizerische Bodenkredit-Anstalt (SBKA), which was integrated into SKA in 1976, and Fides Treuhand-Vereinigung (taken over by SKA in 1928). Winterthur Insurance (a business unit of CSG since 1997) is not covered.

At the start of 1996, SKA embarked on a review of its business activities during the Second World War. In parallel with the expansion of the Central Corporate Archives (CCA), at the end of 1996 a dedicated team of researchers and banking specialists embarked on a comprehensive program of investigation. Their efforts focused on the following six main issues: dormant accounts, gold trading, refugees' assets, business relations with Germany, business relations with the USA, and the art trade. The particular relevance of these areas derived from the public debate in Switzerland, from the accusations made in the USA against the Swiss banks, and from the ongoing work of the two expert commissions, the Independent Commission of Experts Switzerland – Second World War (ICE) and the Independent Committee of Eminent Persons (ICEP).

'Credit Suisse Group banks during the Second World War' is a subject that covers a wide field and that needs to be narrowed down in terms of both the institutions investigated and the range of subjects covered. This book contains key texts from the original German edition, which presents the full results of CSG's academic research; it is based mainly on sources from within the firm, and principally embraces studies and documentation from the Central Corporate Archives.

The results of the individual studies were influenced greatly by the methods and tools utilized. At all times, the overriding goal of the research was to come as close as possible to the historical truth; the conditions under which the work was carried out were certainly conducive to achieving this goal: CSG's research team had free and unlimited access to all of the documents and files contained within the CCA. At no time was the research work influenced by pressure from the company. Uncovering the historical truth was made much easier by the availability of a new type of archive technology and by the professional structure of the archives. Consequently, the viewing and processing of source material was more comprehensive than would have been possible even a few years ago. Anyone making a serious attempt to write a modern economic history has to be able to rely on cooperation across various disciplines. In the case of this history, the interdisciplinary approach brought together historians, economists and lawyers, creating an effective mechanism for academic discussion. Finally, the interdisciplinary group was further strengthened by banking specialists who were able to subject the relevant facts and discoveries to further review.

Even an 'objective' view of the past inevitably involves a degree of interpretation. Even when the sources used are of outstanding quality, it is impossible to separate the 'truth' from personal perception. Right from the very start of the research work, therefore, many facts not only had to be documented, but also evaluated. Clearly it was not going to be enough merely to judge the past from today's vantage point. Instead, we also had to try to understand the period of the Second World War from the perspective of those who lived through it, placing actions and events in the context of the time and of the relevant personal circumstances.

Research results

International monetary flows and Swiss banking

The global economic crisis that began with the New York stock market crash of October 1929 brought an end to the boom years of the 'Golden Twenties'. Switzerland's banking industry was greatly affected by subsequent developments, and in particular by the currency regulations introduced by Germany in 1931. Swiss banks suddenly found that they were unable to access foreign investments. Given their build-up of exposure to other countries over the course of the 1920s, this was a serious problem – serious enough to cause Comptoir d'Escompte Suisse, the only major bank based in French-speaking Switzerland, to collapse. As the general economic misery in Germany and other European states was increasingly compounded by symptoms of political crisis, Switzerland was pulled ever deeper into the whirlpool of international monetary flows – the phenomenon of 'hot money' was born. Country-hopping capital reacted to the potential insecurities that were flaring up all over Europe and which were helping to weaken financial centers: little of this money was available for long-term investments, and the constant movement also had a negative effect on interest rate trends. Following the devaluation of the Swiss franc in September 1936, greater volumes of hot European – and especially French – money found their way into Switzerland for a time. Swiss assets held abroad also flowed back home. Ultimately, however, the 'Gentlemen's Agreement' struck between the Swiss banks and the SNB in November 1937 combined with growing political tensions in Europe to erode Switzerland's significance as an investment destination. Along with the gold reserves held by many central banks, most European flight capital was evacuated from financial centers on the Continent, initially to London and then in most cases on to North America. The USA was also the main destination for hot money from Switzerland.

Prior to 1945, the Swiss banking industry was not as important as many today seek to imply. The economic and currency crisis of the 1930s prevented Swiss financial institutions from building up a lucrative international business. During the Second World War, the Swiss financial center could not offer the Axis and Allied Powers much more in practical terms than could other neutral financial centers, such as Stockholm or Lisbon. Neither did the clearing agreements that governed the dirigiste payments system, nor the blockade of continental European assets in the USA, nor the restrictive policy pursued by various countries against the Swiss franc leave much room for maneuver. Right up until the end of the Second World War, even leading Swiss banks such as SKA, SVB and Bank Leu trailed well behind major banks in other countries in terms of size and activity. During the 1930s and the war years in Switzerland, it was institutions with foreign commitments that saw the greatest decline in assets and income. Furthermore, the Swiss banks only had limited opportunities to make money from currency dealing, asset management and stock market trading.

Business relations with Germany

Optimizing profits was not the main concern of the boards of directors and executive boards of the CSG banks during the Second World War; their main priority was to ensure the survival of their institutions. They fulfilled this aim, thus meeting their responsibility to employees, stockholders, customers and the Swiss economy as a whole. With Switzerland surrounded by the Axis powers and subjected to restrictions by the Allies, the individual CSG banks had to continue doing some of their business with German customers simply in order to avoid financial collapse. The written sources in the CCA contain no evidence that this controversial business involvement with Germany was discussed as a problem at that time within the bank's management bodies.

The European banking crisis of the early 1930s and the introduction of currency controls in Germany in 1931 caused grave problems for the CSG banks, which had greatly increased their investments in Germany, particularly since the economic boom of the mid-1920s: SKA's German exposure peaked at about Sfr 420 million (December 1930), SVB's at Sfr 196 million (July 1931) and Bank Leu's at Sfr 94 million (July 1931). Most of these assets were suddenly frozen, and there was a real concern that even due interest payments would not find their way back to Switzerland. Against this problematic economic background, which was exacerbated shortly afterwards by political developments and by the general moratorium on currency transfers declared by the government of the German Reich in June 1933, SKA, SVB and Bank Leu had no choice but to start reducing their exposure to Switzerland's Northern neighbor. The three banks had already begun their retreat from Germany during 1930, though they all chose different ways of managing the withdrawal. By the end of the war, SKA had reduced its exposure to about Sfr 7 million, representing a decrease of around 98% on the 1930 figure. Bank Leu's German investments, which were mainly in the form of mortgages, could only be cut back to about Sfr 34 million (–63.8%) by 1945. Meanwhile, over the same period (1930–1945) SVB's total foreign investments went down from approximately Sfr 468 million to Sfr 8.2 million (–98.2%).

A comparison of business policy sources from the three institutions shows that SKA's withdrawal strategy was clearly mapped out and rigorously implemented. The bank was able to do this because of its substantial reserves (1930: Sfr 53.9 million; 1945: Sfr 45 million). By contrast, the huge cost of SVB's exit from German business is shown dramatically by documents relating to its two restructurings of 1933 and 1936. Bankruptcy was only avoided thanks to support from the Federal Government. A similar fate befell Bank Leu, which had to be restructured in 1936/37 owing to liquidity problems, and which simply was not in a position to write off a significant portion of its assets in Germany.

Financial relations with Germany also involved cash accounts, securities accounts and lending business. Here we see the effect of the repressive measures taken by the National Socialist (Nazi) authorities to force people to withdraw assets held abroad – including at Swiss banks – and transfer them back to Germany ('compulsory transfers', 'looted assets'). We are also confronted with the systematic dispossession, particularly of Jews ('aryanization'), the issue of business relations with representatives and corporations of the Nazi system ('problematic' customer relationships), and finally the blocking of German assets in Switzerland in February 1945.

German currency legislation introduced in 1931 made it illegal to buy or export foreign currency without authorization. After taking power, the Nazi regime made currency controls progressively tighter in order to stem the outflow of capital. Infringements were harshly punished and the Nazis developed ever-more refined methods of detecting flight capital. Citing the currency laws, the German authorities forced people who had assets at Swiss banks to withdraw them and make them available to the Nazi state. Where the people who suffered the effects of these laws were resident within the 'Third Reich' (within the boundaries of 31 August 1939), we talk about 'compulsory transfers'; but if the victims lived in the occupied territories, we use the term 'looted assets'. By taking the example of SKA, which had more German customers than any of the other CSG banks studied in this book, we can clearly see the problems faced by all of the institutions concerned. If the bank's officers carried out the customer's transfer instructions, they were ignoring the fact that the customer may have issued this instruction under duress. In most cases it was impossible to ascertain whether pressure had been applied or not. However, the truth is that after the mid-1930s the Nazi's systematic policy of dispossession was known about in Switzerland, too. If the financial institution refused to carry out the instruction, it could possibly be saving the customer's assets from appropriation by the Nazis, but it could also be breaking the law. In addition, such an institution would also be running the risk that the Nazi authorities would punish the customer whose instruction was not carried out: from 1936 onwards, the penalty for breaking the currency laws was death.

Systematic analysis of the CCA sources relating to SKA, SVB and Bank Leu reveal the dilemma in which the responsible parties at that time found themselves. In assessing how best to serve the customer's interests, these people had to weigh up the various risks and decide what was allowed and what was possible. Even from today's perspective, it is not hard to see how burdensome this responsibility must have been.

The cases we have investigated suggest that SKA tended to carry out transfer instructions if they were signed by the customers themselves. However, in two specific circumstances it would refuse to comply with the instruction:

- if the customer had previously agreed with the bank that it should not pay out any money – even to the customer himself – unless it was given a pre-arranged code;
- if a Nazi 'sequestrator' ('Zwangsverwalter') issued the transfer instruction rather than the customer himself.

Customer reaction during and after the war shows that both options – execution or refusal of the transfer instruction – could be right or wrong. The same decision could be right from the customer's perspective in one case because it could save his or her life, for example, but wrong in other cases because it meant that customers lost their money. Our research has proved that SKA was involved in cases of both compulsory transfer (about 200 cases) and looted assets (85 lawsuits after the end of the war).

The CSG banks also had to deal with the Nazi's systematic policy of dispossessing Jews. The key formal instruments used by the Nazis to drive Jews out of German economic life were boycotts by the National Socialist system from 1933, the Nuremberg race laws of 1935, and from 1938 the decrees that paved the way for compulsory expropriation. The banks in Switzerland were affected by these developments in various ways, in some cases as a result of having lent money to Jewish companies, in others of being represented on their boards or supervisory committees. It should be noted that such business relationships were forged prior to the Nazis seizing power, meaning that the question of whether the firms involved were Jewish or not played no role in the banks' considerations at that time.

As intended, the measures taken by the Nazi regime pushed Jewish firms into severe financial hardship and made it impossible for them to service their loans. This put the banks in a difficult position. Essentially they could choose one of two options: either distance themselves from the expropriation policy, or adapt to the new circumstances. If they chose the former, they would have to call in their loans which, because of the limited opportunities to withdraw capital from Germany, would be tantamount to completely writing off the assets concerned. On the other hand, if they decided to learn to live with the process of expropriation, most of the same problems remained because of the stringent foreign exchange controls. Nevertheless, it would still be possible to use assets denominated in 'Sperrmarks' ('blocked marks') to make new investments in Germany – to buy real estate, for example, or to acquire stakes in companies. Some of the assets and shareholdings that were considered for purchase with Sperrmarks were former Jewish assets that had come onto the market as a result of the expropriations and the flight of Jewish owners from Germany. Consequently the banks were driven by circumstance into a fateful spiral.

When identifying cases in which the CSG banks came into contact with the expropriation of Jewish property, researchers had to adhere to carefully defined methods and academic criteria. Research at SKA included analysis of the files from the legal departments at head office and at some branches. For SVB, the investigation covered files from the Zurich branch, which was responsible for most of the bank's business with Germany. Research into Bank Leu was based on systematic analysis of the board of directors' minutes from the relevant years. All of this research turned up 17 cases of 'aryaniza-tion', which are described individually in the original German edition of this book. These provide examples of how Jewish influence was removed from the German econ-omy, and demonstrate the role played by the CSG banks.

The fundamental methodological and academic problem in this context is that there is no definitive list of all the people and companies that were involved in the Nazi's malevolent system. In order to identify such 'problematic' customer relationships – at least where these involved private individuals – researchers consulted both the list of the accused at the Nuremberg war crime trials and the so-called 'Wiesenthal List'. 'Problematic' corporate customers were identified using a list put together by Christopher Simpson, supplemented by information from various academic publica-tions. The complex analysis of possible and actual relations with such customers, which could only be carried out properly once an inventory of the relevant data had been loaded onto computers, produced 14 'person identifications' of SKA customers, one of whom also had an account at SVB, as well as 20 uncertain cases. Of the 14 def-inite customers, 5 opened accounts at the bank only after 1945. In 4 of the other cases, the accounts had been opened prior to 1939 – some even in the 1920s. As far as the size of the 6 accounts that remained at the end of the war is concerned, one contained about Sfr 1 million, one about Sfr 75,000 and two about Sfr 10,000 each. Then there was an account containing Sfr 166, and finally a customer who in 1945 owned a safe deposit box at the bank, the contents of which can no longer be ascertained. The most important point to note in this regard is that only one of these customers was a sen-ior representative of the Nazi's political leadership. This 'Reichskommissar', who was tried and executed at Nuremberg, held a foreign currency account at SKA for just two months in 1935. Turnover on the account was modest. In all other cases, the people involved were either members of the business elite or diplomats.

As well as these contacts with private customers, the Swiss commercial banks also maintained relations with companies in Germany during the war. SKA, for example, traditionally did business with German banks and industrial companies. Political devel-opments meant that these relationships inevitably became problematic, and most were maintained in a reduced form during the war years. In addition, the bank also opened some new relationships with German companies after 1933. The names of a total of 17 companies from various branches of industry have been identified unequivocally ('company identity'). Of these 17, it is worth noting that 15 of the relationships were established prior to 1931, with some dating back to the 19th century.

In mid-September 1944, the Swiss Bankers Association, under pressure from the Allies, recommended 'urgently' that its member banks refrain from doing any business at all with 'enemies of the Allies'. Partly to prevent the movement of German flight capital, and partly to secure German assets in case reparations had to be paid, Switzer-land's Federal Council issued a Decree on 16 February 1945 blocking all German assets held in Switzerland. Ultimately, this action, implemented via a complex proce-

dure under the supervision of the Swiss Compensation Office, not only met the Allies'
demands, but also served the interests of those German customers who had never done
anything wrong during the war. On 29 May 1945, the obligation to report assets held
by Swiss banks and fiduciary agents was introduced. It is no longer possible to reconstruct the individual cases where German assets were blocked and reported by the
CSG banks in 1945; but with the help of a database set up by CSG containing details
of reported German assets, we can estimate that the approximately 8,150 reports made
by the CSG banks accounted for assets worth about Sfr 300 million. This is equivalent to about a quarter of the overall total assets reported in Switzerland of around Sfr
1.4 billion. SKA's reports included 257 safe deposit boxes, or about 9% of the total
number of boxes reported by all banks in Switzerland. These safes were opened on the
orders of the Compensation Office.

The gold trade

The Federal Council Decree of 7 December 1942 marked a turning point in the
history of private Swiss gold trading in the Second World War: the legislation it introduced brought an end to the free market in gold and gave the Swiss National Bank
(SNB) a dirigiste role. For the commercial banks this meant not only much smaller
turnover and profit margins, but also an end to most foreign gold business. It goes
without saying that gold trading, which was not one of the CSG banks' core businesses
even in earlier years, became even less important after 1942. The CSG banks' partici-
pation in Switzerland's role as a hub for gold trading remained small in volume terms
for the duration of the war, but it is undeniable that in 1940/41 gold from the German
Reichsbank found its way to SKA and Bank Leu. In 1943/44, too, SKA, acting for the
account of private clients and with the authorization of the SNB, imported gold coins
and ingots worth between Sfr 1.7 million and a maximum of Sfr 2.7 million from
Germany. We cannot be sure for certain that these deliveries, some of which were
transported elsewhere shortly after their arrival, did not involve looted gold. However,
none of the sources provide any indication that the gold included 'victim's gold'. The
gold transactions carried out with Germany by the CSG banks were characterized by
a 'business as usual' attitude and an absence of critical reflection. This nonchalant
approach can be deduced from the lack of concern about the origins of the gold on
the part of the banks' management bodies. None of the relevant written sources suggest
any awareness of the problem. Bearing in mind the pressure that was being exerted by
the Allies and the fact that their accusations against Germany with regard to looted gold
were known from 1943 at the latest, it is impossible to understand from today's perspective why SKA continued to buy gold from the German Reichsbank at that time.
In September 1944, the executive board of SKA forbade any gold transactions with
enemies of the Allies.

The international gold trade had grown in importance after the First World War.
Trading in gold coins in particular increased as a consequence of the dissolution of the

Latin Monetary Union (1926) and the abandonment of the gold standard by the USA, the United Kingdom and France. Towards the end of the 1930s, state regulations, the widespread retreat from free trade and, finally, the outbreak of war placed fresh constraints on the international gold market. Until it entered the Second World War in December 1941, the USA was by far the largest buyer of gold on the world market. With its enormous demand for gold, together with the freeze it imposed on European assets, the USA sharply drove up the price of gold on the world market. Not only did this approach hurt the international gold market, it also made it more difficult for the SNB to pursue its monetary policy, which was based on ensuring the stability of the Swiss franc. Until the end of 1942, the Swiss gold market was essentially a free market, though it was subject to certain guiding principles on account of the war and the SNB's monetary policy. Private domestic gold trade was conducted mainly in the region bordering France, because in France, unlike in Switzerland's other neighbors, private ownership of gold was still permitted. Rising gold prices and the increasing demand for gold at home and abroad made legal regulation of the Swiss gold trade unavoidable: the Federal Council Decree of 7 December 1942 fixed legal maximum prices for ingots and coins, introduced compulsory licensing for anybody wanting to trade in gold, and subjected all imports and exports to authorization by the SNB. Ironically, the Federal Council Decree triggered a blossoming of the black market, and gold continued to be exported to other countries, not least by smugglers and diplomats. Employees of CSG banks were implicated in two notable illegal transactions of this kind involving the sale of up to Sfr 1 million worth of gold.

The SNB refused to heed early hints and warnings about the origin of the German gold. It even continued to carry out questionable gold transactions after the Allies' warnings had become too loud to ignore in 1943. The intention of the SNB board was to prove in this way that it had always acted in good faith. The political authorities ultimately covered up for the SNB and refrained from bringing those responsible to account.

The SNB was the most important source of gold for the CSG banks, and between 1942 and 1945 it delivered gold with a gross value of approximately Sfr 176.7 million to the three institutions, SKA, SVB and Bank Leu. From the middle of 1943 onwards, a certain amount of looted gold also found its way into circulation via the SNB. The CSG banks' proprietary holdings of gold during the war years – peaking at about Sfr 28 million at SKA, and at less than Sfr 3 million at SVB and Bank Leu – were insignificant compared with the gold reserves held by the central banks. For reasons of security and business policy, at the end of 1942 SKA built up its gold deposits in Argentina by buying gold of American origin. These Argentinean holdings had nothing whatsoever to do with the movement of Nazi flight capital. In the years between 1939 and 1945, the three CSG banks investigated in this study generated income of a few hundred thousand Swiss francs every year from gold business. This figure only increased in 1941 and 1942, and the largest income earned from gold by any of the CSG banks during the war was the approximately Sfr 2 million posted by SKA in 1942. This resulted primarily from sales of gold coins worth about Sfr 160 million, which were conducted that year prior to the implementation of the Federal Council Decree on gold trading of 7 December 1942.

Before the outbreak of the war, the CSG banks' gold business was concentrated mainly on customers from the United Kingdom and France. When the war began, foreign business shifted to the central banks that held deposits at the SNB in Bern – to Germany and, until the middle of 1940, primarily to the USA. Between March and June 1940, for example, SKA sold roughly the same amount of gold to American customers as it acquired from Germany's Reichsbank throughout the entire war. With the gold markets in the USA and Britain closing down, and the risks of sea transport growing all the time, SKA and Bank Leu conducted most of their gold business in 1940 and 1941 with the German Reichsbank. According to the Independent Commission of Experts Switzerland – Second World War (ICE), the Reichsbank delivered gold worth about Sfr 7.4 million to SKA and about Sfr 43.8 million to Bank Leu. CSG's own research shows, however, that the gold deliveries to Bank Leu were actually about Sfr 10 million less than this. Unlike SKA, Bank Leu was practically forced by its outstanding loans in Germany to engage in gold business with the Reichsbank. If it had not done so, it would have risked collapse. Based on the available sources, we can assume that the German gold deliveries to SKA and Bank Leu were carried out on behalf of customers rather than for the banks' own account. However, we have to note that the documents in the CCA dealing with gold business do not permit a clear assessment in every case.

Fides Treuhand-Vereinigung and its art dealings

The significance and scope of the trade in looted art before, during and after the Second World War has been the subject of many investigations over the years. Thanks to the research conducted to date, it is possible to make an assessment of Switzerland's role as a hub for the art trade.

Fides Treuhand-Vereinigung (Fides) was one of the parties involved in the international art trade during the time when the Nazis ruled Germany. Fides did not, however, act as an art dealer. Its role between 1934 and 1942 was to make its expertise as a fiduciary company available to the 'Kunst' ('Art') consortium of which it was a member and whose business it managed. Fides's activities in this regard were motivated by financial considerations, but over and beyond this, its involvement in the art world served another purpose. The company's aim, and more especially the aim of a Jewish lawyer who had emigrated from Germany and who was involved in the consortium, was to use its business channels in order to release capital that was blocked by Germany and to bring works of art out of Nazi Germany. The clients and business partners with whom Fides worked when purchasing art – almost all of them people or institutions from Britain or America – included numerous people of the Jewish faith. Owing to these business relationships, Fides acquired a reputation among art dealers sympathetic to Nazi ideology as a 'Jewish clique'. The mandate given to Fides to use art as a means of liquidating 'Sperrmarks' was an important source of earnings for the company until 1940. Between 1935 and 30 June 1940, the 'Kunst' consortium generated a net profit of around Sfr 1.25 million. After applying the agreed 'profit distribution formula' Fides received about Sfr 533,000. Between October 1940 and the end of the 'Kunst' consortium's activities on 31 December 1942, this share of profits increased by only Sfr 3,300. Over the same period (1935–1940) Fides's gross income as a joint-stock company was Sfr 8.6 million. The art business thus accounted for only about 6% of its earnings.

In the 1930s and early 1940s, Fides's mandate to liquidate Sperrmark-denominated assets, its rehabilitation plans for a hotel in Munich and its involvement in the international art trade were essentially all part of the same business package. Persons whose names have been lost, but who are known to have emigrated from Germany after Hitler seized power, still owned blocked assets in Germany worth RM 8 million. Since it was impossible for them to take this sum out of Germany in their own names, in 1934 they mandated Fides to liquidate the assets. On their behalf, and with the permission of the Reich Ministry of Economics and the Reich Chamber of Fine Arts in Berlin, Fides intended to use RM 4.8 million (60%) to expatriate works of art from Germany to other countries. In return for permission to conduct this business, Fides's clients agreed to invest 40% of the blocked assets – i.e. RM 3.2 million – in Germany. One of the beneficiaries of this investment was Hotel AG in Munich, which owned the famous 'Vier Jahreszeiten' hotel and which was a subject of particular interest to certain leading figures in the Nazi Party in Berlin. In the early 1930s, the company faced bankruptcy. Fides had also taken on the contract to restructure Hotel AG and had granted it a loan of RM 2 million as well as a written-off payment of RM 600,000. Finally, the Reich Chamber of Fine Arts also received a written-off payment of RM 600,000.

Fides's art mandate included handling correspondence with the relevant authorities and structuring the foreign exchange transactions associated with the purchase of works of art. In carrying out this mandate, Fides adhered to the conditions attached to the permission granted by the Ministry of Economics in Berlin, as well as to the relevant legal provisions in Germany and Switzerland. This is made clear by its correspondence with the Swiss Compensation Office, which shows that Fides was granted the authorizations needed to carry out transactions requiring clearing. The plain fact is that the Allies did not put Fides on their blacklist. The British authorities, for example, which in 1942 investigated the transactions associated with Fides's art business, came to the conclusion 'that it was justified in carrying on the transactions'. Between 1935 and 1942, Fides carried out about 1,600 individual transactions, using about 4.5 million Sperrmarks from the total sum of 8 million Sperrmarks to execute the deals. About RM 2.6 million of this was used to buy artworks on the instructions of clients. Fides's business partners and clients came almost without exception from the USA (about 90%) and the United Kingdom (about 10%). The available sources only tell us in a few exceptional cases which works of art were actually taken out of Germany and sent to other countries in this way. What is clear is that brokering rare books became Fides's main business. In 1940, the company continued its mandate to liquidate Sperrmarks separately from the rehabilitation of Hotel AG. When it had to break off business relations with business partners from the USA and UK because of the war, it tried in 1941 to nurture Switzerland as a new market for people interested in works of art from Germany. These efforts proved fruitless, however, because the Compensation Office was not prepared to grant more favorable conditions to Fides than to Switzerland's art dealers. The authorization to conduct art business granted by the Reich Ministry for Economics ran out in spring 1942 before the fiduciary company in Zurich was able to completely liquidate the Sperrmark assets with which it had been entrusted.

In the wake of Fides's financially motivated work as a broker, a number of artworks that had been threatened with destruction were taken out of Germany and sent to other countries, and thus brought to safety. In carrying out these activities during the time of the Nazi dictatorship, Fides was working for American and Jewish interests. This is underlined by the fact that after the end of the war, the company was mandated to handle restitution claims and represent the interests of people deprived of their rights by the Axis countries. Its art brokerage activities during the period 1934–1942 were not interpreted by anyone as discreditable.

Financial relations with the USA

The history of financial relations between Switzerland and the USA was heavily influenced by events between the blocking (1941) and the unblocking (1947/48) of Swiss assets in America. Most of all, developments were dictated by the American demand that the identity of customers be revealed and by Switzerland's refusal to comply with this request on account of its banking secrecy legislation. The years of tense relations between the two countries can largely be attributed to a difference in mentality: American flexibility was set against the Swiss instinct to abide by laws and contracts.

Following the blocking and registration of foreign assets by the American government, Swiss bank offices in New York were subjected to several years of investigations and audits, during which the US authorities had no compunction about forcibly opening letters and sealed documents. Since the start of the blocking, the American Treasury Department was obsessed by the idea that large amounts of enemy assets were being hidden in accounts held at Swiss banks. When the Swiss Bankers Association conducted surveys of its members about the ratio between Swiss and foreign owners of assets deposited in the USA and the proportion of assets accounted for by individual countries, the results showed that most of the people investing in the USA through Swiss banks were of Swiss origin. Of the foreign customers, the French made up by far the largest group, with only a few customers from Axis nations. The USA's extremely negative view of Swiss financial structures overshadowed more positive assessments of Switzerland, such as those expressed by the US State Department when referring, for example, to the country's humanitarian and diplomatic efforts. The American financial authorities continued to exert pressure for decades in an attempt to uncover hidden assets.

Shortly before the start of the war, the board of directors of SKA decided in the interest of shareholders and customers to transfer a portion of the bank's assets 'to whatever place … can be considered the most secure'. To this end, in 1939 the bank opened a subsidiary in New York called Swiss American Corporation, and in 1940 a branch: the Credit Suisse New York Agency.

In the face of Germany's ongoing occupation of Europe, from 10 April 1940 onwards the USA blocked assets that had been taken out of Europe and deposited in America. One of the aims was to protect the owners of this property; the other was to prevent the Axis powers from using the USA as a safe haven for their assets. In a 1941 census, the US Treasury Department called for the registration of all foreign assets along with details of their size and the names of beneficial owners. The Treasury Department reported that the total sum of all foreign deposits, investments, interests and other property in the USA on 14 June 1941 came to about $ 12.7 billion, of which almost $ 6 billion came from countries whose assets had been blocked. More than 132,000 foreign individuals owned assets worth almost $ 2.6 billion; 23,000 foreign legal entities accounted for property worth about $ 8 billion; the remaining $ 2.1 billion belonged mainly to government institutions. Swiss investments came third in terms of size behind the United Kingdom and Canada, but ahead of France and the Netherlands. Swiss assets invested in the USA amounted to approximately $ 1.2 billion (Sfr 5.2 billion), i.e. 9.5% of the total of $ 12.7 billion worldwide assets, or 15% of the European total.

The legal establishment of Swiss banking secrecy in 1934 helped to attract a good deal of investment: by Swiss people who placed a premium on security and discretion, by foreigners who wanted to expatriate their money because of the currency laws in their own countries, but also by people whose lives were in danger. Switzerland's attempt to guarantee banking secrecy even in the USA was met with bitter resistance, however. Essentially there was a head-on collision between two value systems that could not be reconciled. For their part, the Swiss attached less importance to moral principles than to a liberal-individualist one: the protection of property and personal freedom. Meanwhile, representatives of the USA focused exclusively on the implications of the war. As far as they were concerned, the interests of individual states and individual people had to be sacrificed to the common goal, i.e. victory over the evil enemy. Consequently, any action or instrument that did not serve this goal and this goal alone was seen as morally reprehensible. There was similar disquiet on the American side about Switzerland's political commitment to neutrality. At a time when America was calling for 'firm moral convictions', neutrality permitted Switzerland to pursue ad hoc solutions and stand-alone political strategies, i.e. anything that would most effectively assure the survival of a small, encircled country.

The main reason why the American financial authorities suspected that Swiss banks were secretly holding German assets was the existence of an investment form known as the 'omnibus account' ('Sammelkonto'). These accounts were widespread at the time, being cost-effective for customers, and were commonly used in the USA. They were opened in the name of a Swiss financial institution and contained assets owned by a number of different customers. At the US correspondent banks, these accounts were held in the name of the Swiss institution, but for the account and at the risk of this institution's customers. Consequently, the identity of the actual customers, the 'beneficial owners', remained hidden from the American authorities.

Throughout the war, the US Treasury Department and representatives of the Swiss banks negotiated in vain to find a way of revealing the names of the 'beneficial owners' of these accounts. The negotiations were accompanied by progressively more stringent US banking legislation with regard to foreigners. The web of blocking regulations was drawn much tighter. By issuing repeated warnings and using economic sanctions, the Allies increased pressure on neutral countries in an attempt to force them to abandon any form of support for the enemy. As the end of the war approached, America's power increased. For Switzerland, military encirclement by the Axis powers was followed by moral and political isolation by the Allies. Ostracized in this way, Switzerland protested its probity and insisted on the legitimacy of its actions, while the USA stated that it had lost its last shred of trust in the Swiss 'cover-up merchants' and 'profiteers'.

In February 1945, the Swiss government declared – on paper at least– that it was prepared to investigate the ownership structure of assets blocked by the USA. In order to do this it proposed the establishment of a government auditor, a role that was eventually assumed by the Swiss Compensation Office (SCO). A demand put forward by the United States at the beginning of the war was thus finally met. In the 'Currie Agreement' of March 1945, the US concession on unblocking Swiss assets in the USA was linked to the demand that German assets held in Switzerland be blocked. The negotiations, which continued to revolve around the issue of identifying customers, subsequently continued beyond the Washington Agreement of 1946.

Even after the unblocking process had started for several European countries, the Swiss and American negotiators found it difficult to agree on the principles that would govern the unfreezing of Swiss assets. Finally, in November 1946 the US financial authorities agreed that the names of 'beneficial owners', which had to be investigated before any unblocking, would be reported to the Swiss Compensation Office, but not to the American authorities. The Compensation Office thus assumed the role of certifying authority, issuing all persons qualifying for unblocking with a government certificate as required by US General License No. 95. On presentation of a certificate, the US bank holding the assets would automatically unblock them.

In February 1948, the Treasury Department launched a new offensive with the 'Snyder Plan'. This plan stated that all Swiss assets that remained uncertified at the end of the certification period would be seized owing to the 'presumption of enemy ownership' – a presumption that could only be rebutted by revealing the beneficial owner. The motive behind the blocking of assets had thus changed once and for all. Whereas the protection of creditors in occupied countries had been the prime reason to start with, the certification process meant that blocking was now more and more being used as a tool of the Allies' reparation policy: enemy assets and non-certified assets would be used to pay for the reconstruction of Europe. Confiscation ('vesting') of disputed, uncertified assets began in spring 1951, and the battle to have them released continued into the 1970s.

Were the Swiss banks involved in 'cloaking transactions' as repeatedly claimed by the Americans? And after the war did they repatriate German or dormant assets disguised as their own property? The Swiss Compensation Office, which investigated the banks, their activities and their customers in line with American demands, issued the financial institutions with a clean bill of health. Only about 1.7% of SKA's US investments could not be certified; these were confiscated ('vested') by the US authorities.

Dormant assets

Ever since the first days after the end of the Second World War, the Swiss Federation of Jewish Communities (SFJC) has repeatedly raised the issue of dormant assets dating back to the period of Nazi dictatorship; but until recently the Swiss banks had failed to devote sufficient attention to the issue. Whether responding to the various surveys conducted to inventorize dormant accounts, or implementing the Federal Decree of 1962, or responding to individual requests, the banks were less than forthcoming. There were various reasons for this attitude. For a start it reflected the principle of customer protection enshrined in Switzerland's binding legislation on confidentiality, i.e. banking secrecy. The banks were particularly cautious about dormant assets originating in Eastern Europe, fearing that customers or their heirs could be subjected to pressure from Communist-bloc governments. Another reason was that in financial terms, dormant assets were actually a rather minor issue for the banks. Finally, two of the central reasons for the low priority afforded to the problem and for the passive strategy adopted were that dormant assets were dealt with relatively low down in the banks' hierarchies, and that the primary responsibility was lodged with the Swiss Bankers Association.

For a long time, dormant assets were not seen as a top-level matter at either the Swiss Bankers Association or at individual banks: the boards of directors and executive boards barely bothered with the issue. Policy formulation was left to the Bankers Association. Even here the matter was handled mainly by the legal committee rather than by the board of directors on which the top managers of the member banks were represented. At the commercial banks too, legal departments tended to deal with dormant assets, which might have been appropriate from a functional point of view, but which was clearly inadequate in terms of the political and moral dimensions of the whole issue. In fact, the approach taken by the banks and the Bankers Association was based on legal considerations. This was reflected in the banks' response to individual queries, which was no doubt correct in strictly legal terms, but which was often over-bearingly formalistic and lacking in the sensitivity required when dealing with Holocaust victims or their heirs. It was not until 1997 that the problem was addressed in more or less the way proposed by the SFJC 50 years before.

As part of the Washington Agreement of 1946, Switzerland undertook to develop a method that would enable dormant assets to be paid out to victims of the war. The SFJC presented several proposals as to how this might be done. Top of the list were an obligation to report assets belonging to Holocaust victims, which was suggested in 1947, and the methodical search for beneficial owners or their heirs. Assets that could not be linked to a beneficial owner should be added to a fund set up to provide support for victims of the war. The SFJC was convinced that this solution would be possible under international law. It felt that a formal obligation to report was necessary in order to guarantee that the banks' researches were serious and comprehensive. Political and diplomatic representatives of the USA, France, the United Kingdom and Israel, as well as various international Jewish organizations, also repeatedly petitioned the Swiss authorities to work towards a legal solution to the problem. However, the Swiss Bankers Association opposed these proposals, fearing that the publication of a list of names might endanger beneficial owners, especially in Eastern Europe. In addition, the Association pointed out that an obligation to report could not be reconciled with banking secrecy legislation. It also argued that the dormant assets of Holocaust victims did not make up a sufficiently large overall sum to justify special legislation. The Bankers Association emphasized that the banks were doing everything necessary to clear up requests.

While the controversy about a legal solution was going on, in 1947 and 1956 the Swiss Bankers Association conducted surveys of possible dormant assets belonging to victims of the Nazi regime. In addition, the implementation of the Swiss-Polish Agreement of 1949 required the Bankers Association to carry out further surveys. In 1952, Switzerland's Federal Council asked the Federal Department of Justice and Police (FDJP) to draft legislation, which led to yet more lengthy discussions. In 1957, National Councilor Harald Huber submitted a motion requesting the introduction of a legal obligation to report dormant assets. However, Federal Councilor Markus Feldmann (FDJP) recommended that the Federal Council reject the motion owing to the modest results of the Bankers Association's 1956 survey. By contrast, the Federal Political Department (FPD, the Swiss foreign ministry) gave its full backing to a legal solution. Friedrich Traugott Wahlen, another supporter of a legal solution, was elected to the Federal Council in 1958. By 1959 the draft was ready for approval. In 1961 the Federal Council decided to implement the proposal. The two houses of

Switzerland's parliament, the National Council and the Council of States, approved the draft with few amendments in 1962. The 'Federal Decree on Assets in Switzerland Belonging to Foreigners or Stateless Persons Persecuted for Reasons of Race, Religion or Politics' entered into force on 1 September 1963.

This Federal Decree obliged Swiss asset-holding institutions to report all assets that had been dormant since 1945 and whose last-known owner had been a foreigner or stateless person who was known or suspected to have been the victim of racial, religious or political persecution. Any cases that met all three criteria had to be reported.

SKA's head office and Swiss branch offices identified 503 cases that potentially needed to be reported. Following comprehensive internal investigations, the bank finally reported 141 of these (worth a total of Sfr 1.11 million) to the Claims Registry in June 1964. From today's perspective, a problematic aspect of this process was that persons who had been identified as probably or certainly Jewish by the Jewish experts brought in to advise SKA, but whose place of domicile was unknown, were not reported. According to the Swiss Bankers Association's interpretation of the Federal Decree, assets belonging to these persons did not have to be reported. SVB assembled 62 cases from all over Switzerland and reported 22 of these (Sfr 189,204) to the Claims Registry. Bank Leu investigated more than 50 cases at its head office and branches, finally reporting 3 of these (Sfr 929).

Between 1965 and 1970, the Claims Registry sorted out which of the reported assets accorded with the provisions of the Federal Decree. Assets of less than Sfr 500, or less than Sfr 1,000 from 1970 onwards, were usually paid directly into the Swiss government's 'Unclaimed Assets Fund'. Similarly, assets that could not be paid to owners or their heirs – even after the efforts of the General Custodial Trustee ('Generalbeistand') appointed by the Federal Council – were also paid into this fund. Under the 1949/50 agreements signed with Poland and Hungary, money from the fund was transferred to the national banks of these countries in 1975. Two-thirds of the remaining sum was paid to the SFJC in accordance with a further Federal Decree. The final third went to the Swiss refugee aid effort, and the authorities wound up the fund in 1980. The subject of dormant assets then disappeared from the public and political agenda for a number of years.

Renewed calls for a legal solution to the problem of dormant assets were made from 1989 onwards and then with increased force from 1995. This resurgence of interest was prompted in the first instance by the end of the Cold War, and then by events held to commemorate the 50th anniversary of the end of the Second World War, which forcefully reminded people of the horrors of the Holocaust. When the Iron Curtain disappeared, it suddenly became possible to access new information from Eastern European archives about dead or missing victims of the Holocaust. The World Jewish Congress, later supported by the American authorities, dedicated itself to re-evaluating the issue of dormant assets. As a result, enormous political and economic pressure was exerted on the Swiss banks as well as on the Swiss government.

In June 1995, the Swiss Bankers Association decided to carry out another survey of the banks that were represented on its board of directors, asking about the type and size of dormant assets. The banks reported 893 accounts owned by Swiss and foreign customers that had been opened prior to 9 May 1945, that had been left dormant since at least 1985, and that had credit balances of more than Sfr 1,000. These accounts contained a total of Sfr 40.9 million. In September 1995, the Bankers Association extended the investigation to all its member banks. The total amount of dormant assets of foreign customers was published in February 1996. These figures cannot be compared directly with the ones from September 1995. In February 1996 there were 775 accounts worth Sfr 38.7 million, a figure that prompted sharp criticism from Jewish organizations in Switzerland and abroad, which had expected the total to be much higher. Calls for an independent audit of the results finally led to the establishment in May 1996 of the Independent Committee of Eminent Persons (ICEP) under the chairmanship of Paul A. Volcker (hence its alternative name, the 'Volcker Commission'). The Bankers Association's new guidelines on how to deal with dormant assets entered into force on 1 January 1996. The banks now had to identify all dormant accounts in order to make inquiries and surveys easier and to ensure that the accounts were managed properly and in the interests of their prospective owners. A central contact point was also set up at the office of the Banking Ombudsman to help with the search for dormant assets.

The Bankers Association, which had published three lists of names in connection with dormant assets in 1997, introduced new guidelines in July 2000. These stipulated the need to search actively for beneficiaries, and defined the obligation to report assets to the Banking Ombudsman. In February 2001, the ICEP arranged publication of another list of names. Treatment of the associated claims by an independent tribunal will probably take about two years. The claims are covered by the settlement of $ 1.25 billion paid by the major banks in August 1998.

As a result of the events of the Second World War, many of the surviving victims of Nazism, or their heirs, had no precise information about cash accounts, securities accounts and safe deposit boxes held in Switzerland. Others did not have the proofs of identification needed to press a successful legal claim for their assets. Research into how the three CSG banks dealt with requests about actual and supposed assets reveals the following picture. There were generally no apparent differences in the way that the legal departments of three banks carried out their internal research. It is also clear that none of the three banks made any distinction between Holocaust victims and other groups of people. In the period between 1945 and 1995, SKA, for example, investigated practically all requests free of charge where no or only partial proof of identity was presented, searching all the relevant departments at head office and the General Register. If the results were negative, the applicant was told so. These investigations covered about 95% of all accounts in Switzerland. If the applicant paid a fee, the bank would additionally conduct a Swiss-wide or specific regional survey. If the search results were positive, no information was given until the required identification documents were presented (proof of own identity, death or inheritance certificate). SKA gave out extensive information about accounts that still existed, but in a good quarter of the cases investigated, it did not mention accounts that had existed but which had been closed by the time the request was made. When original documents had been lost, SKA often accepted sworn affidavits in their place. The bank was particularly careful with information in response to queries from Communist Eastern Europe, demanding that identification documents be additionally certified by a Swiss Embassy. The fear was that the applicant could be put under pressure by the authorities in his or her home country. To summarize, in cases where the applicant could identify himself adequately, all three of the CSG banks carried out searches. If the research produced a negative result, the bank would communicate this news and return the documents. If assets were identified, it would still take a long time before these were finally paid out if the Holocaust victim concerned did not have the required proofs of identity, and especially if he came from a Communist country in Eastern Europe. In isolated cases, SKA, SVB and Bank Leu also undertook external research on their own initiative, contacting the International Committee of the Red Cross (ICRC), for example, or Jewish organizations, or the Swiss authorities. This only happened occasionally, however, since the banks' desire to protect customers usually precluded any external research.

Refugee assets in Switzerland

The job of providing the accommodation, infrastructure and staff required to look after refugees placed great demands on the Swiss federal authorities and the Swiss army. The fact that there was a war on meant that the authorities only had limited room for maneuver; it also meant that they had to monitor the political, economic and intelligence activities of the refugees. Another goal of state supervision was to impound any ill-gotten assets or looted goods. The analysis of account ledger sheets conducted as part of the study of SVB's fiduciary mandate confirms the results of the official investigation of 1945, according to which there were only a few isolated cases of such dubious assets, disguised as refugee property, arriving in Switzerland. This is the context in which one should view the Federal Council Decree of 12 March 1943, according to which civilians accepted into Switzerland after 1 August 1942 as refugees had to deposit their assets with a fiduciary office. The directives concerning property rights issued by the Police Division of the Federal Department of Justice and Police (FDJP) were based on constitutional principles, which ensured that civilian refugees retained their rights of ownership.

The Federal Government appointed SVB as its fiduciary in this matter, because it had a denser branch network throughout Switzerland than any of the other major Swiss banks. Research into the extensive sources available at SVB and, in particular, the meticulous review of thousands of account ledger sheets and lists of balances confirm that the bank executed its mandate correctly, in accordance with the government's instructions, and in the interests of the refugees.

The mandate was given to SVB in May 1943 in order to professionalize the whole process. Previously, the responsible federal civilian and military authorities had only held refugee assets in custody on an emergency basis. As a result of the additional administrative costs incurred, managing refugee assets was actually a loss-making business for SVB.

Assets were returned to entitled owners in the proper manner. All the accounts and security accounts opened at SVB as part of the mandate were eventually balanced and closed, with the assets paid out or handed over to the refugees. Where this was not possible, the SVB transferred the assets and valuables to the Police Division in Bern.

SVB accounting documentation contained in the Central Corporate Archives (account ledger sheets, lists of balances) allows us to make detailed statements about the financial position of 13,804 civilian refugees whose assets were deposited with SVB in accordance with the Federal Council Decree of 12 March 1943.

In the original German edition of this book, CSG for the first time presents academically researched information about the size and the use of civilian refugees' assets in Switzerland during the Second World War. It has been possible to make statements about the total amount of assets brought into Switzerland by civilian refugees, about the sums paid into and out of accounts in Switzerland, about how these sums were used, and about the total amount taken away by refugees when they finally left the country.

The Police Division instructed SVB to manage the assets and valuables concerned on the basis of the Federal Council Decree of 12 March 1943 and the agreement between the Police Division and SVB of 18 May 1943. This switch to professional management by a bank had become necessary because the large number of refugees taken in by Switzerland in the late summer of 1942 was putting an excessive strain on the staffing capacity and technical expertise of the federal authorities and military units. It was no longer possible for the Police Division of the FDJP to guarantee that assets would be received and processed in accordance with correct banking and accounting practice, or that they would be kept secure in the refugee camps, which had become overcrowded.

Civilian refugees were allowed free access to Sfr 100 in cash from their assets, and Sfr 300 in valuables. These unrestricted amounts did not have to be deposited with SVB. The assets held by SVB remained the property of the civilian refugees, who could access them with permission from the Police Division. Most withdrawals were made to defray small costs incurred in the refugee camps and homes. Civilian refugees who were not called on to work in labor camps and who had enough assets at SVB to pay for accommodation at a hotel or boarding house could arrange for regular transfers to cover their living costs; 936 civilian refugees made withdrawals of this type from SVB, taking out sums of between Sfr 400 and Sfr 1,000 each month.

Because of the war, the Swiss financial sector was subject to a large number of regulations. Some of these – such as the maximum price rules for gold coins (as laid down in the Federal Council Decree of 7 December 1942) or the ban on trading in dollar and sterling banknotes (Federal Council Decree of 2 March 1945) – affected civilian refugees, too. Alongside general account management tasks, the mandate required SVB to exchange foreign currency notes and sell securities as instructed by refugees. It can be shown that in these matters, the civilian refugees enjoyed the same banking services and conditions as any other customers from abroad. The administrative services that SVB performed for the Federal Government included calculating boarding costs on the basis of information supplied by camp managers. Using these calculations, the bank debited the accounts concerned by the appropriate amounts. With the help of rolls from the refugee camps, SVB determined which refugees had money in bank accounts, and transferred a monthly allowance of between Sfr 20 and Sfr 30 to them. The Police Division could access civilian refugees' assets held at SVB in order to make sure that their public debts were settled. These debts included the costs incurred by the state for accommodating the refugees in camps and homes. However, in deference to the modest amount of assets owned by the majority of civilian refugees, the Police Division was reticent about charging board, so refugees with few assets were completely or partially exempted from these expenses. Most boarding costs were thus borne by the Federal Government in the first instance, and secondly by refugee charities.

The complexity of the situation when SVB took on the mandate presented the bank with an enormous challenge. On 25 May 1943, the Police Division thus ordered that a precise inventory be made of refugee assets. It was impossible to correctly allocate all of the valuables, some of which were kept in collective containers, without the help of the owners – especially when the only receipts available were summary rather than individual ones. Given this situation, SVB insisted that the federal authorities and military reconstruct the entire history of the assets from their receipt, via their disbursement in the refugee camps (including details of what they were used for), to their transfer to SVB. The bank created its own special form, known as the 'transfer protocol', to facilitate this process. From the beginning of the mandate onward, SVB documented all asset movements on the appropriate account ledgers. In this way, SVB fulfilled the Police Division's wish to establish complete transparency about the type, the size and the usage of cash assets and valuables brought into the country by refugees. Furthermore, the Police Division, like SVB, wanted to be able to provide the refugees with information about their property at any time, so that complaints and time-consuming research into the whereabouts of assets could be avoided in the future.

As a consequence of the Police Division's instruction to exchange foreign banknotes into Swiss francs, SVB found itself in a delicate position, torn between the interests of the refugees, the Swiss government, and the Allies. One of the ways in which the Allies waged economic warfare was to control monetary flows and the circulation of their own currencies' banknotes. Pressure was exerted on SVB via the British and American Embassies in Bern – the bank was even threatened with inclusion on the 'Blacklist' – in an attempt to make it stop trading in UK sterling and US dollar notes. The Allies feared that large amounts of these notes could be moved into Switzerland disguised as refugee assets, and then converted into Swiss francs for use in the German war effort. Ultimate responsibility for the refugees' assets rested with the Police Division, which had to ensure that the currency conversions were made at the official exchange rate – something that SVB could guarantee. As a result of the war, foreign banknotes owned by the refugees were exposed to massive devaluation. In order to keep exchange rate losses to a minimum, the Police Division ordered that SVB had to convert foreign notes no later than one week after receipt. However, when Switzerland gave in to Allied pressure and issued the ban on banknote trading on 2 March 1945, refugees suffered because they could no longer exchange their foreign banknotes into Swiss francs.

Assets were eventually returned by SVB on the orders of the Police Division. Because the manner of repayment was determined by the refugee's location, SVB was saddled with various time-consuming administrative procedures. There were three basic options: refugees who returned to liberated countries prior to the end of the war could be given their assets in the camps as soon as SVB had delivered the bank assets and valuables concerned to the camps in sealed envelopes. Refugees who left Switzerland after the end of the war by specially organized group transportation were given back their assets at the expatriation camps. Finally, refugees who traveled out of Switzerland on their own could withdraw their assets from the nearest branch of SVB or from another bank at the place where they were staying. SVB made efforts to return all assets to their owners. Where this was not possible, the assets were transferred to the Police Division. Systematic analysis of the relevant documents in the Central Corporate Archives confirms that all of the assets held in cash accounts and securities accounts were paid out or delivered to the entitled refugees or to the Police Division. Consequently, there are no dormant refugee accounts at SVB.

Overall, managing refugee assets was not a profitable business for SVB. In fact, looking after the large number of small accounts consumed so much time and effort that the bank made a loss on the operation. It simply could not cover the costs generated by all the services it provided, such as transferring allowances, calculating boarding costs, and settling insurance premiums and tax debts, not to mention taking care of the entire bookkeeping.

SVB managed the assets of 13,804 civilian refugees in total. A breakdown of clients by nationality shows that the largest groups were Italian (25.7%), French (22.8%) and Polish (14.9%). Broken down by religion, 48.8% of all civilian refugees were Jewish, while 36.6% were Catholics. Because we still have a complete inventory of refugee assets, as well as extensive accounting documentation, we are able to make a rough estimate of the size of refugee assets: over the course of the fiduciary mandate (1943–1956) SVB looked after cash account assets worth approximately Sfr 17 million. Added to this, the assets held in safekeeping accounts came to at least Sfr 11.4 million. The approximately 100,000 items classed as 'valuables' included gold coins, jewelry and precious stones, watches, cameras and securities. Cash assets were deposited in no fewer than 34 different currencies. About a quarter of the civilian refugees registered in Switzerland imported total cash assets of around Sfr 2 million. The other Sfr 15 million of cash was transferred as support payments from Switzerland or abroad by civilian refugees after coming to Switzerland, or paid to them for work they did, or received as income on assets already invested at other banks in Switzerland. Of the grand total of about Sfr 28.4 million of assets, an estimated Sfr 16.1 million remained in Switzerland. Civilian refugees spent about Sfr 13.9 million of this on living expenses, and about Sfr 2.2 million on other items. Repayments of boarding costs to the Swiss government came to approximately Sfr 0.9 million.

Joseph Jung

Born 1955; studied Swiss history, modern history, history of law and German at the University of Fribourg; doctorate 1987; Assistant Professor at Zurich's Federal Institute of Technology and Visiting Professor at the University of Fribourg; Head of Foundations, Corporate History and Archives, Credit Suisse Group, Zurich. Has published widely on cultural and financial topics; see p. 237 for selected works.

Schweizerische Kreditanstalt: caught in the middle of Swiss-American financial relations 1941–1953

A study by Credit Suisse Group

Contents

*F*rom the early 1930s onward, money belonging to European customers began to pour out of Europe and into America. Increasingly restrictive German currency legislation gave further impetus to this flight of capital across the Atlantic. The complex form taken by some investments in the USA, along with the banking secrecy laws introduced by Switzerland in 1935, fed the American finance authorities' mistrust of Swiss banks during the war and the years thereafter. One investment product in particular, the collective account, became a focal point of their criticism. Because these 'omnibus accounts' were opened in the name of a (Swiss) financial institution, the identity of the individual bank customers behind the accounts (the 'beneficial owners') was concealed from American officials.

From 10 April 1940, as the German army was sweeping across Europe, the United States started blocking assets deposited in the USA by continental European owners. Registration of foreign assets with the US government was followed by several years of investigation by the Treasury Department into the Swiss banks' New York offices, during the course of which even sealed documents were forcibly opened. The reports that resulted from these audits criticized the Swiss banks because these institutions, invoking Switzerland's banking secrecy laws, would not disclose the names of beneficial owners. The Treasury Department assumed that American blocking rules were being evaded in the name of Swiss banking secrecy; numerous negotiations with Swiss bank officials took place throughout the war in an attempt to find a means by which the names of the beneficial owners could be disclosed. However, these talks were largely unsuccessful, and blocking regulations became increasingly restrictive. In spring 1946, the American asset freeze was revoked as part of the Washington Agreement; at the end of 1946, Switzerland's government gave the Swiss Compensation Office the job of certifying the blocked assets. Non-certified assets were subjected to a blanket presumption of enemy ownership and were confiscated ('vested') by the Americans from spring 1951 onwards (a process which came to an end in 1953).

Working from a substantial number of internal and external sources, we will examine Schweizerische Kreditanstalt (SKA) in the context of the very fraught financial relations that existed between Switzerland and the USA. What unfolds is a long history of failure to reach a consensus within Switzerland itself, a failure which was reflected in constant maneuvering and ultimately in the postponement of decisions. As a consequence, Switzerland laid itself open to serious reproach by the Allies.

1 Allied blocking and monitoring of assets: impact on Schweizerische Kreditanstalt's business activities, 1941–1945

1.1 Before the asset freeze

New investment institutions in North America: the establishment of Swiss American Corporation and the Credit Suisse New York Agency

With the flow of capital out of Switzerland beginning to increase, the establishment of a bank office in New York had been discussed at SKA's headquarters from the mid-1930s onwards. This idea was rejected, however, on the grounds that there was no point in setting up an additional 'vehicle' abroad that could not promise to generate profit.[1] Nonetheless, SKA established various new investment institutions overseas. The Custodian Trust Company (CTC), set up together with Fides in 1938, was popular with customers, particularly since its investment arrangements with the Bank of Montreal included special security measures to protect assets in the event of war. CTC's offices were in Charlottetown, Prince Edward Island (Canada).

The volume of foreign deposits held in Switzerland decreased with the decline in the number of German, Austrian, Czech and Italian customers. Only the French clientele remained well represented. The serious political crisis at the end of September 1938 made it clear to the Swiss financial services industry that even centers such as London, which had always been considered safe, were not impervious to international developments, and that in the event of war deposits there would not be freely accessible. For a variety of reasons, only the United States ultimately offered a secure venue for business activities.[2] The executive board felt that a 'foothold in New York' would satisfy the wishes of many existing customers, attract new customers and win back former customers.[3] As a result of an exploratory trip to New York in the fall of 1938 by SKA executive board member Joseph Straessle, SKA learned that the Jewish bank Speyer & Co., New York, was in liquidation owing to the advanced age of its owner. Speyer & Co. enjoyed a good reputation in both America and Europe. A takeover would present an opportunity to 'aryanize' the bank 'amicably'.[4] However, in December 1938 the board of directors' finance committee decided not to purchase the Jewish establishment for the time being, because SKA wanted to avoid being identified as a Jewish sympathizer. Finally, in July 1939, SKA opened its own base in New York in the form of its subsidiary, Swiss American Corporation (Swissam).[5] Suitable office space 'with the appropriate cachet'[6] was rented near Wall Street in the building previously occupied by the liquidated Speyer & Co. at 24–26 Pine Street; several of Speyer's lead-

Chronology of Swiss-American financial relations (1939–1951)

1939	28 June: Founding of Swiss American Corporation in New York (subsidiary of SKA).
	Mid-July: Swiss American Corporation commences business.
1940	9 May: Opening of the New York Agency (SKA's first foreign branch office).
1941	14 June: US Treasury Department tightens control of financial transactions with continental Europe.
	Following the gradual blocking of assets belonging to Axis countries and Axis-occupied territories, all continental European assets located in the United States are blocked.
1941	18 December: First War Powers Act – creation of the Office of Alien Property (OAP) for the purpose of vesting enemy assets in the United States.
1943	20 October: Escalated blocking of Swiss assets in the United States under General Ruling No. 17.
1945	16 February: Federal Council blocks German assets in Switzerland.
	8 March: Conclusion of the Currie Agreement between Switzerland and the Allies.
	30 October: Allied Control Council issues Law No. 5 on the Vesting and Marshalling of German External Assets Abroad.
1946	25 May: Conclusion of the Washington Agreement.
	22 November: Certification Agreement between Switzerland and the United States.
	27 December: Federal Council instructs the Swiss Compensation Office (SCO) to certify blocked Swiss assets in the United States.
1947	From March: Certification of blocked Swiss assets in the United States by the Swiss Compensation Office.
1948	February: Under the Snyder Plan, a presumption of enemy ownership is applied without exception to all uncertified Swiss assets in the United States so that they can ultimately be vested and used as aid under the Marshall Plan.
1951	Vesting of uncertified Swiss assets in the United States begins. The campaign to release these assets lasted into the 1970s. Only about 1.7% of all SKA's blocked US investments were vested.

ing stockbrokers were hired.[7] Swissam's major activity was investment banking, with an emphasis on underwriting, equities trading, bonds, real estate and mortgages, and stockbrokerage. As a 'business corporation', Swissam was not permitted to accept customer money and invest it for its own account; customer deposits could be maintained, however, 'as long as the accounts were active'.[8] Like the arrangement with the Custodian Trust Company, Swissam customers also had the opportunity to invest their assets via SKA bank offices in Switzerland using a numbered or pseudonym account and stipulating a right of access in the United States in the event of the military occupation of Switzerland.

The new subsidiary in America replaced the investment facilities previously available within Europe: since 1922, SKA customers, motivated primarily by a desire for geographical diversification, had deposited assets with SKA's subsidiary N.V. Effecten-Maatschappij, Amsterdam (EMA), which EMA reinvested primarily in the United States. Following the American blocking of assets from occupied territories and the decree issued by the Royal Netherlands Government exiled in London on 24 May 1940, EMA's accounts were blocked as Dutch assets, even though many of them belonged to Swiss citizens resident in Switzerland. A special license made it possible to transfer EMA omnibus accounts from various US deposit banks to Swissam, though these accounts remained blocked under the name of EMA, which was wound up in 1941.[9]

Key terms relating to the blocking and unblocking of assets

account	In English, this term encompasses both the German concepts of 'securities account' ('Depot') and 'cash account' ('Konto'). Because a securities account cannot be maintained without a cash account, the term 'account' will be used here to include both types of accounts, although strictly speaking securities account management practices can differ from those for cash accounts.
omnibus account	American term for an account integrating the assets and/or securities of several different customers. Omnibus accounts were managed in the name of a financial institution and kept in a US deposit bank. The names of the individual customers were not disclosed to the US deposit bank. The term 'collective securities account' ('Kollektivdepot' or 'Sammeldepot') was also used synonymously for 'omnibus securities account'.
rubric account, sub-account	A special account that was attached to an omnibus account and that was the property of an individual customer or group of customers.
beneficial owner	The owner of the economic benefit of an asset; has a direct claim to the asset.
interest	Any type of direct or indirect claim or entitlement to an asset.
(general) license	Government permission under US law to engage in activities otherwise prohibited by Executive Orders Nos. 8389 and 8785, which froze continental European assets and prohibited transactions with blocked assets. In addition to generally applicable licenses, special licenses were also issued.
national	A 'national' was a citizen of a given country or a resident of a given country, as defined under US law in General License No. 17 (20 October 1943). Swiss living abroad had 'dual nationality' according to this license.
certification/certificate	Government authentication issued by the Swiss Compensation Office in 1947 and 1948. The United States insisted that the Swiss government authenticate, or certify, that the conditions laid down in General License No. 95 and other agreements with the United States were met before regulated assets were unblocked.
to vest/vesting	The confiscation by the United States during and after the war of property belonging to citizens of certain foreign countries ('enemy assets'). Property rights were transferred to the US government.
to escheat/escheatment	The reversion of dormant property to the US government – a legal construct that releases banks from responsibility for the dormant assets.
to refund	Property that reverted to the state could be returned to the beneficiary or his heirs upon presentation of specific documentation.

SKA's management was not initially drawn to the idea of having an SKA branch office in New York, as it already had good relations with a number of American banks with which it could conduct its American transactions. However, once the war had begun, the proposal took on a new importance and new urgency, especially since a US branch would be in a position to carry on dealing with European business.[10] SKA's managers considered it their duty 'in the interest of our shareholders, to transfer a portion of our assets to whatever place can currently be considered the most secure'.[11] SBV (Schweizerischer Bankverein, known internationally as Swiss Bank Corporation, or SBC) had already established a branch office in New York, and SKA's customers expected an equivalent facility. The SKA New York Agency was opened on 9 May 1940 in the same building as Swissam.[12] The Agency promoted itself among its European clientele as an expert on the US market for commercial banking business and securities transactions,

Relocation of business offices during times of war

The German annexation ('Anschluss') of Austria and its occupation of Czechoslovakia showed only too clearly how companies could easily be taken over by an occupying force using pseudo-legal means. Consequently, after the Netherlands, Belgium and Norway were occupied, their governments in exile guaranteed businesses in their respective countries secure domiciles abroad. In October 1939, the Swiss Federal Council issued a decree providing for the automatic relocation of the seat of government and of the domicile of Swiss businesses in the event that Switzerland was invaded or occupied.[13] At the same time, all executive powers associated with the old government or business domicile would be severed. Likewise, 'invasion clauses' permitted banks to amend arrangements for customers investing overseas: customer services that would normally have been offered in Switzerland could be automatically halted and transferred to a previously designated person overseas.[14]

The Federal Council Decree of 30 October 1939 on the relocation of legal entities and commercial companies during wartime gave the Swiss government the right to transfer the domicile of a Swiss company in an occupied area or in an area threatened with occupation to the place where the Swiss government had taken its seat. If the seat of government were relocated abroad, all affected companies would then automatically be able to maintain their legal domicile at that location. Swiss firms that wanted to avail themselves of this opportunity had to enter their names on a list kept by the Commercial Registry; in the event of war, the company's domicile would then be changed automatically by official act ('statutory change of domicile', Article 1). It was also possible for a company's executive board to designate an alternative place of business within Switzerland ('voluntary change of domicile', Article 6). As soon as the new domicile became legally effective, the old business address would become invalid and, if possible, be removed from the Commercial Register. Should operations continue at the old domicile, the authorities would convert the office concerned into a branch. The mandates of board members, managers, and agents remaining in occupied areas would be automatically revoked for the enterprise as a whole and would be strictly limited to local operations.

SKA, too, decided that it would relocate its head office in the event of war. This decision was made legally valid on 22 November 1939 by the Federal Department of Justice and Police (FDJP).[15]

for general American business, and for stock brokerage and currency transactions.[16] In contrast to Swissam, SKA's Agency was allowed to engage in all banking activities in the United States. The only exception was that the Agency could not accept money from US companies and US private citizens. The permitted activities were conducted without change for the next 24 years, with an emphasis on services for foreign customers – particularly the numerous foreign citizens who had taken up residence in the United States.[17] The board of directors made it clear when the Agency was established that it 'should distance itself from any speculative transactions, whether in securities or hard currency. It should conduct its bank transactions according to the fundamental principles that we have established for our existing branch network…'[18] Both Swissam and the Agency were established under American law. This meant that American law governed the business activities as well as the assets of SKA's New York offices. After the United States entered the Second World War, SKA's offices in the United States became subject not only to normal peacetime laws, but also to American war legislation.

Whereas prior to the establishment of SKA's own offices in New York, SKA had held accounts at various US correspondent banks, after May 1940 it placed most dollar assets at the New York Agency.[19] Branch offices in Switzerland were instructed to direct as many sale and stock orders as possible to the New York Agency or Swissam, 'with allowances to be made only for Brown Brothers Harriman & Co., and, to an even lesser extent, J. P. Morgan & Co.'.[20] The volume of investments increased rapidly; the Agency employed 37 employees, Swissam 25.[21]

Case study: securities accounts held by SKA's Kreuzlingen branch at American correspondent banks from 1930 to 1945

When discussing the opening of SKA customer accounts in the United States between 1930 and 1945, we have to distinguish between two separate periods: the years before the establishment of Swissam and the Agency on the one hand, and the years thereafter on the other. Until the turning point came in 1939/1940, all of SKA's deposited assets in the United States were kept at American correspondent banks. But once SKA had established its own US offices, it could offer its customers the choice of depositing their investments with Swissam or the Agency, or with an American correspondent bank. A case study of the SKA branch in the town of Kreuzlingen (located by Switzerland's border with Germany), where documents from the relevant period remain largely intact, demonstrates the extent to which SKA investment customers chose one or the other option.

From 1930 to 1945, all securities account customers at the Kreuzlingen branch were listed in four large ledgers along with details of their securities.[22] In addition to information on the number of customers investing overseas and the type of accounts used, the documents also indicate the designated American correspondent bank and the point in time at which the customers purchased their assets or transferred them to the United States. Of a total of 648 securities account customers at the branch[23], 69 customers (i.e. 10.6% of the total) are listed as investors in North America between 1930 and 1945. Of these 69 depositors, 55 were Swiss, 7 were German, 3 were stateless, and one was Italian; there was one Polish couple and 2 customers whose citizenship was not specified. According to the entries, the branch's US investments were all placed in collective securities accounts with larger 'home banks', mostly 'under the direction of our Zurich head office'. As with other small and mid-sized SKA branches, the Kreuzlingen branch did not maintain collective securities accounts in North America under its own name, but rather entrusted its customers to a larger organization. Thus a three-tiered system was created: the owner of the securities (the beneficial owner) had contact with his branch, and the branch had contact with head office. Head office was designated as the 'legal owner' of the collective securities account in the United States. Only head office had any contact with the US correspondent bank, and the beneficial owner was not disclosed to the American bank. It was virtually inevitable that this would give rise to suspicions in the United States that the assets in such accounts were being willfully hidden because they belonged to the enemy.

Arrangements for SKA customers abroad

One problem with the Swiss banks' collective accounts, which otherwise provided excellent protection for Swiss and foreign customers, was that the depositor could only access his assets through the Swiss 'home bank'. Because the customer had to consider the possibility of an enemy takeover of the financial institution, the banks thus offered special arrangements for overseas deposits. These allowed the customer to access his assets independently, in the same way as a direct depositor, in the event of war. The customer would thus continue to be protected by Swiss banking secrecy even if war broke out. The customer's identity could remain undisclosed in America until the 'change-over', i.e. the transfer of the overseas account by separate contract to a direct-access arrangement. Given the Allied enemy legislation on the one hand and Swiss banking secrecy on the other, it was inevitable that these 'secret contracts in sealed envelopes' between the customer and the bank would lead to speculation and suspicion on the part of the Americans. Two such arrangements that SKA offered before the Second World War are discussed below.[24]

Custodian Trust Company, Charlottetown, Prince Edward Island, Canada

The Custodian Trust Company (CTC) in Charlottetown, Canada, was founded by Fides and SKA in September 1938, at a time when the uncertain political situation in Europe was prompting 'many of our foreign and domestic customers to approach us about accessing their securities located abroad, primarily in America and England, in the event of a military conflict'.[25] The Royal Trust Company, Montreal, managed CTC. Agreements made between customers and CTC for the event of war or invasion were a significant part of the arrangement. In the event of war, customer responsibility was to be 'changed-over' to the previously designated, secure Canadian location. The connection to the Swiss bank office that had maintained a collective account in its own name with CTC in times of peace would be severed, and the customer would be able to access his assets in Canada or London upon presentation of the proper identification. This arrangement was very popular among SKA and Fides customers up until the Commonwealth Blockade of 1940.[26]

SKA's securities deposits with CTC consisted of a number of 'sub-accounts' belonging to individual customers. These sub-accounts were managed under keywords. Delivery orders on behalf of the true owners were filled out in triplicate and sent to CTC, Royal Trust Montreal, and Royal Trust London. These orders were placed in sealed envelopes along with other personal information: customer identification with signature samples and photographs, a list of securities transferred by the customer, an indemnification for CTC signed by the customer, and a standard form letter setting forth the details of the change-over formalities.[27] The joint right of access for Fides and SKA was to expire automatically in the event that war was declared on Switzerland or if Switzerland was occupied. SKA's name would be automatically removed and the accounts would be maintained under the keyword 'CTC'. According to the 5 January 1939 minutes of the SKA board of directors, 'the depositor's name [was] therefore unknown to Custodian Trust; in the event the feared events [should come to pass], these customers ... [could present themselves to] Montreal, London, or Charlotte[town] ... give the keyword, and, after properly identifying themselves, gain access to their securities. In this way, we could accommodate entirely the wishes of our clients.' Head office advised interested customers 'to set these accounts up in advance as joint survivorship accounts so that more than one person could be authorized to dispose fully of the assets upon appropriate identification in London or Montreal'.[28]

Upon CTC's inquiry, Fides declared in the fall of 1939 that the sub-accounts it had opened did not contain enemy assets and that the customers concerned were not citizens of countries that were at war with Great Britain.[29]

SKA customer arrangements
with Swiss American Corporation

After the establishment of SKA's subsidiary Swiss American Corporation (Swissam), similar deposits were managed via SKA's head office and branches as rubric accounts in the form of pseudonym or numbered accounts.[30] These arrangements were less complicated than those at CTC. Certain information was placed in a sealed envelope: a letter to Swissam consistent with the war clause; a sample signature; handwritten instructions from the customer about the handling of securities, opening of cash accounts, and retention of correspondence; and instructions for contacting the customer directly. After a change-over had been executed, all customer instructions had to be submitted in handwritten form; only then could they be carried out. The letter also contained a short, handwritten statement of indemnity from the customer. The 'Agreement' between Swissam and the customer and a power of attorney (optional) signed by the grantee was also enclosed in the envelope. Instructions on what to do with the envelope were detailed in a letter to Swissam; this described the circumstances under which the envelope was to be opened (war clauses) and included a statement noting that the arrangement was irrevocable and valid for an unlimited period.[31]

With respect to these specially designated accounts ('earmarked accounts'), the lawyers for the SKA offices in New York instructed Swissam not to open the sealed envelopes when the event triggering the legal transfer of the customer to the American bank office (the 'change-over') occurred, but rather to wait until the customer concerned came forward and identified him/herself in the prescribed manner. Prior investigation of the beneficial owner's identity would not be necessary or indeed practicable, since the account was being maintained for an unknown person. If the United States entered the war, it was foreseeable that the Alien Property Administration would order the immediate opening of the sealed envelopes.[32]

SKA's post-war arrangements

In the 1950s, when Europe was worrying about the prospects of an imminent new war, the 'CREDMONT Arrangement' replaced earlier arrangements. This allowed the customer to authorize a bank to transfer his North American securities to a rubric account at Credit Suisse (Canada) in Montreal. A letter with specific information about the conditions under which the envelope could be opened accompanied the sealed envelope. Opening such an envelope required approval from a CREDMONT board member. To access his assets, a customer had to appear in person in Montreal and have his fingerprints compared with the copy of the fingerprints in the envelope. These 'sealed envelope arrangements' were still in general use for smaller depositors and third-party banks up to the 1980s.

Before SKA's own offices opened in 1939 and 1940, the correspondent banks most favored by head office in Zurich were Brown Brothers Harriman, J. P. Morgan, Guaranty Trust, and Bankers Trust, according to documents from the Kreuzlingen branch.[33] Of the total of 69 Kreuzlingen branch customers who kept securities in American banks between 1930 and 1945, 54 customers (about 78%) arranged for SKA to deposit their securities with the above American correspondents. Many customers distributed their investments among different correspondent banks in order to reduce their risk exposure. The choice of bank was dictated not only by the level of fees charged, but also by arrangements made between the banks for reasons of reciprocity. Cost considerations meant that it was not worth transferring securities already held locally.

Some isolated North American deposits begin to appear in the account ledgers from 1930 on. As the following list of purchase orders issued by customers of the Kreuzlingen branch between 1930 and 1945 indicates, demand for securities held in US securities accounts increased markedly in 1936. Investments peaked in 1936 and 1937. There was a spurt of investments when the Credit Suisse New York Agency opened in May 1940, but this collapsed again in October 1940.[34] After the Americans blocked Swiss assets in June 1941, investments were only sporadic until 1943; the documents

SKA: number of purchase orders issued by the Kreuzlingen branch for accounts held at North American correspondent banks (1930–1945)

	1930–1935	1936–1937	1938–1940	1941–1943	1944–1945	Total	% per bank
Brown Brothers Harriman & Co., New York		42	23	7	8	80	28.4
Credit Suisse New York Agency			37	9	8	54	19.2
J. P. Morgan, New York		24	11	1	2	38	13.5
Guaranty Trust, New York	5	13	10	3	5	36	12.8
Bankers Trust, New York	9	7	4	1	6	27	9.6
National City Bank, New York	4		1	3		8	2.8
Bank of the Manhattan Co., New York		6	3			9	3.2
Bank of Montreal, Montreal			4	1		5	1.8
A. Iselin & Co., New York	5	4				9	3.2
Swiss American Corporation, New York					2	2	0.7
SBC New York Agency			1		5	6	2.1
Dillon Read & Co., New York	2					2	0.7
Hallgarten & Co., New York					1	1	0.3
Royal Bank of Canada, Montreal					1	1	0.3
Chase National Bank of the City of New York					1	1	0.3
Central Hanover Bank & Trust Co., New York			3			3	1.1
Total	25	96	97	25	39	282	100

show the emergence of a cautious revival in interest in 1944 and 1945. Payments for purchase orders from customers of the Kreuzlingen branch show that from 1930 to 1945, a smaller proportion of securities invested in North America were deposited at Swiss bank agencies (25% of purchase orders), while the majority (75%) were deposited at American banks.

Developments prior to the freeze imposed by the USA on all continental European assets on 14 June 1941

While CTC in Canada successfully booked deposits worth between Sfr 180 million and Sfr 190 million by the time the war started, from June 1940 onwards the arrangement became unsatisfactory for customers. This was because of the Commonwealth Blockade. After November 1940, Canadian securities could no longer be traded without authenticated certificates of ownership.[35] Swissam also reported a downturn in business, as well as noticeably longer approval periods for accounts of Swiss origin whenever there was the slightest uncertainty about the actual nationality of the owner.[36]

At the end of May 1940, Swissam informed Zurich that some sealed envelopes that were needed to open rubric accounts had not arrived. The executive board sent a letter to the branch offices, stating: 'We ask you to keep in mind that all of your correspondence will be examined by a censor.'[37] In February 1941, the executive board advised against physically transporting American securities to New York, which could now take months, because the British authorities had been withholding mail in Bermuda for some time. Securities could only be sent to New York at the customer's risk.[38] The Agency asked head office and the branches not to mention certain subjects when writing to New York. The Agency management explained that until then, Swiss banks had been 'warmly received' in the United States. The domestic banks, however, were generally unhappy about foreign institutions establishing full-scale branches. 'Under these circumstances, we should expect the bank examiners to put not only our balance sheets under the microscope, but our entire business management. […] There must be no mention in our correspondence of tax evasion.'[39]

Both the Agency and Swissam reported high staffing levels at the beginning of 1941. Space in the Speyer Building was tight, so offices were rented for both companies at Goldman Sachs & Co. at 30 Pine Street.[40] However, the founders' expectations of success were not fulfilled. In the summer of 1940, the influx of dollar-denominated assets ebbed. A comparison of the Agency's balance sheets from 1 June 1940 and 27 August 1942 reveals that dollar investments with US banks decreased from about $ 20 million in 1940 to less than $ 3 million in 1942.[41] The 'Final Report, Swiss Bank Investigation', a US Treasury Department audit report, published figures on SKA's US investments held at the Agency itself and at American correspondent banks for June 1940 and June 1941. These figures clearly show that even in June 1941 – a year after the establishment of the Credit Suisse New York Agency – the majority of US investments were still held at American correspondent banks.[42]

SKA: investments held at the Credit Suisse New York Agency and at banks in the United States (June 1940/41)

(in 1000 $)		1940	1941
New York Agency	Securities	18 250	19 912
	Cash	30 373	27 518
Other banks in the USA		101 368	55 979
Total		149 991	103 409

In the fall of 1940, the Swiss public became 'concerned about possible blocking measures that the United States of America might take against Switzerland'[43]; this led to a substantial repatriation of capital back to Switzerland from the beginning of 1941.[44] In response to an inquiry from the banks, the Federal Political Department (FPD) stated that 'blocking measures against non-combatant or non-occupied European states are not anticipated by the relevant US agencies'. Customer inquiries were met with the response that 'Swiss debt to the USA is miniscule compared to our claims on that country, and therefore a block [should be seen as] only a temporary measure and not as a confiscation'.[45] Bankers in New York, however, took the possibility of a block on Swiss assets very seriously at a time when Switzerland was encircled by the Axis powers.[46]

In a submission of 14 December 1940 to the relevant US government agencies, Eduard A. Feer, a member of the Swiss Legation in Washington, referred to the rumors that were circulating about blocking measures.[47] Undersecretary of State Sumner Welles sent him the following response on 17 December 1940: '[…] No action of this type is in immediate prospect.'[48] However, the various US government agencies held different opinions about freezing Swiss assets. While the State Department was critical of such a plan, in the Treasury Department 'Secretary Morgenthau and some of his legal counsel could not be dissuaded from their conviction that freezing [Swiss assets] was the only means of exercising the desired control over transactions with foreign money'.[49] In a note from the FPD to Secretary of State Cordell Hull in February 1941 describing the impact of an asset freeze on Switzerland's economic and monetary policies, the Swiss banks declared their readiness 'to make every effort to avoid conflict with measures taken by the United States, and in particular to eschew violations of the American blocking requirements'.[50] Walter Fessler, a member of the SKA executive board, had talks with the Treasury Department in April. He emphasized that Switzerland rejected a block on Swiss assets for reasons of principle and that, by virtue of its neutrality and its democratic government, Switzerland could not be subjected to these restrictions. Moreover, American accusations and data on the volume of Swiss-German business were heavily exaggerated. It was true that Switzerland was engaged in business with the Germans, but only on condition that it did not violate American or Swiss law in the process.[51] At the beginning of June 1941, Bern suggested sending a special delegation to America to explain Switzerland's unique situation. The Swiss envoy, however, felt that the timing was bad because the 'USA is entirely absorbed with its own problems' and its political direction was not yet certain.[52]

On 14 June 1941, President Franklin Delano Roosevelt ordered the blocking of all assets belonging to the countries of continental Europe.

Blocked assets in the United States: the Treasury Department census

On 14 June 1941, the US ordered that the 'Census of Foreign-Owned Assets in the United States' be taken immediately; the cut-off date for assets of occupied countries was 30 June 1940. The results were published in 1945.[53] The census yielded information on the structure of foreign-owned assets in the United States and on the owners. It served not only as the statistical basis for implementing the freeze, but also for the subsequent unblocking of assets. Ultimately, it was also an important source of information for the reconstruction of war-damaged areas. The registration requirement applied to all legal entities and natural persons who were managing property for 'foreign countries' (from the perspective of the United States) or for nationals (on the basis of domicile) of such countries.

About 565,000 completed 'TFR-300' forms were submitted. The total value of assets meeting the above definition as of 14 June 1941 was $ 12.7 billion. Two-thirds of this amount belonged to 84,000 persons living in Europe; about one-seventh belonged

Foreign investments in the United States by country (14 June 1941)

	Value of investments ($ m)	Percentage of total European investments	Percentage of total worldwide investments
United Kingdom	3 238.9	39.9	25.4
Canada	1 709.2	–	13.4
Switzerland	1 210.6	14.9	9.5
France	1 040.5	12.8	8.2
Netherlands	976.7	12.0	7.7
Sweden	366.2	4.5	2.9
China	356.4	–	2.8
Belgium	312.7	3.8	2.4
Philippines	276.8	–	2.2
Argentina	233.4	–	1.8
Germany	198.0	2.4	1.5
Cuba	171.8	–	1.3
Panama	170.1	–	1.3
Japan	160.5	–	1.2
Mexico	159.8	–	1.2
Italy	129.6	1.6	1.1
Spain	59.8	0.7	0.5
Portugal	59.7	0.7	0.5
Romania	19.5	0.2	0.2
Hungary	9.9	0.1	0.1
Other countries	1 878.6	–	14.8
Total worldwide	12 738.7	–	100.0
Of which Europe	*8 127.6*	*100.0*	*63.8*

to 29,000 persons in Canada. The remainder was split fairly evenly between Latin America and Asia. Dollar assets belonging to persons from countries affected by the blocking rules came to about $ 6 billion, or $ 8 billion incuding gold and securities. More than 132,000 'foreign individuals' held assets in the United States worth $ 2.6 billion. Many of them had assets worth less than $ 5,000. Twenty-three thousand foreign corporations held property worth about $ 8 billion; $ 2.1 billion had been invested in the US by government institutions. In the Treasury Department's view, this was a large sum, but not large enough to threaten the American economy. Switzerland was the third largest foreign investor, ranking behind the United Kingdom and Canada but ahead of France and the Netherlands. Swiss assets in the United States accounted for 9.5% of the total from all countries and 14.9% of the total from European countries.[54]

1.2 Blocking foreign assets in the USA:
first phase, 14 June 1941 to 20 October 1943

Reasons for extending the asset freeze to Switzerland

Following the gradual blocking of assets belonging to the Axis powers and Axis-occupied countries, the American decree (Executive Order No. 8785) of 14 June 1941 blocked all continental European assets, including Swedish and Swiss property. Bern authorized its Minister in Washington, Karl Bruggmann, to convey the Swiss government's surprise and dismay in a note to Secretary of State Cordell Hull.[55]

Unlike business circles in Switzerland, which optimistically believed that negotiations could result in a speedy and general easing of restrictions or perhaps even a total exemption for all Swiss financial transactions, the Swiss Legation in Washington and branches of Swiss firms in the United States considered the situation far graver. In his keynote report to the FPD, Minister Bruggmann in Washington emphasized the 'deep-rooted mistrust' felt by the responsible offices in the American government. It was difficult to disabuse Americans of their 'largely inaccurate ideas about the amount of German and Italian assets in Switzerland' and, above all, of their suspicions about the Swiss banks' role as intermediaries – a role that they had purportedly played for the enemies of Great Britain up until June 1941. 'The principal accusations involve the flight of American-held Axis assets through Switzerland, the transfer of Axis assets to Swiss persons, trade in Sperrmarks [blocked marks], the repatriation of German and Italian dollar bonds, the purchase of dollar banknotes, etc. It is assumed that such activity is still being conducted to the extent possible, even today.' Swiss banking secrecy was considered an effective means of cloaking assets; the possibility of opening discreet numbered accounts and 'the apparent willingness of certain banks to enter into all kinds of machinations that were conceivable only under the protection of banking secrecy' gave rise to mistrust in a country where banks were strictly regulated by the authorities. There was no confidence in the Swiss professional associations either, Bruggmann said, because in the USA the equivalent institutions represented the US banks' business interests; so it was assumed that the Swiss Bankers Association and stock exchange associations did the same. Another main reason for the mistrust was, the minister continued, that in Switzerland it was customary to issue bearer shares, whereas in the United States only registered shares – which facilitated reliable monitoring of ownership – were permitted. Even if their activities were perfectly legitimate, Bruggmann felt compelled to criticize Swiss businesses in the United States for committing blunders and tactical errors in relations with American officials, thus fueling the Americans' preconceived notions.[56]

Scope of General License No. 50 and the question
of a Swiss government guarantee

Under a new regulation (General License No. 50 of 20 June 1941) the American government granted Switzerland and the SNB a specific right of codetermination, though only for internal Swiss transactions. In America's view, more frequent use of this 'license' was desirable as long as there was official confirmation that it was not being used to benefit Germany, Italy, or the citizens of these countries.[57] The SNB refused to assume responsibility for ensuring that the banks complied with the blocking orders or for monitoring their implementation.[58] This refusal was prompted not least by the SNB's interests in the United States – it did not want to endanger its gold and dollar reserves – and by the fact that the financial transactions were so complicated that 'neither the National Bank nor any other government office was in a position to determine whether the transactions complied with the American rules or not …'.[59] The banks continued on the one hand to stand up for banking secrecy, while on the other calling for an official guarantor: the conditions under which they were operating – particularly with regard to asset transfers between blocked accounts – would only improve if a guarantor was in place. The banks' main demand was to have their own general license, or improved cooperation with the SNB on the basis of General License No. 50.

Gentlemen's Agreement on payment transactions with the US:
merchandise dollars and finance dollars

Before the SNB would address specific bank requests, it insisted on a firm agreement with the banks regarding dollar transactions: the Swiss Bankers Association (SBA) grudgingly signed the 'Gentlemen's Agreement' with the SNB on 17 September 1941, dividing payment transactions with the United States into two categories: payments for merchandise, and payments for financial transactions. Payments for exported merchandise, for the cost of diplomatic representation, and for insurance transactions were made with 'export dollars' or 'merchandise dollars' at a fixed rate of exchange and under guarantee from the SNB. The banks could use dollars for financing purposes without restriction in the form of 'finance dollars'.[60] The banks regarded the Agreement as temporary. In particular, they wanted to come to an agreement with the SNB on the open question of transfers of dollar-denominated interest payments received in the United States. The banks hoped that the SNB would take over their blocked interest income in the United States and make the equivalent amount available to them in Swiss currency.[61] In signing the Gentlemen's Agreement, the SNB had expected that dollar credits and debits would be roughly equal; but this was not the case. Instead, the supply of dollars used to pay for exports remained much greater than the demand for dollars to pay for goods that could be imported into Switzerland from dollar areas. By the end of June 1943, Switzerland's blocked currency holdings in the United States had risen by another Sfr 161 million.[62]

Since income earned on these assets could not be transferred to Switzerland, there was a danger of devaluation. Tax assessments in March 1942 acknowledged a 30% reduction in value on the claims concerned.[63]

Conflicts of interest

The conflict between the various Swiss interest groups on the one hand and between Switzerland and the Allies on the other intensified with Switzerland's rejection of the US request for it to provide government or SNB oversight for the implementation of the American decrees. In October 1943, this conflict resulted in the escalation of American regulations in the form of General Ruling No. 17.

In June 1941, the banks proposed the establishment of a consortium within the Bankers Association to function as the supervisory body responsible for transactions with the United States. The Swiss government recommended to the United States that it accept this internal bank solution, but US authorities refused to accept a non-governmental supervisory body.[64] A framework agreement between the banks and the Bankers Association was then proposed, on the basis of which the US Treasury Department would have approved applications. Negotiations with Washington, mediated by the Swiss envoy, progressed at a sluggish pace.[65] Chairman of the SKA board Adolf Jöhr was of the opinion that Switzerland's representatives in Washington were far too timid in handling this matter, whereas for political reasons the FPD had reservations about taking a more aggressive stance. Jöhr regretted that the Swiss were unable to propose an organization to the Americans that would be able to provide the requested guarantees.[66]

From December 1941 to August 1943, complaints were repeatedly raised within SKA's board of directors about the protracted negotiations, the lack of results, the parties' lack of interest, and the rejection of proposals. There is a record of a fierce argument with SNB President Ernst Weber, who apparently made no effort to support the banks[67] and who rejected the takeover of finance dollars by the SNB.[68] In a detailed and long-awaited report from Legation Counselor Robert Kohli of the FPD, Kohli made a new proposal for the government to take over blocked dollars in return for naming the beneficiaries, as well as a suggestion concerning the creation of 'Sperrfranken' ('blocked francs') to the equivalent value of the dollars taken over by the government; this proposal was dismissed as unattractive.[69] A plan to permit the SNB to take over blocked dollars from income earned on Swiss-owned American securities was rejected by the SNB itself – a decision which, according to the SKA board of directors, was 'unfortunate'. Three other plans were likewise dismissed.[70] No progress was made in the negotiations. The establishment of a trust[71] under License No. 50 and plans to regulate American coupon payments[72] were circulated for approval.

Swissam concentrated its business activities almost exclusively on the American continent, with underwriting activities at the forefront.[73] Transactions between America and Switzerland decreased dramatically. The Americans' opportunities to engage in trade with Switzerland were also limited because every contact with the Swiss was considered an indirect contact with the enemy under the Trading with the Enemy controls.[74] Trade between Zurich and New York became increasingly complicated. With the outbreak of war, SKA began sending all mailed communications in duplicate for security reasons ('Original by Air Mail, Duplicate by Steamer Mail'). In November 1942, mail deliveries between Switzerland, France and the Allies came to a complete halt. All communication had to be by telegram.[75] Business telegrams between Switzerland and the New York offices were encrypted by special code, the use of which for personal purposes was strongly prohibited by the censor.[76]

On 9 February 1943, Karl Bruggmann, the Swiss Minister in Washington, briefed Marcel Pilet-Golaz, the head of the FPD, on the Treasury Departments' blocking practices.[77] An improvement in the situation was not anticipated because the freezing policy was being 'implemented by blocking fanatics who enjoyed the full confidence of Secretary Morgenthau, who himself is too little acquainted with the subject to form his own opinion'. Bruggmann urgently requested Pilet-Golaz to reinforce the Legation with a financial adviser and proposed former SKA executive board member Joseph Straessle, who had been vice chairman of Swissam's board of directors in New York since 1942.[78] Straessle's knowledge of the Swiss and American economies was unparalleled. He had good relations with the banks, knew all about the complicated relations with the Treasury Department, was trusted by the Americans, and had the complete confidence of the Swiss government.[79] Straessle's tenure as financial adviser to the Swiss Legation in Washington began on 1 November 1943.[80]

On 25 May 1943, Peter Vieli, the Swiss envoy to Rome and former member of the SKA executive board, reported to Adolf Jöhr that a former manager of the papal finances, who had just returned from a trip to the United States, had been 'very struck by the extraordinarily hostile mentality prevalent in all American circles towards Europe as a whole'. The assets of neutral countries, above all Switzerland, were from the American perspective 'nothing more than camouflaged German money'. Vieli emphasized the urgency of proving beyond doubt the purely Swiss origin of the money.[81]

1.3 American investigations of Swiss companies in New York

On 14 June 1941, the Treasury Department ordered American banks to register the amounts held in all blocked accounts as of 30 June 1940 or 14 June 1941, along with details of the type of ownership and exact descriptions of the securities and their owners. This information was to be entered on TFR-300 forms, which were due in by the end of October.[82] This placed a tremendous burden especially on small Swiss branches – work in the evening and on weekends, the suspension of vacations – and there was grave concern about the feasibility of submitting all the required figures according to instructions within such a short period of time.[83] From the first day of the freezing, American auditors – the National Banking Examiners[84] – appeared on site at the New York offices of the Swiss banks, the assumption being that Germany was using Swiss banks as intermediaries.[85] At the same time, the search was on for loopholes in the American financial blockade policy.[86] From the very beginning, the Americans were suspicious of the Swiss offices' business practices and of the connections to South America that the Swiss banks maintained through their New York agencies. After examining these relationships, the second phase of the investigation involved an audit of all documents held by Swiss banking institutions in New York to determine customer identity.[87]

SKA's board of directors in Zurich wondered why the investigations were limited to foreign agencies and did not include American depository banks, which were certain to be holding a larger volume of 'suspicious' assets thanks to their pre-war contacts with Europe.[88] But this antipathy on the part of American bankers towards their Swiss competitors was not new. As early as 1927, for example, the big Swiss banks succeeded in frustrating the efforts of the National City Bank of New York to open an office in Zurich. With the flight of capital overseas in the 1930s, however, the Swiss banks began to lose investors, as noted in an internal Treasury report from 1942. When they subsequently inquired if the American banks would oppose the opening of a Swiss agency in New York, the answer was 'of course an emphatic "yes"'. SKA circumvented this opposition by forming an investment company, and placing the most highly qualified persons at its head: Joseph Straessle, 'one of the two great old men in Swiss banking', and, on the American side, George N. Lindsay, a former partner at Speyer Bank. In the meantime, the strong man of SBV, Armand Dreyfuss, obtained a license to establish a New York Agency by playing off the New York bankers against each other. Consequently, an American banking license could no longer be withheld from SKA. According to the Banking Examiners' assessment, the management of both of the Swiss agencies was characterized by absolute loyalty to Switzerland and its institutions; furthermore, the upper management consisted predominantly of Swiss nationals, and compensation for the lower positions was shamefully low; in spite of the most exacting supervision, the assessment went on to say, it was difficult or impossible to catch on to the banking practices of the Swiss. The potential for expansion was identified as the greatest threat posed by the three bank offices, and for that reason alone they should not be allowed to remain in business. Their activities could be carried out more effectively by US banks.[89]

The Swiss banks were severely criticized in the Treasury Department's 'Final Report'[90] on investigations into Swiss banks operating in New York; the 'Criminal Report'[91] released by the Treasury Department in November 1942 was also very critical. Both reports testify to the meticulous investigative work and to the high level of knowledge the American regulators acquired with respect to Swiss banking activities in New York. In their 'Final Report', Treasury Department inspectors considered revoking Swiss banking secrecy in the United States.[92] On 3 March 1943, the Credit Suisse New York Agency sent new instructions, effective immediately, to head office in Zurich regarding the omnibus accounts: for every purchase and sale of securities, the name, address, and nationality of the current, previous and subsequent beneficial owners had to be submitted to the American authorities and recorded, and the original securities had to be enclosed. All instructions that were still in effect at that time were annulled by the Agency on the basis of the new rule.[93] The Agency questioned why the new rule did not apply to American banks. George N. Lindsay from Swissam explained the Americans' behavior: 'They [the Treasury Department] are interested in seeing the reaction of Zurich in the present, and are only able to do so through the men stationed on the premises before instructions to all American Banks will go forward.' A Treasury Department memorandum recorded the shock and the familiar sense of discrimination felt by Swiss bankers in New York.[94]

Officials of the three Swiss bank institutions were accused in the Criminal Report of intentionally falsifying Treasury Forms. They were ordered to appear at hearings to testify and explain their behavior.[95] The hearings for the Credit Suisse New York Agency and Swissam took place on 22 and 23 April 1943 in the form of an 'investigatory interrogation' – a session of questioning typically conducted at the end of an investigation to place facts in a wider context and to present an opportunity for explanations.[96] The first day was devoted to general queries regarding head office, its organization, and business policy, while the second day was taken up entirely with TFR-300 reports that allegedly had not been filled out accurately. According to a memorandum from the responsible Treasury supervisor, Credit Suisse New York Agency's defense was that although official Agency documents were shared with the Treasury Department, other available customer and correspondent files had not been taken into account. Upon the conclusion of the bank investigations, it was decided that three Agency employees would meticulously review all files, correspondence, index cards, and other documents to record 'once and for all' all known names and enter them on TFR-300 forms. When asked about the high cost of this action, the Agency representative's answer was 'simple and to the point: "what can we do about it?"' The hearing, which was not conducted under oath, was felt by the Americans to be generally positive, such that the Foreign Funds Attorney who was asked for an adjournment responded, 'the matter, gentlemen, is closed'. The Credit Suisse New York Agency, however, was left with the uneasy feeling that investigations could resume at any time.[97] The bank's managers were subject to particular scrutiny by Treasury officials. A memorandum about the head of Swissam, George N. Lindsay, expressly mentions that head office in Switzerland held Lindsay in high esteem and that he was valuable to the Swiss because of his excellent relationships with Wall Street. Nevertheless, his loyalty to the United States was also noted: 'Mr. Lindsay was definitely in favor of the foreign policy of the United States Government [...] nor is there anything at all in this correspondence to indicate that Mr. Lindsay tends in any slight degree whatever to the mentality that believes "you can do business with Hitler".'[98]

On 9 April 1943, the Swiss Consul in New York, Victor Nef, submitted a final report to the FPD on the Treasury inspections. He reported that 'the review of files at most of the larger firms subjected to this inquisition appears to be more or less over. The regulators have collected a considerable amount of material from all the firms under investigation, some of which was copied by hand, but most of which was photocopied. [They are ...] still busy with the translation, review, and analysis of the information. Every once in a while a regulator or two shows up at one of the given firms to check additional materials and to obtain clarifications [...] by asking questions in person. In certain cases, the questions are asked under oath, but usually they are not because certain of the regulators have suggested that, for example, the oath of a Swiss banker is worthless. [...] With the exception of smaller, obviously unintentional infringements of the require- ments, it does not appear that any "incriminating" evidence was found, with one possible exception. [...] The investigation has extended to all of the larger Swiss firms so far, in- cluding Nestlé, Maggi, SBV, SKA, Swiss American Corporation, Swiss Re, Winterthur, La Suisse, Sandoz, Geigy, Ciba, Hoffmann-La Roche, Thorens, Paillard and others [...].'[99]

On 11 August 1943, Treasury Supervisor Joseph W. Sinnott, the 'Treasury Repre- sentative ... stationed on the premises of Credit Suisse, New York Agency', com- mented briefly on the Credit Suisse New York Agency managers, and on the actions described in the reports as 'criminal': 'Your representative believes the management conservative and responsible. It recognizes the difficulties placed before it under the Executive Order, and unless an about-face takes place after supervision is removed, any violations to the present will likely be unintentional and minor.'[100] This evaluation marked the end of the US Treasury investigations and coincided with the withdrawal of the Bank Supervisor from the New York Agency.[101]

Omnibus accounts: the focal point of American criticism

Omnibus accounts were a key subject of the Treasury Department's bank audits because with this type of account, the New York agencies of Swiss banks only knew the identity of the foreign 'home' bank, not of each individual depositor with the home bank. The Treasury Department's Final Report makes the following statement, albeit with no date given, on the significance of omnibus accounts for the Credit Suisse New York Agency: 'At the Agency of Credit Suisse 43,500,000 $ in securities and in cash are on deposit for owners whose names are not known while only about 5,600,000 $ in cash and securities are held apparently in the names of actual owners.'[102]

The Final Report defined omnibus accounts thus: 'An omnibus account is any ac- count in which the property of more than one person is mingled and which is held in one bank in the name of another bank, through which the actual owners deal. There is no sure way in which anyone in New York can tell whether a particular account is an omnibus account or not. And there is no certainty that a sub-account contains prop- erty of only one person. When the head office at Basle of the Swiss Bank Corporation opens an account with its New York Agency, there is normally nothing in the records of the New York Agency to indicate who or what is the owner of this account or how many people share in it.'[103] With the omnibus accounts, the depository bank did not know the beneficial owners of the deposited assets; any contact between the depository bank and these owners had to be conducted through the intermediary Swiss bank office.

As for the operational subdivisions within the omnibus accounts, the Final Report stated that as a rule, they contained numerous securities accounts but usually only a single dollar cash account. The reason for this was that the customers' securities were booked in separate sub-accounts, while accumulated interest from the various assets was credited to a single dollar account (an 'ordinary' or 'regular' account).[104]

Advantages of omnibus accounts for Swiss bank depositors

The maintenance of omnibus accounts and the New York agencies' bookkeeping practice of placing customer assets in the name of either head office or a Swiss branch office enabled the Swiss bankers to avoid mentioning the names of their investors in the ledgers of the US agencies. The protection afforded by Swiss banking secrecy could thus be extended to all customers who wished to place their assets abroad. It should be noted, however, that the assets invested by Swiss banks in the United States were fundamentally subject to American law – including the relevant war measures and the concept of escheatment. The possibility of maintaining anonymity was the highest priority for a great number of Europeans. Even the Final Report itself, which is generally dominated by criticism of the Swiss practice of secrecy, makes this observation: 'The possibility of remaining anonymous was a great advantage to owners in Axis countries who were anxious to preserve property from seizure. It is probable that the discretion of Swiss banks has made escape from Axis countries possible for many people and saved many refugees from poverty.'[105]

The Swiss practice of running omnibus accounts also offered certain tax advantages. 'While accounts that were set up under the name of a physical person were subject to an inheritance tax, the anonymous collective accounts were not. It thus became customary to maintain American investments in a bank's collective account. This applied not only to Swiss investments, but also to those of other countries.'[106] Direct investments were in this respect not very attractive.[107] It could take years to settle inheritance cases involving direct depositors, as demonstrated by wartime and post-war documents from SKA's US attorneys relating to inquiries, extensions, lists of heirs, etc.[108]

While direct customers were subject to the full force of the blocking measures for individual depositors, the requirements of General License No. 43 (later No. 13A) applied to owners of assets deposited in omnibus accounts. Portfolios owned by 'indirect' customers could still be actively managed in spite of the blocking measures; i.e. American securities could be bought and sold.[109] The Treasury Department was absolutely convinced of one point regarding the operational background of this situation, which hindered its monitoring ability: 'As long as the bookkeeping is done in Switzerland and not in New York, there can be almost unlimited change of ownership of the various components of an omnibus account.'[110]

Although assets deposited in the United States by indirect customers were blocked, up until 1942 these customers could still receive credits in Switzerland for interest and dividend earnings. This crediting of amounts from the US to customer accounts in Switzerland was conditional upon the willingness of the Swiss banks to increase the sums held in their own blocked dollar accounts in the United States.[111] At the end of 1942, the Swiss Bankers Association required the Swiss banks to forego the practice of crediting US dividends in Switzerland.[112]

Treasury Department criticism of omnibus accounts

As mentioned above, securities portfolios in omnibus accounts could still be actively managed in spite of the American blocking measures. The US control authorities therefore looked for ways and means to escalate the rules. Customers who had deposited assets at the New York offices through an omnibus account at a Swiss bank branch were not necessarily Swiss nationals, nor were they all Swiss residents. Notwithstanding, the securities accounts were still treated as Swiss property.[113] According to American blocking rules, all transfers not guaranteed by the Swiss government or the SNB under General License No. 50 required special permission from the Treasury Department. For all account movements, legal and beneficial owner relationships had to be disclosed on official forms such as the TFR-300 reports.[114] These measures were intended to prevent the Axis countries from liquidating confiscated assets in the form of Allied securities on the stock exchanges of neutral countries during the war.

In the Criminal Report, the American authorities identified violations of this disclosure requirement by the Swiss banks. For example, a procedural directive from the Credit Suisse New York Agency dated 16 September 1941 regarding the completion of TFR-300 forms stated:[115]

'The reports [TFR-300] we are required to file with the Treasury Department covering property held for account of our head office and branches contain the following question: "State the name, nationality, and address of any person other than the national, having any interest in any property listed above of any nature whatsoever, direct or indirect, including any arising under powers of attorney and any other powers or rights to deal with the property or arising under any agreement restricting the national's use of the property, and describe the nature and amount of such interest."

'Which we propose to answer as follows: "Our records and files do not disclose [the] name and nationality of any possible third-party beneficial owner." When reporting a sub-account or a rubric account where the identity of the beneficial owner is not known to us, the following answer will be inserted: "Our records and files do not indicate [the] name and nationality of [the] presumable beneficial owner designated as ... (name of sub-account) ...".'

Treasury Department officials made the following 'Statement of Fact' in their investigation report: 'As disclosed by its files and records, the New York Agency knew prior to the date said TFR-300 reports were filed: 1. That the securities deposited in substantially all of said depots were actually or beneficially owned by a person other than the depositing bank. 2. The names, addresses and nationalities of the actual or beneficial owners of certain securities deposited in said deposits.'[116]

It was foreseeable that customers' access to their money could be restricted or suspended via the blocking measures. The Final Report emphasized that the Swiss banks considered it not merely a service, but rather their obligation to protect their customers from such dangers.[117] According to Marco Durrer, the Swiss banks prepared special emergency authorizations in case American officials restricted or suspended an account holder's ability to dispose of his assets: should that occur, the assets were to be made over to persons who were not affected by the freeze.[118]

The Criminal Report refers to arrangements to conceal information at Swissam: 'Credit Suisse made available to its clients the plan of concealment and identity of funds deposited with Swissam … after the issuance of Executive Order 8389, when certain transactions involving property subject to the jurisdiction of the United States in which nationals of certain foreign countries had an interest were prohibited except by license from the United States Treasury, knowledge of actual ownership of the funds deposited in the United States became important and such a plan to conceal ownership could be effectively used to evade the purposes of the Order.'[119]

The friction between the Swiss emergency authorizations and the American freezing requirements is addressed in numerous places in the Final Report. Swissam managers began confronting this problem as early as May 1940, and Swissam's lawyers stated: 'If the change-over takes place, there will be no transfer of securities nor any change in ownership whatever. […] There is no change of ownership, legal or beneficial, whatsoever.'[120] On the lawyers' advice, the emergency authorizations, which were kept in sealed envelopes at the New York institutions, were not opened upon the outbreak of war, nor upon the blocking. It was not until early 1942, in fact, that a great number of seals were broken, the accompanying documents searched, and bank correspondence and numerous other sealed documents read by the American investigating authorities.[121] Transfers of property rights of the sort described above by Durrer were not reported by the American inspectors in their Final Report. It can therefore be assumed that no such irregularities were found at the Swiss banks operating in New York – contrary to American expectations. Neither did CSG find any cases of a change in owner when in 1997/98 it examined the archives for remaining rubric customer cards dating from the period between 1940 and 1947.

Before the investigation of the Swiss banks came to a close, Bernhard Bernstein, who headed the investigation, produced a report in July 1942 which included recommendations for further American action.[122] Since practically all accounts were blocked as property of the depository institution, the beneficial owners were free to conduct transfers and assignments to the extent the depository bank would permit. The 'ultimate owners' of the assets – a Belgian, a Dutchman, and a Greek, for example – could transfer their assets (voluntarily or otherwise) to a German, Japanese, and Italian, who could then transfer them to a Swiss, a Portuguese and a Spaniard (for obvious reasons) – and all these transactions could be completed without a license and without informing the American bank.[123]

As the only appropriate cure for such abuse, Bernstein insisted that the depository banks disclose their beneficial owners and block the property of the persons concerned. It was understood that after the war, the assets should only be paid back to those persons who could prove that they were beneficial owners with no Axis interests. Ascertaining the beneficial owners alone would not have been so difficult, Bernstein maintained, as demonstrated in Canada, where the government insisted on disclosure of the beneficial owners of omnibus accounts. Swissam managed sub-accounts on behalf of SKA in a collective securities account with the Custodian Trust Company, Charlottetown, under such names as 'Harvard', 'Justice', and 'Museum'. On 20 January 1941, Bernstein went on, Swissam had disclosed to the Canadians the identity of all the depositors concerned.[124]

1.4 Blocking foreign assets in the USA: second phase, 20 October 1943 to the end of 1944

Blocking assets under General Ruling No. 17

Negotiations between the representatives of Swiss interests and the Allies to find an acceptable solution regarding the identification of Swiss property dragged on, which the Americans blamed on their partners' delaying tactics. Seen in this light, the escalation of the American position, which led to the issuance of General Ruling No. 17 on 20 October 1943, appears understandable.[125] 'You Swiss, you had the chance to provide the proof that the money deposited with you actually belonged to you. You did not provide the proof, therefore you will have to suffer the consequences.'[126]

General Ruling No. 17, which was obviously issued as a measure against Switzerland, served the purpose of 'separating assets and securities held in the United States in the name of Swiss banks and financial institutions into those for which proof of Swiss ownership as defined by the American embargo rules has been provided, and on the other hand, those for which the proof has not been provided'.[127] Securities could henceforward only be sold upon disclosure of the name, nationality and domicile of the actual owner or, where applicable, of all those who had acquired or retained any interest in them since 8 April 1940 or since the date of the purchase. Coupon payments could only be collected if the owner's name, nationality and domicile were disclosed. If this mandatory information was not provided, the proceeds of the transaction would be credited to a blocked special account (a 'General Ruling No. 6 account') until the ownership details had been established.[128] Purchases and transactions could only be carried out for 'nationals', defined as Swiss citizens living in Switzerland who were not blacklisted. The first means of establishing these nationals' identity was proposed under General Ruling No. 17 (Section 2) and involved identifying the buyer's nationality, name and domicile. A second means was a statement (a certificate) from the depository bank that the holder of the securities was a Swiss national (Section 3), whereby the accuracy of the information was subject to review by American officials at some later point in time. A third means was to conduct securities transactions according to the 'Swedish system' as provided by General License No 50.[129]

Joseph Straessle reported from Washington on discussions with the Treasury Department that he had conducted jointly with Minister Bruggmann.[130] It seemed that there was no possibility of discussing the new rule with leading representatives of the Department:

'The entire Ruling No. 17 is being handled by the Foreign Funds Division, now headed by Mr. Pehle. The leading men in this division are mostly young attorneys who are making every effort to win their laurels. Their attitude toward our country is so biased and unfriendly that it will be no small task to surmount it. They make the accusation that all of our economic and financial actions show that we are subject to German pressure and that we apparently are willing to make concessions to our northern neighbor that we do not likewise extend to the Allies.'

'Minister Bruggmann protested against this with caustic words and used every argument possible. Regrettably, these people are convinced that they know best about everything, and that they understand our relationships and needs better than we ourselves do. They are particularly opposed to our alleged extension of credit to Germany. In my opinion, the Treasury's rigid approach to us is primarily occasioned by the large clearing surplus in Germany's favor and by the simultaneous refusal of the Swiss National Bank to hand over gold francs blocked in the United States for the duration of the war.'

Straessle considered whether 'in light of the not so distant end of the war in Europe and the enormous influence of the United States on post-war political and economic developments, [it] would not be appropriate to give our policy in this area a new direction before it is too late. In my opinion, this can only be done if we are willing to carry through one hundred percent with the matter, i.e. among others things, eliminating the market for freely convertible Swiss francs. Of course, this requires that the National Bank be prepared to distribute the Swiss francs needed from here on.' This was, in his opinion, the best way of establishing a more favorable atmosphere.

Of the alternatives that the new American law permitted, Straessle lobbied for adoption of the 'Swedish system'. This would prevent Americans from looking into the Swiss banking system and would enable the unblocking to be effected quickly and jointly later on. In particular, he remarked that 'an American audit will certainly investigate every last detail of the initiation and processing of individual transactions; on the one hand this could reveal some highly unflattering circumstances, and on the other it could cause endless complications and delays in the matter of releasing all Swiss property'.

The Swiss Embargo Commission for its part raised the question of whether such a law could even be considered, given that it discriminated against foreign customers. On the other hand, it would be equally unsatisfactory to inform the Americans 'that significant foreign, and specifically French assets [were held] in Switzerland', because this 'would inevitably create the desire to disclose the same'. Genuine Swiss interests in the United States were, however, 'so significant that they must not be endangered by efforts to protect foreign [interests]'.[131]

An 'absolutely muddled situation' prevailed in Switzerland.[132] A series of new plans for account control were discussed and rejected.[133] Concepts oriented towards the Swedish system, such as the proposal to have the SNB supervise certification, as suggested by Legation Counselor Robert Kohli, or the idea of control by the Compensation Office, which the Americans would have accepted, were vetoed by the SNB, supposedly on the grounds of banking secrecy. As a consensus among the Swiss banks seemed impossible and General Ruling No. 17 was due to take effect at the beginning of 1944, SKA's executive board decided of its own accord to allow 'identification' of securities accounts, after consulting with and in the interests of its customers, in accordance with the regulation given in Section 2 of General Ruling No. 17. In the course of the debate, 'certification' of the accounts was rejected because this would be inconsistent with banking law and banking secrecy in particular. Moreover, SKA's legal department opposed certification, although at first glance this would have seemed to be advantageous for customers in that their names would have remained secret. Presumably, however, these names would have had to be disclosed in the course of a later audit: there was nothing to suggest that the investigation by American officials would be cursory or only based on random sampling.[134] Management notified its customers on 6 November 1943 and asked them to authorize the bank to share their name, place of residence and nationality with 'our New York friends' when placing orders for the New York Stock Exchange.[135] On 3 January 1944, a reminder letter was sent to customers who had yet to give their consent to being identified. The letter notified them that American credits for which the customer's name was not provided would be transferred to the much more restrictive blocked special accounts under General Ruling No. 6.[136]

Escalated blocking rules under General Ruling No. 6

American inheritance tax was often a factor to be considered by owners of both 'identified' and 'certified' deposits.[137] Disclosure of the names of securities owners enabled the IRS to track movements on securities accounts.[138] 'All assets deposited in the United States for the account of the testator, including all North American securities that the testator held outside of the United States', were subject to American inheritance tax.[139] SKA sent a letter to the heirs of all its customers who had died since 8 April 1940, which was the deadline applicable to customer identification, and requested authorization to register the death, to change the identification, and to implement the inheritance tax procedure in the United States.[140] In the event that authorization was denied, no further transactions could be conducted through the blocked account. American bonds and dollar assets held in Switzerland were also registered, but without recognizing a tax liability. American securities located in Switzerland were accompanied by a 'Statement on Non-Enemy Property' in addition to the mandatory Swiss declaration (Swiss Affidavit Convention A of April 1943) because the assumption was that the new American regulation on the identification of Swiss property would also be extended to securities located in Switzerland.[141] Submitting a US tax statement within 15 months of the customer's death, or at the very least requesting an extension, was critical. Extensions were often required because the disrupted postal service could delay the whole process for months or years.[142]

Under General Ruling No. 17, the owners of omnibus accounts held at the Credit Suisse New York Agency had to reveal all details of changes in ownership of stocks and bonds. Assets could only be transferred out of blocked accounts with special permission. Applications to legalize past transfers had to state the name, nationality, and place of residence of all persons who were directly or indirectly affected by the transfer of assets. Moreover, the reason for the asset transfer, the purchase price paid, and other relevant information on the change of ownership had to be provided.[143] J. P. Morgan reported that it had sorted omnibus account securities identified by SKA (head office in Zurich) according to the name of the beneficial owner. Credit and debit payments in connection with assets owned by Swiss nationals were carried out collectively through SKA's 'original cash accounts'. For non-Swiss owners of securities, new accounts were opened once their nationality was known.[144]

In the course of the identification process, SKA's head office directed bank staff's attention to the American definition of a 'national' under General Ruling No. 17. A Swiss living in Liège, Belgium, would be identified as a Swiss national in the Swiss securities declaration – and consequently also in the American documents. However, according to General Ruling No. 17, this person would be a national of Belgium and Switzerland (dual nationality). The bank asked its employees to exercise particular care in filling out the forms required under American law, as 'any such errors' would likely 'make the US Treasury Department mistrustful of Swiss bank statements'.[145] As for determining the citizenship of Credit Suisse New York Agency's corporate customers, the American correspondent banks noted that a new Treasury Department interpretation was issued on 16 June 1944: the Credit Suisse New York Agency was required to review all nationality information for its corporate customers to date, to sort investments by owner's nationality, and to segregate the portion of shares owned by shareholders of unknown nationality. Identifying information now had to be provided for earlier customers of the firm as well.[146]

Since April 1940, the Treasury Department had permitted certain payments to be made from blocked accounts in favor of private persons who lived in or came from blocked countries. Essentially these were to meet the living expenses of a narrowly defined group of persons described as emigrants and refugees. Instead of payments under General License No. 32, certain payments from identified or certified accounts could now be made abroad on the basis of a Special License (valid from 22 April 1944 to 28 February 1945).[147] Transfers of support payments to Switzerland required not only an American General or Special License, but also permission from the SNB, which had to accept the dollars and pay their equivalent in Swiss francs to the beneficiary. The SNB, which was in principle cautious where dollars that were not being used for trade in commodities were concerned, stated on numerous occasions that it never refused to make payments to those in need when permission had been granted by the Americans.

Allied warnings and their consequences

At the beginning of March 1944, the Bankers Association discussed whether to send a delegation to the Treasury Department 'to dispel the Americans' mistrust, which is based on the erroneous assumption that there are piles of German-owned American securities in Switzerland'.[148] A survey taken by SKA of its customers from Axis countries and their ownership of American securities revealed that holdings of such paper were 'remarkably small'.[149]

Since the fall of 1943, lengthy negotiations between the Allies and the Swiss banks had been going on in London. At the beginning of 1944, the Swiss banks were threatened by the Allies with the warning that a list was being compiled of all transactions considered 'imprudent' and 'promoting the enemy war effort'. Offenses involving prohibited transactions would result in inclusion on blacklists. In the summer of 1944, the Swiss delegation to the continuing negotiations with the Allies (the Lisbon Round) achieved a softening of the original text; the Bankers Association's new proposals, however, were rejected. The Allies accused Switzerland of willfully stalling the negotiations. 'If the Swedes are stubborn, the Swiss were the cube of stubbornness.'[150] Ultimately, the Allies decided not to issue an express warning: each bank was to decide for itself whether it would continue to carry out certain transactions that were objectionable to the Allies. If they did, however, they would have to suffer the consequences.[151] Bretton Woods Resolution No. VI required the neutral countries to refrain from receiving enemy assets, to refrain from covering up such assets, to put these assets at the disposal of the victorious powers once the war had ended, and to facilitate their surrender.[152]

The Bankers Association recommended a series of procedural rules to the banks in a circular. Top of the list came the Allies' demand not to accommodate in any way the transfer of looted assets and flight capital to Switzerland. The banks were urgently asked to comply strictly with all the relevant legal requirements for all transactions involving assets abroad. The banks were bound by the general principle 'that under the prevailing circumstances, it would be in the banks' own interest to exercise the greatest caution and restraint in all transactions with foreign countries'.[153] In the view of the chairman of SKA's board of directors, the Allies were proceeding on the principle that all foreign securities, bank notes, etc. held in Switzerland were to be considered looted assets until proven otherwise. The Bankers Association objected that in Switzerland it was taken for granted that no bank would consent to receive and hold stolen assets. The more efforts were made to accommodate the Allies' demands, the greater the cause would be to suspect that not everything was in order. 'As far as our institution is concerned, we are of the conviction that we have taken the right path with respect to money belonging to the Allies' enemies; there are no indications that such flight capital or stolen assets have been left with us.'[154]

A few days earlier, SKA's executive board had issued instructions to its branch offices in the spirit of the Bankers Association's recommendations: 'A few months ago, we called your attention to the fact that in business transactions with enemies as defined by Allied legislation, or in transactions that could directly or indirectly benefit the Allies' enemies, the utmost restraint must be exercised. [...] As a result of subsequent developments, we feel compelled to notify you again that the previously released directives are to be followed strictly and zealously. [...] Effective immediately, we strictly prohibit the following types of transactions: 1. The import and export and all trade in pounds and dollars for one's own account or a third-party account. Currency and gold transactions, whether spot or forward, with enemies of the government of Great Britain or the USA. 2. The opening of any new account of any type for or on behalf of enemies [...]. 3. The receipt of deposits ... of any kind for or on behalf of enemies [...]. 4. The purchase and sale as well as the receipt of any securities issued by the enemy [...]. 5. Purchases and sales, or the facilitation of transactions, or the extension of any credit involving assets in which the enemy ... has a direct or indirect interest [...]. 6. The extension of loans, advances or account overdrafts, or any other financial services that in any way facilitate or enable trade with the enemy [...]. 7. The extension of new loans, advances or overdraft provisions to enemies [...]. 8. The continuation upon maturity of previously provided overdraft provisions or credit relief [...]. 9a. Currency transactions, whether spot or forward, or the purchase, sale or receipt of deposits of gold or silver in the name of or on behalf of an enemy [...]. 9b. Currency transactions for non-enemies for the purpose of making payments to enemies [...]. 10. Financial transactions or business contacts where Swiss banks or "Swiss nationals" hold assets but the beneficial ownership lies with an enemy [...].'[155]

On 30 September 1944, the Bankers Association advised the banks in an amendment: '1. Not to open new accounts for businesses or persons domiciled in combatant or occupied countries. 2. Not to accept any payments or bonds, gold or other securities into existing accounts belonging to such businesses or persons if the balance of the relevant customer assets would significantly exceed the maximum balance recorded in 1943.'[156]

In a 'briefing note', SKA addressed the interpretation and application of the enemy regulations and emphasized 'that non-observance of the regulations issued by the Allied governments with respect to the definition of enemies and trading with the enemy [could] result in grave consequences'. Specific reference was made to the retaliatory threat made by the Allied governments of inclusion on the 'Statutory List' and the 'Proclaimed List' (the 'graylist' and the 'blacklist').[157]

A delegation of Swiss bankers stayed in Washington in the second half of 1944 to take part in the ongoing negotiations. At the conclusion, they reported that the Americans were impressed with the Swiss banks' new affidavit convention but would only accept the system if the SNB or the Swiss government was prepared to guarantee control of the regime.[158] This was to be considered their final position.[159]

At a meeting of SKA's board of directors on 14 December 1944, the state of Swiss-American financial relations was discussed at length. The Allied governments were still not satisfied with the banks' measures, and the Allied position was likewise unacceptable to the Swiss banks. The Allies expected 'that we will assist in future in uncovering every transaction involving looted assets or flight capital, that we will act almost as policemen and, above all, that we will even uncover any earlier transfers of assets; this is an unreasonable demand which we must of course refuse'.[160] The Americans were not going to release Swiss assets unless their Swiss ownership had been clearly demonstrated; legal entities had to prove the absence of enemy ownership. Swiss people domiciled abroad were not considered Swiss. 'The control measures under Ruling [No.] 17 (provision of satisfactory evidence and a verified statement) were interpreted such that the names and addresses of all interested persons had to be disclosed in every case.' Treasury Department representatives would want to resolve special cases directly with the banks.[161] They were particularly mistrustful of holding companies, although it was noted that holding companies were much more likely to have been accommodated by notaries, lawyers, and other private persons than by the Swiss banks.[162] When it came to holding companies in Liechtenstein, the Allies suspected 'that prominent German statesmen have stashed their assets there'. Following a survey on this topic SKA was relieved to find that it had only participated in four Liechtenstein holding companies and that only one of these was created during the war (in 1943). The Allies were interested in these holding companies' capital and above all in the assets they managed.[163] 'For our part […] we have no reservations; it is worth proving our goodwill to the Allies to the fullest extent, so that the suspicions raised against Switzerland can finally be refuted as untenable.'[164] The chairman of the board of directors commented that 'the demands made by the Allies are analogous to the extension of the Inquisition to commerce'. Nothing would satisfy the Allies. The parties were in the same position as two years before; in the end, some kind of Swiss government body would have to assume responsibility for the criteria and methods used to ascertain Swiss ownership of property, as had already been the practice in Spain, Portugal, and Sweden for some time.[165]

The number of regulations and technical instructions covering bank transactions with the United States increased daily. Telegrams bearing new Treasury Department requirements were constantly arriving at SKA's head office; their original contents were forwarded to the branch offices. Head office directed its questions to the New York Agency, which in turn would make inquiries to American banks or to the Treasury Department and send explanatory telegrams back to Zurich.

After November 1944, a foreign bank had to produce a sworn certificate before transferring securities and cash amounts from one blocked account to another. The certificate had to give the name and nationality (including the date of naturalization where applicable) of the beneficial owner. In addition, a statement had to be attached that no other person held a direct or indirect interest in the assets. For each certificate, the issuing bank had to consent to provide the American authorities with complete access to the relevant files at all times so that the information could be verified. On the advice of the American consulate, SKA's management decided 'to sign and notarize the form in each individual case'. If there was to be a subsequent verification process, the bank reserved the right to obtain the customer's prior consent in every case.[166]

If there was a change in the ownership of securities in Switzerland owing to an inheritance, this change would be registered in New York, and the Agency would note 'that according to General Ruling No. 17, this change in ownership will only be valid if the Treasury Department grants approval in the form of a license'. To request such a license, it was necessary to provide a statement or a 'document attesting to ownership, such as a will [or] a purchase receipt' that could be verified at any time by US consular representatives. SKA's head office emphasized that it would only provide the statement and access to the files with the customer's consent.[167] At the end of October 1944, many American banks, including Swiss American Corporation, received licenses in connection with special General Ruling No. 6 blocked accounts. On the basis of these new licenses, securities could be bought and sold for the account of customers whose securities were not identified. Proceeds from 'non-identified accounts' had to be placed in a General Ruling No. 6 account, from which it was possible to purchase North American securities. These securities were then deposited in a newly opened 'General Ruling No. 6 account under General Ruling No. 17'.[168]

After his stay in the United States from October 1944 to January 1945, member of the SKA board of directors Wilhelm M. Keller reported his alarm at the ill-will toward Switzerland that stemmed from 'the Americans' belief that they had documentary proof of Swiss attempts to use false data to cloak German interests. It is very important for Switzerland that this matter is clarified.'[169] SKA was accused of carrying out illegal gold and bond transactions with Germany.[170] SKA strongly objected: 'Schweizerische Kreditanstalt has never engaged in any such transactions, either from its head office or its branches. […] To us, it is inconceivable how our institution can be associated with such transactions, and we declare with the utmost certainty that any assertion of this nature is pure invention.' The bank urgently requested that 'the source of these unfounded accusations about our bank be revealed'.[171] Legation Counselor Kohli conveyed information from the Swiss Legation in Washington to SKA in a letter of 13 March 1945. The Treasury Department did not dispute that 'most banks would take care not to engage in further transactions involving securities, etc. originating from Germany or from the previously occupied areas because of the associated risk'. It was, however, conceivable that a few individual employees might try to get rid of shares acquired earlier in order to avoid criticism from the bank's executive board, which is why the warnings were issued. The Treasury Department was aware that many denunciations and reports were unreliable; it emphasized nonetheless that 'the cases we have in mind appear utterly credible given the source and the nature of the description'.[172] SKA responded that the Treasury Department itself 'seemed to have little confidence in either the "fairly precise picture of the degree of reliability" of the denunciations and reports and "their utter credibility given the source and the nature of the description"'. The bank understood that mistrust of the Swiss banks may unfortunately have been reinforced by the fact that Switzerland had not been able to commit to 'offering an official guarantee for the identification of Swiss ownership of American securities and bank assets that Washington had requested and that other European governments had been offering for some time'.[173]

In December 1944, America threatened to revoke an offer it had made in the fall of that year to deliver merchandise. With Switzerland seemingly intent, in American eyes, on assisting Germany to the bitter end, the Americans wanted to make it clear once and for all that Swiss policy needed to be altered radically.[174] An article to this effect appeared in the *New York Herald Tribune* that provoked an out-and-out press campaign against Switzerland. As the FPD subsequently noted, Switzerland was threatened with 'the isolation of our country to an extent previously unknown'.[175] The Swiss press reacted strongly. For the first time, the problem of asset blocking became a topic of public debate in Switzerland.[176] In a much-read article in the *Neue Zürcher Zeitung,* an effort was made to explain the American point of view to the Swiss public.[177]

SKA's board of directors made it clear that the time for concessions had come and that the SNB would have to offer the requested government guarantee, because otherwise, 'they will say in America that you can't trust the Swiss banks because the Swiss National Bank itself doesn't trust the banks in its own country'.[178] There was 'a widespread opinion that the banks would thwart any effort to shed light on banking secrecy, but the situation is such that the banks are also fighting for the release of blocked Swiss dollars. The banks, too, therefore advised their customers to identify their accounts in America. If the Allies were going to claim that the banks had cloaked funds for prominent Germans, they should name names in such cases and of course investigate. A general lifting of banking secrecy is out of the question. It is to be hoped that the earlier request of the Swiss banks would finally be met, and a special Swiss office would take on the task of checking all documents pertaining to Swiss assets in America, and issuing the necessary statement if all was in order.'[179]

On 1 February 1945, Federal Councilor Max Petitpierre became the new head of the FPD. At the same time, Minister Walter Stucki took charge of the FPD Foreign Affairs Division, ushering in a change of tack. The new men decided to pursue a new policy: Swiss federal officials would play a much more active political role from now on. Stucki, who was 'generally regarded as a forceful and difficult character'[180], and, in contrast to his predecessors, was also known for his competence in economic and financial matters, announced a new direction in Switzerland's policy towards the US. The wait-and-see approach of the conservative bankers had to give way to an active policy promoted by open-minded thinkers. Under pressure from the Currie negotiations that Switzerland had initiated with the Allies in Bern, the Federal Council decided on 16 February 1945 to block all German assets in Switzerland. On 20 February the Federal Council approved the government-controlled certification of Swiss property in the United States and the grant of executive authority to the Swiss Compensation Office in Zurich. Two more years of slow-moving negotiations passed before this body could finally begin its work.

2 End of American blocking measures: certification of blocked assets by the Swiss Compensation Office, 1947–1948

2.1 Legal basis

Over the course of 1945 and 1946, the Allies concluded bilateral unblocking agreements with a number of European countries. After the conclusion of the Washington Agreement, Switzerland could claim to be the first neutral country to be unblocked under General License No. 95.[181] Established as the official control office and guarantor for transfer and clearings institutions, the Swiss Compensation Office was granted authority to monitor the blocking and marshalling of German assets in Switzerland on 16 February 1945 (Compensation Office, Department for German Assets). On 20 February 1945, the Compensation Office was also given the mandate to develop an 'irreproachable and guaranteed control system' for the segregation and certification of Swiss blocked property in the United States.[182] On 27 December 1946, the Federal Council formally charged it with the certification of these assets in the name of the government (Compensation Office, Department for US Certification).

This chapter is based principally on materials from the Compensation Office's Department for US Certification found in the Federal Archives in Bern (BAR), from Credit Suisse Group's Central Corporate Archives (CCA), and from the archives of the Credit Suisse New York Agency and Swissam.[183]

Swiss-American Certification Agreement of 22 November 1946

As was the case with the other continental European countries that the United States had previously placed under General License No. 95[184], the fundamental principles of unblocking for Switzerland were set forth in the agreement of 22 November 1946 between US Treasury Secretary John W. Snyder and Federal Councilor Max Petitpierre[185], and in the Federal Council Decrees of 27 December 1946.[186] They were in principle the same for all countries and centered on certifying the absence of 'enemy interests' as well as establishing certifiability and eligibility for certification.

The main task of the government offices assigned to conduct the certification process in General License No. 95 countries (in Switzerland this was the Compensation Office) was to determine for each individual case whether a person regarded as an enemy had an interest in the blocked assets. For this purpose, an 'interest' was defined as any type of direct or indirect claim to the assets.[187]

For each asset to be unblocked, the Treasury Department required an official statement – a certificate – to the effect that there were no enemy interests in the asset as

From the Safehaven Program (1943) to the Currie Agreement (8 March 1945)

Towards the end of the war, the Allies took measures to prevent long-term German rearmament.[188] One such measure was the Safehaven Program begun in 1943. This program was intended to prevent German assets from flowing into neutral countries. It aimed to secure German assets located outside Germany and use them to finance reparations. For the purposes of the program, both public and private German assets abroad were classified as potential military resources.

The Allies insisted that Switzerland suspend Swiss exports to Germany as well as transit traffic through the Gotthard. They criticized the SNB for allegedly accepting German and Italian gold of dubious provenance. They complained further about Swiss private banks acting as intermediaries or conducting credit transactions with the Axis powers or their camouflaged customers. The Allies had significant means of exerting pressure because they had, for example, an effective monopoly on the allocation of resources and transportation in Europe. The blacklists were still in effect, and Swiss assets in the United States remained blocked. Further sanctions were feared.

Switzerland's supply problems became increasingly acute toward the end of the war. Neither the Allies nor Germany were in a position to help supply Switzerland. In addition, the Swiss government was plagued by other concerns. Those among the Allies who considered Switzerland to be German-friendly were becoming increasingly vociferous. Finally, the Swiss government proposed that an Anglo-American delegation come to Switzerland to examine all the unresolved issues. In a letter dated 19 January 1945 responding to Swiss President Eduard von Steiger, President Roosevelt gave great weight to the renegotiation of bilateral economic relations, and he therefore named his personal assistant, Laughlin Currie, chief of the US delegation.

In parallel with the negotiations with the Allies that began on 12 February 1945 in Bern, Switzerland was conducting discussions with a German delegation, also in Bern, on the extension of the Swiss-German economic agreement that was due to expire on 15 February. As it turned out, Switzerland was unable to simultaneously negotiate an advantageous treaty with both the Allies and Germany. The Swiss government's strategy focused on negotiating with Germany in such a way that the Germans themselves would announce that they could not enter into a new economic agreement.

At the beginning of the negotiations with the Allies, the Swiss delegation was presented with a text based on Bretton Woods Resolution VI. The Swiss delegation, however, did not want to commit to the Allied Safehaven Program and invoked principles of international law to demonstrate that Allied demands were inconsistent with the international Hague Conventions. A solution specific to Switzerland's situation had to be found.

On 16 February 1945, four days after negotiations began, the Federal Council decided to block all German assets located in Switzerland. For the first time, foreign residents of Switzerland were also affected by a Swiss blockade. The resolution was hastily put into force under conditions of great secrecy. Convinced that Switzerland would not be able to avoid blocking German assets anyway, Switzerland's chief negotiator, Walter Stucki, pushed to have the asset freeze implemented at the very beginning of the session – as a sign of goodwill intended to positively influence the atmosphere of the negotiations. The blocking resolution did indeed elicit the hoped-for reaction from Currie, the leader of the US delegation. Attacks in the US press abated notably, and even US Treasury Secretary Henry Morgenthau had kind words to say.

With respect to the inventory of blocked German assets, the Allies demanded that Switzerland conduct a survey of all capital assets, both public and private, belonging to the Axis Powers as well as countries occupied by the Germans. The Swiss Bankers Association followed this part of the negotiations with concern, because an investigation of foreign assets threatened to have a negative impact on Switzerland's position on the international capital market. In the end, the Federal Council chose a compromise solution: Switzerland was prepared to investigate all blocked assets in Switzerland, but expressly did not commit itself to showing the results to a foreign government.

On 20 February 1945, the Federal Council decided to comply with the demands of the US government and have assets that had been blocked in the United States controlled by a Swiss government office, the Swiss Compensation Office (SCO), which had been established in 1934 as the state regulator and guarantor for transfer and clearing institutions in Switzerland. Two new divisions were added to the Swiss Compensation Office: the Department for German Assets and the Department for US Certification.

The Currie Agreement with the Allies was sealed by an exchange of notes on 8 March 1945. Switzerland had made various financial policy concessions to put an end to its isolation. In its final report to Treasury Secretary Morgenthau, the US delegation commented very positively on the Swiss arrangements for the blocking and inventory of foreign assets. In return, the Allies opened up transit through France and extended allocations of food, animal feed, and raw materials without supply obligations. The Allied concessions also included transportation of these goods on their own ships. As for the blacklists and the unblocking of Swiss assets in the United States, no agreement was reached.

Initially, the Allies used the Currie Agreement as a template for other Safehaven agreements, but the initial euphoria quickly subsided. Differences in opinion over the implementation of the agreement emerged early on.

Opinions differed on the issue of disclosing bank customers' names. The Swiss Bankers Association espoused certification by means of its affidavit system, which had already been accepted in dealings with Britain, Belgium, and Argentina. Customers would give their bank a binding statement about the provenance of their assets, and the banks would issue confirmations to the Bankers Association. To uphold bank customer secrecy, these sworn statements used numbers instead of customer names. The Compensation Office would have the right to conduct audits during which the banks would reveal customer identities. Walter Stucki and Max Schwab, Chief Executive Officer of the Compensation Office, were against this proposal. In carrying out the obligation to identify blocked German assets in Switzerland, problems similar to those with the certification of Swiss assets in the United States arose: the question of the disclosure of names led to differences between the government and the Bankers Association. Under pressure from the US Treasury Department, the Federal Council finally decided that for both the certification of Swiss assets in the United States and the survey of German assets in Switzerland, the names of the owners would have to be given to the Compensation Office. The Federal Council Decrees of 3 July 1945 temporarily rescinded banking secrecy for this purpose.

A further controversy delayed the beginning of certification: the Federal Finance Administration insisted that only those assets for which a tax receipt from a Swiss tax official was available should be certified. In August 1946, there was still no agreement on the form this tax receipt should take. The intent was to make certification dependent on the payment of taxes, but also to avoid driving large amounts of untaxed capital out of the Swiss economy. The federal tax agency seemed to be content with a relatively benign approach toward tax evaders. A general amnesty was, however, ruled out.

defined by Treasury Department regulations. 'Enemies' were defined as Germans and Japanese based on nationality and domicile, and Hungarians, Romanians, and Bulgarians based on domicile alone.

General License No. 95 relied on the concept of domicile.[189] Three categories of person were defined with reference to country of domicile:

1. Country of domicile in the Generally Licensed Trade Area under General License No. 53 (primarily the countries of South and Central America) where assets were accessible and trade was unrestricted. Persons domiciled in this region had to be certified by Switzerland if their assets had been deposited in the United States via a Swiss financial institution.[190]

2. Country of domicile under General License No. 95 (continental European countries).[191] All persons living in Switzerland were required to obtain their certification from the Swiss Compensation Office; they were in principle eligible for certification regardless of their nationality.[192] A person was considered as de facto domiciled in

Switzerland if there was an 'intention to remain for the long term'. Foreigners had to have a valid resident alien identification document and had to have lived in Switzerland for a minimum of one year (or in special circumstances, six months) at the time of submission of their certification application.[193] Persons living outside Switzerland in the General License No. 95 areas had to be certified in Switzerland if their assets had been deposited by intermediary Swiss financial institutions. To do this, they needed a 'cross certificate' from the certifying agency in their country of residence documenting that no enemy interests were involved. In some cases, obtaining the cross certificates could be highly problematic: persons who had invested their assets in Switzerland or via Switzerland before the war in spite of the harsh currency restrictions and criminal penalties imposed by their home country risked high fines or imprisonment after the war if those facts came to light.

3. Country of domicile Germany and Japan, as well as Hungary, Romania and Bulgaria, as of 1 January 1945.[194] Assets belonging to Germans and Japanese remained blocked under General Ruling No. 11A and were confiscated ('vested'). There were no agreements with Hungary, Romania or Bulgaria; assets belonging to residents of these countries remained blocked.

For legal entities and their property, essentially the same domicile rules were in effect as those for natural persons described above. A distinction was made between 'operating companies' (factories, banks, insurance companies, businesses) and 'non-operating companies' (holding companies, investment trusts, family trusts, estates, etc.). Operating companies were eligible for certification if the interests considered enemy-owned accounted for less than 25% of the company's capital. As with natural persons, cross certificates had to be presented for capital located in General License No. 95 countries. The American authorities were to be contacted in especially complex cases. Non-operating companies were, however, only fully eligible for certification if all persons holding an interest in the company satisfied the criteria for certification eligibility. The assets of interested parties who were eligible for certification were proportionally certified. Articles 1 and 9 of the Certification Agreement established that the ownership of organizations and institutions must be carefully scrutinized because representatives and front men acting for the enemy could be involved. The Treasury Department promised to inform the Swiss government on an ongoing basis about persons that the Americans suspected of such activity. A 'graylist' was given to the Compensation Office for comment.[195] Investigation of companies was complicated; it relied on the cooperation of the companies themselves and required that the Compensation Office auditors had industry-specific knowledge.[196] As a result, the highest degree of uncertainty arose in this certification category.[197]

The concept of the beneficial owner applied: certifiability was determined by who had an economic interest in an asset. Customers who had invested their assets in the United States before the American freeze (by 14 June 1941 at the latest) had two choices: they could either apply directly to the US bank, or arrange for a Swiss banking institution to act as intermediary and invest their assets in its name in a collective ac-

The Washington Agreement (25 May 1946)

Truman, Churchill and Stalin set forth the guidelines of the Allied reparations policy in the Potsdam Declaration.[198] The Declaration adopted the key points of the Safehaven Program with respect to German assets in foreign countries. German assets located in neutral countries reverted to the countries controlling the Western zone of occupation, whereas the Soviet Union claimed all German assets that were located in the areas occupied by the Red Army. The conference resolutions were communicated to the neutral countries in a note dated 3/4 August 1945.

The Federal Council tried to treat this matter as routine business and did not respond to the note until 27 September 1945: there was no legal basis for the Allied claims; access to the assets of foreign persons in Switzerland had never been permitted before. To have German private citizens pay for the war debt of the German state through the confiscation of their assets was based on the idea of collective guilt and was therefore inconsistent with Western legal concepts.

On 30 October 1945, the Allied Control Council issued Law No. 5 on the Vesting and Marshalling of German External Assets, which revoked the entitlement of German natural persons and legal entities in Germany and abroad to their assets located outside Germany. This marked the beginning of a fundamental disagreement between the Allies and Switzerland. At the Paris Conference, 18 countries agreed that proceeds from German assets in neutral countries should be used for reparations.

In spite of the release of Control Council Law No. 5, the Allies did not come closer to achieving their goal of confiscating German assets in neutral countries. Treasury Department representatives pushed harder and harder for sanctions against Switzerland, while the State Department emphasized that Switzerland's involvement was relatively small, in the order of $ 250 to $ 500 million. The Treasury Department itself was pressuring Great Britain, but London was not enthusiastic about further trade restrictions and began to relax control over Swiss accounts in August 1945.

On 20 August 1945, the Federal Council voted in favor of the Americans' unblocking conditions as set forth in the 'Moskowitz Proposal', with a few amendments. Subsequently, however, no agreement was reached. At the end of October 1945, the Safehaven attaché in Bern, James Harold Mann, advised against starting to unblock Swiss assets in the United States because Switzerland had allegedly not fulfilled its Safehaven obligations. In addition, the Swiss government was informed of the decision to call off the negotiations that were under way.

On 23 November 1945, the Federal Council decided to send a delegation to Washington. Their agenda included the following points: 1. recognition of Allied Control Council Law No. 5; 2. escalation of Switzerland's control and blocking legislation; 3. discussion of the SNB's gold transactions from 1939 to 1945; 4. German patents and trademarks; 5. the establishment of a mixed Commission; 6. the repatriation of German citizens; 7. blacklists; 8. Swiss assets in Allied countries.

During the Washington negotiations, the Allies continued to pursue their goal of obtaining the release of German assets for use as reparations. They were able to pressure Switzerland by threatening to keep the roughly $ 1.2 billion of Swiss assets in the United States blocked until the question of German assets in Switzerland was resolved. In addition, the Allies' blacklists were still in effect. Finally, the Western Allied governments had considerable influence on public opinion in the free world, which put additional pressure on a Switzerland already isolated in terms of foreign policy.

On 22 February 1946, the Federal Council appointed the members of the Washington negotiating delegation and placed them under the leadership of Minister Walter Stucki. The main argument of the Swiss delegation was that Allied Control Council Law No. 5 was inapplicable to assets located in Switzerland: Swiss law extended the protection of property to foreigners, and the Allies' demands were diametrically opposed to international private law.

After six plenary sessions, the negotiations became bogged down in all the key areas, and Minister Stucki returned to Bern to receive new instructions. In a memorandum of 29 March 1946, the Allies described their demands and for the first time showed a willingness to compromise on the issue of the ultimate distribution of German assets: a Swiss governmental body should liquidate the German assets under the supervision of a mixed Allied-Swiss Commission. The proceeds would be placed in a fund, a portion of which would go to Switzerland.

Once the negotiations resumed on 12 April,

the head of the Swiss delegation announced that Switzerland was willing to allocate Sfr 100 million for European reconstruction – as a gesture of goodwill, but without acknowledging any legal obligation. The Allies demanded $ 130 million to settle the gold question, as well as two-thirds of the proceeds from German assets. The French rejected as an insult the payment of Sfr 100 million proposed by the Swiss. On 2 May 1946, Stucki made a final offer to the Allies: Sfr 250 million to settle the gold question and a fifty-fifty split with the Allies on the proceeds from German assets. Stucki described the whole package as a voluntary contribution to European reconstruction. Switzerland for its part would not recognize the Allies' legal right to make a claim. After three weeks, the Allies finally informed the Swiss that their offer had been accepted, and on 25 May 1946, the Agreement was signed. Both sides had been compelled to downsize their goals: the Allies could count as a victory Switzerland's consent to liquidate German assets and pay 50% of the proceeds to the Allies, in addition to the one-time settlement payment from Switzerland of Sfr 250 million for 'looted gold'. The Swiss counted among their successes the revocation of the asset freeze in the United States and, in particular, the immediate un-

blocking of resources belonging to the Swiss government and the SNB, the immediate removal of all Swiss companies from the blacklists, and the designation of a Swiss governmental agency responsible for the liquidation of German assets.

By now, there was a degree of clarity about the fundamentals and basic procedure of unblocking Swiss assets: the Compensation Office would be granted a great deal of authority. Natural persons with domicile in Switzerland and Liechtenstein were eligible for certification. Legal entities had to prove that at least 75% of their equity capital was Swiss-owned and 75% of their liabilities were owed to Swiss. At the end of summer 1946, the United States proposed negotiations in Switzerland on the final resolution of a certification agreement. On 28 October 1946, Orvis Schmidt, the director of the Foreign Funds Control Division, went to Bern to discuss the application of the American General Licenses Nos. 94 and 95 with representatives of the FPD, the Compensation Office, and the Bankers Association. On 22 November 1946, US Secretary of the Treasury John W. Snyder and the head of the FPD, Federal Councilor Max Petitpierre, signed the Certification Agreement. Switzerland was the first neutral country to have its assets unblocked by the United States.

count in the United States. The Agreement further established that claims of indirect creditors were to be treated the same as those of direct creditors.

First and foremost among non-certifiable assets were those of Germans and Japanese (whether or not domiciled in Germany or Japan), followed by assets owned by persons in Hungary, Romania, or Bulgaria. The principle of uninterrupted ownership applied: as a rule, assets were certifiable only if persons who were eligible for certification had held their interests in them continuously since the designated date. The designated date for Switzerland was 14 June 1941.[199] Proof of uninterrupted legitimate ownership had to be produced upon any change in ownership.

Tax auditing was a genuine Swiss request relating to American certification conditions.[200] The issuance of a certificate by the Compensation Office was made dependent on the proper Swiss taxation of assets deposited in the United States.[201] Applicants who could not produce a receipt of payment from the tax agency could choose to make a cash deposit with the Federal Tax Administration worth 50% of the assets to be certified; the Compensation Office would then evaluate the certification application for those assets. The deposit could be retrieved when it could be shown that the assets had been declared. A stubborn rumor circulated in the United States that innumerable Swiss tax evaders were trying to get their investments released without obtaining certification from the Compensation Office and were applying directly to the Treasury Department, in some cases through their American attorneys.[202] It was mostly the small investors, for whom avoiding tax control was not worth the effort, who opted for the process requiring the 50% deposit.[203]

The Compensation Office's authority encompassed the review of all documents submitted, control and auditing at customer, bank and government levels, and the preparation of the government certificates according to precisely defined rules. The 'Consultative Commission' acted as the advisory body on the Swiss side of the Compensation Office. It was responsible for handling fundamental questions of procedure and interpretation, as well as some specific cases.[204] The Consultative Commission also acted as a board of appeals against decisions taken by the Compensation Office. It could call forward experts but could not issue binding orders to the Compensation Office. Questions that could not be resolved internally in Switzerland had to be forwarded to the Treasury Department.[205]

2.2 Technical process of certification

The Compensation Office carried out the actual technical certification of assets from 1 February 1947 to 31 December 1948 as instructed. A distinction was made between the process for certifying Swiss assets located in the United States and the one for certifying American assets located in Switzerland. Different procedures were also required for the different domicile categories: Swiss in Switzerland, foreigners in Switzerland, legal entities in Switzerland, applicants from the Principality of Liechtenstein, Swiss abroad, foreigners abroad, and legal entities abroad.[206]

Process for direct creditors

The American banks registered directly held assets with US Treasury officials at the beginning of the blockade. To initiate the certification process, a customer had to submit a direct customer form to the Compensation Office, attesting with his or her signature to the accuracy of the information. The Compensation Office then reviewed the certification eligibility of persons with interests in the assets and the certifiability of the registered assets themselves. As with the process for bank customers described below, the assets that had been checked were then sent to the United States with the certificate and with the name of the owner left on the documents. If his country of residence was a General License No. 95 country, a foreigner who was a direct customer would submit his certification application in his home country. If his country of residence was one of the General License No. 53 countries, his assets would be unblocked without further formalities, as long as he was not on the 'Proclaimed List'.

Process for bank customers

In its review of indirect customers with deposits in omnibus accounts, the Compensation Office relied heavily on the preliminary work done by the authorized Swiss banks, though it expressly reserved the right to carry out its own audits.[209] The banks were obliged to designate and train special officers for certification processing. In its invitation to designated staff from all branches to attend a training conference, SKA's executive board emphasized the following: 'The thoroughly correct processing of certification work is the executive board's highest priority.'[210]

The banks collected statements that had been signed by customers to confirm the accuracy of the information provided, then checked them against their own records for certification eligibility and certifiability, and issued a bank certificate to the Compensation Office. When forwarding the applications to the Compensation Office, the banks issued the following confirmation: 'We declare that to the best of our knowledge and belief we have verified the accuracy of the information in the customer statement(s) on which this bank certificate relies, and that we are unaware of any facts that contradict the customer statement(s) or cast doubt on its/their accuracy.'[211]

The authorized banks were held liable for the consequences of any incorrect certification where they were at fault: 'Whoever violates this order or its official implementing rules and regulations or hinders or attempts to hinder official measures in any way, and in particular, whoever falsely obtains Swiss Compensation Offices certificates, whoever gives false information or withholds material facts or presents documents that he knows, or should know, contain information that is not consistent with the facts or is no longer consistent with the facts, whoever misuses or forges or falsifies certificates or related declarations from the Swiss Compensation Office or any other documents (certified statements, affidavits, or other legal documents) or presents them as valid or uses them when they are forged, falsified or invalid will be punished by a fine of up to Sfr 30,000 or by imprisonment of up to five years or both. [...] Negligence is also a punishable offence.'[212]

Unblocking indirect investments under General License No. 95: case studies

Mr. O. E., head of one of SKA's branch offices, had indirect investments. His blocked assets in the United States were held in SKA Zurich's collective account at the Credit Suisse New York Agency, as disclosed when the relevant correspondence was opened during the 1942 Treasury investigation. Apparently, these securities were originally held by SBV in New York but were transferred to the Credit Suisse New York Agency in August 1940 upon O. E.'s request.[213] As a loyal branch manager, O. E. took the directive from head office to heart and transferred his investments from SBV's agency to SKA's own agency once it had opened, in May 1940. In October 1943, O. E.'s accounts were closed, according to information in the customer register. O. E.'s wife obtained the certification and unblocking of his Agency assets by applying through SKA Zurich; SBV Geneva also issued a certificate.

Swissam also held indirect investments belonging to 'Credit Suisse, Zurich, Rubric 31431 W. S., Swiss citizen', as registered with the Federal Reserve Bank on a TFR-300 form in November 1941. In the course of the 1942 Treasury investigation, a sealed envelope deposited by the Credit Suisse New York Agency with Swissam labeled '31431 W. S.' was opened. It contained a custodian agreement between SKA Zurich and the customer W. S. dated 2 November 1939, a power of attorney for his wife G. S., and instructions concerning the free disposal of the securities upon the occurrence of certain described events.[214] Documents from the Compensation Office reveal that the investments in the rubric account had been placed with the Custodian Trust Company, Charlottetown, Canada, via Fides Treuhand-Vereinigung, Zurich. The certification of the deposit was conducted jointly for Mr. W. S. and Mrs. G. S.

Certification of bank customers required a Customer K Form (or an uninterrupted sequence of K Forms for every change in ownership since 14 June 1941), and customers domiciled abroad needed to submit a personally signed 'cross certificate' to the bank.[215] The bank was responsible for checking that persons who had held interests in the assets since 14 June 1941 had been continuously eligible for certification. The signed customer forms remained in the bank's possession and were kept in case of possible audits by the Compensation Office.

Confirmation of a tax declaration was also required. The confirmation contained the customer's name and address; his domicile for tax purposes as of 1 January 1945; a list of assets; the dated signature of the taxpayer; and the dated signature and stamp of the designated tax administration.

A Bank Certificate B (or, if there had been a change in authorized bank since 14 June 1941, an uninterrupted sequence of Certificate Bs from the institutions that had managed the assets) was given to the Compensation Office by the bank to prove the continuous certifiability of the assets. For investments held in the name of the authorized bank on behalf of a second authorized bank, a supplementary Bank Certificate B2 was required that had to be verified, along with the Customer Form, by the second bank. Form B provided the Compensation Office with the name of the depository bank in the United States, the name and address of the customer, the customer's nationality, the securities and cash accounts (listed individually along with the balance and exchange rate as at 31 December 1946). The authorized bank attested to its statements with double signatures. The description of the penalties was clearly visible on the first page.

Unblocking under General License No. 53: case studies

Under American regulations, investments belonging to persons with nationality and domicile in one of the countries in the Generally Licensed Trade Area (an area defined by General License No. 53) were not blocked. On condition that there was direct customer contact with the American banks, and as long as the given customers were not on the American blacklists, they could freely dispose of their assets in the United States.

By contrast, investments were blocked if they belonged to customers who were domiciled in the Generally Licensed Trade Area but who were nationals of a blocked country. After 30 May 1946, however, it was possible to unblock assets under General License No. 53 if the applicant had maintained his domicile from a certain date and was not blacklisted.

Customers domiciled in the Generally Licensed Trade Area who invested their assets through a bank in a third country were subject to the American regulations for the third country (General License No. 53 for Generally Licensed Trade Area countries, General License No. 95 for continental Europe, and General Ruling No. 11 for enemy countries), and the unblocking procedure – assuming it was even permitted – had to be conducted by that third country. Accordingly, blocked assets that had been invested via Swiss financial institutions were subject to General License No. 95 unblocking regulations, which referred applicants to the Compensation Office.[216]

The Credit Suisse New York Agency archives contain some dossiers for direct customers from the Generally Licensed Trade Area:

Engineer E. L. and his wife opened an account on 13 August 1942 with the Credit Suisse New York Agency, listing 'New Goldfields, Venezuela' as their address. The Swiss couple knew that their account would be blocked on the basis of their nationality; nonetheless, they wanted to transfer support payments under General License No. 32 from their Swiss bank account to their daughter in Switzerland. On 4 June 1946, the account was unblocked under General License No. 53A.[217]

Mrs. T. S. from Mexico City opened an account with the Agency in order to make monthly transfers under General License No. 32. The amounts transferred each month were $ 100 from November 1942, $ 200 from February 1943, $ 500 from March 1943, and $ 1,000 in 1945. Her account was unblocked on 4 June 1946 under General License No. 53. Mrs. T. S. gave heartfelt thanks for the Agency staff's kind support and willingness to help.[218]

Mrs. C. W. from Tehran held direct investments with the Agency after 19 November 1940. Problems arose because she did not have the same name as her husband, whose nationality was not known to the Agency. Mrs. C. W. told the Credit Suisse New York Agency that her husband was of Hungarian nationality. Moreover, she stated that she had resided in Tehran since 1935. On 5 March 1947, her assets were unblocked under General License No. 53 based on a certificate issued by the American Embassy in Tehran.[219]

The certification application from authorized Bank Z was submitted to the Compensation Office together with three copies.[220] The application indicated the name and address of the authorized bank submitting the application, the precise designation of the account to be unblocked, and the designated US depository.[221] Securities and dollar accounts were also listed here, as on the bank certificates, and the bank provided two signatures. The owner's name was omitted because these forms were ultimately sent to the United States after the Compensation Office had reviewed and stamped them as certified (showing the date of certification and the certification number). The original (white certificate) went to the US depository bank; the first carbon (pink certificate) went to the Foreign Funds Control Division in the Treasury Department in Washington. The second carbon served as a receipt for the bank submitting the application, the third as a copy for the Compensation Office. Banking secrecy was thus preserved because though the Compensation Office knew the names of bank customers, the American authorities did not.

Power of attorney for customer declarations

Customers could not simply appoint a representative to sign declarations on their behalf. A special power of attorney was required that could only be used if the beneficiary was unable to sign his or her own name and if the bank had no doubts about the details of ownership. To establish such a power of attorney for persons abroad, very specific information was required about the relationship between the grantor and the grantee.[222]

2.3 Changes in the procedural requirements for certification

The Snyder Plan and the shortening of certification periods

The certification process was made easier in some respects as an indirect result of the USA unilaterally bringing forward the deadline for certification: without forewarning, the Snyder Plan of 2 February 1948 designated 1 June 1948 as the new deadline. Thereafter, all non-certified assets could be investigated as presumed enemy assets and – on that basis – confiscated and given to countries in need of assistance.[223] This helped to shore up the currency laws which European countries qualifying for Marshall Plan assistance were using to help them gain control over their citizens' hidden, unregistered private dollar assets.[224] According to American estimates, there was about $ 700 million in blocked assets in the United States at the end of 1947, the bulk of which was accounted for by concealed assets belonging to French citizens domiciled in France. Their direct deposits in the United States were estimated by the French Finance Ministry to be between $ 100 million and $ 150 million, while their indirect deposits invested via Switzerland were estimated at $ 200 million to $ 250 million. French customers knew that the regulations meant that Switzerland could not certify assets without a cross certificate – which would entail disclosing the customer's identity in his country of domicile. This is why so many of them had not registered their assets for certification at that point in time.[225] Treasury Secretary John W. Snyder noted in his letter of 2 February 1948 that under normal circumstances the American government would not support the partial confiscation of private property by third countries. However, he went on, this was an extraordinary time: many European countries were dependent on dollars for their survival as free nations, and American taxpayers were making substantial payments for European reconstruction; what is more, concealing property ran contrary to the law and to the national interests of the given countries. Consequently, Snyder continued, the requests of these countries were being supported. There was no alternative to the threat of confiscation.

From the Swiss point of view, the Snyder Plan made it clear that the original goal set forth in the Certification Agreement, i.e. to segregate enemy assets, was no longer the priority; instead the main aim was to register assets managed by Switzerland with the tax authorities and use these assets for financial aid under the Marshall Plan.[226] There was no question that France was pressuring the United States heavily at this time. At the same time, if not before, Swiss officials were pushing for new negotiations with the United States for an extension of the certification period and for relief from certain certification requirements in order to accelerate the process. Not least, they wanted to state a clear objection to the anticipated presumption of enemy ownership for assets that had been deposited in America through third countries. The concept of the presumption of enemy ownership appeared to be specifically directed at the Swiss banks. It seemed to Switzerland like a form of 'discrimination and a threat to Switzerland's position as an international financial center'.[227]

Subsequently, the end of the certification period was extended by order of the American President first to 30 September[228] and finally, upon Switzerland's request, to 31 December 1948.[229] The Federal Council Decree of 27 December 1946 on the certification of Swiss assets in the United States lapsed at the end of December 1948.[230] By 15 December 1948, certificates had been issued for assets worth more than $ 4.25 billion, but a significant number of cases remained open. Most of these involved applications that the Compensation Office could or would not certify without consulting American officials, or pending applications based on temporary registration by the banks. Because of the notoriously long turn-around time at the American Justice Department's Alien Property Office, it was anticipated that the Compensation Office would have to conduct further investigations and controls in 1949. For that reason, the Federal Council added another two years to the effective period of the Federal Council Decree of 27 December 1946 as a precaution.[231] The Compensation Office concluded its work with the issue of a Final Report in April 1949.[232] The Federal Council Decree of 27 December 1946 was rescinded on 31 March 1950, though the Consultative Commission continued to operate until December 1950 because of the issue of fee reimbursement.[233]

At the end of 1950, in addition to the problem of the threatened confiscation of many assets belonging to businesses in which Germans had an interest, the issue of unblocking assets of former Swiss women who had married Germans remained unresolved. It had not been possible to reach agreement with the Americans on this. A solution for isolated cases was found only in the context of the sequestration regulations.

Easing of the certification process

In January 1948, the Bankers Association announced that it would generally take at least a month from the receipt of a certification application to the unblocking of the assets concerned in the United States. Efforts were made to find ways of accelerating the process. The greater demands particularly affected the Compensation Office's Department for Business Investigations, which, because of the excessive number of trivial

Research on dormant accounts at SKA's New York institutions (1997–1999)

In conjunction with CSG's own research into dormant assets at the Swiss banks operating in New York, in January 1997 the New York State Banking Department called for an investigation into customer accounts maintained at SKA institutions in New York during the war years.

Using various customer lists from the Credit Suisse Agency and Swissam that were found in the National Archives in Washington, initial research was begun at CSG's head office in Zurich. The main goal of this and subsequent research projects was to find out what happened to assets held in wartime accounts once the war was over. Specifically, proof was sought that beneficial owners were able to dispose of their assets after the war. This proof could be demonstrated by the presence of one or more of the following:

a) a Swiss certificate for assets blocked in the United States;
b) evidence that a customer relationship was continued in New York after the war;
c) evidence that a customer relationship was continued in Switzerland after the war;
d) evidence that the customer was unquestionably domiciled in a territory that was not affected by the war or that was designated by the United States as an unblocked area.[234]

In the middle of February 1997, Credit Suisse First Boston hired the consulting firm Deloitte & Touche to conduct research on all customer-related documents from the war years held in the archives of the former Credit Suisse New York Agency and Swissam. The goal of this thorough investigation was to analyze all documents archived in New York that related to accounts from the time the two agencies were opened to the end of 1945. Particular attention was paid to the question of whether beneficial owners were able to dispose of their assets after they were unblocked. In the course of the approximately two-year investigation involving 239 Deloitte & Touche employees and a total of 122,000 person-hours, 10,091 archive boxes from the Agency were reviewed as well as 10,607 archive boxes from Swissam; 4,400 square feet of office space were rented in Manhattan to accommodate this project.

CSG also analyzed numerous customer lists from the Agency and Swissam and used the various sources of identification to create a list of the names of all customers who had held investments with SKA institutions in New York during the war and whose names were known in the United States: there were 1,620 entries for Swissam customers (of which 1,283 were individual account holders) and 1,304 customer entries for the Agency (of which 892 were individual account holders).[235]

CSG employees in Switzerland found out all about the mechanics of blocking and subsequent unblocking of Swiss assets in the United States. A key step here was the retrieval of a large amount of archived material on customer names from the Compensation Office's USA Certification Department that was stored in the Swiss Federal Archives in Bern (BAR): documents relating to post-war Swiss bank accounts (for the years 1947 and 1948) and the files on assets in the United States certified by the Compensation Office remain largely intact.

Compensation Office file cards naming applicants for certification[236] were particularly relevant to the investigation, as were the fee invoices, and the Compensation Office's control ledgers, which also included certificate numbers. The Compensation Office's application card catalog contains approximately 60,000 names, and the control ledgers contain about 72,000 written confirmations of certification for assets deposited either with Swiss financial institutions in the United States or with American correspondent banks.[237] Of the certificates issued by the Compensation Office, 16,514 were for assets belonging to SKA customers. For SVB, the number of certifications was 1,853; for Bank Leu, 987; for Hofmann & Cie., 170; for the Aargauische Hypothekenbank, 92; and for Bank in Wädenswil, 6.

In order that this considerable amount of data could be used for individual investigations, the Compensation Office card catalog had to be copied. CSG submitted a written request to the Swiss Federal Archives in September 1997 to copy the cards for former US customers. Because the cards contained information on customers of various Swiss banks, the Federal Archives sent a written inquiry to the Swiss Bankers Association asking if it wanted to express an opinion on CSG's plan. The Bankers Association circulated this letter among its members for comment and informed them that CSG was willing to allow other affected banks access to the data. Once the Bankers Association had given its consent, the Federal Archives signed an agreement with CSG in July 1998 on the use of data in its Compensation Office 'Certification' collection. This agreement established among other things that CSG could use the documents from the Compensation Office for internal bank research in connection with investigations of its business activities during and after the Second World War. Moreover, this document established that CSG would be entitled, after prior written consultation with the Archives, to share copied records with third parties provided that these third parties used them to help review the business activities of Swiss banks during and after the Second World War.[238]

The Federal Archives' directors allowed CSG to install two of its own high-performance copiers in a separate room in order to do the work as quickly as possible. Four CSG employees made the application card catalog accessible within three weeks for internal bank research.

Reviewing the over-sized control ledgers used to record issued certificates proved to be more complicated. Because the entries were in chrono-logical rather than alphabetical order, the information had to be entered manually into a specially designed database so that it could be accessed easily when researching individual customer cases. Numerous CSG employees spent more than four months in total entering this information into their laptop computers in Bern.

The customer information thus retrieved was then compared against the consolidated customer list for the Credit Suisse New York Agency and Swissam. By checking various aspects, it was thus possible to identify 'evidence of survival' for 95% of the Agency's 'individual account holders' and 60% of Swissam's investigated customers. For a significant number of customers, the list comparison yielded evidence of a continuing relationship with bank offices in Switzerland after the war. For a small number of customers, the American freeze meant that their investments had been confiscated ('vested') or escheated to the state because of dormancy, though in some cases and under certain conditions these were later returned ('refunded').

cases it was having to handle, was struggling to keep up. The Swiss cited the following reasons for certification delays:

- The inability of many foreigners to provide a cross certificate.[239]
- Unblocking regulations still applicable to residents of countries that were neither in the Generally Licensed Trade Area nor in the General License No. 95 area, which meant that these assets could not be unblocked at all.[240]
- Problems for companies organized under Swiss law that could not be certified because of blocked foreign interests or interests of more than 25% which could not be certified.
- The impossibility of certifying a Swiss company domiciled in Switzerland but at least part-owned by Germans. (Once the German stake had been separated out, however, such a company could register for certification.)
- Tax concerns of certain Swiss customers.
- The US's rejection of the proposed provision for a certification-free limit of $ 5,000 that would have removed many trivial cases from the process.[241]

On 10 November 1947, the Treasury Department raised the limit on assets requiring a cross certificate from $ 100 to $ 5,000 for bank customers resident in General License No. 95 countries (effective retroactively from 25 August 1947), with cash and securities of up to $ 5,000 treated as separate property. The Treasury Department, however, continued to support the basic mandatory cross certificate requirement. Consequently, the essential problem with cross certification remained unresolved: foreign investors whose assets were placed in the United States by Swiss banks – for tax reasons or in order to avoid domestic currency restrictions – could not obtain a cross certificate from the officials in their countries of domicile.[242]

To protect the small saver, and to compensate for US intransigence on cross certification[243], assets worth $ 5,000 or less on 1 February 1948 in any cash account or securities account were automatically unblocked under the new General License No. 97 of 27 February 1948. Cash and securities were considered as separate assets; every account was considered individually. The rule did not apply to assets belonging to natural persons, regardless of their nationality, residing in Germany, Japan, Hungary, Romania, and Bulgaria, but it did cover persons who left those countries during the effective period of the license. The principle of General License No. 97 was extended to Swiss bank collective accounts in April 1948 on the condition that the Compensation Office checked to ensure that the principle was being applied correctly. The $ 5,000 limit (as of 1 August 1947) applied per person and per account within the collective account. As with normal certification, certification under General License No. 97 also had to satisfy the requirements of the Swiss tax administration.[244] After General License No. 97 was introduced, the Compensation Office returned applications and their enclosed documents to direct customers with assets of less than $ 5,000. A duplicated letter informed these customers about the automatic unblocking of their assets. The following sentence from the text was underlined: 'We request […] that you have the American depository bank confirm without delay that your assets have been unblocked.'[245]

Swiss people living abroad in General License No. 95 countries whose dollar assets were managed by a Swiss bank had to furnish a cross certificate from their country of residence. Assets belonging to Swiss in the Generally Licensed Trade Area could be certified without either a waiting period or cross certification, while assets belonging to Swiss in enemy countries (Germany, Japan, Hungary, Romania, Bulgaria, and Italy) were not eligible for certification at all. When the United States decided on 2 February 1948 to conclude the certification process on 1 June 1948, protecting the assets of Swiss living abroad became the highest priority. On 26 February 1948, the FPD, backed by the Federal Council, issued a decree concerning an exemption for Swiss living abroad. These Swiss were deemed 'persons resident in Switzerland'. The 1 March 1948 process for Swiss abroad allowed them to avoid contacting the authorities in their country of residence. Swiss abroad could be certified under the Swiss procedure upon the condition that they applied to the Compensation Office in person in Switzerland if they were direct customers, or to their bank if they were bank customers, presenting proof of their domicile, citizenship, a Swiss address and a tax certificate.[246] A prerequisite for direct customers was that they provided the American bank institution with the address of their Swiss domicile and that all future correspondence be conducted through the Swiss address.

Unblocking according to the process for Swiss people abroad: case study

Mr. R. L.-T., a Swiss resident in Italy, made some substantial investments with EMA via SKA Zurich. Blocked omnibus accounts held at the liquidated Dutch SKA subsidiary were transferred to Swissam. The Treasury Department learnt Mr. R. L.-T.'s name when a file containing telegraphed instructions was opened, because in July 1941 shares had been acquired for R. L.-T. from another customer in the EMA account. In 1947, R. L.-T. had to present an Italian cross certificate in order to be certified – in March 1948 he was certified under the process for Swiss people abroad. He used his wife's family home in the canton of Glarus as his Swiss address.[247]

Swiss Compensation Office Instruction No. 1 stated that foreigners residing in Switzerland who wanted their assets certified required a valid alien resident permit A, B, C, or D, or proof that they had resided in Switzerland for a minimum of six months. Once the period for certification was shortened, Switzerland reduced the minimum period of residence from six months to three months (or in hardship cases, to one month) without consulting the Americans.[248]

During the negotiations in Washington, the Americans said that reducing the period of residence would encourage French people to move to Switzerland in order to obtain certification. The Swiss delegation attempted 'in the arduous and at times very tense negotiations to make clear' that 'the question of who is a "resident" for purposes of certification will be determined under Swiss law and authority as per our agreement'. The delegation claimed that the new rule on the required period of residence was modeled on the US procedure for immediate unblocking upon presentation of an American immigration visa, and that there was no question of changing the reduced period that was already in effect.[249]

Because of the critical shortage of hard currency, French citizens were compelled to surrender their foreign currency after the war. It was, in fact, impossible for French customers to apply for a cross certificate from the French 'Office des Changes', which they needed in order to be certified in Switzerland, without being subjected to a 25% 'taxe de légitimation' (validation tax), compulsory repatriation of their assets to France, and compulsory conversion of their assets at a rate that was fixed below the dollar rate. Customers could, moreover, expect to be audited for tax and currency law violations; given the social position of some of the people concerned, this could be a sensitive matter.[250] In 1947, French customers were waiting for the next developments on this issue. With France in urgent need of currency, the American financial authorities gave in to French pressure and developed rules under the Snyder Plan to more effectively compel French and Swiss customers to comply. The Swiss banks and officials searched for ways out of this situation during months of tedious follow-up negotiations in Washington. Thereafter, a compromise acceptable to Washington was sought in the more favorable atmosphere of the Swiss-French economic negotiations in Paris. The problem had to be resolved in such a way that the Swiss would not subsequently be criticized for 'casually turning French capital held in a fiduciary capacity over to the

Americans'.[251] No deviations from the cross certification system would be tolerated; it was conceivable, however, that an agreement could be reached with the 'Office de Changes' whereby certificates could be issued on the basis of anonymous, numbered statements from Swiss banks in exchange for an amnesty fee paid by the creditor (a minimum of 25% of the assets concerned); the Swiss in turn would require that the remaining dollar amount owed to the customer be left alone.[252] Meanwhile, customers in Paris had figured out that instead of going through the arduous Swiss process, they could hire American lawyers whose fees ranged from 17% to 25% of the amount certified.[253] For those who could not produce a US immigration visa, it was possible to temporarily change their residence to a Central American country, where the unblocking could be completed in a matter of days.[254] The abuses in the certification process discovered by the Compensation Office from May 1948 onwards included such 'cunning maneuvers' by the French.[255]

A solution finally emerged in May 1948 in the form of anonymous cross certification that was not subject to the control of the Compensation Office and which became known as the 'sugar' or 'merchandise' method.[256] Once the responsible French official had checked the assets for enemy ownership, without forwarding information to the government, a cross certificate was issued along with a 25% 'taxe de légitimation'.[257] The unblocked dollars had to be made available to French importers who could buy goods that France needed, especially sugar, on the open market.[258] The owner received his assets in French francs at a fixed dollar rate of exchange below the market rate – but the importer often credited the owner for both the tax and the exchange rate differential, so that in the end the arrangement turned out to be quite favorable for the owner. From August 1948, certificates were issued under a new agreement for assets that had been registered with the Compensation Office before 2 June: 50% of all assets were repatriated to France and placed on the free market in Paris via transfers or simple sales transactions. The other 50% was paid to a collective account maintained by the Banque de France in New York to facilitate French-Swiss payment transactions. A special fee of 27% was also assessed against the owner. This method was recommended because it was also in Switzerland's interest.[259]

2.4 Abuses of the certification process

As previously mentioned, applicants who were domiciled in a General License No. 95 country had to provide the Compensation Office with a cross certificate from the foreign body responsible for certification. Because many bank creditors wanted to avoid the tax consequences of official registration, they played for time in the hope that the Americans would revoke the mandatory cross certificate requirement in due course. As the American position became increasingly unyielding and the certification period was made even shorter, the affected bank creditors began to look for other solutions.

Two types of abuse aimed at circumventing cross certification were discovered: the falsification of Swiss resident permits and resident alien identification documents, and the improper use of proof of domicile in countries included in the 'Generally Licensed Trade Area' defined by General License No. 53. In several cases, the Compensation Office approved certification applications that contained false domicile information and false resident alien identification documents. These cases involved bank customers of French nationality in particular.[260] After an official preliminary investigation, the Federal Prosecutor's Office launched a criminal investigation in June 1948 that involved the cooperation of the local police authorities as well as of Compensation Office representatives.[261] At the behest of the Federal Department of Justice and Police (FDJP), the Federal Council resolved on 10 August 1948 to hand the investigation over to the Federal Criminal Court.[262]

The modified Swiss domicile rules of March 1948 opened up a legal means of avoiding cross certification by permitting foreigners resident in Switzerland for only three months to claim Swiss domicile, and with it the accompanying certification eligibility. In spite of this easing of regulations, the Compensation Office became aware at the end of May 1948 of suspected abuses in connection with the certification process for blocked assets in the United States. French bank customers had apparently used false information to obtain Swiss identification cards in the cantons of Valais and Fribourg. This had been done, allegedly, by using government officials, bank functionaries, and private persons as intermediaries. For the most part, the resident alien identification documents contained incorrect information about the date of issue or the date of entry into the country. In many cases, a pre-1 June 1947 date of issue was given. Untruthful information of this sort gave the impression that the holder of the resident alien permit was already resident in Switzerland prior to the effective date for certification eligibility.[263] Middlemen working for French customers charged their clients substantial commissions. Banks and bank functionaries also demanded special fees for services in this area. According to information contained in the Compensation Office's final report, civil servants involved in issuing the resident alien permits did not receive kickbacks; they were acting exclusively in the fiscal interests of their cantons.[264] Abuses in the certification process observed in Switzerland were criticized by the Americans and led to prompt intervention by the Treasury Department.

In addition to improprieties in Switzerland, there were also problems with proofs of domicile from countries belonging to the Generally Licensed Trade Area under General License No. 53. Certain foreigners, particularly French people, were able to avoid cross certification by obtaining residence permits from countries not subject to the American blocking legislation. With the help of middlemen – in Switzerland and other countries – French bank customers obtained these permits in exchange for payment without ever having resided in the given countries. In the course of the court investigation, such domicile permits were found from countries such as Cuba, Mexico, Venezuela, Peru, and Brazil. The Treasury Department vehemently protested and demanded that certifications for all customers from the General License No. 53 area be suspended.[265]

With the consent of the FPD and bank representatives, the Compensation Office ordered an internal Swiss freeze on the contested certified assets held at Swiss banks instead of a certificate recall. As with the Swiss resident alien permits, in the course of investigations into proofs of foreign domicile, banks and asset management companies were identified that had wrongfully assisted in obtaining the documents.[266] However, the official report on the abuses stated that these cases were of limited relevance to the actual goal of asset certification: 'It can be said that the fraud was not intended […] to certify "enemy" assets, but rather, to avoid penalties of a fiscal nature […]. We can state that these irregularities, which were not aimed at obtaining certification of assets belonging to the enemies of the United States, should in any event be considered as minor infractions.'[267]

2.5 Compensation Office's criticism of the American position during implementation of the certification process

In the Agreement of 22 November 1946, the Americans had given express assurance that individual cases that could not be certified on the basis of the regulations alone could be forwarded to the Treasury Department, where they would be 'treated sympathetically'.[268] Be that as it may, the Compensation Office's annual report for 1947 notes that 'experiences to date […] have not met expectations'. The processing of special cases was sluggish; the Treasury Department delegates to Bern (James H. Mann, Walter W. Ostrow, and Donald W. Curtis) did not have decision making authority, were to some extent ill-prepared for their jobs, and were required to forward all inquiries to Washington.[269] For its part, the Treasury Department said that the slowness of its dealings with its Swiss correspondents could be explained by the large workload, and by the fact that no case could be settled bilaterally and in isolation. Apart from anything else, each case was different and had to be investigated by several US departments.

Moreover, there was no consensus on the extent to which the Treasury Department should be consulted on all matters. An internal Compensation Office memorandum recorded the opinion of a 'significant source' that it was time to quit trying to parse the meaning of the correspondence from November 1946 and reporting all problems to James H. Mann, as the situation in the United States had fundamentally changed. Psychologically, at least, the war against Germany seemed amazingly far away in the past. It was time now to line up against the Russians. The Americans wanted to end the freeze, which had become an anachronism. The 'New Dealers' and 'hardliners' around James H. Mann would soon cease to be political players.[270]

Before the certification process began, the Compensation Office had emphasized in a discussion with representatives from the Treasury Department that it would be very conscientious about certification work. 'Where there is the slightest doubt, there will be no certification. The Compensation Office has incurred considerable costs in connection with certification; circumventions of the Compensation Office should not,

87

therefore, be facilitated by releasing accounts in the United States to people who have traveled there expressly for this purpose.'[271] Consequently, the Swiss Compensation Office was particularly displeased by the fact that American officials unblocked the assets of wealthy Swiss who circumvented the certification process by engaging American attorneys as intermediaries. Events of this nature caused a number of people to question whether the Americans were actually following their own rules on certification.[272]

2.6 Swiss Federal Political Department's position on the agreement and its implementation

In the conclusion to its official report on the investigations into abuses in the certification process, the FPD made a statement of principle with regard to the Agreement and its implementation. The report praised the loyal cooperation of Swiss officials with the United States in what was often a difficult climate and added:

'The certification process was a regime that was imposed on Switzerland from the outside. Its origin and motivation lay in the economic warfare being waged by the United States. However, it was alien to public order and the legal system in Switzerland, and indeed called for the application of American law on foreign territory with respect to the segregation of enemy assets. Economic warfare was thus extended to the neutral territory of Switzerland, which the Swiss government resolutely – and with varying degrees of success – resisted.'[273]

The further the implementation of the Agreement progressed, the clearer it became that the two sides were not complying exactly with its provisions. On the American side, the promised sympathetic approach was not forthcoming. Moreover, the Agreement was reinterpreted during the process in such a way that it took on a new meaning. As a result, the law was no longer clear – a fact that is crucial to any assessment of the abuses discussed above. While there is no justification for the maneuvers employed to circumvent the measures, the fuzziness of the legal situation is nonetheless a factor that should be considered when trying to understand the situation.

For their part, Swiss officials also deviated from the original text of the treaty when they created the special procedure for Swiss abroad – though in Swiss eyes this was a legitimate defensive measure. The certification procedure was not clearly regulated; its provisions were incomplete and extremely complicated. It required the Compensation Office to review innumerable, barely comprehensible, detailed instructions out of all proportion to the technical requirements of certification. Swiss law is based on the fundamental principle of the right to freely dispose of private property. As certain foreigners tried to regain their rights through the certification process, they ran into problems caused by rules that were diametrically opposed to the basic tenets of Swiss law.

The report concluded that the complicated circumstances, the complex legal basis of the certification rules, the differences between legal concepts in the United States and Switzerland, and the way the United States unilaterally changed the goal of certification all needed to be considered in order to understand how difficult the problems were that Switzerland had to resolve. The report also noted that Swiss officials dutifully fulfilled their assignments and thus that they could also be trusted in future. From the point of view of international relations, the certification of non-enemy assets was not compromised by the points mentioned.

In an annex to the final report of 1949, the Compensation Office presented an overview of assets in the United States that had been certified by Switzerland.[274]

Assets certified by Switzerland, by customer category (1947/48)

(Sfr m)	Total	Assets managed by Swiss banks	Assets managed directly by customers
Swiss in Switzerland	1488.2	859.5	628.7
Foreigners in Switzerland	725.6	400.9	324.7
Legal entities in Switzerland	1465.9	499.4	966.5
Principality of Liechtenstein	115.9	41.0	74.9
Swiss abroad	36.3	31.9	4.4
Foreigners abroad	418.8	372.9	45.9
Legal entities abroad	129.8	129.8	–
Total	4380.5	2335.4	2045.1
Total (%)	100.0	53.3	46.7

3 US vesting of non-certified assets 1951–1953

The program designed in February 1948 by the head of the US Treasury Department John M. Snyder (the 'Snyder Plan') stated that all non-certified assets still blocked in the United States would be subject to a blanket presumption of enemy ownership. They could thus be 'vested' (confiscated) and ultimately used as part of the assistance being granted under the Marshall Plan.

Following the expiration of the official certification period, the efforts of Swiss financial institutions with regard to non-certified assets concentrated primarily on investments held in omnibus accounts. Vesting of the contested assets by the United States in 1951 was inevitable. German assets that were held by Swiss financial institutions in omnibus accounts in the United States were faced with the possibility of double seizure (by the Americans and the Swiss, in what was known as a sequestration conflict). The liquidation of German assets in Switzerland under the Washington Agreement, which had been postponed for a long time, was ultimately abandoned in the changed political climate of the 1950s. As a consequence, the Swiss focused on securing the refund of vested assets and on sorting out individual unresolved cases. In numerous cases of different types, Swiss officials intervened with the support of the Swiss Legation in Washington. In some hardship cases, vested assets were returned. The final decisions on sequestration conflicts and similar cases were taken in the 1970s.

3.1 Conclusion of the certification process

The revocation of General License No. 95 on 31 December 1948 essentially brought an end to certification and unblocking. By the end of 1948, certification had led to the release of approximately Sfr 4.4 billion of blocked Swiss assets in the United States. About Sfr 400 million of assets remained uncertified.[275] Non-certified assets included securities and cash held by Swiss banks in omnibus accounts at American correspondent banks.

There were many reasons why some assets in the United States were not certified. Some of the blocked assets were utterly uncertifiable from the American point of view because they were German or Japanese enemy assets, or assets in which there were Bulgarian, Romanian, or Hungarian interests. Some owners intentionally chose not to seek certification because they were afraid of the fiscal or confiscatory consequences in their countries of domicile. Uncertified assets also played a major role in unresolved sequestration conflicts.[276]

Switzerland was not the only country affected by the Snyder Plan. The proposed vestings were aimed at blocked assets in the United States that originated from other European countries as well. The broad-brush presumption of enemy ownership was supposed to bring an end to this chapter of American economic warfare.[277]

Swiss officials and bankers expressed concern about the American vesting program. The Bankers Association established a 'Special Committee for Uncertified Dollar Assets' in the summer of 1948.[278] The banking community focused primarily on blocked dollar assets held in omnibus accounts and blocked securities accounts held by Swiss banks at American correspondents. Uncertified dollars in omnibus accounts are therefore the focal point of the following comments. In spite of all the efforts by Swiss officials and bankers, the vesting of uncertified Swiss assets in early 1951 under the Snyder Plan could not be prevented. After 1951, Swiss efforts focused on the return of vested assets and on the resolution of individual unresolved cases. In the meantime, the political situation had changed fundamentally. Relations had normalized between the United States and the Federal Republic of Germany, while relations between the United States and Eastern European countries had become much worse as the Cold War had taken hold.

The Washington Agreement is the starting point for questions regarding uncertified, blocked Swiss assets in the United States; the associated issues also have to be considered in the context of the planned liquidation of German assets in Switzerland, which was also proposed under the Agreement.

3.2 Problems in implementing the Washington Agreement

Liquidation of German assets in Switzerland

In the negotiations that resulted in the Washington Agreement, Switzerland consistently maintained the view that foreign private property could not be sequestered until provisions were made for effective and appropriate compensation. German citizens should be compensated in German currency at a uniform rate of exchange for any of their assets that were liquidated in Switzerland. Half of the resources needed to do this were to be provided by Switzerland out of Swiss assets held in Germany in German currency; the Allies, who were at that time the only ones with access to German currency, would come up with the other half. Half of the proceeds from the liquidation of the German assets in Switzerland was to be allocated to the Allies for European reconstruction, and the other half would remain in Switzerland.[279]

The liquidation of German assets deposited in Switzerland as proposed by the Washington Agreement was not carried out, however. Impediments to liquidation arose from both the Agreement itself and from the rapidly changing political climate in the years after the war. One of the first problems with implementation concerned the setting of a uniform exchange rate for paying compensation in German currency. Without consensus on this question, the Federal Council did not want to proceed with the liquidation of German assets.[280]

Following the German currency reform of 20 June 1948, the Allies no longer had access to German currency. Initially they maintained that they could pass on their obligation under the Washington Agreement to provide half of the compensation for confiscations to the Federal Republic of Germany, which was created in 1949. However, owing to the changed nature of political relations between the Allies and the Federal Republic, it was no longer appropriate to insist that the compensation payments be made. Moreover, the government of the Federal Republic of Germany now needed to be included in negotiations on implementing the liquidation of German assets in Switzerland.[281]

After lengthy discussions, which were particularly intense in 1951, the agreement on Swiss-based German assets was concluded between Switzerland and the Federal Republic of Germany on 26 August 1952; the transfer agreement between Switzerland, France, the United Kingdom and the United States was signed two days later. The former regulated the release of blocked German assets in Switzerland. The latter released Switzerland from all obligations under the Washington Agreement with respect to the liquidation of German assets in Switzerland. In return, Switzerland had to make a payment of Sfr 121.5 million to the Allies out of funds from the Federal Republic of Germany.[282]

However, the German government did not have this amount of Swiss francs available. On 6 August 1951, a bank consortium led by SKA announced its willingness to extend a loan to the Federal Republic of Germany to cover the transfer fee.[283] Funds to repay this loan were raised from German owners of blocked assets in Switzerland. Assets were unblocked without a requirement to register with the German authorities as long as the owners were willing to transfer a third of the total unblocked amount to the Federal Republic of Germany – an option chosen by 98% of owners. Assets of beneficial owners who refused this option were liquidated. The proceeds of the liquidation were paid to the owners in Germany in German currency, but only after deduction of a significant tax.[284]

Sequestration conflicts

According to the agreements signed at Yalta (February 1945), Potsdam (summer of 1945), and Paris (January 1946), German assets – above all private assets belonging to German citizens abroad – were to be confiscated and used in the reconstruction of war-torn countries. With concrete material interests at stake, jurisdictional conflicts arose between national sequestration authorities in the implementation of this policy. The most hotly contested issue centered on which country should be responsible for the confiscation of which enemy assets.[285]

Sequestration conflicts between Switzerland and the United States stemmed from the two countries' differing understanding of the concept of property. These differences surfaced most clearly in the tussle over omnibus accounts. The real bone of contention here concerned Swiss bank assets that had been placed in omnibus accounts at American correspondent banks to cover dollar-denominated customer assets. The Swiss and continental European view that dollar investments in omnibus accounts were the sole property of the custodian conflicted with the Anglo-Saxon legal tradition from which American law is derived. The latter distinguishes between the legal owner who holds title – i.e. a defensible claim to ownership – in the property, and the beneficial owner, who ultimately has a right to the economic benefit of the assets. The beneficial owner can be the same person as the legal owner, but does not have to be. From the American point of view, the risk clauses used by the Swiss banks could be considered an indication of a customer's ownership interest, i.e. as evidence of beneficial ownership of the covering assets held in the United States.[286] Because of the risk clause, it was the customers rather than the banks that would suffer from the confiscation of these assets. The customers therefore had an economic interest in the fate of the covering assets.

In the Washington negotiations, the main aim was to find a practical solution for the majority of unblocking cases; this aim was achieved. The problems with interpretation and implementation of the agreement that arose from the different legal traditions may have been acknowledged, but actually solving these problems was left to those who had to implement the Agreement on the ground. In the Allies' view, the provisions in the Agreement for the liquidation of German assets applied only to assets physically located in Switzerland.[287] According to this interpretation, the sequestration in the United States of assets that were considered German under the concept of beneficial ownership was exclusively a matter for the American authorities. Because the Washington Agreement did not define the 'Swiss' assets that the United States was obliged to release, vital questions of demarcation remained unanswered. German assets that had come to the United States via Switzerland were exposed to the danger of double seizure because of the various possible interpretations of the Agreement.

After all efforts to regulate the various sequestration conflicts by multilateral agreement had failed, Switzerland resorted to bilateral agreements. In 1950, it concluded agreements with Great Britain, Norway, and the Netherlands; in 1953 and 1954, with France, Denmark, and Canada.[288] In negotiations between Switzerland and the United States, proposals for solving the disputed issues were worked out and submitted to the two governments in the summer of 1949.[289] Further negotiations in early 1951 resulted in an agreement ready for signing. In the American view, however, it no longer made sense to enter into a sequestration agreement at this time because by 1952, thanks to the German transfer agreement with the Allies and the agreement with the Federal Republic of Germany, German assets no longer had to be liquidated as originally envisaged by the Washington Agreement. Swiss diplomatic efforts were unsuccessful.[290]

3.3 Vesting of non-certified assets based solely on the presumption of enemy ownership

The conclusion of the certification process on 31 December 1948 did not result in the automatic vesting of blocked assets in the United States by the Office of Alien Property, the American agency charged with managing enemy property.[291] This office could release assets upon request in the event that non-enemy ownership could be indisputably proved. However, owners from General License No. 95 countries receiving Marshall aid had to take into account that the relevant authorities in their respective countries of domicile would be informed of their application for unblocking. It was also possible for dollar assets belonging to persons domiciled in Hungary, Bulgaria, Romania, Poland and Czechoslovakia to be unblocked, especially if the owners were victims of the Nazi regime. In such cases, the American practice was not to inform the home country.[292]

The Swiss took very seriously the possibility that the Snyder Plan could be implemented in such a way that a mere presumption of enemy ownership would suffice to permit the vesting of blocked Swiss (and other European) assets. The discovery of violations in the certification process hurt relations between Switzerland and the United States, and leading officials in the US Office of Alien Property were known to be negatively disposed towards Switzerland.

Swiss defensive measures

In the summer of 1948, the Swiss had no information about when and to what degree to expect the vesting of non-certified assets, or about how this would be accomplished, or about what legal remedies would be available to defend against vesting.

The certification agreement expressly anticipated a discussion between the governments of the United States and Switzerland before the adoption of a final decision on non-certified blocked assets. Now, however, the American side intended to go ahead with the vesting unilaterally.[293]

On 11 August 1948, the Bankers Association identified the following categories of owners of assets that remained uncertified:[294] 1. Swiss abroad; 2. persons domiciled in Switzerland who had not yet submitted a unblocking application because of tax concerns; 3. owners of assets that had been certified but subsequently reblocked by American officials[295]; 4. persons who could not or did not want to provide cross certificates; 5. persons domiciled in the General License Trade Area whose assets had been blocked by Switzerland for violations regarding residence documents; 6. cases still pending with the Swiss Compensation Office as of 1 September 1948; 7. non-certifiable assets of legal entities (i.e. those in which Germans or blocked non-enemies had more than a 25% interest); and 8. German assets in Swiss bank cash accounts in the United States.

At the end of August 1948, the Special Committee[296] defined its political program: it made contact with the Legation in Washington, hired American and Swiss attorneys to give legal opinions on vesting, and planned a press campaign against vesting solely on the presumption of enemy ownership. The Swiss banks' main priority was to have dollar assets that were still blocked at American correspondent banks reviewed and unblocked. In the view of bank representatives, these assets were the property of the given bank and therefore should be unblocked as Swiss assets without any further ado, even if they were being used to back customers' dollar assets. The Bankers Association requested banks to press ahead with their inquiries into assets that were still blocked and to submit applications for the other unresolved cases.[297] By the end of 1948, there was still Sfr 400 million-worth of uncertified assets in the United States. The report on a further survey by the Bankers Association dated 14 March 1949 is not available.[298]

In the spring of 1949, there were increasing signs that the vesting of uncertified assets was imminent. The Swiss Legation in Washington was unable to obtain anything from the American government more than a promise that Switzerland would be informed 30 days before the implementation of any confiscatory measures.[299] The FPD discussed its position with the Compensation Office and the Bankers Association. Upon notification of vesting, the Legation would raise the following objections with the American government: 1. unilateral American measures were not permitted under the certification agreement; 2. unresolved sequestration conflicts should be exempted from vesting because they were to be the subject of negotiations scheduled to begin in June 1949; 3. certification cases still pending with American officials were supposed to be exempt from vesting; 4. there should be no vesting of assets that had already been certified. The American government was also to be reminded that the payment of compensation for vested assets was, in the Swiss view, a condition of earlier agreements. Sequestered dollar assets of Swiss banks should thus be protected, especially against claims from German customers.[300]

Vesting begins

Swiss officials and businessmen were taken by surprise by the press release issued on 11 October 1950 by the US Department of Justice announcing the publication of Public Circular No. 39.[301] This circular required the registration of all assets worth more than $ 1,000 with the Office of Alien Property on a newly printed form by 15 November 1950. The intention was to gather the information required to issue vesting orders under the Snyder Plan. Applications for unblocking could still be submitted under certain circumstances. While outstanding unblocking cases were still being processed, the assets concerned would not be vested. After vesting, however, confiscated assets would only be returned as laid down in Articles 9 and 32 of the Trading with the Enemy Act, i.e. through an administrative return process or a petition for return. The measures set forth in Public Circular No. 39 applied to assets from 23 countries, mostly in continental Europe.[302]

Within a few days, the FPD, the Bankers Association, and the Swiss Compensation Office had agreed upon a joint plan of action.[303] The Bankers Association advised the banks in a number of circulars, and issued instructions on how to comply with the registration requirements.[304] Regarding uncertified assets in omnibus accounts, the Bankers Association advised the banks on 24 October 1950 to submit unblocking applications.[305] On 4 November 1950, however, this advice was recalled without explanation, before being reinstated on 1 December 1950. Enquiries by the attorney Otto C. Sommerich had revealed that US officials were not willing to consider Swiss arguments regarding property in omnibus accounts, because they insisted as before on complete disclosure of the identity of customers to whom a Swiss creditor bank had dollar obligations. Meanwhile, the Bankers Association expressed grave doubts about whether under these circumstances unblocking applications would provide any protection at all against vesting orders.[307] Initially, the Compensation Office seemed negatively disposed toward the unblocking: it was afraid that if such applications were only submitted for non-German interests, American officials would conclude that all blocked assets for which no unblocking application had been submitted were German assets.[308]

The announcement of vesting at the end of 1950 raised basic questions about whether vesting on the mere presumption of enemy ownership should be contested using the legal remedies provided under the Trading with the Enemy Act. SKA estimated the chances of success of legal action in the United States at less than 50%.[309] The Bankers Association and some non-member banks also adopted a wait-and-see approach. The rejection of legal action against the general vesting orders was perhaps influenced by the fact that the vesting of cover assets in omnibus accounts did not affect the banks' own financial interests. The risk clauses in the General Terms and Conditions shifted the consequences of confiscation to the customers. Customers clearly could not bring claims for compensation.

Vesting orders regarding SKA's investments were issued in the spring and summer of 1951.[310] These orders compelled the American banks to transfer the assets concerned to the Office of Alien Property. Publication of the vesting orders in the US Federal Register marked the beginning of a two-year period during which an administrative refunding procedure or legal refunding suit could be initiated.

Although it was consistent with both American and international law, the vesting of enemy assets invested in the United States was irreconcilable with the Swiss concept of neutrality and the interests of bank customers. The precise volume of assets confiscated under vesting orders is not known. Individual banks reported the following amounts of vested assets (securities and cash accounts) in response to the Bankers Association's request of 20 June 1952:[311] SKA $ 1,818,300; Bank Leu $ 44,687; SBG $ 435,145. For SKA, the amount confiscated was equivalent to only about 1.7% of the approximately $ 103 million of assets blocked in 1941.[312] When compared to the original amount of Swiss assets blocked in the United States ($ 1.2 billion), the vested assets were relatively insignificant. Nevertheless, individual bank customers were hit hard by these measures.

Assets used to cover the claims of persons residing in countries behind the Iron Curtain were not vested at this time. They remained blocked, however. The exact volume of assets involved is not known in these cases either, although reports from some individual banks to the Bankers Association are still available:[313] SKA $ 2,356,600; SVB $ 6,800; SBG $ 27,285. According to a press release from 1955, this freeze was only a 'control' measure since it was planned that these assets would be returned to their owners after the liberation of the countries involved from Soviet rule.[314]

3.4 Aftermath of the US asset freeze

Over the two-year period during which legal measures could be taken against vesting orders based on mere presumption of enemy ownership, which had been issued in spring 1951, relations with the Federal Republic of Germany had normalized to such an extent that the confiscation of private German property was no longer an issue as far as the Allies were concerned. However, the assets that had recently been confiscated by the United States were not returned, and neither was an automatic resolution of sequestration conflicts and similar problems with the USA possible.[315]

In the spring of 1953, the two-year period for appealing against vesting orders was coming to an end. Max Ott, the General Secretary of the Compensation Office, used the opportunity to try and include the big banks in his plan to make one last effort to persuade the American government to sign the sequestration agreement that had been negotiated long ago and that would have resolved numerous outstanding problems.[316] The vehement reaction of the major banks during the discussion was followed by a polite though unambiguous letter from the Bankers Association in which its own rejection of the plan was explained in detail.[317] In the light of the relatively small amounts involved for the banks, it is understandable that they wanted to keep a low profile.

At the request of the Swiss Compensation Office, the Bankers Association asked the banks on 21 April 1953 to submit requests to the Office of Alien Property for the return of confiscated dollar assets from blocked omnibus accounts. By submitting a request to the Office of Alien Property to initiate the administrative refunding process, the two-year deadline for submitting legal refunding suits could be suspended.[318] All of

Blocking and sequestration: case studies

In 1940, a lawyer from Chur opened a cash account and a securities account with SKA Chur in his own name as trustee of the E. and the S. Trusts.[319] J. R. W. S., a German, had an interest in the trusts, but he died in 1946. The blocked assets that had been invested in Switzerland were released in 1955 upon the heirs' request. However, the assets, which SKA Chur had transferred to the Credit Suisse New York Agency, were vested in 1951 under the Snyder Plan. The heirs tried at least until 1974 to obtain their return from the United States, as well as compensation from the Federal Republic of Germany under its Reparations Law.[320]

S. v. M., born in Germany in 1940, was the daughter of the Swiss-American dual national C. v. M. and a German mother.[321] The Gestapo deported her father in 1940. Mother and child remained in Germany. $ 1,700 was bequeathed to the needy S. v. M. by an American relative, but this legacy was confiscated as enemy assets because the child had been resident in Germany. What is more, the Americans' view was that the father had lost his American citizenship by swearing an oath of allegiance and actively serving in the Swiss Army. The FPD, the Legation in Washington, and even Minister Walter Stucki himself intervened on behalf of the girl. It was considered outrageous a Swiss child would be dispossessed solely because she had lived in Germany during the war. Efforts to return the vested legacy dragged on from 1953 to 1956. During the restitution proceedings, the Office of Alien Property took the position that the child S. v. M. had voluntarily chosen to live in Germany during the war years because children were deemed to have the same status as their mothers. The Office of Alien Property also considered the father's oath and active service in the Swiss Army to be voluntary. In the course of the compensation proceedings, a number of US court decisions established that the oath and active service were not voluntary on the part of American-Swiss dual citizens and that the oath did not constitute a rejection of American citizenship in any way. As a result of this new legal situation and after jumping through numerous bureaucratic hoops, father and daughter were recognized as American citizens, which enabled the legacy to be returned.

E. A. M., an SKA employee until 1940, managed the assets of a number of German citizens as a private fiduciary agent.[322] The funds managed by E. A. M. included significant assets belonging to W. T. R. Sr., a German living in Hungary, some of which had been deposited at American banks by SKA. E. A. M. was of the opinion that W. T. R. Sr. had transferred his assets to his son, W. T. R. Jr., an American citizen, in 1940, and so he had the assets held in America certified. The Compensation Office revoked the certificates in 1948 after it discovered in the course of an audit that it was utterly unclear whether the assets had indeed been transferred from the father to the son. Moreover, not only W. T. R. Sr., but also other (German) persons had interests in the assets. W. T. R. Jr. was not the sole heir of W. T. R. Sr., who died in 1946. The revocation of the certificates led to the reblocking and subsequent vesting of the assets that still remained in the United States. The Compensation Office was still handling the case in 1956.[323]

SKA's branch offices were promptly advised to submit return requests and to distribute circulars, which had already been prepared, to German customers whose assets in America had been vested, informing them about the basic legal remedies available to them in the United States and about the relevant deadlines. The prospects of a successful appeal through the administrative process for the return of property were questionable given the applicable American legislation; neither did litigation in court look promising. With an eye to possible changes in the American position, and also in part to win time for any subsequent claims, SKA nevertheless advised those who were divested of their property to submit return requests. The bank offered its help in administrative matters but also made clear that it would not assume any responsibility for the fate of the assets that had been vested in America.[324]

Dormant assets and enemy assets in the USA: case studies

Dormant assets

Both the United States and Switzerland attach a great deal of importance to private property; however, as a result of their different legal systems, business practices and customs, they treat dormant assets differently. Under American law, dormant assets become the property of the state (escheatment) after five to ten years.[325] After transfer to the state, the authorities are responsible for returning the assets to their beneficial owners should they subsequently come forward. The Credit Suisse New York Agency became subject to such a law in 1952 and implemented the requisite process by means of an internal directive. Requests for assets to be refunded to the owners or their heirs had to be thoroughly documented. Eastern European victims of National Socialism or their heirs could only have their confiscated assets returned if the beneficiary of the dormant assets lived outside the Communist sphere of influence. Victims resident in Eastern Europe could not have their assets returned.[326]

The fate of a few individual customers that are documented in CSG's archived files in Switzerland and in New York are presented here as examples. Information available in the correspondence files is in some instances very detailed, in others, full of gaps; in many cases, decisive information is missing.

Escheatment

P. J., who had a Budapest address in 1941, invested about $ 5,000 with the Credit Suisse New York Agency in 1945. On 10 March 1948, he asked SKA Lausanne to make monthly transfers of $ 200 for his family (three children). Under General License No. 32, citizens of Hungary, Romania, and Bulgaria whose assets in the United States remained blocked were allowed in June 1946 to receive funds from blocked accounts in hardship cases, which was the case with P. J. In 1950, the Treasury Department revoked General License No. 32 and P. J. disappeared from view. In 1961, the Agency made inquiries to this customer's authorized agent in Spring Lake, which did not yield any information. The remaining assets were registered with the State of New York as dormant (with a copy sent to Zurich), and were transferred to the state on 3 November 1961. An inventory of dormant assets in 1962 identified an account in Switzerland holding Sfr 22.30 in the name of P. J., with an address in Reichenberg, Czechoslovakia.[327]

P. B. opened an account in June 1940 at the Credit Suisse New York Agency. He asked the bank to be careful when composing telegrams concerning his transfers. In February 1946, he inquired about the possibility of obtaining the necessary approvals. The bank requested additional information regarding his nationality and place of residence, which he did not provide. In March 1948, monthly transfers to P. B. were arranged by forwarding them to his authorized agent in Vienna under new Treasury Department licenses. On 17 August 1948, P. B. asked the Agency to suspend the monthly transfers. P. B. asked for access to all of his assets because he wanted to begin a new life after having experienced persecution and internment in a concentration camp. The Alien Property Control acknowledged receipt of his letter and responded that a decision would take some time because of the large number of pending requests. From June 1948 to July 1949, the bank paid out a total of $ 3,000. There was still $ 7,000 in his account. In August 1948, P.B. canceled his earlier instructions. There was no further correspondence with him until 1959. In September 1959, P.B. tried to obtain a new Treasury Department license for monthly transfers; in January 1960, the Agency informed him that the Justice Department had denied his request on the grounds of the change in US policy towards Hungary. He could withdraw only $ 50 per month in the United States to purchase clothes, food and medicine. An authorized agent in Pennsylvania undertook to receive the money on P. B.'s behalf. In April 1960, permission for an export license was granted; however, in June 1960, the agent announced that he was no longer willing to receive the money on behalf of P. B. From September 1960 on, Mrs. A. V. in Miami received the monthly transfers. Then all correspondence ceased. By 1970, the Agency still had not heard from P. B., so it prepared to transfer the remaining assets of $ 234 to the state. There is no further record confirming the transfer or any subsequent claims.[328]

Escheatment and refunding

Mrs. I. R. and Mrs. A. L., residents of Oradea, Romania, opened an account with the Credit Suisse New York Agency. It was blocked on 10 October 1940. In 1947, L. I., I. R.'s nephew, contacted the bank and informed it that I. R. and A. L. had perished in Auschwitz. However, a sister of I. R. wrote from Australia stating that I. R. and A. L. had died in Oradea. A court document with a death certificate from Hungary was rejected by the Agency. The assets went to the State of New York. The Office of Alien Property subsequently remitted the assets to 'Estate R.' and 'Estate L.'.[329]

P. B. opened an account in the name of A. K., a Romanian Jew. All account correspondence was sent directly to A. K. On 10 October 1940, the account was blocked. On 4 November 1957, the Agency transferred the assets ($ 2,851) to the State of New York. In March 1960, A. K. contacted the Agency. The State of New York refused the first request for return because the applicant had not provided sufficient identification. In 1973, A. K. wrote: 'I did it because I was Jewish and was and am living in Romania.' The State required confirmation of his signature from the American Consulate in Romania, which was not possible. However, the money was paid out in September 1973.[330]

I. R. M. invested his assets with the Credit Suisse New York Agency in June 1940. After the war, the Agency sent him information on the licenses and the new rules. It informed him that the bank had taken steps to avoid vesting. In November 1956, it transferred his dormant funds to the State of New York. In December 1970, the Agency received a letter from I. R. M. requesting information on the balance of his account and explaining that he had emigrated to Israel. In 1971, the State of New York requested additional documentation. I. R. M.'s request for the return of his assets was approved in September 1971 and the balance of $ 1,123.25 was transferred to another bank for him.[331]

Enemy assets

Only a small number of customers were explicitly named on the 'Treasury Lists' as Germans. Their residence, however, was given as 'unknown' rather than 'Germany'.[332] General License No. 95 ordered that unblocking be carried out on the basis of proof of residence. This rule did not apply to Germans and Japanese, for whom either nationality or residence were decisive. In such cases, unblocking could only be done by direct application to the Treasury Department, if at all.[333]

One key question remains today: did the money held in the US by Swiss banks include significant assets belonging to German customers, as the American authorities claimed at the time?

From the beginning of the war, the Swiss banks had always emphasized that German investments in the United States were minimal – which was certainly true in comparison to the large volume of French investments.[334] What happened to these assets? Did the banks try to have them unblocked?[335] And what became of enemy assets that were never unblocked?

There is no question that some German Jews attempted to save their assets by sending them to the United States. Such transfers would only be natural, since emigration applications had to be accompanied by a list of assets. Regardless, not many German customers invested their assets in the United States, or if they did, they tended to transfer them back at the beginning of the war.[336] The lists of US depositors from the Kreuzlingen branch indicate that, as instructed, German assets in SKA omnibus accounts were not certified. The fate of German deposits in the United States can be traced by referring to the official 'vesting orders' issued by the US authorities and listed in the Federal Register. Direct customer deposits, and after 1951, certain portions of the Swiss banks' omnibus accounts, assets belonging to businesses controlled by Germans or in which Germans held shares, securities, insurance policies, real estate, patents, copyrights[337], etc. were confiscated from the beginning of the blocking, but even more after the end of the unblocking process.[338] Persons living in Germany, or Germans outside of Germany, who wanted their assets unblocked because they were 'bona fide victims' had to apply directly to the Treasury Department. Various examples from the archives illustrate this situation.

In the Central Corporate Archives, for instance, there is a memorandum from the Kreuzlingen branch about the German customer E. S., who was deported to a camp in France (the Camp de Milles, near Marseilles) in 1941 because of his Jewish faith. The equivalent of Sfr 17,000 was transferred to the New York Agency upon his urgent request. His name appeared regularly on the Agency's list of names until 1945 with 'near Marseilles' as his domicile and a balance of $ 3,800 (at the official rate of exchange). The remaining dormant assets in Kreuzlingen were transferred to the collective account for dormant assets in 1963.[339] Nothing more is known about the assets in New York; after 1945, the name E.S. appears neither in the customer logs nor in the dossiers and lists of dormant accounts transferred to the government. No further records were found in the American archives.

According to research done during the Treasury investigation, the securities account 'Credit Suisse Zurich, rubric 8230 G.G.' was declared as bank property by Swissam on 30 June 1940. There was no information on other persons with interest in these assets. After opening correspondence with management and searching the customer dossiers kept by one of the employees, it was discovered that the rubric account had been transferred via the Basel branch with a personal introduction from the branch manager himself in August 1939. The head of Swissam thanked the Basel manager for bringing him this lucrative customer and was 'delighted to take care of his personal affairs'. The correspondence shows that the customer, who was German, was only to be referred to by his rubric number. It was also made clear, though, that any inquiries from the American authorities were to be answered truthfully. In September 1939, Swissam asked the Basel branch for an asset management mandate signed by the customer and was told: 'Mr. G. G. was put into a concentration camp under suspicion of being pro-German; [...] one should take care of his affairs to the best of his interest until it is possible to get in touch with him. [...] so far as I know him, he is anything else but a friend of the Nazi government. Moreover, he is, as I told you before, in possession of a Suisse [sic] passport.' On 13 March 1941, i.e. before the freeze, Swissam received an order from the Basel branch to close the securities account and account No. 8230 in New York, and to transfer them back to Basel.[340]

On 6 October 1948, G. P. T. who is mentioned in the records under various names, along with a Barcelona address and Spanish nationality, was certified upon request from Bank Hofmann, Zurich, with assets of approximately $ 13,000 (Blocked Account A. Hofmann & Cie. held at Chase National Bank of the City of New York). In the course of an audit of Bank Hofmann, which showed there was 'no cause for complaint with respect to the certification process', a complaint was made on 4 April 1949 by the Department for the Liquidation of German Assets regarding the case of a certain G. P. T. because it appeared to involve a German citizen. The remaining balance of certified assets in the account was reblocked. G. P. T. held a German passport that had been issued in 1944 by the General Consulate in Spain. In March 1945, he was taken into custody by the

Spanish police for deportation to Germany, and then held until 25 January 1947 in Internment Camp No. 72 in Ludwigsburg. In 1948, he traveled illegally back to Spain under a false name, was identified in Bilbao, but subsequently received a resident alien permit. The investigation showed that G. P. T. was not a Spanish-German dual citizen, as stated in his papers, but rather was exclusively German and therefore his blocked assets totaling $ 4,350 were to be confiscated.[341] In 1953, the Office of Alien Property reported that G. P. T. had been a captain in the Abwehr (the German military intelligence service) during the war and had also lived in Germany.[342]

The securities account ledgers from the Kreuzlingen branch, including records naming securities account customers, have survived in the Central Corporate Archives.[343] Assets were listed clearly in the ledgers; the nationality of the holders of securities was provided as well as details of the mandate for managing the portfolio.[344] Of the branch's 69 customers who invested in North America, there were, in addition to Swiss customers, one Italian, a Polish married couple, seven Germans, three stateless persons, and two persons with unknown nationality. Six of the seven Germans lived in Switzerland. In compliance with American law, these Germans were not certified by Switzerland, with one exception.[345] The American enemy rules were thus satisfied. The assets of the remaining foreigners were unblocked in accordance with the relevant licenses by the Compensation Office.[346] This finding strengthens the oft-repeated assertion of the Swiss banks that there were no grounds for American suspicions that large quantities of enemy assets were hidden in the Swiss banks' collective accounts.

The Compensation Office asked James H. Mann, Treasury attaché to the American Legation in Bern, about Professor T. N., a Bank Leu customer who, upon the invitation of the French occupation troops lived for a time in Germany where he held a university chair. Certification was approved on condition that the normal certification requirements were satisfied and that the case would not establish precedent.[347]

G. B., a German citizen resident in Germany, had run up a debit balance on his account at the Kreuzlingen branch and thus pledged his other assets as security. Correspondence between James H. Mann and Reinhard Hohl dated 25 November 1946 shows that the right to liquidate the pledged assets was permitted under certain conditions – which were met in this instance.[348] The Treasury Department approved certification.[349]

The Office of Alien Property's vesting orders were published in the US Federal Register, as were its 'return orders' for returning confiscated property on the basis of claims.[350] In 1951, vesting orders were issued in 24 cases where the beneficial owners of uncertified portions of omnibus accounts came from enemy countries.[351] In 9 of these cases, the American depository bank was the Credit Suisse New York Agency; in 3 it was Swissam. In 7 of these cases, complaints were filed in court for the return of the assets.

Towards the mid-1950s, there was a shift in public opinion in the United States. The view became widespread that the uncompensated appropriation of privately held assets – even 'enemy assets' or 'presumed enemy assets' – that occurred during and after the war was not only inconsistent with American law but also ran counter to US foreign policy interests.[352] From 1954 on, the government of the Federal Republic of Germany lobbied for the return of its citizens' assets. On 30 November 1955, the leading Swiss newspaper *Neue Zürcher Zeitung* reported on a Senate Subcommittee hearing about proposed amendments to the Trading with the Enemy Act that would allow the full or partial return of vested assets.[353]

The available sources do not tell us to what extent such political efforts in the United States succeeded in securing the return of assets to SKA customers. The SKA legal department's extensive file on property return questions ends with a memorandum dated 2 February 1955, stating that the time for submitting return forms for vested assets was due to expire on 9 February 1955.[354] From the bank's point of view, no further action was required on its part. Nonetheless, the resolution of certain individual blocking and sequestration cases dragged on into the 1960s and 1970s.

4 Appendix

4.1 Investments in North America

In this chapter, the technical structure of Swiss investments in North America prior to and during the Second World War is explained with the help of illustrations. Explanations are given for basic terms, such as indirect investments, omnibus accounts, rubric accounts, as well as for the fundamental concept of the 'beneficial owner'.

Two basic types of accounts were offered in North America.[355] On the one hand, an account (securities account or cash account) could be opened by the customer himself. The account owner in such cases was in direct contact with the American depository bank, which knew him by name. No records of such investments were kept in Switzerland; in the event that Switzerland was invaded, the occupier would find no trace of them.[356] It was assumed that with such direct accounts, the customer and the economic beneficiary of the assets, i.e. the beneficial owner, were the same person.

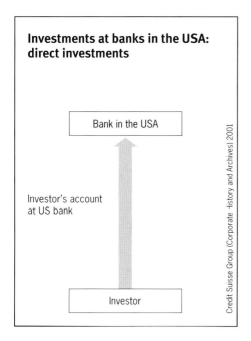

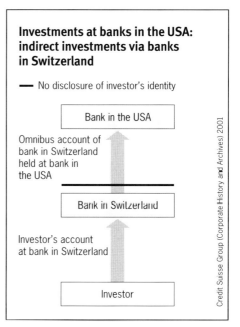

With the second type of account, the 'omnibus account', the beneficial owner of the assets had no direct contact with the depository bank in the United States.[357] The American depository bank did not know the identity of the beneficial owner of the deposited assets because this beneficial owner had no direct contact with the American bank. All contact was conducted through the 'home bank', i.e. the financial institution chosen by the customer, generally in his country of domicile, that then placed the securities or currency in the US depository bank by order and for account of the customer, but in the name of the home bank. The home bank thus acted as the link between the owner of the securities and the American depository bank; it was the fiduciary owner of the securities under Swiss law. It was also entirely possible that customers investing in America through the home bank included other Swiss banks – i.e. ones that did not deposit their assets directly in the United States, but preferred to deposit assets for their own account and for their customers through a (larger) intermediary Swiss home bank.

Customers were free to make direct deposits overseas. The home bank could be of assistance, but all correspondence was sent directly between the American bank and

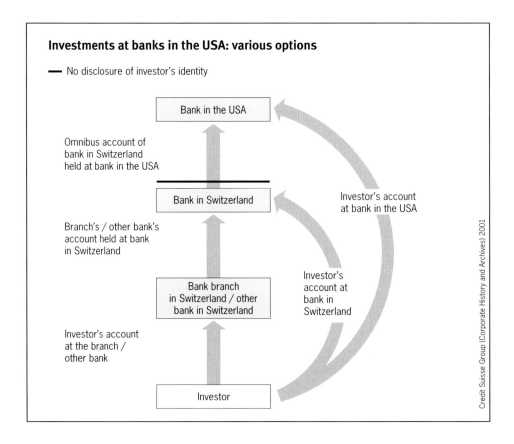

Investments at banks in the USA: various options

— No disclosure of investor's identity

Bank in the USA

Omnibus account of
bank in Switzerland
held at bank in the USA

Bank in Switzerland

Investor's account
at bank in the USA

Branch's / other bank's
account held at bank
in Switzerland

Bank branch
in Switzerland / other
bank in Switzerland

Investor's
account at
bank in
Switzerland

Investor's account
at the branch /
other bank

Investor

Credit Suisse Group (Corporate History and Archives) 2001

the customer. The customer could directly influence his assets, and access them as long as he presented himself to the bank in the USA. The personal effort and costs, however, were not negligible. Direct deposits were therefore usually made by customers with substantial private assets, and above all by businesses, foundations, holding companies, and trusts. Direct customers accounted for about 10% of all Swiss investors.[358] In areas of Switzerland that encouraged financial development (e.g. Chiasso, Glarus) and in Liechtenstein, the proportion of direct depositors was fairly high, while this type of investment was less common in rural areas. Foreign depositors, above all the French, often patronized banks in the border regions (Geneva, Lausanne, Basel). They tended to prefer the more cost-effective and anonymous indirect form of investment.

The majority of investors sought the assistance offered by a banking institution and had the bank manage their assets. Such investments were run via omnibus accounts. Customers who wanted to spread the risk diversified their US investments. They would, therefore, invest in different branches of the home bank, in its subsidiaries or in other Swiss banking institutions that maintained deposits in the United States. As a result, their assets were invested in various omnibus accounts at various American depositary banks. In some cases, investors chose a mixture of direct and indirect investment.

There could be any number of relationships between banking institutions, or between customers and banks, and these could be configured in many different ways: between the home bank and the correspondent US depository bank (several omnibus accounts opened by the home bank), between the home bank and various US depository banks, between subsidiaries or other banks and the home bank.[359] All kinds of combinations were possible: direct investments with a US depository bank (individual investments), investments in the United States through a home bank intermediary (omnibus account in the United States), or through a third bank (the third bank would hold an omnibus account at the home bank, and this would then be integrated into the home bank's omnibus account at the US depository bank).

As well as a securities account and the obligatory dollar account, an omnibus account could incorporate numerous sub-accounts owned by a single customer, or by several customers, and these could have a variety of functions and designations: at the Swiss American Corporation, SKA's subsidiary, they were called rubric accounts; at the Credit Suisse New York Agency, sub-accounts or special accounts. Rubric and sub-accounts were also held as numbered or pseudonym accounts for purposes of anonymity. These specially designated indirect investments could be subject to instructions from customers, such as arrangements for specific rights of access in the event of war. Upon the occurrence of the specifically described event, the assets would be managed in the omnibus account, but under a separately designated 'rubric'. Once the event occurred – and as long as the proper identification was made in person and according to previous instructions – the customer could have direct access to his assets overseas in the same way as a direct depositor.

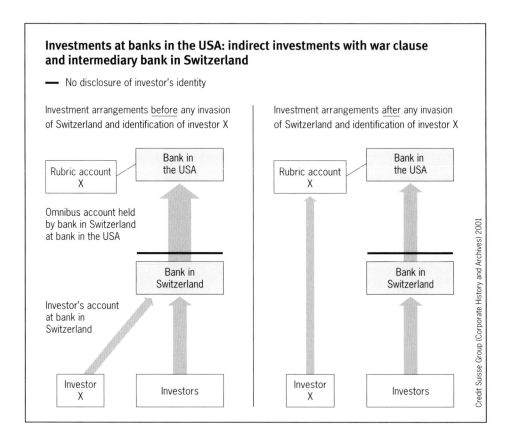

Investments at banks in the USA: indirect investments with war clause and intermediary bank in Switzerland

— No disclosure of investor's identity

Investment arrangements <u>before</u> any invasion of Switzerland and identification of investor X

Investment arrangements <u>after</u> any invasion of Switzerland and identification of investor X

Rubric account X — Bank in the USA

Omnibus account held by bank in Switzerland at bank in the USA

Bank in Switzerland

Investor's account at bank in Switzerland

Investor X — Investors

Rubric account X — Bank in the USA

Bank in Switzerland

Investor X — Investors

Credit Suisse Group (Corporate History and Archives) 2001

4.2 American regulation and control of foreign property 1940–1953

The following description of the American regulatory regime is written from the viewpoint of US law and US technical literature. The first part lists the most important rules concerning the asset freeze, which increased in severity from 1940 on, and the most important licenses that permitted transactions with certain blocked assets. The rules on the international unblocking of frozen assets and on the vesting of enemy assets date from the post-war period.

Establishment of foreign property controls

Even before entering the war, the United States adopted measures intended to prevent Germany from removing assets belonging to conquered nations from the United States.[360] After Germany invaded Denmark and Norway, President Franklin Delano Roosevelt signed Executive Order No. 8389 on 10 April 1940, which prohibited transactions and froze assets in which Norway and Denmark, or nationals of these countries, had an interest. From this point forward, transactions had to be expressly approved by license from the Treasury Department.[361] The Treasury Department entrusted implementation of the Executive Order to the newly created Division of Foreign Funds

Control, which introduced further measures to block assets belonging to enemy nationals and nationals of countries affected by the war.

The expansion of the war in Europe and Asia resulted in a gradual extension in the reach of the asset freeze.[362] On 14 June 1941, this process culminated in an amendment of Executive Order No. 8389 that prohibited transactions with virtually all of continental Europe: Germany, German-controlled territory, and neutral countries. On that same date, the Treasury Department issued regulations under the Order that defined the types of property to be frozen and the process for applying for licenses to conduct specific transactions.[363] The Order specified five types of transaction that fell under the Freezing Program. It applied to all transactions that were done by, or for, or upon instructions from a country listed in the Order or its nationals, as well as to all transactions involving the property of such nations. The transactions that were expressly prohibited were:

- Transfers from a US bank to another US bank or to a bank outside the United States
- All payments by or to a bank in the United States
- All foreign currency transactions conducted in the United States
- All exports of gold and silver (coins, bars) or currency out of the United States
- All transfers abroad of debts or property by US citizens[364]

Accordingly, under the Executive Order, a national of Switzerland would have been unable to deposit currency at a US bank, to withdraw it from a US bank, transfer it between two US banks or order a transfer between a US bank and a foreign bank.[365] Likewise, the export of gold, silver, or currency out of the United States was forbidden, as were securities transactions. These prohibitions remained in effect until a General License permitting the transactions could be obtained. Under US embargo legislation, the concept of a national was based on both citizenship and domicile. A 'blocked national' was defined as an individual who had been resident in a country subject to the asset freeze since a specified date (which depended on the country concerned), or who was a subject, citizen, or resident of the given country as defined by American law.[366] By contrast, the definition of 'enemy' was determined solely by domicile.

In 1941, the Treasury Department conducted a census of all property frozen to date: it required persons and institutions that had custody, control, or possession of foreign-owned property in the United States to register the total amount and the type of assets involved. The Treasury's intention in carrying out the survey was to ascertain the amount and type of foreign assets in the USA, as well as the identity of the owners and their relationship to the assets concerned.[367] Once the United States entered the war, policy toward foreign-owned assets changed. There was a shift from the previous practice of neutralizing these assets to vesting 'enemy-owned' assets for the benefit of America's war chest.[368] On 18 December 1941, the President signed the First War Powers Act.[369] Among the special powers this gave him, it authorized him to establish an Office of Alien Property headed by the Alien Property Custodian for the purpose of vesting enemy assets in the United States' favor, and preventing transactions prejudicial to US interests.[370] The vesting aspect was particularly significant because before the United States formally entered the Second World War, it had been entitled to block foreign assets but not to take them over or confiscate them.[371] On 15 October 1946, the Office of Alien Property was transferred from the Office for Emergency Management to the Office of the Attorney General in the Department of Justice.[372]

Regulation of frozen assets during the war

The overarching principle of the Foreign Funds Control Division was that no change in title or in the beneficial ownership of blocked assets was permitted without a Treasury Department license. This enabled the Treasury Department to ensure that foreign assets would not be used against the United States.

General Licenses

General Licenses permitted certain categories of transactions with frozen assets. In addition, in certain cases, individuals were allowed to apply directly to the Treasury Department for a special license covering specific transactions. The following General Licenses were particularly relevant to the embargo against Switzerland:

General License No. 32:[373] This license and others permitted monthly payments for living expenses to individuals residing in blocked countries. It authorized payments of up to $ 200 per household per month for individuals residing in blocked countries (e.g. Swiss citizens living in Switzerland) under certain conditions.[374]

General Licenses Nos. 42 and 42A:[375] These licenses conferred on citizens of blocked countries who had resided in the United States for a specific period of time the status of 'generally licensed nationals'; as such, they had full access to their assets in the United States. This status affected individuals who were domiciled and resident in the United States on or since 17 June 1940; after 1942, this status was extended to individuals residing in the United States on 23 February 1942.

General License No. 43:[376] On 14 June 1941, just when Executive Order No. 8389 was revised to prohibit transactions with Germany, countries controlled by Germany, and neutral countries in continental Europe, the US offices of SKA and SBV were granted General Licenses as 'generally licensed nationals'. This allowed them to carry out business on their own account. The licenses treated the foreign bank agencies in the United States as American financial institutions ('domestic banks') but this treatment did not extend to their overseas offices. The licenses granted to foreign banks doing business in the United States (Nos. 13, 14, 18, 19, 21, 22, 40, 43, 62, 66, 69, and 81) were combined in General License No. 13A on 29 September 1943.[377]

General License No. 50:[378] This license permitted all otherwise embargoed transactions provided that they were carried out by order of and for the account of the Swiss government or the SNB, or for Swiss nationals if the SNB approved the transaction. Such transactions could be conducted under this license provided that the assets did not belong to other blocked countries or their nationals and that no blacklisted persons had an interest in the assets. In the event, however, the SNB refused to guarantee transactions in favor of Swiss citizens under the conditions of General License No. 50.[379]

General License No. 53:[380] This license authorized free trade within certain regions, including the American Republics, the British Commonwealth, and the USSR. No special license was required for normal trade with nationals of blocked countries residing in this trade area unless they appeared on the blacklist.

General Rulings

The General Rulings (as well as the Public Circulars and Public Interpretations) issued by the Treasury Department interpreted the General Licenses, implemented Foreign Funds Control Programs, and responded to questions concerning general licenses.[381] The following General Rulings are relevant to the blocking of Swiss assets:

General Ruling No. 4:[382] This ruling defined terms used in Executive Order No. 8389, its revisions, related regulations, rulings, and licenses. Under this ruling, an 'interest', for example, was defined as any kind of direct or indirect claim on assets. A 'generally licensed national' was 'a person within the United States who was not a national of any blocked country'.[383] The term 'domestic bank' was defined as a bank office in the United States that was established under and subject to the laws of the United States. The New York offices of SKA and SBV were considered domestic banks. A 'blocked account' was an account in which a blocked country or a person from a blocked country had a direct or indirect interest; all transactions made through a blocked account were subject to a licensing requirement.

General Ruling No. 5:[384] This ruling introduced a procedure for ascertaining that securities entering the United States were free of enemy interests. Under this procedure, persons bringing securities into the United States from June 1940 onwards were required to deposit them with a Federal Reserve Bank. The owners could submit applications for the release of the assets, which would be granted as long as the absence of enemy interests could be verified.

General Ruling No. 6:[385] This ruling permitted the Federal Reserve Bank to transfer into blocked accounts all securities sent to it under General Ruling No. 5 pending the determination on the presence of enemy assets. It also regulated the release of securities held by the Federal Reserve Bank. Under this ruling, securities that had been transferred to a blocked account could earn dividends or interest and could be sold by the bank maintaining the blocked account; however, the income or the proceeds of sales had to remain in the blocked account.[386]

Amendment to General Ruling No. 6:[387] This amendment, issued on 27 June 1941, designated the defined accounts as General Ruling No. 6 accounts. It required that General Licenses authorizing payments, transfers or withdrawals from an account specify whether they also applied to General Ruling No. 6 accounts. Assets blocked in a General Ruling No. 6 Account could be transferred only to another type of blocked account and only by special license.

General Ruling No. 11:[388] This ruling, issued on 18 March 1942, adapted the provisions of the 1917 Trading with the Enemy Act to the changed conditions of the Second World War. It prohibited all transactions and all communications with enemy nationals.[389] This included the import and export of merchandise or trading goods (including securities and currency) as well as actual and attempted communication by mail, telegram, telephone or other means. Enemy nationals were defined as 'the Government of any country against which the United States has declared war (Germany, Italy and Japan) and the Governments of Bulgaria, Hungary and Romania, and any agent, instrumentality or representative of the foregoing Governments, or other persons acting therefor'.[390] This ruling also prohibited any future license from authorizing trade or communication with an enemy national unless such licenses made specific reference to this ruling.

General Ruling No. 17:[391] This ruling, issued on 20 October 1943, prohibited the purchase and sale of securities as well as the receipt of dividends, interest, or other income on securities held in an account for the benefit of a bank or financial institution located in a blocked country that was not specifically licensed as a 'generally licensed national'. This ruling limited omnibus account transactions. As with General License No. 6 accounts, omnibus account transactions could only be conducted if the General License or Special License approving the transaction specifically referred to General Ruling No. 17. Transactions were only approved if the US depository bank could identify the beneficial owner of securities or if it could provide certification, i.e. proof of the absence of enemy interests in the assets involved in the transaction.

Post-war unblocking of frozen assets

After the war, the Treasury Department started to remove freezing restrictions and paved the way for the release of frozen assets.[392] As to current commercial transactions, it removed all restrictions so that all dollars accruing as of a specified point in time were 'free' dollars. With regard to assets that were still frozen, a blanket unfreezing was undesirable because of the possibility that the unblocked assets could be used by enemy underground organizations. Because enemy assets were meant to be used for the payment of reparations, the Treasury Department established a procedure to ensure by means of licensing that an asset was not enemy-owned and therefore could be unblocked.

General Licenses

General Licenses Nos. 90 and 91:[393] These licenses, issued in April and May 1945, established a procedure for unblocking assets belonging to French and Belgians residing in France or Belgium. These licenses included 'conduit clauses' under which a transaction could be authorized only after the designated agency of the French or Belgian government verified that no enemy-owned assets were involved.

General License No. 94:[394] Starting on 5 October 1945, successive steps were taken to lift all freezing controls on current transactions. Under General License No. 94 of 7 December 1945, most current transactions were permitted that had previously been blocked. All future transactions were permitted without restrictions. Assets that were already frozen and the income they generated remained blocked, however. The license applied to all blocked countries except Portugal, Spain, Sweden, Switzerland, Liechtenstein, Tangiers, Germany, and Japan. The exclusion of the neutral countries was meant to apply pressure on them so that they would facilitate the examination of blocked accounts.[395] On 30 November 1946, Switzerland and Liechtenstein were included in General License No. 94.[396]

General License No. 95:[397] The Treasury Department outlined the unblocking procedure in General License No. 95. Supplementary provisions for individual countries were set forth in an exchange of letters between the US Secretary of the Treasury and the respective foreign finance ministers. The basic agreement required certification by the government of the country in which the owner resided before assets could be released. The certificate verified that the assets were not enemy-owned. General License No. 95 imposed serious penalties for the falsification of certificates[398] and reserved to the United States the right to reblock improperly certified property.[399]

General License No. 97:[400] Prior to expiry of the certification period, General License No. 97, issued on 27 February 1948, released all accounts containing assets of less than $ 5,000 as of 1 February 1948. Accounts belonging to individuals residing in Germany, Japan, Hungary, Romania, and Bulgaria were excluded, as were accounts belonging to companies organized under the laws of those countries. In cases where one customer owned more than one account, each account was assessed separately under General License No. 97, even if all these accounts were managed by the same US financial institution.[401]

The United States signed the certification agreement with Switzerland on 22 November 1946. Swiss assets located in the United States could be certified according to instructions issued on 1 February 1947[402] by the control agency – the Swiss Compensation Office – if the owner, creditor or other persons holding interests in the assets satisfied specific eligibility requirements ('certification eligibility')[403] and if the assets themselves also satisfied specific requirements ('certifiability'[404]).

Generally speaking, the Treasury Department did not accept applications for unblocking that were sent directly to it, because it had neither the jurisdiction nor the means to investigate ownership in other sovereign countries.[405] Certification had to be obtained from the government of one's home country. The most notable exceptions were for US citizens residing in blocked countries, victims of National Socialist persecution[406], religious organizations, persons who had permanently emigrated from a blocked country and in certain cases, for interests in trusts and estates.[407]

Vesting and refunding property

The Alien Property Custodian was authorized to vest the property of certain foreign nationals during war or during a national emergency. 'Vesting' meant the US government took title to the property.[408] After the Office of Alien Property acquired title by issuing a vesting order, it would then obtain physical possession of the affected assets and administer them until they were liquidated at the earliest possible time.[409]

After the war – during the certification process and thereafter – assets that were identified as enemy-owned were vested. Before an asset could be vested, it had to be blocked. Executive Order No. 9567 of 8 June 1945 authorized the Alien Property Custodian to vest all enemy-owned assets located in the United States that belonged to German or Japanese nationals.[410] In 1945 and 1946, the Office of Alien Property vested all assets located in the United States that belonged to German or Japanese nationals residing in enemy countries, and also 'under special circumstances' if they did not reside in enemy countries – as well as non-liquid assets acquired in the United States before 7 December 1945 belonging to Hungarian, Romanian, and Bulgarian nationals.[411]

In 1946 and 1947, Congress enacted legislation that authorized the Alien Property Custodian to return vested property to most classes of foreign nationals who were not hostile to the United States, including 'technical enemies' and victims of persecution.[412] There was no authorization for the return of property to persons who voluntarily remained in enemy countries – Germany, Japan, Bulgaria, Hungary, Romania – during the war, or for citizens of an enemy country who resided in enemy territory at any point during the war. Moreover, the Custodian was not authorized to return property to corporations subject to the laws of an enemy country.[413]

As with the certification of assets, the US government also entered into agreements with foreign governments regarding vesting; these placed the responsibility for determining the presence of enemy interests in vested property on the foreign governments.[414] Persons whose property was vested could obtain the return of their assets by filing suit[415] or filing a formal administrative petition with the Office of Alien Property. Since both actions were matters of public record, it was unlikely that a foreign national could effect the return of vested assets without his government finding out. On 9 October 1950, the Alien Property Custodian announced that individuals with an interest in blocked assets in the United States must register in anticipation of a possible vesting of their assets.[416] The Office of Alien Property concluded its vesting program in April 1953.[417]

Conclusion of the certification process

By 30 June 1947, the provisional end-date of the certification process in Switzerland, many owners of blocked assets still had not submitted applications for certification. Individuals acting as nominees for enemies had nothing to gain and much to lose by disclosing the presence of enemy interests. Individuals who had not paid taxes on their dollar assets could be subject to back payments. Inhabitants of war-devastated countries faced the prospect that their own government would force them to exchange their dollar assets for domestic currency.[418]

At the beginning of the blocking, the American government rejected any procedure that would have disclosed owner identity or the location of assets to foreign governments. However, with the advent of the Marshall Plan, the prevailing view in the Treasury Department was that an open exchange of information with foreign governments would relieve the burden on American taxpayers, while the refusal to share information had already resulted in the loss of significant amounts of assets that could have been used for reconstruction. Therefore, the deadline for submitting applications for certification was extended first to 1 June 1948 and subsequently to 31 December 1948.[419] All assets that were still blocked at that time would become subject to the jurisdiction of the Justice Department's Office of Alien Property. An inventory of the blocked assets was then taken and information was provided to governments receiving aid under the Marshall Plan about the frozen assets of their citizens.[420] The certification process formally ended with the revocation of General License No. 95.[421] Although General Licenses Nos. 94, 95, and 97 unblocked a considerable amount of assets and exempted additional classes of assets from blocking restrictions, none of these licenses changed the formal status of the blocked countries and their nationals. Assets that had not been certified under General License No. 95 or released under General License No. 97 thus remained blocked and subject to all wartime restrictions.

The American government assumed that the bulk of the assets that remained blocked involved enemy interests in one way or another, and moved quickly to determine their true provenance and to vest the property where appropriate. According to the circular that required all American financial institutions to take a census of all blocked assets, 'blocked countries' included Austria, Belgium, Bulgaria, Czechoslovakia, Denmark, Estonia, Finland, France (including Monaco), Germany, Greece, Hungary, Italy, Japan, Latvia, Liechtenstein, Lithuania, Luxembourg, the Netherlands, Norway, Poland, Romania, Sweden, and Switzerland.[422] From 1950 to 1953, not only the property of known enemies was vested, but also property belonging to unknown persons, such as that held in omnibus or rubric accounts. In the US government's view, any person holding an interest in such property could apply for the return of assets that had been vested improperly, provided that this person was willing to disclose his identity and produce proof that he was not an enemy.

On 24 June 1953, General Licenses Nos. 101 and 102 removed all remaining freezing controls for Western Europe and Japan and unblocked all accounts with assets under $ 100.[423] Because of the Cold War, all assets remained frozen that belonged to the governments or nationals of Bulgaria, Romania, Czechoslovakia, Poland, Estonia, the German Democratic Republic, Hungary, Latvia, or Lithuania.[424] Under the new licenses, a resident of a blocked country could secure the return of assets over $ 5,000 at this point without any certification, as long as the country was not one of the ones blocked in the wake of the Cold War and as long as the assets had not been vested, or targeted for vesting, by the Office of Alien Property. If the latter were the case, the person would have to prove to the American government that he was not an enemy and that no enemy had an interest in the assets concerned.

5 Sources

The blocking and unblocking of assets by the United States was a matter of grave significance to SKA. Accordingly, there are records in CSG's Central Corporate Archives (CCA) in Zurich that document this historic process on many different levels: the minutes of SKA board meetings record regular discussions and reports; memoranda from meetings and discussions, as well as circulars and instructions can be found in a remarkably diverse array of files from all levels of the business hierarchy. Important records – above all dealing with the impenetrable final phase of vestings in the United States – have been kept by SKA's legal department.

The bank archives of the Credit Suisse New York Agency and Swissam in New York hold information relating to the war and the post-war era in their main ledgers and in customer dossiers stored in large cartons. Customer dossiers contained in six cartons from the archives of the bank's former US legal counsel provide additional information (Milbank, Tweed and Hope Archives).

The technical instructions on unblocking and the certification of Swiss assets are largely based on the complete set of documents from the Swiss Compensation Office (SCO), Division for US Certification, held in the Swiss Federal Archives (BAR) in Bern (BAR, E 7160-02 (-) 1968/27, Vols. 1–394). The 394 volumes hold records, correspondence, forms, customer card catalogs (128 volumes), fee invoices (252 volumes) and certification ledgers (14 volumes); in the notes to this study, documents from these files are abbreviated to BAR, SCO USA, Vol. […]. We also investigated the Federal Archives files of Federal Councilor Eduard von Steiger, Federal Department of Justice and Police (BAR, E 4001 (c) –/1) and the files of the Swiss Legation in Washington (BAR, E 2200 Washington 1970/72).

The relevant files of the Swiss Legation in Washington for the war period are contained in the Diplomatic Documents of Switzerland (DDS); the subsequent period of vesting and reclaiming is documented in the detailed files of the Federal Archives. Documents on the attitude of the Swiss banks over the course of the certification process are scattered throughout the archives of the Swiss Bankers Association (SBA).

Sources documenting the American point of view are from the Treasury Department collection of the National Archives and Records Administration in Washington (NARA). All materials relating to the Swiss banks were entered into a database in 1997/98. Particularly relevant to this study are the detailed documents, customer lists, and individual records and reports on the Treasury investigations conducted at the

Swiss banks in New York from 1941 to 1943, as well as the reports on the Safehaven Program.

The two Treasury Department audit reports from the end of 1942 and the beginning of 1943, the 'Criminal Report' and the 'Final Report, Swiss bank Investigation', informed both the general background research on the business activities of the New York Agency and Swissam and our understanding of the various business records. These two reports – the latter of which survives only in an undated draft version – record on the one hand the high level of the Treasury Department's knowledge of Swiss bank activities in the United States, and on the other, the massive American criticism of Swiss banking secrecy.

In addition to the above mentioned database on relevant bank records in the National Archives in Washington, two other databases created by CSG in 1997/98 are worth mentioning: they contain all the certifications issued by the Compensation Office as well as the address catalogs of all affected customers from the Swiss Federal Archives in Bern.

The works of Marco Durrer (1984) and Linus von Castelmur (1992) make valuable contributions to the study of Swiss-American financial relations during and immediately after the Second World War.

Documents from the National Archives in Washington and other American documents used in this study are shown below; a full list of the literature used is given in the bibliography at the end of this book, p. 236. A complete list of documents used can be found in the original German edition of this book, 'Zwischen Bundeshaus und Paradeplatz. Die Banken der Credit Suisse Group im Zweiten Weltkrieg' by Joseph Jung.

National Archives and Records Administration, Washington, D.C. (NARA)

Bernstein Bernhard, re: Swiss Investigation, 3 July 1942. Records of the Office of Alien Property. Foreign Funds Control General Correspondence, 1942–1960. NARA, RG 131; Entry – Swiss Banks; Box 450 [Bernstein Report, 3 July 1942].

Foreign Service Posts of the Department of State. Confidential File, 1938–1949. NARA, RG 84; Entry 3228; Box 10 [NARA, RG 84, Box 10].

General Records of the Department of State. Decimal Files, 1945–1949. NARA, RG 59; Box 4178, 4206 [NARA, RG 59, Box …].

Records of the Office of Alien Property. Foreign Funds Control General Correspondence, 1942–1960. NARA, RG 131; Entry – Swiss Banks; Box 446, 450, 459 [NARA, RG 131, Box …].

Report on Credit Suisse, New York Agency, New York, N.Y. Close of Business 14 June 1941. Records of the Office of Alien Property. Foreign Funds Control General Correspondence, 1942–1960. NARA, RG 131; Entry – Swiss Banks; Box 450 [TFR-300 reports].

US Department of the Treasury, Criminal Report, re: Credit Suisse, Credit Suisse New York Agency, Swiss American Corporation, 3 November 1942. Records of the Office of Alien Property. /F/. NARA, RG 131; Entry – Swiss Banks; Box 449 [Criminal Report, 3 November 1942].

US Department of the Treasury, Final Report, Swiss Bank Investigation, undated. Records of the Office of Alien Property. Foreign Funds Control General Correspondence, 1942–1960. NARA, RG 131; Entry – Swiss Banks; Box 450 [Final Report].

US Department of the Treasury, In the Matter of Credit Suisse, New York Agency, Swiss American Corporation, 22/23 April 1943. Records of the Office of Alien Property. Foreign Funds Control General Correspondence, 1942–1960. NARA, RG 131; Entry – Swiss Banks; Box 446 [Hearing, 22/23 April1943].

Miscellaneous American documents (law reporters, etc.)

Federal Register, 1940–1953 [Fed. Reg.].

House of Representative Documents, 1947 [H.R. Doc.].

House of Representative Report, 1941 [H.R. Rep.].

Office of Alien Property Custodian, Annual Report 1949, Washington 1950 [OAP Report 1949].

Office of Alien Property Custodian, Annual Report 1950, Washington 1951 [OAP Report 1950].

Senate Report, 1941 [S. Rep.].

Statement from John S. Richards, in: Supplemental Appropriations Hearings before the Subcommittee of the House Committee on Appropriations, 80th Congress, 1948, p. 181f. [Richards, Hearings].

Statutes at Large, 1917–1947 [Stat.].

US Treasury Department, Foreign Assets Control. Chronology of important regulatory documents 1940–1946, Office of the Chief Clerk, Records Administration, Washington 1946 [Treasury Department, Chronology].

United States Code, 1994 [USC].

6 Notes

1 Cf. minutes of the SKA board of directors, 11 May 1939, p. 41. CCA.

2 Cf. Joseph Straessle on the state of international business. Minutes of the SKA finance committee, 12 December 1938, p. 66. CCA.

3 Adolf Jöhr in minutes of the SKA board of directors, 11 May 1939, p. 41. CCA.

4 Minutes of the SKA finance committee, 12 December 1938, p. 69. CCA.

5 With a rival organization already present in New York, opening preparations were conducted hastily and in secret. Swiss American Corporation was often confused with the New York office of Swiss Bank Corporation (the English name of Schweizerischer Bankverein) by both American and Swiss officials.

6 Minutes of the SKA finance committee, 5 June 1939, p. 124. CCA.

7 Two former Speyer partners held seats on Swissam's board of directors: George N. Lindsay, a respected and experienced investment banker and broker; and Otto de Neufville. The president of Nestlé Milk Products, Daniel F. Norton, and Joseph Straessle (member of the SKA executive board) were also board members. In May 1940, Henri Wegmann, who enjoyed the confidence of his bosses in Switzerland, assumed the leadership of the newly opened Agency, serving as business manager. Cf. minutes of the SKA board of directors, 6 July 1939, p. 54. CCA.

8 Minutes of the SKA board of directors, 6 July 1939, p. 55. Cf. minutes of the SKA board of directors, 11 May 1939, p. 39. CCA.

9 SKA's head office had an arrangement with EMA whereby all EMA accounts in the United States would be transferred to SKA's name upon the outbreak of war; but this was not allowed under the Dutch-American blocking rules. SKA's attempts prior to 14 June 1941, the date on which Swiss assets were blocked, to release the assets of the Dutch company in liquidation were strongly rebuffed by both the United States and the Dutch government in exile. Once transferred to Swissam accounts, the blocked assets were maintained in 'separate' or 'special' accounts for Effecten-Maatschappij, Amsterdam. CCA.

10 Key players in Washington were of the opinion that instructions issued from occupied Swiss territory could never be carried out in the United States, which meant that the Agency would be protected. Cf. minutes of the SKA board of directors, 18 January 1940, p. 126. CCA.

11 Minutes of the SKA board of directors, 18 January 1940, p. 131. CCA.

12 The New York State Banking Department issued the banking license on 12 April 1940.

13 Cf. Federal Council Decree on the relocation of legal entities and businesses during wartime, 30 October 1939. AS 1939, Vol. 55, p. 1301–1303; Reeves, Displaced Corporations, p. 205–213.

14 Cf. closed custody account cards, Swiss American Corporation, 1939–1965. CCA.

15 Cf. correspondence with the Commercial Registry, Ra SKA. CCA. The Federal Council Decree of 15 May 1945 expressly revoked the Federal Council Decree on the relocation of legal entities and commercial companies during wartime. AS 1945, Vol. 61, p. 310.

16 Cf. Dossier 'Bank S'. Credit Suisse New York Agency Archives.

17 Cf. SKA Bulletin, Special Edition, 40 Years of CS USA, 1990, No. 6. CCA; Criminal Report, 3 November 1942, p. 2. NARA, RG 131, Box 449.

18 Minutes of the SKA board of directors, 15 February 1940, p. 146. CCA.

19 SKA's policy differed from that of SBV, which transferred practically all of its investments to its own agency in New York once this had been set up. SKA, however, left most of the funds that it already held at various American banks where they were. Cf. Final Report, p. 15. NARA, RG 131, Box 450.

20 SKA executive board circulars to branch offices, 6 December 1940; 15 January 1941. CCA.

21 Cf. information on Alfred Schwarzenbach's return from a trip to New York. Schwarzenbach was vice-chairman of SKA's board of directors. Minutes of the SKA board of directors, 11 July 1940, p. 190. CCA.

22 Cf. Kreuzlingen branch, free securities accounts. CCA.

23 Of the total of 648 securities account customers at the Kreuzlingen branch between 1930 and 1945, 215 were women (marital status: 75 single; 71 married, 48 of whom had an account 'with spousal approval'; one married but with legally separate property; 4 divorced; 65 widowed).

24 American deposit banks also offered arrangements similar to SKA's. Brown Brothers Harriman registered with the Treasury Department 31 sealed customer letters in an SKA Bern 'general account'; this account incorporated sub-accounts for individuals whose identities were unknown to the bank. Cf. memorandum from George Owen, 3 August 1942. NARA, RG 131, Box 446.

25 SKA finance committee minutes, 5 January 1939, p. 83; letter from Fides to CTC, 13 September 1938. CCA. CTC was initially intended only for clients of Fides, SKA and EMA. EMA was a 100% owned subsidiary of Bank in Zürich; SKA had taken over Bank in Zürich in 1907. Eidgenössische Bank, Zurich, entered into this arrangement in the summer of 1939. Cf. letter from Fides to Leo Gerstle, 26 July 1939. CCA.

26 Cf. minutes of the SKA board of directors, 5 January 1939, p. 4; letter from Fides dated 19 September 1938 to Ludwig Peyer-Rheinhardt, Fides Schaffhausen branch. CCA. – 'As you already know, the Royal Trust Company, Montreal, is the only shareholder in CTC. However, CTC is indirectly controlled by us in that we have an option on CTC shares that lapses on the outbreak of war. The Royal Trust Company has full responsibility for the business management of CTC. The Royal Trust Company is one of Canada's leading fiduciary firms and has a relationship with the Bank of Montreal, Canada's leading bank, that is roughly analogous to our relationship to Schweizerische Kreditanstalt.' Letter from Fides to the Fides branch in Lausanne, 22 September 1938. CCA.

27 Cf. minutes of the SKA board of directors, 5 January 1939, p. 4. CCA.

28 Information from head office to customers concerning rubric accounts held at the Custodian Trust Company. CCA. Cf. minutes of the Fides board of directors, 2 December 1938, p. 7f. CCA.

29 Cf. correspondence between Fides and CTC from the fall of 1939. CCA.

30 Various forms of accounts were accepted: pure numbered accounts, numbered accounts with initials, pseudonym accounts or numbered accounts with pseudonyms. Cf. closed custody account cards, Swiss American Corporation, 1939–1965. CCA.

31 Cf. closed custody account cards, Swiss American Corporation, 1939–1965. CCA.

32 Cf. letter from Donald Mackenzie to Swissam, 29 November 1939. Milbank, Tweed & Hope Archives.

33 According to a list compiled by American bank examiners in New York during their investigations, the US banks most favored by SKA (other than the Credit Suisse New York Agency and Swissam) were J.P. Morgan as the top securities correspondent, Guaranty Trust (deposits at which decreased by half between 1940 and 1941) second, and Brown Brothers Harriman third. SKA was in contact with a total of 19 US banks. Cf. 'Securities accounts held for Credit Suisse by New York banks other than Credit Suisse, New York Agency and Swiss American Corporation'. NARA, RG 131, Box 446.

34 The United States began blocking foreign assets in April 1940. Interest in US investments declined as the danger of a more extensive asset freeze grew. Cf. p. 46. For more information on the figures used in the table 'SKA: number of purchase orders issued by the Kreuzlingen branch for accounts held at North American correspondent banks (1930–1945)', cf. Kreuzlingen branch, free accounts. CCA.

35 Cf. minutes of the SKA board of directors, 1 March 1941. CCA.

36 George N. Lindsay, the head of Swissam, wondered whether the prolongation of the waiting period for written permission stemmed from a conscious intention to cause more difficulties for Swiss investments. There was a need to identify any other restrictions that might be in store for Swissam's work. Cf. letter from George N. Lindsay to John Lockwood, 24 August 1940. Milbank, Tweed & Hope Archives.

37 Letter from Swissam to the SKA executive board. CCA.

38 Cf. circular from the SKA executive board to branches, agencies, and deposit counters, 20 February 1941. CCA.

39 Circular from the SKA executive board to branch offices, 7 June 1940. CCA.

40 Cf. minutes of the SKA board of directors, 24 April 1941, p. 49; 29 May 1941, p. 52. CCA.

41 This was primarily because profit-generating investments were made, while the amount of dollar investments held in the name of head office and the branch offices was dramatically reduced. Cf. Final Report, p. 21. NARA, RG 131, Box 450. For more information about the dating of this report, see Note 90.

42 For more information on the figures used in the table 'SKA: investments held at the Credit Suisse New York Agency and at banks in the United States (June 1940/41)', cf. Final Report, p. 15. NARA, RG 131, Box 450.

43 Circular from the executive board to all branches, agencies, and deposit counters, 12 September 1940. CCA.

44 Cf. minutes of the SKA board of directors, 21 August 1941, p. 77. CCA.

45 Bulletin from the executive board to all branches, agencies, and deposit counters, 12 September 1940. CCA.

46 Feeling that his presence was vital in New York for an indefinite period of time, Joseph Straessle stepped down from the executive board in Zurich. Cf. minutes of the SKA board of directors, 14 November 1940, p. 225. CCA. – Straessle nominally remained as director at Swissam but was in practice more of a 'watchdog' in New York. Cf. transcript of testimony from George N. Lindsay, General Manager, Swissam, in the course of Treasury Department hearings, 22/23 April 1943, p. 52. NARA, RG 131, Box 446.

47 'There have circulated many rumors about hemispheric politics and an economic or even a financial blockade of the entire European continent. From a purely administrative point of view, it may appear as a tempting simplification to make no exceptions while proceeding in this direction. But, since Switzerland is defending her exceptional position as a free economy country against all contrary influences, she has a right to demand this position to be respected.' DDS, Vol. 13, No. 424, Annex 1.

48 DDS, Vol. 13, No. 424, Annex 2.

49 The Swiss envoy to Washington, Karl Bruggmann, to the FPD, 12 February 1941. DDS, Vol. 14, No. 9.

50 DDS, Vol. 14, No. 13.

51 Cf. memorandum, Treasury Department, 18 April 1941. NARA, RG 131, Box 450.

52 Cf. DDS, Vol. 14, No. 47.

53 Cf. 'Census of Foreign-Owned Assets in the United States', United States Treasury Department, Office of the Secretary, Washington D.C., 1945, Appendix I, p. 52. BAR, SCO USA, Vol. 7. The basis of the survey was the TFR-300 Form, which was issued in a series of eight: forms to declare property owned by individuals not engaged in business, property owned by individuals engaged in business and by organizations, forms for organizations (primarily corporations), for foreign holdings, for banks and safe deposit companies, for banks to report deposit accounts, collection items, cashiers and certified checks, bank acceptances, and letters of credit, for banks to report securities in their custody or held by them as collateral for nationals or to report funds held in the custody department, and forms for brokers and insurers. – For more information on the figures used in the table 'Foreign investments in the United States by country (14 June 1941)', cf. 'Census of Foreign-Owned Assets in the United States', United States Treasury Department, Office of the Secretary, Washington, D.C., 1945. Appendix II, Table 1, p. 61–63. BAR, SCO USA, Vol. 7. Government and reserve bank investments are not included.

54 Cf. 'Census of Foreign-Owned Assets in the United States', United States Treasury Department, Office of the Secretary, Washington D.C., 1945. BAR, SCO USA, Vol. 7.

55 Cf. FPD to the Swiss Legation in Washington, 16 July 1941. DDS, Vol. 14, No. 58, Annex.

56 According to Karl Bruggmann, American mistrust of Switzerland was based on: 1. the country's geographical location and its consequent extensive economic dependency on the Axis powers; 2. the role of Swiss banks and insurance companies as depositories of international capital; 3. the differences (banking secrecy) between the legal concepts underlying the Swiss and American banking industries; 4. the financial interconnections between Switzerland and the rest of the continent (finance companies). Cf. Karl Bruggmann's report, Washington, to the FPD, 15 September 1942. DDS, Vol. 14, No. 235.

57 Cf. Swiss Legation in Washington to the FPD, 14 July 1941. DDS, Vol. 14, No. 58. – As long as the

Swiss government took 'reasonable steps' to guarantee the trustworthiness of these transactions, it was possible to make payments to private Swiss persons under General License No. 50. Cf. Durrer, Finanzbeziehungen, p. 53.

58 Cf. minutes of the SKA board of directors, 26 June 1941, p. 67; 21 August 1941, p. 80; 13 November 1941, p. 113. CCA.

59 Minutes of SNB's board of directors, 1941, No. 496, cited in Durrer, Finanzbeziehungen, p. 55. – Because of the SNB's 'substantial currency reserves deposited in New York, and also out of general considerations, it could not take the risk of conducting General License No. 50 transactions that might violate the American rules. As a result, it could only assume responsibility for those operations with which it was intimately acquainted.' Robert Kohli (FPD) on the financial situation in December 1942. BAR, SCO USA, Vol. 14.

60 Cf. Gentlemen's Agreement between the SNB and the Swiss Banks, banks' text of the agreement and explanatory letter from the SBA, 24 September 1941. CCA. – Adolf Jöhr remarked that the banks were more or less coerced into signing the Agreement. The SNB apparently did not permit the Swiss envoy to negotiate the problem of asset transfers between blocked accounts until the dollar transfer issue was resolved to its satisfaction. He saw a pattern familiar from the countless negotiations about the clearing agreement for payments with Germany in which he had participated in his former capacity as President of the SBA's Germany Protection Committee: goods and insurance transactions and the needs of diplomatic representations were prioritized over financial transactions (i.e. the principle of 'Work before Capital'). Cf. minutes of the SKA board of directors, 18 September 1941, p. 96f. CCA.

61 In response to a Treasury examiner who asked about the various exchange rates for the Swiss franc, Walter Niklaus (Credit Suisse New York Agency) explained the SNB's position as follows: The SNB was interested in promoting commerce and would exchange US dollars at the official rate ($ 23 for Sfr 100) if shipments of cheese, watches and the like were involved. On the other hand, the SNB did not deem it desirable to cooperate with persons who had invested their assets in the United States out of fear; income from such investments was not converted at the official rate. Because the supply of Swiss francs on the free market was lower than demand, the price was higher. Cf. confidential Treasury Department report, 'Censorship report on correspondence relating to Swiss francs and the Credit Service, New York', 30 November 1942. NARA, RG 131, Box 446.

62 The SNB's currency reserves in the United States were Sfr 2,290.1 million on 14 June 1941 and Sfr 2,451.1 million on 30 June 1943. These reserves stemmed from export surpluses, dollar transfers for payments in Swiss francs to Swiss legations in Europe, payments of Switzerland's expenses for representing foreign interests, payments to the International Committee of the Red Cross, and to Americans living in Switzerland and to foreign refugees to defray their living expenses. Information kindly supplied by Patrick Halbeisen, Head of SNB Archives, 4 May 2001. Cf. 'Die blockierten Guthaben der Schweiz in den Vereinigten Staaten von Amerika' ('Blocked Swiss assets in the United States of America'), 20 February 1945. DDS, Vol. 15, No. 371.

63 Cf. Robert Kohli (FPD) on the financial situation in December 1942. BAR, SCO USA, Vol. 14.

64 Cf. minutes of the SKA board of directors, 26 June 1941, p. 67f. CCA.

65 Cf. minutes of the SKA board of directors, 13 November 1941, p. 113. CCA.

66 Cf. minutes of the SKA board of directors, 11 December 1941, p. 121; 8 January 1942, p. 125; 5 February 1942, p. 141. CCA.

67 Cf. minutes of the SKA board of directors, 6 March 1942, p. 148; 2 April 1942, p. 161f. CCA.

68 Cf. minutes of the SKA board of directors, 4 June 1942, p. 176. CCA.

69 Cf. minutes of the SKA board of directors, 27 August 1943, p. 202; 24 September 1942, p. 206; 17 December 1942, p. 238; 14 January 1943, p. 248f. CCA.

70 Cf. minutes of the SKA board of directors, 5 April 1943, p. 280; 13 May 1943, p. 286f. CCA.

71 Cf. minutes of the SKA board of directors, 8 July 1943, p. 300f. CCA.

72 Cf. minutes of the SKA board of directors, 26 August 1943, p. 313. CCA.

73 Cf. hearing 22/23 April 1943, p. 21. NARA, RG 131, Box 446.

74 'It is unlawful for any person in the United States to engage in any form of business or commercial communication or intercourse with Switzerland as a means of indirectly communicating with the en-

emy.' 'Summary of United States Freezing Controls with respect to Switzerland', undated. NARA, RG 59, Box 4206.

75 Minutes of the SKA board of directors, 11 February 1943, p. 255; 13 May 1943, p. 285; 8 July 1943, p. 297. CCA. After a three-year stay in the United States, Hans Klaus reported on bank communications between New York and Europe: After laborious censorship by the US authorities and transportation by ship to Europe under Klaus's supervision, two large containers of bank correspondence for banks and customers were stored at the Swiss Legation in Lisbon, but no one had any idea about how or when this correspondence could be further transported.

76 For more information about measures taken by censors in the United States, cf. circular from SKA management to branches and head office departments prohibiting explicit confirmation of telegram texts by mail, 13 August 1942; circular prohibiting the commingling of business and personal communications, 16 December 1942. CCA.

77 Cf. discussion with Mr. Thomas H. McKittrick, President of the BIS, Basel. Karl Bruggmann, Washington, to Federal Council member Marcel Pilet-Golaz, 9 February 1943. DDS, Vol. 14, No. 300.

78 Telegram to the FPD, 30 October 1942. DDS, Vol. 14, No. 300, Note 6. – Joseph Straessle served on various missions, including – with the approval of the US State Department – as the official Swiss delegate to the exchange of diplomats in Lourenço Marques. Cf. telegram from Joseph Straessle to the SKA chairman of the board, 27 May 1942, cited in the Treasury Department letter to Gibbs Lyons, 10 June 1942. NARA, RG 131, Box 450.

79 In a discussion on 5 November 1942 with Peter Vieli, who was sent to Bern by Adolf Jöhr and who supported hiring Straessle at the Legation in Washington, Federal Council member Marcel Pilet-Golaz noted that it would be possible to integrate Straessle into the Legation. SKA saw no problem with this. Straessle was exceptionally intelligent and highly skilled; he had already heard from Envoy Bruggmann. Bruggmann added: 'Perhaps we would have an interest in having Straessle at this time after all. He has certain "Jewish" qualities, and this is perhaps not a bad thing in dealing with the Treasury Department.' DDS, Vol. 14, No. 300, Note 6.

80 Cf. DDS, Vol. 14, No. 300, Note 7.

81 CCA.

82 Cf. Public Circular No. 4, Treasury Department. A complicated and detailed series of questions. BAR, SCO USA, Vol. 7.

83 Certain special files containing additional customer correspondence and customer names were not reviewed at this time, which later caused Treasury inspectors to criticize the banks for knowingly covering up relevant information. After the registration requirement was issued, SKA's New York institutions endeavored to report the amount of assets in a timely manner, whereas the Treasury Department was primarily interested in identifying owners, a fact that only became apparent once the Treasury investigation was underway. Cf. hearing, 22/23 April 1943, p. 61ff., 192. NARA, RG 131, Box 446.

84 Cf. SKA finance committee minutes, 21 August 1941, p. 42. CCA.

85 'It is probable that various fascist chieftains have used Swiss banks to conceal or to send to other countries wealth which they have put aside against a day of reckoning. There is an equal probability that the Nazi government, or its agents, have made use of the Swiss banks as a channel through which looted assets can be realized, sabotage in outside countries financed, and economic warfare waged against us in other ways.' Final Report, p. 49. NARA, RG 131, Box 450.

86 'In 1938 and 1939 because of the fear of confiscation, in the event of invasion, there was a heavy flow of Swiss and other foreign capital to the United States. The owners of such capital were obviously desirous of concealing their identity. The Swiss banks including particularly Credit Suisse having an established tradition of "cloaking" and concealment of funds, were extensively used for this purpose.' Criminal Report, 3 November 1942, p. 4. NARA, RG 131, BOX 449.

87 The first phase of the bank investigation through May 1942 aimed to 'check on all current operations'; the second phase aimed to review all other files (focusing on transfers between Italian and German owners to American owners, bank behavior, opening sealed envelopes with secret instructions, and identifying owners of numbered accounts). Letter from E.H. Foley, Inter Office Communication, Treasury Department, to Henry Morgenthau, 2 June 1942. NARA, RG 131, Box 450.

88 Cf. report by Hans Klaus upon his return from New York after a three-year assignment. Minutes of the SKA board of directors, 8 July 1943, p. 297. CCA.

89 Letter from Estella Reiner and Gabriel Kerekes to Lawrence S. Lesser, Inter Office Communication, Treasury Department, 14 September 1942. NARA, RG 131, Box 446.

90 'Final Report Swiss Bank Investigation', undated, containing numerous hand-written notes and corrections that make it clear that this version is not the final one. The Report must have been compiled towards the end of 1942, judging by the dated information on the balance sheets and profit and loss accounts of the New York bank agencies; a survey of bank officials on the 'conclusion of the investigations' was conducted in April 1943. A final, dated copy of the report has yet to be located in the archives. NARA, RG 131, Box 450.

91 The Treasury Department's Criminal Report of 3 November 1942 catalogues the Swiss banking institutions' violations of American rules in the United States. NARA, RG 131, Box 449.

92 'Although Swiss tradition and law support the system of anonymous accounts and this fact has been from time to time offered as a reason for the fact that we do not know the owners of much of the property in custody at the Swiss agencies in New York, there is really no reason why we should not find out. Swiss law need not take effect in this country when it runs counter to American law. And much can be done to learn owners' names, even when they are not known to the agencies in New York.' Final Report, p. 42. NARA, RG 131, Box 450. – No documents were found in the Central Corporate Archives recording the reactions of SKA head office to the new rules; the first recorded mention of Swiss opinion is from the fall of 1943, following the release of General Ruling No. 17, the fundamental premises of which corresponded generally with this report.

93 Cf. 'Copy of cable sent on 3 March 1943 by the Credit Suisse New York Agency to Credit Suisse, Direction General, Zurich'. NARA, RG 131, Box 450.

94 Memorandum from Joseph W. Sinnott, Treasury Supervisor for the Credit Suisse New York Agency, to the Federal Reserve Bank, 4 March 1943. NARA, RG 131, Box 450.

95 Cf. letter from Lawrence S. Lesser to Henry Morgenthau and Randolph E. Paul, 28 November 1942. NARA, RG 131, Box 446.

96 The questioning ranged from general questions about Switzerland, SKA, and the New York bank institutions, their forms of organization, and responsibilities, to the files and recording systems in general, the various types of accounts and how they were organized; there were also questions about individual documents and about the conflict between the files found and the falsified forms submitted to the Treasury Department. Cf. Opening Remarks, 5 April 1943. NARA, RG 131, Box 459.

97 Memorandum from Joseph W. Sinnott, the Treasury Supervisor for the Credit Suisse New York Agency, to the Federal Reserve Bank, Foreign Funds Control, 1 May 1943. NARA, RG 131, Box 450.

98 Memorandum from George H. Owen 'Re: Organization of Swiss American Corporation', 11 July 1942, p. 4. NARA, RG 131, Box 450.

99 Report from Victor Nef, Swiss Consul, New York, to the FPD, 9 April 1943, DDS, Vol. 14, No. 235, Note 9.

100 Information note from Treasury Representative Joseph W. Sinnott, Supervisor for the Credit Suisse New York Agency, to fellow employees, saying 'that the US Treasury Department will no longer require representation at that institution after August 11, 1943'. Letter from Joseph W. Sinnott to the Federal Reserve Bank, 11 August 1943. NARA, RG 131, Box 450.

101 Treasury Department supervision was terminated on 11 August 1943. Cf. letter from Chas. N. Van Houten, Foreign Funds Control, to the National City Bank of New York, 6 August 1943. NARA, RG 131, Box 450.

102 'The corresponding figures at the Swiss Bank Corporation are approximately $ 194,000,000 in cash and securities held for unknown owners, and approximately $ 61,000,000 in named accounts.' These amounts are presumably the interim figures for the business year 1942. By far the lion's share of assets in omnibus accounts transferred from Switzerland to the United States was not placed with the Swiss agencies, but rather with American banks. Final Report, p. 15, 41. NARA, RG 131, Box 450.

103 Final Report, p. 57. NARA, RG 131, Box 450.

104 '[…] the income, when it was in the form of dollars, was not kept separate from other dollars. If it were

in a separate account, no debit to the account could be made without a license and the dollars would be truly blocked. When the dollars sink into a reservoir of many other dollars, all held in the name of the Zurich office, there is no way in which either the Treasury Department or the Agency can tell what names may be found on the Zurich books opposite various quantities of those dollars.' Final Report, p. 62f. NARA, RG 131, Box 450.

105 Final Report, p. 49. NARA, RG 131, Box 450.

106 Letter from Robert Kohli (FPD), 19 January 1945, cited in Durrer, Finanzbeziehungen, p. 125.

107 According to general estimates, they accounted for only about 10% of all Swiss investments; cf. Robert Kohli (FPD) on the financial situation in December 1942. BAR, SCO USA, Vol. 14.

108 Cf. Milbank, Tweed & Hope Archives.

109 A General License permitted stocks quoted on an American stock exchange as well as bonds to be bought with funds from blocked accounts. Cf. Schweizerischer Bankverein, Basel (publisher), 'Vereinigte Staaten Embargo. Wichtigste Vorschriften auf dem Gebiet des Zahlungs- und Kapitalverkehrs unter besonderer Berücksichtigung der die Schweiz betreffenden Massnahmen' ('US embargo. Key regulations on payment and capital transactions with particular reference to the measures affecting Switzerland'), Oct. 1943, p. 16. CCA. – '[...] the bulk of each ordinary account consists of assets of clients of the depositing branch. As a result, those clients, about whom we [the US Treasury] know little or nothing, are able to buy and sell American securities with little concern for freezing control.' Final Report, p. 59. NARA, RG 131, Box 450.

110 Final Report, p. 60. NARA, RG 131, Box 450.

111 'The owner of securities in an omnibus account held at the New York Agency in the name of a Swiss office of one of these Banks can receive in Switzerland income accruing from his investment. Interest or dividends are credited to a blocked account in New York, but the New York Agency can, by the simple act of notifying the Swiss office that they are received, insure their crediting to the Swiss owner.' Final Report, p. 61. NARA, RG 131, Box 450.

112 Cf. minutes of the SKA board of directors, 17 December 1942, p. 238. CCA.

113 'Accounts were treated as Swiss when a reasonably careful examination would have disclosed an interest of some other nationality.' Final Report, p. 51. NARA, RG 131, Box 450.

114 Cf. Durrer, Finanzbeziehungen, p. 129.

115 Criminal Report, 3 November 1942, p 10. NARA, RG 131, Box 449.

116 Criminal Report, 3 November 1942, p. 11f. NARA, RG 131, Box 449. The cited passages are taken from the customer examples provided in the Criminal Report.

117 Cf. Final Report, p. 46. NARA, RG 131, Box 450.

118 Durrer states that in each case, the person who would assume the rights of the account holder affected by the asset freeze and have the authority to access the assets was designated in advance and spelled out in a sealed letter signed by the account holder. This released the Swiss bank agencies in New York from the responsibility of having to determine themselves how to apply emergency instructions. More detailed instructions concerning the conditions and timing of a change of ownership were set forth on the envelope or in a cover letter. Four scenarios were envisaged: 1. express and written instructions from the owner of the assets; 2. a notice published simultaneously in the 'New York Times' and the 'Herald Tribune' that Switzerland had become militarily involved in the war; 3. instructions sent by telegram from the bank office located in Switzerland; and 4. instructions from one or more persons authorized to act on behalf of the given bank. Cf. Durrer, Finanzbeziehungen, p. 128.

119 Criminal Report, 3 November 1942, p. 5. NARA, RG 131, Box 449.

120 Memorandum 'Re: Conference with Lindsay, de Neufville, and Shepperd on 15 May 1940', p. 3. Milbank, Tweed & Hope Archives.

121 Final Report, p. 48. NARA, RG 131, Box 450.

122 Cf. Bernstein Report, 3 July 1942. NARA, RG 131, Box 450.

123 The depository bank had an express interest in not knowing the identity of the actual owners of omnibus accounts, because as soon as a bank knew who the beneficial owner was, it could be held responsible for losses caused by violation of instructions. Cf. Bernstein Report, p. 2, Note 2. NARA, RG 131, Box 450.

124 Cf. Bernstein Report, 3 July 1942, p. 4–6. NARA, RG 131, Box 450.

125 The introduction of General Ruling No. 17 was planned for 20 November 1943, but was postponed by 50 days to 8 January 1944 and again to 31 January 1944 thanks to the efforts of the Swiss Legation in Washington. Cf. Report of the Swiss Financial Adviser to the Swiss Legation, Joseph Straessle, to the Chief of the FPD's Foreign Policy Department, Pierre Bonna, 30 November 1943. DDS, Vol. 15, No. 45.

126 The Swiss envoy in Lisbon, citing Emil Froelich, a manager with Swiss Re, in a report dated 19 March 1943 to Federal Council member Marcel Pilet-Golaz: The American freezing was not a currency control like those in other countries, but rather the complete negation of all property rights until the true ownership relationship (propriété réelle) could be proved. $ 7.5 billion were blocked and were considered as American collateral; the newspapers reported that it would be used to compensate war expenses. Sfr 1.7 billion in Swiss assets were very solidly blocked and would perhaps one day have to share the fate of German assets. DDS, Vol. 14, No. 300, Note 2.

127 SBA communiqué to the banks, 12 November 1943. CCA.

128 Cf. FPD memorandum on the new US financial ruling, described by Robert Kohli (FPD Embargo Commission), 28 October 1943. DDS, Vol. 15, No. 29; minutes of the SKA board of directors, 18 November 1943, p. 330f. CCA.

129 Under the 'Swedish system', all transactions involving blocked assets were conducted through Sveriges Riksbank. The banks were obliged to provide Sveriges Riksbank with precise customer information for the attention of the American authorities, such as name, nationality, residence of the beneficiaries, and the purpose of the transaction. Sveriges Riksbank ensured that changes in ownership and interest payments were made only for purely Swedish property. Cf. Durrer, Finanzbeziehungen, p. 61. – SKA's board of directors was of the opinion that the only advantage of the Swedish system was that the customer information was released not to the Americans but to a domestic office. Sweden already had currency controls, and all transactions were monitored. Sveriges Riksbank regularly exchanged dollars for its own currency, which the SNB categorically refused to do. Unlike the SNB, Sveriges Riksbank could afford to do this because its transactions were modest in volume. Cf. minutes of the SKA board of directors, 18 November 1943, p. 330. CCA.

130 Cf. Report of the Swiss Financial Adviser to the Swiss Legation, Joseph Straessle, to the Chief of the FPD's Foreign Policy Department, Pierre Bonna, 30 November 1943. DDS, Vol. 15, No. 45.

131 Cf. FPD notice on the new US financial ruling, signed by Robert Kohli (FPD Embargo Commission), 28 October 1943. DDS, Vol. 15, No. 29.

132 Minutes of the meeting on financial relations with the United States (SNB, FPD, FDF, Chamber of Commerce, Trade and Industry Association, etc.), 6 January 1944. DDS, Vol. 15, No. 66.

133 A plan that would have made the SBA responsible for the supervision was rejected by the United States, which insisted on a General Ruling No. 17 procedure or the Swedish system. The SBA was preparing comments in mid-December to be submitted to the Federal Council in support of staying under General Ruling No. 17. Cf. minutes of SKA's board of directors, 16 December 1943, p. 339f. CCA. – Robert Kohli (FPD) spoke of a 'confused comment from the Bankers Association'. DDS, Vol. 15, No. 66.

134 With regard to the system of customer certification that the Swiss institutions in the United States (Swissam, the Legation in Washington) preferred, it was noted that: 'A greater responsibility would be transferred to the bank through the certification process; moreover, the bank would be subject to supervision by a foreign authority. In the event of a review, the American consulate will contact the bank, not the customers. No one can say how and to what extent this control will be exercised. It is a matter of concern that, given the American war mentality, control will be rigorous. The danger cannot therefore be dismissed that banking secrecy will be affected by this control. […] It will be a sensitive issue if they ask to examine the books, because then a sphere of confidentiality will be surrendered that will affect more than just the customers concerned. […] It contradicts our concept of public law to have foreign government offices exercising functions that are to a certain extent official. The entire Swiss affidavit system is designed to prevent the intervention of foreign offices.' Memorandum, SKA Ra, 19 November 1943. CCA.

135 Letter from management to customers dated 6 November 1943, CCA. The text of the form to be signed by the customers read: 'I authorize you to disclose my name, residence and nationality to the American Treasury Department via your New York agents, and I expressly declare that the accumulated interest and dividends from my American securities are my personal and exclusive property and that no other persons have an interest therein of any kind. I likewise consent to your sharing the necessary information with your New York friends in the event of sales and purchases of American securities.' Cf. also minutes of the SKA board of directors, 13 January 1944, p. 6. CCA.

136 Cf. letters from SKA management and branch offices to customers, 3 January 1944. CCA.

137 Cf. letter from the FDP, Foreign Affairs Division, to the SBA, 21 September 1944; 30 November 1944. CCA.

138 Cf. minutes of the SKA board of directors, 18 November 1943, p. 331. CCA.

139 Cf. letter from SKA management and branch offices to customers, 24 March 1944. CCA.

140 Cf. SKA circular to branch offices, 6 December 1944. CCA. The name, address and nationality of all heirs, and all American assets (including those not deposited with SKA) were to be disclosed.

141 Cf. letter to the Securities Exchange Association in Zurich, 5 January 1944. CCA. – Securities had to be identified as 'legitimate instruments' before they could be sold on Swiss stock exchanges. This was done by attaching an affidavit, i.e. a sworn statement attesting to uninterrupted ownership since a specified date and/or the non-enemy status of the owner. The Allies' security precautions were having an increasing impact on the securities market in Switzerland. While there was a need at the beginning of the American blockade against German-occupied lands to exclude unauthorized creditors (by means of a 'Green Affidavit' for trading American securities, according to the SBA directive of 5 February 1941), once the blockade was extended to the neutral countries, proof of Swiss ownership had to be provided (the 'Red Securities Affidavit' from the Swiss Securities Exchange Association and a 'New Statement' for the 'Proof of Swiss Ownership', 1 September 1941; Directive from the Securities Exchange Association in Zurich, 25 August 1941). Following the discovery of a significant affidavit counterfeiting ring and after the requisite improvements were subsequently made to the system, SKA decided on 1 December 1942 to unilaterally identify deposited securities. In April 1943, the SBA put forward a new affidavit convention (Convention A 'On Proof of Swiss-Owned Property', including the 'Blue USA Securities Affidavit', augmented after the issuance of General Ruling No. 17 by the 'Statement on Non-Enemy Property'). The SBA Convention L Affidavits followed the American 'warning' in 1944. All of the affidavits were unilateral measures taken by Switzerland; recognition of these affidavits by foreign authorities was achieved subsequently by means of intergovernmental agreements. A new USA affidavit was created in 1947/48 for unblocking and certifying American securities (the 'Beige USA Affidavit No. XIII' of 28 January 1947). Cf. Bank Leu Collected Affidavits, NAB, and 'Affidavit Conventions' File, SKA Ra. CCA.

142 Cf. SKA circular to branch offices, 6 December 1944. CCA.

143 Cf. copy of Credit Suisse New York Agency telegram to head office and circulation to the branch offices, 16 March 1944. CCA.

144 Cf. e.g. 'Swiss-French', 'Swiss-Dutch', etc. Copy of Credit Suisse New York Agency telegram to head office and circulation to the branch offices, 17 February 1944. CCA.

145 Information on nationality and residence was equally important to the American authorities in identifying assets and 'isolating enemy assets under General Ruling No. 17'. Owing to the presumption of common interests, a Swiss living abroad in an enemy country was treated the same as a citizen of an enemy state. The American interpretation of the concept of nationality caused complications particularly during the unblocking and certification phase after 1946 and especially with regard to the separation out of Swiss property belonging to Swiss living abroad. Cf. SKA management circular to the branch offices of 11 September 1944 with reference to a notice from the SBA. CCA.

146 Cf. telegram from the Credit Suisse New York Agency and instructions from head office to the branch offices, 31 July 1944. CCA.

147 Cf. Special License No. NY 618496. Support for living and travel expenses of the beneficiary and his family members. Management instructions to the branch offices of 20 June 1944. CCA. Extension and Amendment of the Special License on 23 April 1945. Support was limited to a maximum of $ 1,000

per month for Americans domiciled abroad, for private persons with domicile in and nationality of Portugal, Spain, Sweden, Switzerland, as well as for private persons or citizens of blocked countries with domicile in the Generally Licensed Trade Area or in a non-blocked country. Support payments of up to $ 500 per month were permitted to former US citizens or citizens of non-blocked countries with foreign domicile or private persons domiciled in Portugal, Spain, Sweden, and Switzerland since 8 April 1940. A maximum of $ 250 was allowed for private persons domiciled in Portugal, Spain, Sweden, or Switzerland since 1 January 1943.

148 Minutes of the SKA board of directors, 23 March 1944, p. 24f. CCA.

149 Minutes of the SKA board of directors, 6 July 1944, p. 54. CCA.

150 Dean Acheson, Assistant Secretary of State, caustically warned the neutral countries that this was the last chance for them to join the side of the victors. 'The time-consuming and difficult negotiations with the Swiss and the Swedish were […] becoming increasingly tiresome. He found the Swiss particularly intractable.' Cited in Schiemann, Neutralität, p. 101f.

151 Cf. minutes of the SKA board of directors, 20 September 1944, p. 73f. CCA.

152 Cf. Schiemann, Neutralität, p. 100f.

153 'First off, we have to be aware of the danger of the movement of looted assets and flight capital to our country under today's circumstances. […] Collaboration of any kind in the movement of such assets [must] be avoided at all costs. Even passive collaboration, such as producing balance sheets, accounts, asset statements, etc. with fictitious liabilities, transferring existing asset positions to anonymous accounts or accounts under other names for the purpose of covering up the true state of affairs, could facilitate such movements or even enable it. […] We should be particularly careful that the actual and factual relationships are put down in each instance, so that the legal form in which the assets may be deposited or represented is not considered decisive on its own. For example, with fiduciary property, it is not the fiduciary arrangements that are decisive, but rather the actual details of ownership. The same principle also applies to the management of assets that in fact belong to foreigners, or to which they are indirectly entitled but which are held abroad in the name of or for the account of Swiss banks […], because actual beneficial ownership is the only decisive criterion that a bank may apply when applying the foreign requirements.' SBA circular to the banks, 11 September 1944. CCA.

154 Minutes of the SKA board of directors, 20 September 1944, p. 74f. CCA.

155 Instructions from SKA's executive board classified 'highly confidential', 15 September 1944. CCA.

156 SBA circular, 30 September 1944. CCA.

157 Cf. 'Orientierende Notiz betreffend die Interpretation und die Anwendung des Feindbegriffes und der Massnahmen bezüglich des Handels mit dem Feind seitens der alliierten Regierungen' ('Briefing note on the interpretation and application of the term "enemy" and Allied government measures regarding trading with the enemy'), anonymous author (SKA), 27 October 1944. CCA.

158 Cf. SBA Affidavit Convention L, 1 October 1944. SBA Archives. Transactions with foreign securities were forbidden without an affidavit.

159 Cf. memorandum from the Swiss banking delegation in the USA, cited in an FPD letter to the SBA, 11 December 1944. DDS, Vol. 15, No. 313.

160 Peter Vieli on the British-American warning. Minutes of the SKA board of directors, 14 December 1944, p. 102f. CCA.

161 Reports from the SBA delegation in the United States, report by Henri Grandjean. Minutes of the SKA board of directors 14 December 1944, p. 159. CCA.

162 'The SBA has recently been informed that managers of Swiss banks have been summoned to Allied consulates to respond to questions about holding companies on whose boards the persons concerned have sat, or with which the bank concerned has been involved. Our bank was summoned only once for such questioning.' Minutes of the SKA board of directors, 14 December 1944, p. 102. CCA.

163 A British report dated 18 December 1944 on cloaking enemy assets via holding companies in Switzerland and Liechtenstein ascertained that only a few small-scale private assets owned by German Jewish refugees could be identified. Paul Rossy from the SNB, Henri Grandjean and Peter Vieli from SKA, Maurice Golay and Albert C. Nussbaumer from SBV, and Albert Caflisch, General Secretary of the SBA, were noted as being particularly helpful during the survey. The author of the report added: 'If we

were Hitler and Goering, we would not expect the holding companies handling our loot to do their transactions through such banks as the Credit Suisse, but through some small private bank in the back-streets of Zurich.' British Legation in Bern to the Ministry of Economic Warfare, 18 December 1944. NARA, RG 59, Box 4178.

164 Minutes of the SKA board of directors, 14 December 1922, p. 102. CCA.

165 Minutes of the SKA board of directors, 14 December 1922, p. 103. CCA.

166 Instructions from SKA executive board to the branch offices, 10 November 1944, CCA.

167 Instructions from the SKA executive board to the branch offices, 27 December 1944. CCA.

168 'Upon sale, securities are withdrawn from our non-identified securities account and the proceeds credited to a General Ruling No. 6 account. Amounts thus generated – but not old assets – can be used to purchase North American and Canadian stocks quoted on the American markets, as can coupons and dividend payments credited to the account or to be credited to the account from non-identified securities accounts. The acquired securities will be placed in a new account designated "General Ruling No. 6 account under General Ruling No. 17".' Instructions from SKA's executive board, 5 January 1945 (German text); Circular letter, 30 October 1944; 2 November 1944 (English text). CCA.

169 Minutes of the SKA board of directors, 1 March 1945, p. 129f. CCA.

170 'According to confidential information from the Swiss Legation in Washington, the American Treasury Department has supposedly received information to the effect that some Swiss banks are currently going to great lengths to sell off gold and bonds that come from Germany.' Note from Robert Kohli (FPD) to Adolf Jöhr, 14 December 1944. CCA.

171 Henri Grandjean and Wilhelm S. Merian to Robert Kohli (FPD), Bern, 18 December 1944. CCA.

172 Note from Robert Kohli (FPD) to Adolf Jöhr, 13 March 1945. CCA.

173 Adolf Jöhr's response to Robert Kohli (FPD), 26 March 1945, at a point during the Currie negotiations when the certification of Swiss assets and the intervention of the SCO had already been agreed upon. In defense, Robert Kohli responded that as early as 1943, after the issuance of General Ruling No. 17, the FPD had urged the SNB and the banks to adopt an identification system. Unfortunately, this effort had not succeeded. Letter from Robert Kohli (FPD) to Adolf Jöhr, 28 March 1945. CCA.

174 Cf. Leo T. Crowley, head of the Foreign Economic Administration, 29 December 1944, cited in Schiemann, Neutralität, p. 135.

175 Walter Stucki, Chief of the foreign policy division of the FPD, to the National Council Commission on Foreign Affairs, 7 March 1945. DDS, Vol.15, No. 390.

176 Cf. press clippings in Schiemann, Neutralität, p. 137.

177 Cf. Walter Bosshard, 'Das Problem der blockierten schweizerischen Guthaben – Der amerikanische Standpunkt' ('The Problem of Blocked Swiss Assets – The American Point of View'), in: NZZ, 26 December 1944. NZZ's US correspondent, Walter Bosshard, called for understanding of the Allied position and for cooperation.

178 Minutes of the SKA board of directors, 8 February 1945, p. 122. CCA.

179 Minutes of the SKA board of directors, 8 February 1945, p. 122. CCA.

180 Walter H. Sholes, American Consul General, Basel, to the State Department, 16 January 1945. NARA, RG 84, Box 10.

181 Certification and Unblocking under General License No. 95. Countries and dates of unblocking: France (5 October 1945), Belgium (20 November 1945), Norway (29 December 1945), Finland (29 December 1945), the Netherlands (13 February 1946), Czechoslovakia (26 April 1946), Luxembourg (26 April 1946), Denmark (14 June 1946), Greece (15 October 1946), Switzerland and Liechtenstein (30 November 1946), Poland (7 January 1947), Austria (16 January 1947), Sweden (28 March 1947) and Italy (29 August 1947).

182 Minutes of the Federal Council meeting, 20 February 1945. BAR, SCO USA, Vol. 9. The control system was set forth in numerous SCO instructions (Instructions Nos. 1–11, 1 February 1947 – 9 October 1948). BAR, SCO USA, Vol. 1.

183 Cf. BAR, E 7160-02(-) 1968/27, Vols. 1–394, 1944 to 1955.

184 France, Belgium, Norway, Finland, the Netherlands, Czechoslovakia, Luxembourg, Denmark, Greece.

185 Cf. 'Agreement between Switzerland and the United States of America on the Unblocking of Swiss As-

sets in America, 22 November 1946'. AS 1946, Vol. 62, p. 989–998; correspondence between James H. Mann, American Treasury Department representative in Bern, and Legation Counselor Reinhard Hohl, Head of the FPD's Legal, Financial, and Transportation Affairs Office, 25 November 1946. BAR, SCO USA, Vol. 7; correspondence between James H. Mann and Reinhard Hohl, 10 November 1946. BAR, SCO USA, Vol. 4. – After the certification process had begun at the SCO, an employee reflected on the negotiations of November 1946 and referred in a note dated 11 March 1947 to the negotiators' considerable insider knowledge, which remained crucial for the SCO's work: 'The negotiations with Mr. Orvis Schmidt in the first days of November had a unique character in terms of the time available, the participants, the balance of power, and even the texts that served as the basis for negotiations. The personal recollections of the participants were necessary and valuable in interpreting the confusing agglomeration of principles, the detailed rules, and the gaps in the texts at issue.' Note on certification, 11 March 1947. BAR, SCO USA, Vol. 8.

186 Cf. Federal Council Decree on the certification of Swiss assets in the United States of America, 27 December 1946 (extended on 20 December 1948). AS 1946, Vol. 62, p. 1097–1100; AS 1948, Vol. 1948, p. 1207; Federal Council Decree on the marshalling of non-certifiable assets, 27 December 1946. AS 1946, Vol. 62, p. 1104–1100.

187 Interests included ownership, possession, rights of lien, usufructuary rights, patents, life insurance policies, etc.

188 For more on the subjects covered in this box, cf. e.g. Castelmur, Finanzbeziehungen, p. 23–26; Durrer, Finanzbeziehungen, p. 184–251; Schiemann, Neutralität, p. 125–153.

189 Only the concept of domicile applied to unblocking regulations, whereas for blocking regulations, the concepts of domicile and nationality were combined. This combination remained in effect with respect to property owned by Germans and Japanese. Cf. SCO Final Report, April 1949, p. 8f. BAR, SCO USA, Vol. 2.

190 As of 30 May 1946, the Generally Licensed Trade Area under General License No. 53 of 17 July 1941 included the countries of South and Central America, the British Empire, Soviet Russia, the Faroe Islands, the Dutch West Indies, the Belgian Congo, Rwanda-Burundi, Greenland, Iceland, Syria, Lebanon, the New Hebrides, French Equatorial Africa, Cameroon, New Caledonia, Tahiti, the French settlements in India; as of 1 January 1947, also China, Indochina, Dutch East Indies and Turkey; as of 17 July 1947, Tangiers; as of 29 May 1948, Spain; as of 19 July 1948, Yugoslavia; and as of 2 September 1948, Portugal. The blacklists ('The Proclaimed Lists of Certain Blocked Nationals') published by the Americans in monthly updates governed control and blocking in these places, as well as in neutral European countries. In April 1946, the blacklists still included 5,500 names, roughly 640 of which were from Switzerland, 500 from Spain, 360 from Sweden, and 200 from Portugal. Cf. 'Die Überreste des Wirtschaftskrieges' ('The Remains of the Economic War'), in NZZ, 15 April 1946. – To be certified in Switzerland, Germans and Japanese domiciled in these places had to prove that the American blocking rules did not apply to them. Cf. Instructions, No. 1, § 13. BAR, SCO USA, Vol. 1.

191 For the countries covered in General License No. 95, see Note 181 in this study.

192 The only exception was for enemies of the United States domiciled in Switzerland, i.e. persons of German or Japanese nationality.

193 The minimum period of residency required to attain domicile in Switzerland was reduced from six to three months in March 1948. Those who attained domicile in Switzerland were eligible for certification.

194 Also Italy in certain circumstances. A certification agreement was signed with Italy on 29 August 1947. As of 5 May 1947, all types of businesses organized under Swiss law in which Italy, Hungary, Romania, or Bulgaria had an interest were certified upon confirmation from the given countries. Natural persons from Hungary, Romania, and Bulgaria were excluded. Cf. correspondence between James H. Mann, Treasury Department Representative, and Reinhard Hohl, FPD, Bern, 5 June 1947. BAR, SCO USA, Vol. 6. – 'Bona fide victims', i.e. those persecuted by the German National Socialist regime or the Italian Fascist government, could apply directly to the American authorities or indirectly through the SCO if they could present the necessary proof. Cf. Instructions, No. 1, § 45. BAR, SCO USA, Vol. 1; letter from Donald J. McGrew, Treasury Department, to Max Schwab, SCO, 9 July 1947. BAR, SCO USA, Vol. 6. – The American authorities did not revisit their regulations until 1955/56, when the Pres-

ident signed a law that definitively confiscated the assets of legal entities in Romania, Bulgaria, and Hungary, which had become state-owned property after the Communists had assumed power in those countries. The confiscation of assets belonging to natural persons, however, was expressly halted by this law and transformed into a mere 'controlled confiscation' so that the assets could be returned to the owners after these countries were liberated from Soviet rule. Cf. 'Zweierlei Mass bei der Vermögens-rückgabe' ('Dual Standards for Returning Assets'), in: Kurier, 5/6 November 1955; NZZ, 30 November 1955.

195 'Treasury officials' submitted a confidential list (the 'graylist') of 11 names of legal and natural persons to the SCO in Bern on 20 March 1948 for review. Cf. BAR, SCO USA, Vol. 8.

196 Following complaints that qualified SCO employees were being overworked, it was calculated that a newly hired employee needed at least one year to become competent in the subject matter. New employees had to be treated with care so that they could eventually relieve their bosses who were 'spending so much of their free time at home working that they could not reasonably be expected to maintain that pace over time'. In addition to understaffing, lack of workspace was a topic of discussion. Note from the Department for US Certification to the SCO President, 11 March 1947. BAR, SCO USA, Vol. 8.

197 In 1947/48, in addition to its diverse agenda, the 'Consultative Commission' was given 27 cases for review, 20 of which were complex cases involving companies, trusts and family foundations located in Switzerland or abroad in which various nationalities held 'interests'. Cf. minutes of the Consultative Commission meetings, 1947 and 1948. BAR, SCO USA, Vols. 2/3.

198 For more on the subjects covered in this box, cf. e.g. Castelmur, Finanzbeziehungen, p. 27–95; Durrer, Finanzbeziehungen, p. 251–285; Schiemann, Neutralität, p. 183–232.

199 Under Executive Order No. 8389, assets deposited in the United States belonging to the following countries and their nationals were blocked on the dates indicated: 8 April 1940, Norway and Denmark; 10 May 1940, the Netherlands, Belgium and Luxembourg; 17 June 1940, France (including Monaco); 10 July 1940, Latvia, Lithuania, and Estonia; 9 October 1940, Romania; 4 March 1941, Bulgaria, 13 March 1941, Hungary; 24 March 1941, Yugoslavia; 28 April 1941, Greece; 14 June 1941, Albania, Andorra, Austria, Czechoslovakia, Danzig (Gdansk), Finland, Germany, Italy, Liechtenstein, Poland, Portugal, San Marino, Spain, Sweden, Switzerland, the USSR, China, Japan, Thailand, Hong Kong.

200 Cf. Federal Council Decree on precautionary measures to insure tax control during the certification of Swiss assets in the United States of America, 26 November 1946. AS 1946, Vol. 62, p. 986–988; Federal Council Decree on tax control during the certification of Swiss assets in the United States of America, 27 December 1946. AS 1946, Vol. 62, p. 1101–1103.

201 As of 25 November 1946.

202 Cf. SCO Final Report, April 1949, p. 44. BAR, SCO USA, Vol. 2.

203 Cf. SCO memorandum, 24 July 1947. BAR, SCO USA, Vol. 6.

204 The FPD, the FDEA, the SBA, the Association of Licensed Swiss Insurance Companies, the Industry Association, and the SCO were represented.

205 'It is agreed that, owing to questions that arise from time to time in the course of the process set forth in the enclosed agreement, a meeting will be arranged with the aim of achieving mutually satisfactory solutions and ensuring the smooth implementation of the process.' Agreement between Switzerland and the United States of America on Unblocking Swiss Assets in America, 22 November 1946, Art. 1. AS 1946, Vol. 62, p. 989–998.

206 The certification process for American assets located in Switzerland lies beyond the scope of this study.

207 Cf. Dossier for M. W. Credit Suisse New York Agency Archives.

208 Cf. Dossier for L. W. Credit Suisse New York Agency Archives.

209 Description of process for natural persons. The following banks that currently belong to CSG were entered on the 'List of Banks Authorized to Assist in the Certification Process for Swiss Assets in the United States' (company names as used at that time): A. Hofmann & Co. A.G., Aargauische Hypothekenbank, Aktiengesellschaft Leu & Co., Allgemeine Aargauische Ersparniskasse, Bank Wädenswil, Ersparniskasse Olten, Gewerbekasse Baden, Lüscher & Co., Schweizerische Kreditanstalt, Schweizerische Volksbank, Verwaltungsgesellschaft 'Affida'. SCO, May 1947. BAR, SCO USA, Vol. 4.

210 SKA executive board circular to branch offices, 21 February 1947. CCA. Internal directive for head office, 20 February 1947. SBA Archives, F 29–30, No. 324g VII.

211 Instructions, No. 1, § 31. BAR, SCO USA, Vol. 1.

212 Federal Council Decree on the certification of Swiss assets in the United States of America, 27 December 1946, Art. 8. AS 1946, Vol. 62, p. 1097–1100.

213 Cf. SBV to Credit Suisse New York with enclosed non-enemy declaration, 9 August 1940. Criminal Report, 3 November 1942, p. 20. NARA, RG 131, Box 449.

214 Free disposal in the event of Switzerland's entry into the war. The customer added the following handwritten instructions: 'From the foregoing you will note that certain securities are to be put at my disposal and I request you to take all such values into Safe-Custody for my Account. Until you will receive direct instructions from me, kindly deal with the valuables and the respective income as per the following instructions: open a cash account to which all revenues are to be credited. Please do not forward any correspondence but withhold it pending further instructions. Kindly note that when I shall directly get into touch with you for the first time, you will receive my instructions in my own handwriting and only such handwritten instructions should be followed by you. In consideration of your carrying out my instructions given above, I hereby agree to indemnify you against all claims, demands, costs, expenses, losses or damages which may be incurred by you by reason of your carrying out such instructions as aforesaid.' Signed W. S. CCA.

215 The various forms have survived because they were included in the few dossiers on certification abuses that were given to the investigating judge in the summer of 1948 and that were not subsequently destroyed. None of the individual dossiers that underwent normal processing were retained by either the banks or the SCO.

216 CSG reviewed the rules regarding the SCO's certification documents on the basis of certain selected cities (Buenos Aires, Mexico City, and Istanbul): as anticipated, no direct customers were certified by Switzerland. However, an international clientele living in the Generally Licensed Trade Area did do business through the Swiss banks: in Buenos Aires, mostly French and Swiss; in Mexico City, mostly French. Certifications in the General License No. 53 zone did not require a cross certificate from the country of origin; the cities that were investigated – typical destinations for immigrants – were therefore attractive as places of residence, even if only temporarily, for those seeking a tax haven.

217 Cf. Dossier for E. L., Credit Suisse New York Agency Archives.

218 'Deeply grateful to you for the kind attention you have shown our exchange of correspondence, I remain, Yours very truly, T. S.' Dossier for T. S. Credit Suisse New York Agency Archives.

219 Cf. Dossier for C. W. Credit Suisse New York Agency Archives.

220 For each US depository institution (and, where appropriate, for various divisions within depositories), a separate certification application had to be submitted. Because customers often kept their securities and cash accounts in a number of different places, they ended up with several certificates.

221 Cf. e.g.: General Ruling No. 6 Account, Ordinary Blocked Dollar Account, Identified Blocked Dollar Account.

222 SCO, Instructions, No. 1. BAR, SCO US, Vol. 1. The 'Catalog of Questions' circulated by SKA management to the branch offices on 2 July 1947 is a good example. CCA: '7. Power of Attorney for Persons Abroad […] a) What is the business or other relationship between the grantee and the grantor? b) When was the power of attorney granted? c) Were was the grantee domiciled at the time the power was granted? d) What is the practical purpose of the power of attorney according to the interested parties, and to what extent will the grantee be entitled to the assets to be certified? e) Has the power ever been exercised? If yes, in what way? f) Are there any agreements between the grantor and the grantee that would partially or fully nullify the power? g) Can the power only be exercised under certain conditions (e.g. an agreement, or the death of the grantor)? h) Do you know of any facts that would confirm or cast doubt on the accuracy of the statements made by the interested parties in questions a–g? i) Is the American depository institution aware of the power?'

223 German and Japanese assets were to be transferred to the Office of Alien Property and confiscated; Hungarian, Romanian, and Bulgarian assets were to be transferred and remain blocked until agreements were concluded with the respective countries; Finnish, Polish, and Czechoslovakian

blocked assets were to be transferred and remain blocked until further notice; Yugoslavian, Estonian, Latvian, and Lithuanian blocked assets were to be transferred and remain blocked until various pending international issues were resolved; Spanish and Portuguese assets remained blocked during ongoing negotiations with Spain and Portugal on looted gold and the treatment of German assets. Cf. Forex (Foreign Exchange Control) Service, 1 March 1948 (Additional Sheet to No. 5, Vol. 2), 'Proposed Measures Regarding Blocked European Assets which have not yet Been Certified'. BAR, SCO USA, Vol. 17.

224 Cf. summary of the Snyder Plan in 'Die amerikanischen Massnahmen gegen europäische Fluchtkapitalien, Ausdehnung und Verschärfung des Zertifizierungsverfahrens' ('American Measures to Counter European Capital Flight, Extension and Intensification of the Certification Process'), in: NZZ, 4 February 1948.

225 The 'abuses in the certification process', which resulted in a year of legal wrangling in Switzerland, involved customers in this at-risk group of French currency-law and tax refugees.

226 Owners subject to the presumption of enemy ownership had to release their names to the American authorities, which would then forward this information to the government of the owner's country of residence. Owing to the presumption of enemy ownership, the Swiss banks were to be compelled to disclose the identity of their customers. Cf. 'Schweizerisch-amerikanische Verhandlungen in Washington über die Beendigung des schweizerischen Zertifizierungsverfahrens. Instruktionen an die schweizerische Verhandlungsdelegation' ('Swiss-American Negotiations in Washington on the Conclusion of the Swiss Certification Process. Instructions to the Swiss delegation to the negotiations'). FPD to the Federal Council, 19 February 1948. BAR, E 4001 (C), Vol. 303.

227 The FPD emphasized that compulsory measures such as the presumption of enemy ownership were to be disregarded and a mutually acceptable solution should be sought along the lines, for example, of the proposal from the Swiss banks that French customers should be offered subscription to a bond whose proceeds would go to the benefit of the French government in a manner to be defined. FPD to the Federal Council, 19 February 1948. BAR, E 4001 (C), Vol. 303.

228 Cf. Instructions, No. 9, 26 August 1948. BAR, SCO USA, Vol. 1.

229 Cf. Instructions, No. 11, 9 October 1948. BAR, SCO USA, Vol. 1.

230 Cf. limit on the effective period, based on Art. 2 of the Federal Decree rescinding the Federal Council's extraordinary powers of 6 December 1945. AS 1945, Vol. 61, p. 1049–1051.

231 Cf. FPD to the Federal Council, 15 December 1948. BAR, E 4001 (C), Vol. 303.

232 A supplement to the Final Report of April was issued on 21 December 1949. Cf. SCO Final Report, April 1949. BAR, SCO USA, Vol. 2.

233 Cf. FPD to the SBA Secretary on the fulfillment of the mandate of the Consultative Commission, 23 December 1950. Private Files, Robert Dunant. SBA Archives, F29–30.

234 'Generally Licensed Trade Area' under General License No. 53.

235 Information in the United States that was used to create the names list came from: 1. Treasury Department TFR-300 Reports from 1941 (customer documents with information, as at June 1940 and June 1941 and subsequent amendments). NARA, RG 131, Box 450; 2. reports from the Treasury investigations from 1941 to 1943 of Swiss banks in the United States; cases in the Criminal Report of names falsely reported or unreported on TFR-300 Forms (these involved customers whose names the auditors found in sealed envelopes or in special customer correspondence files, i.e. 'indirect customers' whose assets in omnibus accounts were considered to belong to the bank and thus were registered with the Treasury Department as bank property. NARA, RG 131, Box 449); 3. main ledgers of the Credit Suisse New York Agency, issued monthly, listing direct customers; 4. other records in the Credit Suisse New York Archives, above all, files from Milbank, Tweed & Hope, SKA's New York law firm during the war, and the few remaining customer correspondence files after the war.

236 Certification applications had to be signed by the customer. An application thus proves evidence of customer contact in 1947 or 1948, ruling out the possibility of dormancy.

237 The number of certification receipts exceeds the number of persons who registered for certification because cash accounts and securities accounts had to be certified separately. Consequently, there would sometimes be more than one certification per customer. The figures cited include both direct creditors and bank customers of all involved Swiss financial institutions.

238 Cf. agreement between the Swiss Federal Archives (BAR) and CSG, 7/8 July 1998. CCA.

239 Mainly because of tax issues and currency restrictions.

240 'Non-certifiable interests of blocked lands under General License No. 95 (Spain, Portugal, Yugoslavia, Albania, Hungary, Romania, Bulgaria, the former Baltic countries, Trieste)' for which the SCO proposed to send multiple applications to the Treasury Department, which undertook to deal with the claims if thoroughly checked in advance by the SCO. SCO proposals regarding the removal of impediments to the certification process, 17 December 1947. BAR, SCO USA, Vol. 6.

241 Cf. SBA comments on the SCO's letter of 23 December 1947 re: the acceleration, simplification, and conclusion of the certification process of 9 January 1948. CCA. Highly confidential SCO letter to Federal Councilor Petitpierre of 23 December 1947. Private Files, Robert Dunant. SBA Archives, F 29–30.

242 Washington officials insisted on cross certificates, and even bona fide victims from France were not exempted from this requirement. Cf. correspondence from Walter W. Ostrow, Treasury Representative at the US Embassy in Bern, to the SCO, 15 December 1947; 19 December 1947. BAR, SCO USA, Vol. 6.

243 Cf. letter from Franz Kappeler (FPD) to the SCO, 16 September 1948; correspondence with the Treasury Department. BAR, SCO USA, Vol. 6.

244 Cf. instructions, No. 5, § 104, 11 May 1948. BAR, SCO USA, Vol. 1. – 'If a Swiss bank manages both a dollar account and a securities account for the same person, the two are treated as *one* account in contrast to the rules for direct customers under General License No. 97.' Ibid.

245 Correspondence with direct customers. BAR, SCO USA, Vol. 165.

246 Cf. tax certificate under the special procedure for Swiss abroad. Notice from the SBA to the banks, 3 March 1948. CCA. – The applicable form required certification by a government office confirming Swiss citizenship. Cf. circular from the Federal Department of Justice and Police to the Cantonal Police Departments, 8 March 1948. BAR, SCO USA, Vol. 14.

247 Cf. Criminal Report, Exhibit II, p. 19. NARA, RG 131, Box 449.

248 Cf. SBA, 'Confidentiel, aux members de la commission embargo USA: Mesures autonomes suisses en vue de faciliter la procédure de certification en Suisse' ('Confidential, to members of the USA embargo committee: Autonomous Swiss measures designed to facilitate the certification procedure in Switzerland'), 13 March 1948. CCA.

249 'Stand der schweizerisch-amerikanischen Zertifizierungsverhandlungen in Washington' ('Status of the Swiss-American certification negotiations in Washington'), 12 April 1948. Private Files, Robert Dunant. SBA Archives, F 29–30.

250 Cf. 'Refuge en Suisse de capitaux français' ('Swiss Refuge for French Capital'), undated treatise by an anonymous author, paragraph VIII: 'La cross certification française anonyme' ('Anonymous French Cross Certification'), p. 24. BAR, E 4001 (C), Vol. 303.

251 FPD to the Swiss Legation in Washington (Karl Bruggman), 14 April 1948. Private Files, Robert Dunant. SBA Archives, F 29–30.

252 Cf. FPD to the Federal Council, 5 April 1948: 'Schweizerisch-französische Verhandlungen in Paris betreffend die Zertifizierung der durch schweizerische Banken verwalteten französischen Vermögenswerte in den USA. Instruktionen an die schweizerische Verhandlungsdelegation' ('Swiss-French negotiations in Paris concerning the certification of French assets in the United States managed by Swiss banks. Instructions to the Swiss delegation to the negotiations'). Private Files, Robert Dunant. SBA Archives, F 29–30.

253 French customers could have their assets unblocked under individual licenses directly in the United States, where, interestingly, at least one lawyer was practicing who had formerly worked at the American Embassy for the Treasury Department on control and certification. Cf. 'Refuge en Suisse de capitaux français' ('Swiss Refuge for French Capital'), p. 27. BAR, E 4001 (C), Vol. 303.

254 Cf. FPD to the Swiss Legation in Washington (Karl Bruggmann), 14 April 1948. Private files, Robert Dunant. SBA Archives, F 29–30.

255 See the certification of French customers based on false domicile statements from Switzerland and Central America, p. 85f. of this study.

256 'La voie marchandise', or 'la voie sucre', or 'la voie des importateurs'. Cf. 'Refuge en Suisse de capitaux français' ('Swiss Refuge for French Capital'), BAR, E 4001 (C), Vol. 303.

257 SKA's executive board informed its branch offices on 10 May 1948: 'Without officially divulging the name of the person seeking certification to the Office de Changes, we can tell you that the person involved is very closely linked to our establishment.' CCA.

258 The first to make use of this solution and to make it popular among Swiss bankers was R. L. in connection with Fides, Basel. R. L. single-handedly unblocked about $ 12 million by these means. The total amount of assets unblocked in this way greatly exceeds this sum. Cf. 'Refuge en Suisse de capitaux français' ('Swiss Refuge for French Capital'), p. 27. BAR, E 4001 (C), Vol. 303.

259 Cf. notice from the SBA to the banks regarding the unblocking of French assets managed by Swiss banks in the United States, 14 August 1948. SBA Archives, F 29–30, No. 324g VII.

260 All assets belonging to persons domiciled in countries in the Generally Licensed Trade Area and certified by the SCO after 1 March 1948 were blocked with immediate effect. Cf. SBA notice to the banks, 24 July 1948. CCA; SCO Final Report, April 1949, p. 32f. BAR, SCO USA, Vol. 2.

261 In its Order of 14 June 1948, the Federal Council authorized the Federal Prosecutor's Office to launch and conduct a thorough investigation. Cf. BAR, SCO USA, Vol. 18.

262 Cf. SCO Final Report, April 1949, p. 36. BAR, SCO USA, Vol. 2. – The Swiss press declared the complicity of Swiss officials, notaries and bank officers unacceptable – calling it 'financial banditry' – and blamed them for triggering the repressive American acts. Voix ouvrière, 30 July 1948. In contrast, 'Der Bund' remarked on 15 June 1948 that the matter 'was much less serious than portrayed in certain circles'.

263 'The false date of issue regularly corresponded with a date for entry into Switzerland indicated in the applicant's passport. Accordingly, the resident alien identification document would show not the date of the last trip into Switzerland under the heading "Entry into Switzerland", but rather a date prior to 1 June 1947 that was consistent with a date in the passport for entry into Switzerland.' In the canton of Valais, 22 cases of certification made on the basis of false resident alien ID information were discovered by 15 March 1949. The total amount unblocked in these cases was $ 5.95 million. In the canton of Fribourg, 41 cases of wrongful certification were identified by mid-March 1949. The total amount unblocked in these cases was $ 9.12 million. SCO Final Report, April 1949, p. 37. BAR, SCO USA, Vol. 2.

264 'A uniform tax of Sfr 400 per person was assessed in the community of Sion; the name of the taxpayer did not appear anywhere on the tax receipt; rather, a note might be made such as "16 persons at Sfr 400 = Sfr 6,400". The taxes were not paid until certification was completed. As a result of this practice, no taxes at all were paid in many cases where sometimes substantially antedated resident alien identification documents were involved, because the certification was impeded by the intervening investigations.' SCO Final Report, April 1949, p. 38. BAR, SCO USA, Vol. 2.

265 'On 6 July 1948, the Treasury Department asked the SCO to suspend the issuance of certificates for assets in which persons domiciled in General License No. 53 […] countries had an interest. On 21 July 1948, it further requested that all certificates that were issued from 1 March 1948 to 19 June 1948 for persons domiciled in the Generally Licensed Trade Area be suspended or revoked, and then re-examined. Such a general recall of the certificates, however, would have had enormous consequences for the Swiss banks (a new block on omnibus accounts that would surely also include the assets of persons who had been legitimately certified).' An internal Swiss block by the Swiss banks on the certified assets in question was instituted instead of a recall – a precaution that the SCO had already undertaken on its own initiative for a portion of the assets even prior to the Order. SCO Final Report, April 1949, p. 33f. BAR, SCO USA, Vol. 2.

266 By mid-March 1949, 42 cases had been discovered where certification had been obtained for a total of $ 4.99 million on the basis of falsified proofs of domicile. Cf. SCO Final Report, April 1949, p. 40f. BAR, SCO USA, Vol. 2.

267 FPD, 'Rapport Officiel sur les infractions à la procédure de certification' ('Official report on violations of the certification process'), undated. SBA Archives F 29–30, No. 324 g VII.

268 Contact should be established 'with the goal of finding mutually acceptable solutions and ensuring smooth implementation'. Agreement between Switzerland and the United States of America on the Unblocking of Swiss Assets in America, 22 November 1946, § 1. AS 1946, Vol. 62, p. 989–998. Cf. SCO Annual Report 1947. BAR, SCO USA, Vol. 2.

269 James H. Mann left his government position in the course of 1947 and began practicing law in Washington in January 1948. In this capacity, he was able to take advantage of his knowledge to attract an international clientele. Cf. BAR, SCO USA, Vol. 17. 'Whereas his predecessor, Mr. Mann, at least had knowledge of the subject matter (though he had no decision-making authority) as a result of his role in the certification process and his previous employment with the Treasury Department, his successor, Mr. Ostrow, lacks even that knowledge and is nothing more than a conveyer of information. […] Experience shows further that as a rule, it takes weeks or several months before Washington responds to the concerns we put to Ostrow for forwarding to W.' Handwritten SCO note on Walter W. Ostrow, Treasury Department representative in Bern after James H. Mann's departure. BAR, SCO USA, Vol. 18.

270 'The Americans desire to be rid of the Freezing which they regard as anachronistical. Of course, there is a little group of people, which includes Mr. Mann, that feel differently, but this group is dwindling and is rapidly being entirely eliminated from public life. Mr. Mann has been known to declare publicly that Switzerland is a nation of Nazis. Like Morgenthau who brought this group of people into the Government Mann would like Germany, and Switzerland for that matter, to be turned into a cow pasture. [...] Accordingly, when the Swiss take problems to Mr. Mann, they are not only creating entirely unnecessary difficulties for themselves, but they are displeasing the Americans.' Confidential memorandum on Mann, SCO, 5 March 1947. BAR, SCO USA, Vol. 16.

271 Max Schwab, SCO, in a conversation with staff of the American Legation in Bern, 29 January 1947. Cf. BAR, SCO USA, Vol. 6.

272 Cf. SCO Final Report, April 1949, p. 44. BAR, SCO USA, Vol. 2.

273 FPD, 'Rapport Officiel sur les infractions à la procédure de certification', 28 September 1951, p. 16–18. SBA Archives, F 29–30, No. 324 g VII.

274 For more information on the figures used in the table 'Assets certified by Switzerland, by customer category (1947/48)', cf. SCO Final Report, April 1949, Annex I. BAR, SCO USA, Vol. 2.

275 Cf. SCO Final Report, April 1949, Annex I. BAR, SCO USA, Vol. 2; Federal Council Report to the Federal Assembly on the Implementation of the Agreement Concluded in Washington on 25 May 1946, 13 April 1949. BBl, 101. (1949), Vol. I, p. 769; Castelmur, Finanzbeziehungen, p. 156f.

276 The blocked assets of Interhandel alone with respect to General Aniline and Film Corp. were said to have been worth $ 60 to $ 80 million. Castelmur, Finanzbeziehungen, p. 242.

277 Cf. Castelmur, Finanzbeziehungen, p. 144f.

278 Cf. SBA letter re: the establishment of a special committee for uncertified dollar assets, 6 September 1948. BAR, SCO USA, Vol. 14.

279 Cf. message from the Federal Council to the Federal Assembly regarding approval of the financial agreement concluded in Washington, 14 June 1946. BBl, 98 (1946), Bd. II 2, p. 714–741.

280 Cf. Federal Council Report to the Federal Assembly on the implementation of the agreement concluded in Washington on 25 May 1946, 13 April 1949. BBl, 101 (1949), Vol. I, p. 769–791.

281 Cf. message from the Federal Council to the Federal Assembly regarding German assets in Switzerland, 29 August 1952. BBl, 104 (1952), Vol. III, p. 1–17.

282 Cf. message from the Federal Council to the Federal Assembly regarding German assets in Switzerland, 29 August 1952. BBl, 104 (1952), Vol. III, p. 1–17.

283 Cf. Castelmur, Finanzbeziehungen, p. 325ff.

284 Cf. Federal Council Report to the Federal Assembly on German Assets in Switzerland, 1945–1958, 22 August 1958. BBl, 110 (1958), Vol. II, p. 629–651.

285 In short, this meant that an answer had to be found to the question of whether, for example, Swiss or French officials should be the ones to sequester assets located in France belonging to a Swiss company controlled by German interests. Under Swiss law, assets which a Swiss company had invested abroad were considered Swiss property. It therefore followed that assets invested abroad belonging to a German-controlled Swiss company should not be confiscated by foreign sequestration authorities. The company, including its assets located abroad, was supposed to be liquidated by Switzerland under the Washington Agreement, with half of the proceeds of the liquidation going to Switzerland. More complex sequestration questions arose in connection with companies in which Germans owned shares but did not have control, or in inheritance cases involving German beneficiaries, trusts with German bene-

ficiaries, etc. Cf. Federal Council Report to the Federal Assembly on the implementation of the agreement concluded in Washington on 25 May 1946, 13 April 1949. BBl, 101 (1949), Vol. I, p. 769–791.

286 SKA used the following risk clause that was presented to the customer when an account was opened: 'This serves as notice that your assets have been [...] deposited in an account in our name and at our disposal but that you retain the risk.' SBV's risk clause for foreign currency accounts served as the model for this text: 'Your assets are invested in our name but for your account and under your responsibility in the country of the currency in which your account is run. Any assets in this account are subject to the current and future laws, measures, restrictions, fines, and taxes in Switzerland and abroad that apply to our customers and to us. Your assets do not confer the right on you to their equivalent in bank notes or coin in the given currency.' SKA form with note, Ra SKA, 5 January 1949. CCA.

287 Cf. Castelmur, Finanzbeziehungen, p. 238f.

288 Cf. Federal Council report to the Federal Assembly on German assets in Switzerland, 1945–1958, 22 August 1958. BBl, 110 (1958), Vol. II, p. 629–651.

289 The SBA set forth its wishes and proposals in a letter dated 29 April 1949 to the chief negotiator, Walter Stucki. Cf. CCA; memorandum re: the agreement between Switzerland and the United States on disputed claims to German assets, 19 July 1949, cited in Castelmur, Finanzbeziehungen, p. 242, Note 43.

290 Cf. Castelmur, Finanzbeziehungen, p. 244.

291 Cf. Department of Justice press release, 29 September 1948, Treasury Department, Chronology.

292 SBA Circular No. D19, 14 March 1949. CCA.

293 The numerous Swiss efforts to intervene in the imminent sequestration of all blocked assets in the United States are mentioned in an FPD letter dated 3 May 1949 to the SCO and SBA. Cf. CCA.

294 Cf. SCO to the FPD, 23 July 1948; SBA letter, 11 August 1948. SBA Archives, F 29–30, No. 324g VII.

295 The well-documented case of the stateless G. v. K., who had lived in Switzerland since 1941, provides a good example. Her assets had been held at Bankers Trust in New York since June 1940, i.e. since before the effective date for certification of 14 June 1941. These were certified and unblocked in the summer of 1948. The OAP reblocked them shortly thereafter. The Swiss Legation, which intervened with the OAP to obtain their re-release after the SCO had reviewed the case and shown the certification to be correct, was laconically informed: 'Information received in this Office indicates that the property in the name of Miss G. v. K. may be property in which there is an enemy interest. On the basis of such information, this Office directed that the property of Miss G. v. K. within the United States be reblocked and a full investigation of this matter is presently being conducted.' BAR, SCO USA, Vol. 391. In an inventory taken by the Swiss Legation in Washington in 1951, this case was listed as still pending. Cf. BAR, E 2200 Washington 1970/72, Vol. 16.

296 The Committee consisted of C. de Loës of Hentsch & Cie, Geneva; Otto Hegetschweiler and Paul von Fellenberg, SKA, Zurich; Paul Gmür-Henggeler, attorney, Zurich; Fritz Liebrich, SBV, Basel; Adolf Jann, SBG, Zurich. FPD representatives also attended Committee meetings. Cf. minutes of the meetings of 26 August 1948 and 19 October 1950. CCA.

297 Cf. SBA circular, 6 September 1948; SKA notice to the SBA, 24 September 1948. CCA. SKA registered $ 4 million of blocked cash assets for the Credit Suisse New York Agency (regular blocked accounts $ 3.1 million; identified accounts $ 0.1 million; General Ruling No. 6 accounts $ 0.8 million).

298 On 14 March 1949, the SCO asked the banks to list securities and dollar assets held at correspondent banks in the United States according to the owners' country of domicile: Switzerland, including Liechtenstein; free countries, including General License No. 53 countries; General License No. 95 countries divided into a) Marshall Plan countries, b) non-Marshall Plan countries (Finland, Poland, Czechoslovakia), non-licensed countries (the Baltic countries, Hungary, Romania, Bulgaria) and enemy countries (Germany, Japan). CCA.

299 Cf. FPD to the SCO and the SBA, 3 May 1949. CCA.

300 In the same letter, the banks were advised to notify their customers about the possibility of direct unblocking. As a precaution, the SCO was authorized to submit a form for the relevant pending cases. Apparently the assumption was that assets being processed for direct unblocking would not be subject to vesting. General claims from German customers for refunding had already been mentioned in the

28 April 1949 FPD letter to the SBA. The letter reiterates the Swiss position that bank assets in the United States that remained blocked had to be released under the Washington Agreement. At the same time, banks were asked to look into whether they would be confronted with claims for refunds from German customers in the event of vesting. Cf. CCA.

301 Cf. Department of Justice press release, 11 October 1950, Treasury Department, Chronology. – The surprise caused can be gauged from the frenzy triggered by the press release in Switzerland. Because the American government had been authorized by Congress to conclude sequestration agreements shortly before, the Swiss had expected a sequestration agreement to be concluded in the near future. In mid-November 1950, the SCO still thought that negotiations were imminent. Cf. memorandum, Ra SKA re: American official measures regarding blocked assets, 14 November 1950. CCA.

302 'Reports on Form OAP-700 are hereby required to be filed on or before November 15, 1950, with re-spect to all property subject to the jurisdiction of the United States on the opening of business on Oc-tober 2, 1950, in which on that date any blocked country or national thereof had an interest, except that no report shall be required with respect to property specifically exempted by paragraph (c) hereof. As used throughout this section (Circular) the term "blocked country" shall mean Austria, Belgium, Bulgaria, Czechoslovakia, Denmark, Estonia, Finland, France (including Monaco), Germany, Greece, Hungary, Italy, Japan, Latvia, Liechtenstein, Lithuania, Luxembourg, the Netherlands, Norway, Poland, Romania, Sweden and Switzerland […].' Public Circular No. 39, 9 October 1950. CCA.

303 Cf. minutes of the Special Committee meeting on uncertified dollar assets on 19 October 1950 (repre-sentatives from the FPD and from Walter Stucki's office also attended the meeting); SBA to the FPD, 24 October 1950, CCA. – The efforts of the Legation in Washington were fruitless. American officials were no longer willing to negotiate about uncertified assets. Cf. memorandum, Ra SKA re: American official measures regarding blocked assets, 14 November 1950. CCA.

304 The balance of a blocked omnibus account was to be treated as a purely Swiss claim: 'The balance of this account belongs to us and no customer has any claim whatever against it.' Contrary to the SBA's advice, SKA had its American correspondent banks put the following statement concerning its rights on the registration forms for blocked assets: 'Credit Suisse, Zurich, claim that the balance of this ac-count is their personal property and constitutes a cover which they have created in order to be able to satisfy claims expressed in dollars which clients of theirs may have against them. Pursuant to Swiss Law clients of a Swiss bank have no personal rights whatsoever in an investment which such bank at its own discretion has made in the USA.' SKA circular to all branches in Switzerland, 6 November 1950. Cf. SBA circulars dated 24 October 1950 and 4 November 1950. CCA.

305 These recommendations were based on legal opinions from Paul Gmür-Henggeler (Switzerland) and Otto C. Sommerich (USA). CCA.

306 Cf. letters from James H. Mann to the SCO, 29 January 1947; 17 March 1947. BAR, SCO USA, Vol. 6.

307 Cf. SBA circulars dated 24 October 1950; 4 November 1950; 6 November 1950; 1 December 1950. CCA; BAR, SCO USA, Vol. 4.

308 Cf. memorandum, Ra SKA re: American official measures regarding blocked assets, 14 November 1950. CCA.

309 Cf. memorandum, Ra SKA, 27 December 1950. CCA.

310 The OAP's vesting orders provided the following justification: 'In re: Accounts maintained in the name of Credit Suisse, Zurich, Switzerland, and owned by persons whose names are unknown […] 2. That the property described in subparagraph 1 hereof is owned or controlled by, payable or deliverable to, held on behalf of or on account of, or owing to, or is evidence of ownership or control by persons, names unknown, who, if individuals, there is reasonable cause to believe are residents of a designated enemy country and which, if partnerships, associations, corporations, or other organizations, there is reasonable cause to believe are organized under the laws of a designated enemy country on or since the effective date of Executive Order 8389, as amended, have had their principal places of business in a designated enemy country […].' Vesting order No. 17976, 31 May 1951; 6 Fed. Reg., 16 June 1951.

311 Cf. SKA to the SBA, 28 June 1952; Bank Leu to the SBA, 27 June 1952; SBG to the SBA, 30 June 1952. SBA Archives, No. 324 k II. It appears from SKA's notice that the vestings overwhelmingly in-volved German bank customers.

312 Final Report, p. 15. NARA, RG 131, Box 450.

313 Cf. SKA to the SBA, 28 June 1952; SVB to the SBA, 3 July 1952; SBG to the SBA, 30 June 1952. SBA Archives, F 29–30, No. 324 k II.

314 Cf. Kurier, 5/6 November 1955.

315 The resolution of open questions and the expeditious settlement of open cases was not helped by the submission at the beginning of 1953 of an investigative report by a Senate subcommittee led by Senator Willis Smith, which criticized serious shortcomings in the leadership of the OAP and the extremely sluggish treatment of many individual cases. Personnel changes had already been made at the top of the organization when the investigation was initiated in 1952. Cf. Karl Bruggmann (referring to an earlier letter dated 18 June 1952) to the FPD, 12 February 1953. BAR, E 2200 Washington 1970/72, Vol. 9. Even the formal end of the vesting program as a step toward the normalization of relations with the Federal Republic of Germany in 1953 had no immediate effect.

316 In talks on 20 March 1953, the SCO advised representatives of the big banks to file claims with the Department of Justice for the return of vested assets from their blocked omnibus accounts and to initiate legal proceedings which they hoped would have a positive effect on the American officials with respect to signing a sequestration conflict agreement. The SCO let it be known that if the banks did not comply it would not shrink from advising German customers to initiate litigation to secure restitution; the bank representatives in attendance perceived this as a threat. They vehemently opposed any such idea and made it clear that they had no cause to rehash the issues that had been resolved in 1950. Litigation was out of the question, especially for the two major banks that maintained offices in New York. Cf. memorandum Ra SKA re: Vested Assets in Omnibus Accounts in America, 23 March 1953. CCA.

317 A copy of the 10 April 1953 letter from the SBA to the SCO was enclosed with the 11 April 1953 letter to the members of SBA's board of directors. CCA.

318 Cf. SBA Circular No. 2173, 21 April 1953. CCA.

319 Cf. Dossier J. R. W. S. Erben. CCA; Vesting Order No. 17474, 6 Fed. Reg. 2241 (1951), 10 March 1951.

320 It cannot be determined on the basis of existing records in the Central Corporate Archives whether these efforts were successful or not.

321 Cf. BAR, E 2200 Washington 1970/72, Vol. 16.

322 Cf. Dossier for W. T. R. BAR, SCO USA, Vol. 391; Dossier E. A. M. BAR, E 2200 Washington 1970/72, Vol.16.

323 It cannot be determined on the basis of existing records whether the vested assets were ever returned to the beneficiaries.

324 Cf. SKA Circular (with letter for customers) to all branch offices in Switzerland, 15 April 1954; 21 April 1953. CCA.

325 For more information on dormant assets in the United States, see p. 183.

326 In addition to German and Japanese assets, the assets of Eastern European customers were also confiscated on principle as enemy assets. While the Federal Republic of Germany was able to reach a settlement agreement for German customers who suffered a loss, the Americans did not discuss a settlement with the Communist regimes of Eastern Europe because it was assumed that the released assets would go not to the beneficiaries, but to the state.

327 Cf. Dossier for P. J., Credit Suisse New York Agency Archives.

328 Cf. Dossier for P. B., Credit Suisse New York Agency Archives.

329 Cf. Dossier for A. L., Credit Suisse New York Agency Archives.

330 Cf. Dossier for A. K., Credit Suisse New York Agency Archives.

331 Cf. Dossier for I. R. M., Credit Suisse New York Agency Archives.

332 For example, the family B. v. S. had investments with Swissam. N. B. v. S. was listed as residing in Canada in 1941 and was certified by Switzerland under General License No. 95.

333 In cases of 'bona fide victims', victims of National Socialism.

334 SBA discussion with the Federal Council about sending a delegation to the negotiations in Washington '[…] to eliminate the mistrust that exists over there owing to the false assumption that a large number of American stock portfolios in Switzerland belong to Germans'. Minutes of the SKA board of directors, 23 March 1944, p. 24f. CCA.

335 The Americans repeatedly insisted that German assets had been cloaked and transferred back to Switzerland as the banks' own property. Neither the SCO or the Central Corporate Archives contain substantive records relating to bank assets and the certification thereof. In the light of the meticulous government review of all assets submitted for certification, and given the financial and above all political risk of engaging in such highly prohibited bank transactions – especially at a time when business policy was heavily focused on new American business – the assumptions made by the Americans seem extremely implausible.

336 At least, not US investments held in their own name.

337 For example, the copyrights for Richard Strauss's opera 'Intermezzo', his 'Metamorphoses' compositions, and his Etudes for 23 violin solos were vested under Vesting Order No. 500A-289.

338 Example: In 1946, Bank Wehrli was put on the American graylist, which had replaced the blacklist. Some of the bank's deposits or its customers' deposits were subject to vesting orders on the grounds that 'the property described […] is owned or controlled by […] persons, names unknown, who, if individuals, there is reasonable cause to believe are residents of a designated enemy country […]'. 6 Fed. Reg. 7534 (1951).

339 After the Federal Decree of 20 December 1962 (Enforcement Order, 10 June 1963) the SKA branch office in Kreuzlingen registered E. S.'s name as a foreigner with dormant assets on 31 October 1963. His account book showed a balance of Sfr 494.35 as of 1 September 1963. A memorandum from the branch states that E. S. was deported to France as a victim of political persecution in 1941. His last mailing address was listed as 'Groupe A 8, Camp de Milles près de Marseilles'. 'On 16 April 1941, we transferred the sum of Sfr 17,000 to New York and then on 23 February 1942, Sfr 101.80 to the HICEM (a Jewish relief organization), and we have not heard from him since then. We know only that Mr. E. S. tried to expedite the credit to New York in a number of desperate letters, because this seemed to be the only way to escape death.' CCA. AS 1963, Vol. 1963, p. 427–435.

340 Cf. Criminal Report, 3 November 1942. NARA, RG 131, Box 449.

341 Cf. SCO notice from the Customer Control Department to the Department for Certification of Financial Transactions, 7 May 1951; 2 May 1951. BAR, SCO USA, Vol. 391.

342 Cf. OAP notice to the Swiss Legation in Washington, 4 May 1953. BAR, E 2200 Washington 1970/72, Vol. 9.

343 Cf. CCA. See p. 43f. of this study.

344 'US blocked', 'identified', 'normal', 'General Ruling No. 6 deposit', etc.; 'account blocked under Switzerland's German freeze', and the date of unblocking where appropriate.

345 A German resident in Switzerland is mentioned by name in the SCO's files. In response to an inquiry about the case from the Certification Department to the Germany Embargo Division it was noted that the person concerned was permitted to be certified because he had lived in Switzerland since 1929. Cf. BAR, SCO USA, Vol. 188 (Germany Embargo Division, Blocking Inquiries).

346 Mrs. I. S., a resident of Kreuzlingen, was certified as a German citizen although she was in fact stateless.

347 Cf. SCO Correspondence II with the Treasury Department representative in Bern, 12 September 1947. BAR, SCO USA, Vol. 6.

348 Cf. Confidential letter from James H. Mann, Treasury Department representative in Bern, 25 November 1946, to Legation Counsel Reinhard Hohl, Head of the FPD's Legal, Financial, and Transportation Affairs Department in Bern. For more information on liquidation of pledged assets: § 2, a–d. BAR, SCO USA, Vol. 7.

349 Cf. SCO Correspondence I with the Treasury Department representative in Bern, 21 August 1948; 22 October 1948. BAR SCO USA, Vol. 6.

350 Including returned Italian and German-Jewish assets.

351 The following numbers of vesting orders for portions of collective accounts were issued for SKA branches: Zurich 11; Basel 2; Bern 2; Lausanne 2; St. Gallen 2; Chur 1; Geneva 1; Lugano 1; Lucerne 1; Neuchâtel 1.

352 Cf. Reeves, Capital, p. 33f.

353 Cf. 'Opening Statement by Mr. Hermann J. Abs on 10 February 1955'. SBA Archives, F 29–30, No. 324 k II; Kurier, 5/6 November 1955; NZZ, 30 November 1955.

354 Cf. Ra SKA, June 1948 to February 1955. File 'Amerikanische Blockierung, Kommission betreffend Rück-

forderung von als Feindesbesitz beschlagnahmten und dem Alien Property Custodian übergebenen schweizerischen, nicht zertifizierten Aktiven' ('American Blocking, Committee on the Return of Swiss Non-Certified Assets Vested as Enemy Property and Transferred to the Alien Property Custodian'). CCA.

355 The English term 'account' encompasses both the German concepts of 'securities account' ('Depot') and 'cash account' ('Konto'). Because a securities account cannot be maintained without a cash account, the English term 'account' is used here as an overall term to include both types of accounts, although strictly speaking securities account management practices can differ from those for cash accounts. The German terms 'Konto' and 'Kontoinhaber' ('account holder') do not always refer to cash accounts in the sources used, but can be regarded as equivalent to the overall term.

356 In general, no correspondence was sent to these customers. At the time that Swiss American Corporation was founded in New York in 1939, it was hoped that many customers would choose this type of investment. Cf. Hearing, 22/23 April 1943, p. 40. NARA, RG 131. Box 446.

357 An omnibus account customer would not have been granted access to his or her securities if he or she approached the American depository bank directly. Cf. Hearing, 22/23 April 1943, p. 51. NARA, RG 131, Box 446.

358 Cf. Robert Kohli (FPD) on the state of financial relations between Switzerland and the USA, December 1942. BAR, SCO USA, Vol. 14. Spot-checks of contemporary SCO records on the types of investments (in the CSG database in 1998) confirm these earlier estimates.

359 SBG, for example, had direct investments with US custodian banks and also indirect investments via SKA Zurich and SBV Basel; the Berner Kantonalbank made both direct deposits and deposits via SKA Zurich and other banks. Cf. BAR, SCO USA, Vol. 325–339.

360 For an excellent explanation of the freezing process, cf. Reeves, Control, p. 21ff.

361 Executive Order No. 8389, 5 Fed. Reg. 1400 (1940), was issued pursuant to § 5 (b) of the Trading with the Enemy Act, ch. 106, 40 Stat. 411, 415 (1917). § 5 (b) was subsequently amended on 7 May 1940 and again on 18 December 1941. Cf. Joint Res. of 7 May 1940, ch. 185, § 1, 54 Stat. 179; First War Powers Act, ch. 593, § 301, 55 Stat. 838, 839 (1941). The amended version of the Trading with the Enemy Act appears under 50 USC App. § 1 (1994).

362 On 10 May 1940, the Order was extended to the Netherlands, Belgium, and Luxembourg, Executive Order No. 8405, 5 Fed. Reg. 1677 (1940); on 17 June 1940, to France, Executive Order No. 8446, 5 Fed. Reg. 2279 (1940); on 10 July 1940, to Latvia, Estonia, and Lithuania, Executive Order No. 8484, 5 Fed. Reg. 2586 (1940); on 9 October 1940, to Romania, Executive Order No. 8565, 5 Fed. Reg. 4062 (1940); on 4 March 1941, to Bulgaria, Executive Order No. 8701, 6 Fed. Reg. 1285 (1941); on 13 March 1941, to Hungary, Executive Order No. 8711, 6 Fed. Reg. 1443 (1941); on 24 March to Yugoslavia, Executive Order No. 8721, 6 Fed. Reg. 1622 (1941); on 28 April to Greece, Executive Order No. 8746, 6 Fed. Reg. 2187 (1941).

363 Cf. Executive Order No. 8785, 6 Fed. Reg. 2897 (1941).

364 Cf. Executive Order No. 8785, 6 Fed. Reg. 2897 (1941).

365 Cf. Executive Order No. 8785, 6 Fed. Reg. 2897 (1941).

366 In addition, Sections 5 (e) (iii) and (iv) define a national of a given country as any person acting for the benefit or on behalf of any national of the given country, or any person for whom there is reasonable cause to believe is a national. Cf. Executive Order No. 8389, § 5 (e).

367 Cf. 'Regulations of the Secretary', 6 Fed. Reg. 2905 (1941).

368 Cf. Goodman, Foreign Property Controls, p. 769.

369 First War Powers Act, ch. 593, sec. 301, § 5 (b), 55 Stat. 838, 839 (1941) which amended § 5 (b) of the Trading with the Enemy Act, ch. 106, 40 Stat. 411 (1917).

370 S. Rep. No. 77-911, at 2 (1941); H. R. Rep. No. 77-1507, at 3 (1941).

371 Cf. Alk/Moskovitz, Removal, p. 4.

372 Cf. Executive Order No. 9788, 11 Fed. Reg. 11981 (1946).

373 Cf. General License No. 32, 5 Fed. Reg. 3531 (1940); General License No. 32A, 9 Fed. Reg. 1581 (1944); General License No. 33, 5 Fed. Reg. 3634 (1940); General License No. 75, 6 Fed. Reg. 5804 (1941).

374 Cf. amendments to General License No. 32: In 1943 the limit was raised to $ 500 per household for in-

dividuals residing in Portugal, Spain, Finland, Sweden, or Switzerland provided the recipient was a citizen of one of those countries. The $ 200 limit per household still applied to all other blocked nationals residing in any of these countries. Since the overall goal of US policy was to prevent belligerent nations from obtaining US foreign exchange, remittances to nationals of blocked countries residing in blocked countries were handled in a somewhat convoluted fashion. Their blocked account at a domestic US banking institution would be debited for the payment and a blocked account at a domestic US bank belonging to a bank in the blocked country would be credited. The foreign bank would then pay the individual in the country using its own currency, to the extent possible.

375 Cf. General License No. 42, 6 Fed. Reg. 2907 (1941); General License No. 42A, 6 Fed. Reg. 6104 (1941); General License No. 68, 6 Fed. Reg. 3726 (1941); General License No. 68A, 6 Fed. Reg. 6454 (1941). General License No. 42A was originally issued to confer the same privileges granted by General License No. 42 to individuals who met the residency requirement of General License No. 42 but not the domicile requirement. Cf. Treasury Department Press Release No. 17, 27 November 1941. Treasury Department, Chronology. Because of this minor technical difference, the Treasury Department revoked General License No. 42A and formulated General License No. 42 more generously on 23 February 1942, effectively combining the two licenses.

376 Cf. Treasury Department Press Release, 15 June 1941, Treasury Department, Chronology.

377 Cf. General License No. 13A, 8 Fed. Reg. 13228 (1943); Treasury Department Press Release, No. 49, 28 September 1943. Treasury Department, Chronology.

378 Cf. General License No. 50, 6 Fed. Reg. 3057 (1941).

379 Cf. Robert Kohli (FPD) on the financial situation in December 1942, p. 2. BAR, SCO USA, Vol. 14. – The corresponding licenses permitting specific transactions were issued for a number of countries and areas. Payments between the United States and Portugal, Spain (but not Tangiers) and Sweden were handled by the central banks of those countries. Cf. Schweizerischer Bankverein, Basel (publisher), 'Vereinigte Staaten Embargo. Wichtigste Vorschriften auf dem Gebiet des Zahlungs- und Kapitalverkehrs unter besonderer Berücksichtigung der die Schweiz betreffenden Massnahmen' ('US embargo. Key regulations on payment and capital transactions with particular reference to the measures affecting Switzerland'), Oct. 1943, p. 16. CCA.

380 General License No. 53, 6 Fed. Reg. 3556 (1941). This license permitted all transactions in the Generally Licensed Trade Area that were normally associated with the import or export of goods.

381 Cf. Reeves, Control, p. 41, Note 1.

382 Cf. General Ruling No. 4, 5 Fed. Reg. 2133 (1940).

383 Cf. General Ruling No. 4, 5 Fed. Reg. 2133 (1940).

384 Cf. General Ruling No. 5 and amendments, 5 Fed. Reg. 2159 (1940); 7 Fed. Reg. 3770 (1942); 8 Fed. Reg. 12286 (1943).

385 Cf. General Ruling No. 6, 5 Fed. Reg. 2807 (1940).

386 General License No. 29, 5 Fed. Reg. 2807 (1940) extended the authority of General License No. 4 to General Ruling No. 6 accounts.

387 Cf. General Ruling No. 6 as amended, 6 Fed. Reg. 3174 (1941).

388 Cf. General Ruling No. 11, 7 Fed. Reg. 2168 (1942).

389 Cf. Treasury Department Press Release No. 34, 18 March 1942. Treasury Department Chronology.

390 The term 'enemy national' also encompassed individuals on the blacklist (the Proclaimed List of Certain Blocked Nationals); 'enemy territory' was likewise defined.

391 Cf. General Ruling No. 17, 8 Fed. Reg. 14341 (1943); Public Circular No. 21, 8 Fed. Reg. 845 (1943).

392 For a general overview of the unblocking process, cf. Alk/Moskovitz, Removal, p. 7.

393 Cf. General License No. 90, 10 Fed. Reg. 4062 (1945); General License No. 91, 10 Fed. Reg. 14814 (1945).

394 Cf. General License No. 94, 10 Fed. Reg. 14814 (1945); General License No. 5A, 10 Fed. Reg. 12600 (1945).

395 Cf. Littauer, Defrosting, p. 168.

396 Cf. General License No. 94 as amended, 11 Fed. Reg. 13959 (1946).

397 The first agreement on certification procedures was concluded with France (Oct. 1945) and served as a

model for subsequent agreements with other countries. The agreement was amended to include Belgium, General License No. 93, 10 Fed. Reg. 14289 (Nov. 1945). Norway and Finland were next under General License No. 95, 10 Fed. Reg. 15414 (1945). Subsequent agreements with the remaining European countries were concluded by amending General License No. 95 in the following order: the Netherlands, 11 Fed. Reg. 1586 (1946); Czechoslovakia and Luxembourg, 11 Fed. Reg. 4601 (1946); Denmark, 11 Fed. Reg. 6537 (1946); Greece, 11 Fed. Reg. 11987 (1946); Switzerland and Liechtenstein, 11 Fed. Reg. 13960 (1946); Poland, 12 Fed. Reg. 96 (1947); Austria, 12 Fed. Reg. 252 (1947); Sweden, 12 Fed. Reg. 2052 (1947); and Italy, 12 Fed. Reg. 5813 (1947).

398 Cf. Alk/Moskovitz, Removal, p. 12, Note 15.

399 Cf. Goodman, Foreign Property Controls, p. 784, Note 8; Littauer, Defrosting, p. 173, Note 37.

400 Cf. General License No. 97, 12 Fed. Reg. 891 (1948).

401 Cf. Alk/Moskovitz, Removal, p. 23, Note 31.

402 On 27 December 1946, the Federal Council designated the SCO as the agency authorized to investigate and certify assets. From the beginning of the control process, in which a number of 'authorized' banks participated, the SCO periodically amended its instructions. Amendments were issued on 2 May 1947, 1 August 1947, 10 November 1947, 11 May 1948, 17 June 1948, 19 July 1948, 18 August 1948, 26 August 1948, 20 September 1948 and 9 October 1948.

403 The following categories of owners were eligible for certification: 1. natural persons regardless of nationality (except for Germans or Japanese) who were actually and permanently resident in Switzerland; 2. corporations and partnerships whose headquarters were in Switzerland and which were eligible for certification according to a statement from the SCO; 3. individuals, corporations, or partnerships domiciled outside Switzerland and possessing a certificate from another country's certifying authority ('cross certification'); 4. individuals (except for Germans and Japanese), corporations, and partnerships domiciled in the Generally Licensed Trade Area under General License No. 53. Cf. Instructions, No. 1, §§ 10–13. BAR, SCO USA, Vol. 1.

404 To be certified, the assets had to be owned throughout the entire war by an eligible person and either (a) located in the United States and administered exclusively by Switzerland, (b) located in a country not affected by American blocking regulations and administered by Switzerland through the mediation of an American bank in the third country, or (c) located in the United States and administered by Switzerland via a bank in a third country. If the assets had been owned at any time by an ineligible person, they could not be certified. In addition, American securities and bank notes located in Switzerland were eligible for certification. Cf. Instructions, No. 1, §§ 14/15. BAR, SCO USA, Vol. 1.

405 Certain foreign citizens sent their unblocking applications directly to the US Treasury Department because, wanting to evade taxes and controls, they did not want to disclose details of their blocked assets to their own governments. Cf. Richards, Hearings, p. 184, Note 60.

406 If the victim lived in a country eligible for certification, his assets were certified upon submission of the appropriate application.

407 Cf. Alk/Moskovitz, Removal, p. 19, Note 15.

408 In contrast, 'blocking' meant that certain transactions involving the assets were restricted or prohibited, but the property rights remained with those who were beneficial owners at the time the assets were blocked. Cf. § 5 (b) of the First War Powers Act.

409 Cf. H. R. Doc. No. 80-464, 4 (1947).

410 Cf. Executive Order No. 9567, 10 Fed. Reg. 6917 (1945).

411 Cf. H. R. Doc. No. 80-465, 2 (1947).

412 Cf. Act of 8 March 1946, ch. 83, sec. 3, § 304, 60 Stat. 50 (amending § 304 of the First War Powers Act, ch. 593, 55 Stat. 838 [1941]); Act of 8 August 1946, ch. 878, sec. 1, § 305, 60 Stat. 925 (adding § 305 to the First War Powers Act, ch. 593, 55 Stat. 838 [1941]); Act of 5 August 1947, ch. 499, secs. 2, 3, §§ 32 (a) (2) and 33, 61 Stat. 784 (amending §§ 32 [a] [2] and 33 of the Trading with the Enemy Act, ch. 106, 40 Stat, 411 [1917]).

413 Cf. Act of 8 March 1946, ch. 83, sec. 1, § 304, 60 Stat. 50 (amendment to section 304). Before confiscated property could be returned, the Custodian had to determine whether its return was in the interest of the United States.

414 Under these agreements, the foreign governments designated an agency to investigate claims made by owners of vested property and to obtain information on citizenship, residence, and the presence of enemy interests. If the agency determined that there was no enemy interest, it forwarded a certificate along with a Notice of Claim to the OAP. If certification was denied, a statement explaining the negative decision was included. The Custodian reviewed the information from the designated agencies; he was not obliged to return certified property. Cf. Alk/Moskovitz, Removal, p. 28, Note 15.

415 Cf. Trading with the Enemy Act, § 9, 40 Stat. 411, 419 (1917). According to § 9, any person who was not an enemy and who made a claim to the Alien Property Custodian on property that was held by the Custodian or by the Treasurer could file a sworn notice of the claim with the Alien Property Custodian and apply to the President to order reimbursement to the claimant. If the President did not issue the corresponding order within 60 days of the filing of the application, the claimant could file a complaint at the US District Court for the district in which the claimant resided.

416 Cf. Public Circular No. 39, 15 Fed. Reg. 6815 (1950). Under this Circular, the following persons were required to register for possible vesting: all nationals of a blocked country who were in the United States; all persons in the United States holding property directly or indirectly, in which any blocked country or national thereof had any interest of any kind on 2 October 1950; corporations in which a blocked country or its national had any interest on 2 October 1950; every agent or representative in the United States of any blocked country or its nationals who on 2 October 1950 had any information about property subject to US jurisdiction in which a blocked country or its nationals had an interest, provided the agent or representative had not already filed a claim; and any other persons designated by the OAP.

417 Cf. Goodman, Foreign Property Controls, p. 785, Note 8.

418 Cf. Richards, Hearings, p. 183, Note 47.

419 To accommodate the large number of applicants before the 1 June deadline, the SCO accepted provisional certification applications which could be completed after the deadline. Meanwhile, the Treasury Department continued to accept applications after the end of the certification period. Cf. Instructions, Nos. 7–11. BAR, SCO USA, Vol. 1.

420 A census conducted in 1948 just before the transfer of jurisdiction to the Justice Department disclosed that roughly $ 1 billion of assets remained blocked. Cf. OAP Report 1949, p. 7. In 1949, the amount was $ 150 million. Cf. OAP 1950 Annual Report, p. 10. Because Switzerland did not receive aid under the Marshall Plan, it did not receive data on its frozen assets either.

421 Cf. Revocation of General License No. 95 on 25 December 1948, effective 31 December 1948, 13 Fed. Reg. 8326 (1948).

422 Cf. Public Circular No. 39 (9 October 1950). 15 Fed. Reg. 6815 (1950).

423 Cf. General License No. 101 and General License No. 102, 18 Fed. Reg. 3687 (1953).

424 Cf. General License No. 101, 18 Fed. Reg. 3687 (1953).

Dealing with dormant assets: the examples of SKA, SVB and Bank Leu

A study by Credit Suisse Group

Contents

All legal systems have to address the question of what to do when contact is lost with the owner of an asset or the holder of a claim. The Second World War exacerbated this problem of dormant assets for banks in Switzerland and elsewhere. What subsequently made the situation even more difficult was the fact that after 1945 and throughout more than forty years of Cold War, customers from Eastern Europe could not normally contact their bank without putting themselves, or at least their assets, at risk.

As early as in the second half of the 1940s and in the 1950s, the banks took various measures to identify the dormant accounts of Holocaust victims. But it was not until the Federal Decree of 1962 that a comprehensive investigation involving a government registration office was carried out; this lasted until the mid-1970s. The particular efforts made by SKA, SVB and Bank Leu form one of the main focuses of this study.

Twenty years later, the problem of dormant assets suddenly became critical once again, not least because of the changing geopolitical situation brought about by the fall of the Iron Curtain. Even though the Swiss banks had always met their legal obligations – except in a few exceptional cases – they were now forced to admit that they had not been sufficiently sensitive to the psychological and emotional aspects of the dormant assets issue.

Committed negotiations with representatives of Jewish organizations in the USA finally led, in several stages, to a solution that has been welcomed all over the world as exemplary and generous. Settlement of individual cases is based on the work of an independent investigating committee (the Independent Committee of Eminent Persons), wide publication of lists of names in newspapers and on the Internet, and the establishment of an international arbitrator (the Claims Resolution Tribunal). The settlement agreed by Switzerland's major banks in August 1998 provides a secure financial foundation for the whole process. Over and above this, the banks have implemented self-regulatory measures: firstly to prevent the creation of new dormant accounts, and secondly, where dormancy does occur, to immediately launch an active search for the rightful owner of the assets concerned. On the political level, discussions are currently underway in Switzerland about a federal law that would clear up the final remaining legal uncertainties.

1 Dormant assets belonging to victims of National Socialism: attempted solutions up to 1956

1.1 Dormant assets before the Second World War

In November 1935, SKA considered the problem of dormant assets at the executive board level. General manager Adolf Jöhr instructed the bank's legal department 'to examine the issue of a time limitation and of annulment as applicable to deposit books'.[1] Once a legal opinion had been prepared, a survey was carried out of the 14 branches, 5 agencies and 7 deposit counters maintained by SKA at that time.[2] A total of more than 1,720 deposit books were registered for 1935, containing a total sum of Sfr 238,629.85. The average balance was thus around Sfr 138. In 58 cases (3.4%) the balance was in excess of Sfr 1,000. Eighty-six of the account holders (5%) lived abroad. Judging by their names, most of these were probably Swiss émigrés. In 332 cases (19.3%) no domicile was given. Almost all cases concerned deposits that had been transferred to a collective account at an earlier date, but that were still registered under their original deposit book number. The beneficial owners could claim the assets at any time by presenting their deposit books.[3]

However, in 1935, not all such collective items were registered. In April 1925, for example, SKA's head office in Zurich carried out a campaign, seemingly forgotten ten year's later, focusing on 'small balances on deposit books that have not been presented for many years'. As a result of this review, the contents of 293 deposit book accounts, worth a total of Sfr 1,558.05, were transferred to a 'commissions account'.[4] Working from an analysis of results from the 1935 survey, we can assume that, depending on the branch concerned, between 1.4% and 2.4% of all deposit books subsequently became dormant. This happened especially when balances fell to a trivial amount (less than Sfr 25) and thus, in line with the regulations of the time, stopped earning interest.[5] While exercising the necessary caution, we can conclude from the 1925 rebookings that around a quarter of assets declared dormant at that time were later reactivated, though in some cases this did not occur until 40 years later.[6] In 1939, Adolf Jöhr returned to the subject, expressing his regret that the matter had not been settled once and for all in 1935. As far as he was concerned, the 'issue of a time limitation' in particular was leading to legalistic quibbling.[7]

The question of what to do with dormant accounts was considered before the Second World War by Swiss Volksbank (SVB), too. In 1935, SVB decided to transfer assets worth more than Sfr 100 that had been dormant for 10 years to a collective account. The records relating to the individual accounts were, however, to be retained in case the owner should make contact at a later date. Four years later, SVB tackled the problem once again. The bank's executive board issued a circular in 1939 stating that according to CO 127ff. these accounts would expire by limitation 10 years after they were set up, or after the customer last made contact, or after the last entry in the deposit book. However, because it was concerned to maintain its reputation, SVB did not want to invoke this law. The bank considered itself duty-bound to keep its customers' assets intact. Consequently, the executive board ordered that balances of more than Sfr 100 on all savings, deposit or creditor accounts that had remained untouched for 10 years should be registered and the owner identified if at all possible. If the identity of the owner could not be established even after extensive investigation, the assets should be transferred into a collective account under the appropriate heading in the balance sheet. This made it easier to produce net balances, carry out interest calculations and monitor such assets to prevent misuse.[8]

1.2 First attempted solutions by the Federal Government; 1947 survey by the Swiss Bankers Association

In the final act of the Paris Conference on reparations on 21 December 1945, the Allies called on the neutral states to put the dormant assets of victims of National Socialism at the disposal of the Intergovernmental Commission for Refugees, which had been founded in 1938.[9] Some five months later, on 25 May 1946, the signing of the Washington Agreement between Switzerland and the Allies brought some progress. On the same day, the head of the Swiss delegation, Minister Walter Stucki, wrote in three identical letters, marked as secret, to the Allies' three chief negotiators: 'With respect to German assets in Switzerland, I can confirm as of the moment today's Agreement is signed that my government will examine with goodwill the measures required to make available to the three Allied governments for aid purposes the sum of assets held in Switzerland belonging to victims of recent violence committed by the old German government who have died heirless.'[10]

In 1947, the Federal Political Department (FPD, the Swiss foreign ministry) made an attempt to solve the problem of dormant assets belonging to supposed victims of the Nazi regime. Swiss diplomats asked the International Committee of the Red Cross (ICRC) whether it would be possible to use ICRC lists to identify the heirs of these victims. Various institutions in Switzerland, particularly the Bankers Association and the Bar Association, were also asked for their opinion. These bodies referred to the professional confidentiality rules that bound their members and that prevented them from providing any information.[11] As part of the preparations for a legal solution, in September 1947 the FPD called on the Bankers Association to carry out a survey of the number and size of dormant accounts. If the sums involved were really as insignificant as the Bankers Association assumed they were, there would be no need to issue a Federal Decree. The Bankers Association's survey was restricted to the major banks, and the results were declared to be 'without guarantee'.[12]

In an internal directive issued in May 1996, SKA defined 'dormant assets' as follows:[13] 'Accounts, securities accounts and safe deposit boxes are regarded as dormant if the customer concerned has not made contact with the bank for 10 years. Contact is defined as any instruction, message or statement from the customer or his agent that has resulted in a movement on the account or change in the files. If customers have been sent bank communications by mail and this mail has not been returned, they are not regarded as dormant.'

This definition was changed substantially in a revised directive of July 2000. The key concept now was 'event related dormancy' which occurred 'if no communication has been received from the customer or his agent and if the bank can no longer contact the customer or any agent'. Under this definition, dormancy can occur after a minimum period of 10 years.[14]

Until 1995, the terms 'heirless' ('erbenlos') and 'ownerless' ('herrenlos'), which are more vague in legal terms, tended to be used rather than 'dormant' ('nachrichtenlos').[15] The term 'ownerless' is not legally correct, since an asset always has an owner: either the rightful claimant who has not been in contact for a long time, or his heirs, or the bank, or a trustee, or even in some cases the state. 'Heirless' is also imprecise because it disregards the fact that under certain conditions a state or a community can be the 'heir' of a dormant asset. The term 'dormant assets' (in German 'nachrichtenlose Vermögen') is the clearest from the legal point of view; it also takes due account of all the technical banking issues as well as the contractual and inheritance issues associated with this type of asset.

Strictly speaking, the assets themselves are not actually 'dormant': rather, 'dormant' refers to the fact that the bank or the person or organization looking after the assets has not had any communication from this customer for a long time.

Some banking transactions do not require contact with the customer, and so are completely irrelevant to the issue of dormancy, e.g. crediting of interest payments, deduction of charges, execution of standing orders, and asset management mandates where the bank manages the customer's investments at its own discretion.

Except in some quotations, this study uses the term 'dormant' throughout. Only accounts for which there has been no customer contact since 9 May 1945 are relevant to the issue of dormant assets of Holocaust victims.

SVB's executive board, for example, sent out a circular on 19 September 1947 asking its branch offices to provide the following information within eight days:

- 'Details of assets that you hold or manage and that belong to persons who you know have fallen victim to the violent acts of the former German government and who do not have any heirs known to you.'
- 'Details of assets that you hold or manage and that belong to persons who you suspect have fallen victim to the violent acts of the former German government and who do not have any heirs known to you.'
- 'Please give us details of the value of these assets and the number of people among whom this amount is divided, as well as the nationality and the domicile of the original owner.'

The term 'victims of the violent acts of the former German government' applied to citizens of states occupied by Nazi Germany, as well as to German citizens, who had been deported or who had perished in concentration camps and prisons. Property left behind by people subject to the freeze on German assets also had to be registered, since the Swiss

Swiss banks' foreign liabilities 1937–1945

During the period between the wars, large volumes of foreign capital flowed into Switzerland, which was regarded as a crisis-proof, inflation-proof country. Furthermore, as a result of its 1934 Banking Act, Switzerland had introduced banking secrecy on 1 March 1935. Liabilities towards foreign customers increased continuously until the middle of the 1930s. There was a noticeable decline after this as many customers transferred their money to the 'safe havens' of New York and London. Customers from Germany, Austria and Poland also withdrew their assets because of the stricter currency laws imposed by their countries. Foreign liabilities carried by the 63 biggest Swiss banks thus decreased from Sfr 1,471.6 million (1937) to Sfr 1,081.3 million (1939) and then to Sfr 1,027.6 million (1941): a drop of more than 30% over four years. By the end of 1945, however, foreign funds had gone up again to Sfr 1,335.5 million.

Liabilities towards customers from Axis countries or from countries occupied by the Axis powers, which are the important liabilities when identifying dormant assets belonging to Shoah victims, fell from Sfr 977.7 million (1937) to Sfr 672.6 million (1939) and then Sfr 666.6 million (1941). At the end of the war they amounted to Sfr 734.0 million.

Customers from Germany/Austria and Italy accounted for 17.5% (Sfr 257.2 million) of foreign liabilities at Swiss banks in 1937. By the start of the war, this figure had fallen to 14.7% (Sfr 158.6 million). Customers from France were much more important to the Swiss banks, accounting for 35.4% (Sfr 520.4 million) of foreign liabilities in 1937, and 28.2% (Sfr 305.2 million) at the end of 1939. Prior to Germany's partial occupation of France, Sfr 215.2 million (41.4%) was withdrawn from Switzerland, with another Sfr 31.4 million following by the end of 1941.

Although approximately half of the French on-balance-sheet assets were taken out of Switzerland, and despite the fact that the number of territories occupied by the Axis powers increased over the course of the war, French assets never accounted for less than 37.9% (1943) of total customer assets from Axis powers or Axis-occupied territories. By the end of the war, the total volume of French assets had risen again to Sfr 331.6 million (45.2%).[16] At SKA, which accounted for 26.7% of the Swiss banks' foreign liabilities at the end of

1945, the proportion of French customers was even higher. With Sfr 71.797 million of on-balance-sheet liabilities, they accounted for 27.5% of total foreign liabilities at the bank, and 55.1% of total customer money from Axis countries or Axis-occupied territories.[17]

At the end of the war, SKA's other significant foreign customer funds came from Italy (7% of SKA's total foreign liabilities), Germany (3.7%), Romania (3%), Belgium (1.9%), Hungary (1.9%) and the Netherlands (1.6%). For off-balance-sheet assets, too, France accounted for by far the largest share – 48.2% – of potential dormant assets of Shoah victims, followed by Italy (8.8%), Germany (5.3%), Belgium (3.8%) and the Netherlands (2%).[18]

In France, the number of people who died during the Second World War – 600,000 or 1.1% of the total population – was proportionally smaller than in other countries; so we can assume that a relatively smaller number of dormant accounts were attributable to French customers. The same applies – though less markedly – to Jews living in France, of whom about a quarter (76,134 persons) died.[19]

Twelve percent of the people included in the two lists that the Bankers Association published in 1997 came from France. These lists also included the names of 96 French SKA and SVB customers, whose assets came to a total of Sfr 4,167,776 (18% of all published assets at the CSG banks).[20]

Of all the other countries, our study focuses most on Poland, since this is where by far the largest number of Jews were killed, namely 2.9 million or 87.9% of the country's Jewish population.[21] Since at the end of 1945 liabilities towards Polish customers only came to Sfr 2.3 million at all Swiss banks, and Sfr 0.544 million at SKA, it was not expected that many dormant accounts would be found to originate from Polish customers.[22] ICEP discovered 902 potentially dormant Polish accounts.[23] Based on the Polish-Swiss agreement of 1949, the Polish state was paid the sum of Sfr 15,498 in 1960. As part of the implementation of the Registration Decree of 1962, another Sfr 463,955 followed in 1975.[24] In 1997, CSG published only 8 dormant accounts belonging to Polish customers, containing a total of Sfr 92,354.[25]

Compensation Office did not know the fate of the owners.[26] On 7 October 1947, the Bankers Association informed the FPD that the surveyed banks had reported assets worth a total of Sfr 482,000 belonging to presumed victims of German violence. However, the banks could not be absolutely sure that any of these assets fulfilled the given criteria. There were only two items, worth about Sfr 200,000 in total, that the banks presumed did meet the criteria. Another reported Sfr 279,000 concerned assets that had already been declared in connection with the decision taken on 16 February 1945 to freeze German assets.[27]

Even before the Bankers Association delivered its report, the FPD had gained the impression that the Allies were losing interest in dormant accounts. With the survey producing such modest results, the view was also expressed that it would not be expedient to pursue the issue any further. In fact, the matter should only be revisited if one of the interested states suggested it.[28] In November 1947, the Compensation Office rejected the request that it look for possible owners itself, citing an already excessive workload.[29] However, the proponents of statutory regulation did not give up. In 1949 and 1950, Jewish organizations, especially the World Jewish Congress (WJC), the Jewish Agency and the Swiss Federation of Jewish Communities (SFJC), but also the state of Israel, repeatedly pressed for a solution to the problem.[30]

1.3 Swiss Federation of Jewish Communities and Swiss Bankers Association: argument about a legal solution

The aim of the SFJC was to trace legitimate heirs, regardless of any claim to the assets that might be made by home states under international private law, and to pay the remaining dormant assets to surviving Holocaust victims, or to use them for social purposes.[31] It referred to the fact that 6 million Jews had been killed during the Second World War, and maintained that the scale of the tragedy justified a special ruling – not only morally, but also for practical reasons. It also contested that according to its estimates, dormant accounts in Switzerland actually accounted for 'a substantial number of millions of Swiss francs'.[32] Other countries – Sweden for example[33] – had long ago taken steps to solve the problem by means of special regulations on missing persons and dormancy. Furthermore, the SFJC believed that the Bankers Association's actions thus far offered no guarantee that all of the relevant institutions would make serious efforts to help with the investigations, particularly since previous requests for information had not always been met with the most helpful of responses.

At the end of 1947, the SFJC sought to back up these arguments by commissioning a report for internal use from three professors of law, Paul Guggenheim, Charles Knapp and Georges Sauser-Hall.[34] This 'Report on heirless assets in Switzerland belonging to the victims of political, religious or racist persecution' was brought to the attention of Switzerland's governing Federal Council, and was submitted to the FPD and the Bankers Association at the end of 1952 as an 'expert opinion' ('Gutachten').[35] Together with Adolf Schnitzer, Guggenheim produced a second expert opinion in

1953.[36] In 1954, the SFJC submitted another 'report' to the Federal Department of Justice and Police (FDJP)[37], which put forward the following key considerations and proposed solutions with regard to the problem of dormant accounts:

- Duty to report: The introduction of an obligation to report would help to identify the dormant accounts held in Switzerland whose owners had fallen victim to the Nazis. Banks would have to register assets belonging to people who were neither Swiss citizens nor domiciled in Switzerland and who had disappeared during the period between 1 September 1939 and 8 May 1945 in life-threatening circumstances in territory controlled by one of the belligerent countries. 'Life-threatening circumstances' covered the fate of all persons who were arrested, deported, sent to a camp or otherwise seized prior to 8 May 1945 for political, racial or religious reasons in territories controlled by the belligerents. Banks would have to fulfill this duty to report within six months. As a concession to the Bankers Association, the SFJC agreed to the creation of a 'mixed commission' (1947/52) or appeal commission (1954) to investigate uncertain cases.

- Registration office: The report/expert opinion of 1947/52 proposed that the Compensation Office should function as the central reporting office, 'since its other activities have already given it experience of such tasks'. In 1954, the SFJC responded to the Bankers Association's concerns about making the names public by proposing the establishment of a fiduciary institution. This would function as the registration office under the supervision of the federal authorities and it would be obliged to maintain the strictest secrecy with regard to all information received from banks and asset managers.[38]

- Search for rightful owners: Once the relevant accounts had been reported, the next job should be to check whether the assets in question met the registration criteria. The registration office would then have to ask all the surviving owners or their statutory and testamentary heirs – if necessary through appeals in the press – to get in contact with it within six months.

- Verifying the identity of applicants: People registering inheritance claims would be obliged to produce an official death certificate to prove that the account owner had died. If such proof could not be supplied, a missing persons procedure would have to be initiated in accordance with special statutory regulations. Inheritance law in the relevant home country would be used to decide whether and in which form the applicant was a legal heir, though states or communities would not be recognized as heirs. In uncertain cases, an appeals commission would have the final say on any right of inheritance.[39]

- Use of funds: If no entitled person could be found, assets in dormant accounts should be transferred to 'the body stipulated in the Federal Decree' (1947/52), or to an 'inheritance fund' to be used by the Federal Council 'for purposes to be determined at a later date' (1954). The SFJC specified that the money should be used to benefit the victims of the Nazi regime, or for social purposes. In addition, a reserve fund was planned that would help rightful claimants whose claims were received too late, though such claims would still be subject to a time limit of two years.

The Bankers Association categorically refused to have the problem of dormant accounts regulated by means of special legislation. It believed that the existing laws were sufficient, provided they were applied correctly. The Association's main arguments were as follows:[40]

- Creating a central registration office and transferring dormant assets into a fund would in many cases lead to dispossession. The duty to register dormant accounts would place the assets especially of Eastern European customers at risk. Authorities in Eastern Europe could use questionable means to try to appropriate the money for themselves.
- As the survey of 1947 confirmed, dormant accounts belonging to victims of the Nazis were not significant in size and thus did not justify special legislation.
- The banks were doing all they could to investigate inquiries. The problem would solve itself – given time – because the banks would look after the dormant accounts indefinitely and there would be no chance of illegal appropriation.
- A legal obligation to report the accounts would not be consistent with banking secrecy.

Internal discussions at the Bankers Association referred to 'soliciting and importuning' by the Jewish organizations in Switzerland, and to 'organized begging'. A member of the legal commission noted 'that it was often Jewish organizations that initiated such investigations in their own financial interests. But there is little reason for us to feel morally beholden to these so-called charitable organizations.'[41] The Bankers Association was nevertheless ready to make concessions in order to avoid the introduction of a legal obligation to report. They based their stance on the 1953 expert opinion that they commissioned from ex-Federal Judge Plinio Bolla and Professor Werner Niederer.[42] This proposed that the responsible Swiss authorities advise the district guardianship offices by means of a circular letter that under SCC article 393 sections 1 and 3 a custodial trustee could be established for a foreign owner of a dormant account located in Switzerland, even if this person had never lived in Switzerland. This solution would offer the institutions holding dormant assets – primarily the banks – the best protection against any future call upon them to pay up. The Bolla/Niederer expert opinion was clear about the issue of a time limitation: foreign owners of assets deposited in Switzerland would not lose their right to have those assets paid out to them either through limitation or through 'prescription' ('Ersitzung'). It could also be assumed that the foreign creditor or his legal successor (heir) could still enforce his rights against a Swiss debtor even after the limitation deadline if he had been prevented by force majeure from asserting the claim earlier.[43]

The Bolla/Niederer expert opinion, 1953

Based on an analysis of the legal situation at that time, the expert opinion of May 1953 concluded that 'all problems relating to assets located in Switzerland that belong to people subjected to racist (and other) persecution can be resolved in a thoroughly proper way through the relevant Swiss regulations governing conflicts of laws'.

On the question of how many cases there were, Bolla and Niederer stated: 'It is hard to gain a picture of the scale of assets in Switzerland belonging to foreigners who have disappeared. According to information from the Swiss Bankers Association and the Association of Swiss Insurance Companies, there can only be a few cases. The assets that may be held by lawyers, notaries, property managers, fiduciary companies and private individuals are doubtless even smaller. The large number of persecut-

ed people who lost their lives during the war cannot be used as the primary basis for an estimate: it was precisely the better-off of those threatened with persecution that often had the opportunity to escape in time to other countries. By far the largest proportion of the victims of racial persecution came from impecunious sections of the Jewish population in the Eastern states. In addition, the strict currency laws made it difficult to get money out of Germany, Hungary, Romania, etc., and into other countries. What is more, Switzerland was neither the only nor even the preferred investment location for flight capital. It is well known that the USA took in considerable volumes of flight capital from all over Europe, including even Switzerland. Finally, in most cases where persecuted people killed abroad had assets in Switzerland, their heirs are already known or have already taken possession of any legacy.'

1.4 From the Polish-Swiss Agreement of 1949 to the 1956 survey by the Swiss Bankers Association

The most important goal of the negotiations begun by Switzerland and Poland in 1945 was the conclusion of a trade agreement. At the same time, efforts would be made to settle the question of compensation for Swiss citizens who had lost some or all of their property as a result of nationalization by the Communist regime after the Second World War. Finally, the negotiators wanted to solve the problem of dormant assets in Switzerland that supposedly belonged to Polish citizens. Max Troendle, head of the Swiss delegation and minister in the Federal Department of Economic Affairs (FDEA), told the Polish delegates right at the outset that they should have no illusions about the size of these assets.[44] Nevertheless, the Polish delegation suspected that there were significant amounts of money located in Switzerland in the form of dormant accounts and dormant life insurance policies. Meanwhile, the Bankers Association refused the FDEA's request to provide information to unauthorized parties. Neither were the Association's member banks prepared to give the Polish government a confidential list of all asset owners.

As part of the Warsaw Agreement signed on 25 June 1949, the Swiss delegation finally promised in a secret exchange of letters that the Swiss banks and insurers would liquidate dormant accounts belonging to Polish citizens who had been domiciled in Poland on the cut-off date of 1 September 1939, and transfer the proceeds to a Polish government account at the SNB. The Polish government issued a guarantee to the Swiss banks in case the legitimate heirs should claim the money at a later date. Despite this condition, the agreement took little account of the SFJC's view that states could not be legal heirs, or of the banks' concerns about the dormant assets of Eastern European customers.

The SFJC was told about the agreement on 4 November 1949 and the FPD announced its contents in a press release on 1 February 1950.[45] In Switzerland and elsewhere, but especially in Israel, numerous voices were raised against the agreement. *Neue Zürcher Zeitung,* for example, carried the headline 'Dubious Secret Agreement' over an article which said: 'The arrangement for "heirless" assets in the Swiss-Polish Agreement raises serious, fundamental concerns as far as Swiss law is concerned. [...] The other disturbing thing about the Federal Council's behavior is the fact that this confidential exchange of letters relating to the Polish Agreement was not submitted to the Federal Parliament for ratification; only the preparatory commissions were told about it in advance. [...] Be that as it may, we can only hope that when it comes to the ratification of government agreements, our federal parliamentarians will in future know how to prevent such clandestine violations of the law!'[46] The view of the USA, France and the United Kingdom, as expressed in a note to the FPD on 21 March 1950, was that this initially secret exchange of letters contravened the Washington Agreement because it opened up the possibility that assets would be transferred to a state instead of to the owners or their heirs. Meanwhile, Federal Councilor Max Petitpierre was defending the agreement and the originally secret exchange of letters, which had now become public, in response to a motion by National Councilor Werner Schmid. The FPD's response to the Allies was that the Washington Agreement of 1946 did not in any way conflict with a compensation settlement with Poland.[47]

Prompted by the negotiations with Poland, the Bankers Association had already asked its members about dormant Polish assets in April 1949. This survey was repeated with some amendments in 1950 and 1958. SVB and Bank Leu reported only a few assets of this type, but the assets reported by SKA accounted for most of the total registered by all Swiss banks.

The volume of assets registered by member banks went down substantially between the first and the last SBA survey. This reduction can be explained by the changed criteria for recording the assets and the sometimes rather imprecise instructions issued by the Bankers Association, which the banks interpreted in different ways.[48]

- In 1949, the banks listed all people 'domiciled' in Poland whose assets had fallen dormant. One year later, Polish citizenship was added as a limiting criterion. The problem for the banks was that citizenship was rarely recorded when customers first opened their accounts. Unlike SKA, most of the banks did not include the assets of people of unknown citizenship living in Poland in the second survey.
- In 1955, against the background of the Cold War, the FDEA and the Bankers Association carried out another, more precisely formulated survey. Assets now did not have to be registered if the owner's citizenship was unknown. What is more,

Results of the Swiss Bankers Association's surveys of Polish dormant assets (1949–1958); payment to the Polish national bank (1960)

(Sfr)	Swiss banks, total	SKA	SVB	Bank Leu
Results 1949	c. 1 m	n.a.	n.a.	n.a.
Results 1950	598 000	480 000	0	134
Results 1958	17 550	10 605	269	0
Payment 1960	15 498	8 827	0	0

dormant accounts only had to be registered 'if the bank had concrete reason to believe that the owner had disappeared during the war without leaving any heirs'.[49]
- The fall in registered sums can also be explained by the fact that over the years some of the rightful claimants had withdrawn their money.

Finally, in 1960 the banks transferred Sfr 15,498, and the insurance companies Sfr 849 to the Polish national bank's 'N' account at the SNB. Sfr 8,827 came from SKA. The Polish government was not given the names of the original owners for fear that they or their heirs would face reprisals from the Communist regime. On 19 July 1950, Switzerland gave the Hungarian government an assurance similar to the one it had given to Poland on 25 June 1949. This was followed on 3 August 1951 by a similar assurance to the Romanian government, though in neither of these later cases were any payments actually made at the time.[50]

Parliamentary action of 1951

On 26 September 1951, National Councilor Philipp Schmid submitted an inquiry asking the Federal Council to explain whether banks and insurance companies should be obliged by law to report all accounts and securities accounts that contained foreign money and that had been dormant since a particular date to a federal body or to an office stipulated by a federal body.[51] On 22 January 1952, the Federal Council instructed the FDJP to draft a federal act or a federal decree that would provide a solution to the dormant accounts problem, and on which a referendum could be held. The Federal Council stipulated that the assets to be covered by the draft law should be defined as assets transferred into Switzerland before the Second World War by foreigners who had been killed by acts of violence and whose heirs were not in a position to enforce their claims to these assets. The Federal Council referred expressly to the fact that the supposed heirs often failed to press their claims successfully because they were unable to present the necessary identification documents.[52] In the ensuing discussion, the SFJC and the Bankers Association once again played the central roles as lobbyists.

In 1956, Federal President Markus Feldmann, head of the FDJP, asked the Bankers Association to conduct another survey. The 1947 survey was inadequate because it had not been sent to all the banks. Only after a fresh survey could the Federal Council's 1952 instruction to draft a law be withdrawn, if necessary. Feldmann de-

Management of dormant assets by the CSG banks

After the General Custodial Trustee ('Generalbeistand') wrote that they should manage the assets entrusted to them in the interests of the owners, SKA's legal department submitted the following proposal to the executive board in November 1967: 'All cases, at head office and at all the branches, where the customer has not been in contact since the end of the war should be recorded. In all of these cases, all assets should be converted into deposit books (provided the customer has not left express instructions for investing his money and provided the assets concerned are not physical securities, gold, jewelry or other assets deposited by the customer in person). These assets should be monitored particularly carefully by Cb [the central accounting office/internal audit department], and they should not be disposed of before consulting with the legal department.' The executive board agreed with this proposal and in 1968 the bank investigated which 'customers had not been in touch for x years'. A memorandum from the central office on 7 July 1976 shows that until then there had been no long-term ruling on what should be done with this money. The legal department believed that such assets should be kept as long as possible so that the bank was in a position at all times to refute the accusation that it was profiting from money belonging to foreign customers who had not been in contact for a long time.[53]

Until 1996, none of the banks examined in this study, SKA, SVB or Bank Leu, had issued a directive ordering that dormant accounts be managed centrally using a consistent interest rates and fees policy.

Dormant bank accounts were run like any others, though very small amounts were booked – especially at SVB – to collective accounts. In such cases, documentation was sometimes destroyed after 10 years. With dormant securities, it was important to know whether they were subject to an asset management mandate or not. If so, the bank continued to manage the dormant assets as originally instructed by the customer. If there was no such mandate, the bank sought to protect the customer's interests by applying a conservative investment policy (which meant investing in blue-chip instruments such as government bonds or bonds issued by first-class borrowers) and making certain adjustments when individual investments came up for redemption. If rent was not paid on safe deposit boxes, some of the contents were sold to pay the fees; records were always kept of such sales. Because there was no way of contacting the customers, most dormant accounts automatically fell into the category of 'retained mail' accounts, where any correspondence from the bank is retained in the client's file rather than being sent out.

After peaking in the 1960s/1970s, the interest paid on savings products (deposit, investment and private accounts, as well as savings books) trended downwards. At the same time, higher administrative costs and inflation meant that account charges increased continually. Securities investments thus incurred higher account and asset management fees, or higher safe deposit box rents, while savings and current accounts were subject to rising account charges and commissions. Retained mail fees and charges for numbered and pseudonym accounts also increased.

With interest falling and charges going up, smaller dormant accounts were often completely eaten up by fees after a certain amount of time.

clared that the legal machinery would not be set in motion unless the assets concerned came to at least 4 or 5 million Swiss francs.[54] The Bankers Association launched the survey on 20 July 1956. As in 1947, it aimed to find assets belonging to persons who the banks knew or suspected to have been victims of violent acts perpetrated by the former Nazi regime and whose heirs or other rightful claimants were not known. SKA, SVB and Bank Leu together reported 10 dormant accounts to the Bankers Association, worth a total of Sfr 146,595. The figures for each institution were as follows: SKA 5 accounts worth a total of Sfr 63,300, SVB 4 accounts worth a total of Sfr 82,920, and Bank Leu 1 account containing Sfr 375.[55]

SKA declared that it could not say for sure whether any of the registered assets belonged to victims of the 'National Socialist regime' or not. 'This is because the information that assets belonged to such victims is regularly given to us by their heirs; which means that if we do know that this was the case, we also have a claimant for the assets.' With regard to the other cases, it stated: 'In the cases reported to you, our assumptions are based on the information provided by various sources about the whereabouts of our clients. Furthermore, it is very difficult to find out information in such cases, so we can offer no guarantee that out list is complete, despite the fact that it was compiled with great care. Our list does not contain cases involving clients domiciled in German-occupied territory from whom we have not heard since the beginning of the war, unless we have concrete reason to believe that the client was a victim of the former National Socialist government. Without such concrete reasons, it is just as likely that these clients have not been in contact for some other reason, whether it be that they died of natural causes, or that they are still alive but that they are now domiciled in a country behind the Iron Curtain and that they are not, therefore, able to contact us.'[56] SVB's response to the Bankers Association listed 4 persons (names not given), with details of their presumed nationality, last known place of residence, value of the assets and date of last contact. Bank Leu sent the Bankers Association's request, marked 'urgent' to head office departments and branches on 23 July 1956. If in doubt, these were to contact the legal department. Of the three accounts that might possibly qualify, the first had already been closed. In the second case, it was discovered that the owner was still alive. The third identified account proved to be dormant and was reported to Bern as stipulated. Of the other institutions and companies that have since been incorporated into CSG, Fides reported assets of approximately Sfr 60,000 that it 'knew' to have belonged to a victim of the National Socialist government in Germany. Bank Wädenswil reported 'suspected cases' worth a total of about Sfr 10,000.[57]

The Bankers Association informed the FDJP of the results of the survey on 24 September 1956: 3 banks registered assets worth Sfr 36,578 that were known to have belonged to victims of the Nazis; 21 banks, including SKA, SVB and Bank Leu, registered assets worth Sfr 825,832 that they suspected to be the property of victims of National Socialism.[58]

It is not possible to tell from the surviving sources how the individual CSG banks dealt with the problem of dormant accounts in each case. Apart from brief references at executive board meetings, the minutes of the management bodies of SKA, SVB and Bank Leu contain no mention of the subject until 1963. Consequently, the only informative sources we have are the Bankers Association's minutes. At Bank Leu, Jakob Diggelmann, board member and chairman of the Bankers Association's legal commission, was heavily involved in the identification of dormant accounts. He took part, for example, in the meeting with the FDJP on 20 February 1952, as well as the meeting with the FDJP and the SFJC on 4 March 1954. In his opinion, the banks should not give the impression that they wanted to appropriate the dormant assets for themselves.

Fides: asset management in Canada (from fall 1938)

A letter from 1939 firstly shows the kind of measures Fides took to prevent its customers' assets from falling dormant, and secondly documents the trust that customers placed in their asset manager: 'We restrict ourselves [...] to highlighting a point that [...] in our view constitutes the main advantage of our Canadian securities accounts. This is the fact that in the event of a war, the assets continue to be managed by capable, first-class professionals. [...] About 90% of our customers do not intend to have anything at all to do with their Canadian securities accounts in the event of war, but are happy to leave them unseen for years for the Custodian Trust Company Limited to manage. As an example of how far this attitude can go, some new French customers who recently opened securities accounts with $ 6,000,000 decided not to deposit envelopes in London and Montreal. The clients are absolutely aware that this would make it much more difficult to verify their identity and subsequently allow them to dispose of the accounts, but they don't care about this at all because they do not believe that they could be concerned about the securities account during a war, and thus do not want to do so.'[59]

Nevertheless, he was very much against settling the problem by means of a law: 'We should not do anything that would pave the way for an opportunist law that would contradict our concept of public order. We must rigorously oppose the view expressed in the expert opinion produced by the Federation of Jewish Communities, because this view is unworthy of a constitutional state.'[60] SVB executive board member Alfred Wegelin's involvement was just as intense. He was a member of the Bankers Association's legal commission and took part in the first meeting with the FDJP and the SFJC on 17 November 1952 as well as joining the Bankers Association's deputation to Federal Councilor Wahlen on 5 March 1959. He was prepared to make larger concessions than either the Bankers Association or Jakob Diggelmann. At the legal commission's meeting of 7 November 1947, for example, he called for generous treatment of inquiries about assets belonging to the Nazi's victims. At the meeting at the FDJP on 17 November 1952 he conceded that a law could help to solve the problem, though this should not entail compulsory reporting to a central office. Finally, hardly any representatives of SKA took an active part in the Bankers Association's discussions about dormant accounts. The little information available shows that executive board member Eberhard Reinhardt spoke against a legal solution to the problem at the meeting of the Bankers Association on 22 December 1952.[61]

2 The Federal Decree of 1962

2.1 Background

On 20 March 1957, National Councilor Harald Huber submitted a motion calling once again for the introduction of compulsory reporting, as well as a simplified appeals and missing persons procedure for dormant assets of all types. Federal Councilor Markus Feldmann (FDJP), by contrast, used the modest results of the Bankers Association's 1956 survey as a reason to submit a motion to the whole Federal Council on 15 April 1957 proposing that no special law be drafted and that the SFJC be paid a specific sum – without any acknowledgement of legal liability – for victims of National Socialism.[62] The FPD legal department prepared a report for the head of the FPD, Max Petitpierre, in which it called on the government to go ahead with plans to issue a special ruling on dormant accounts belonging to victims of the Nazis.[63] The FDJP then formulated a draft law at the end of 1957.[64]

In December 1958, Friedrich Traugott Wahlen was elected as the successor to Markus Feldmann on the Federal Council. He first headed the FDJP, and then from 1960 the FDEA. As a Member of the Council of States, Wahlen had already made it clear that he preferred a legal solution to the dormant accounts issue, so when the Bankers Association sent a deputation to see him, it once again came armed with all the arguments against such a solution. Wahlen replied, however, that for political reasons there was no possibility of a negative response to the Huber motion and that a special regulation would have to be made.[65]

In spring 1959, Wahlen held out the prospect of a federal act that would define a reporting obligation for all dormant accounts whose last owners were either foreigners or stateless persons about whom no reliable information had been received since the end of the war and who might have fallen victim to political, racist or religious persecution or other violence. On 17 July 1959, Wahlen presented the draft 'Federal Decree on Assets in Switzerland Belonging to Foreign or Stateless Victims of Political, Racist or Religious Persecution'.[66] In September 1959 various newspapers took up the Bankers Association's arguments and declared the proposed draft law superfluous. On the other side, a delegation from the Israeli embassy submitted a request to the FPD for a special regulation on 10 October 1959; on 28 January 1960 the first secretary of the US embassy in Bern, Warren P. Blumberg, repeated the request, and on 1 June 1960 the US embassy sent a diplomatic note on the matter.

One of the decision makers, Federal Councilor Petitpierre, appeared to be undecided. On 29 June 1960, he had told the Federal Council that in view of the expected difficulties he would no longer insist on a special regulation. Three months later he changed his mind, announcing on 5 October that not only out of foreign policy considerations, but also in the interest of those subjected to racial discrimination, a special regulation should be attempted despite all the problems of implementation.[67]

In the winter of 1960/61, the Swiss press began to show renewed interest in the issue of dormant assets; some of the articles written on the subject were very critical of the government's plans. In the *Schweizerische Handels-Zeitung,* for example, the Federal Council's draft was described as a piece of 'foreign policy opportunism'[68] which represented 'an unnecessary breach in our legal system'.[69] Opponents of the Federal Decree found fault with both its content and its form. The foreign press, by contrast, initially paid virtually no attention to the matter. However, a delicate diplomatic situation arose in July 1961, when the Arab press spread the erroneous rumor that Switzerland planned to transfer dormant assets to the state of Israel.[70] At this time, the Eichmann trial was being held in Israel, making a wide global public more aware of Holocaust issues.[71]

Federal Councilor Petitpierre convinced his colleague Ludwig von Moos, the new head of the FDJP, that a regulation was required. In February 1961, von Moos requested that the Federal Council's 1952 decision on the matter be confirmed. On 30 June 1961, the Federal Council submitted the draft law – first commissioned in 1952 and finally formulated in 1959 – to the two-month consultation process among the cantons, political parties and interested professional associations. At the meeting of the Bankers Association's legal commission of 17 August 1961, Alfred Wegelin (SVB) declared himself in favor of paying the dormant assets as quickly as possible to legitimate claimants so that a positive disposition towards the Swiss banks could be engendered among the public. If opposition to the new law was too clear and obvious, many people would start to think that the presumably modest results of the planned measures could be attributed to the intransigence of the banks. He believed that it would be wiser to use constructive criticism to correct the legal inadequacies of the existing draft. The Bankers Association board of directors thus decided on 6 October 1961 not to oppose the law fundamentally but to concentrate primarily on influencing the draft law to take account of the banks' reservations.[72] On 11 December 1961, further talks were held between a delegation from the Bankers Association, Federal Councilors Wahlen and von Moos, and two representatives of the FPD's legal department. Wahlen took the opportunity to emphasize once again that the Federal Council regarded it as a duty to resolve the issue of assets in Switzerland belonging to foreign victims of political, racial or religious persecution by means of a law. Israel's claim to the dormant assets of Holocaust victims was morally justified, he said, and the concerns brought forward by the Bankers Association on the grounds of constitutional law were not shared by the Federal Council.[73] On 4 May 1962, the Swiss government made its submission to the Federal Parliament. Parliament largely went along with the Federal Council's proposals, though the Council of States imposed greater restrictions – compared with the National Council's proposal – on the General Custodial Trustee's powers of authority, and insisted that the reporting obligation be limited to ten years. On 20 December 1962, both houses approved the revised Federal Decree; the Federal Council approved the implementary ordinance on 10 June 1963.[74]

2.2 Interpretation

The Federal Decree of 20 December 1962 obliged Swiss financial institutions to register all assets that bore the following characteristics:[75]

- The last known owner was a foreigner or stateless person.
- The financial institution had not heard anything from the owner since 9 May 1945.
- The financial institution knew or suspected that the owner had fallen victim to racial, religious or political persecution.

Such assets had to be reported to the 'Claims Registry for Assets Belonging to Missing Foreigners' within the FDJP's legal department. If there was any doubt about the duty to report, the case in question was to be submitted to the government office for a decision. Any infringements of the law would be punished by fines of up to Sfr 10,000 or even imprisonment. The Claims Registry was also authorized to have books audited and checked, though there is no reference in the files of SKA, SVB or Bank Leu to any such checks being carried out. The Federal Decree, which was valid for ten years, came into effect on 1 September 1963. Assets had to be registered within six months.[76] In its circular of 27 August 1963, the Bankers Association stated that 'with this Federal Decree' the legislature wanted 'once and for all to solve the problem of assets invested or deposited in Switzerland by victims of National Socialism'; it also said that it was the banks' duty to cooperate faithfully with the official bodies.[77]

The five major banks, SKA, SVB, Bank Leu, SBG and SBV, as well as ZKB, discussed the problem of interpretation and practical implementation at two meetings.[78] Among other things, they decided not to register assets of less than Sfr 100, and to regard Jews who had lived in German-occupied territory as persecuted persons. Following intensive discussions, the banks also decided to register assets owned by people in Communist Eastern Europe and by people of unknown domicile whose names were Jewish. However, they agreed not to include assets that had fallen dormant prior to 1933. Sfr 100 would be deducted from every account to cover expenses and administration – given the small amounts held in some accounts, this seems a less than sensitive decision from today's viewpoint. In cases that required particular effort, the banks could charge even larger fees, though these so-called 'commission revenues' were never high enough to cover costs.[79]

2.3 Implementation

Implementation at SKA

Even before the Federal Decree came into effect, SKA instructed its branches on 11 July 1963 to report the assets concerned to the bank's central accounting office by 30 November. Referring to the penalties threatened by the government, it demanded that the investigation be thorough. Each department was fully responsible for its own actions, though the legal department and central accounting office would be available to help with any uncertainties and questions.[80]

In an initial step, head office and the branches carried out a search based only on the first two criteria stipulated in the Federal Decree, i.e. identifying all accounts that had been dormant since 9 May 1945, and whose last known owners were either foreigners or stateless persons. This search covered deposit books, safe deposit boxes, pseudonym and numbered accounts, accounts belonging to disappeared or unknown creditors, expired or lapsed medium-term notes, and uncashed checks, as well as the accompanying customer correspondence. SKA's general registry, which was a major source since it listed all name accounts in Switzerland, was analyzed by two people independently.

The revised search results – 370 cases at head office, 133 cases at the branches – were then subjected to the Federal Decree's third criteria. In trying to determine whether the owners were also the victims of racial, political or religious persecution, the bank had to rely on old documents, hunches, the memory of employees, and any notes they may have made.[81] A thorough review of every single one of the 503 cases was carried out by the legal department and the central accounting office based on the forms prepared by the departments. 'Very uncertain cases' were passed on to the executive board.

Between 7 and 11 November 1963, SKA's legal department eliminated a large number of cases.[82] It was helped in this work by Rabbi Jakob Teichmann and two experts on Jewish culture, Salcia Landmann and Florence Guggenheim-Grünberg. They decided on the basis of domicile, nationality, first name and family name whether the bank customer in question could possibly be a Jew or not. In nine cases SKA consulted the Centre de Documentation Juive Contemporaine in Paris and the Yad Vashem Martyrs' and Heroes' Memorial Authority in Jerusalem. However, neither institution was able to provide any additional information.[83] On 31 December 1963, the legal department made a progress report to the executive board. It had been very difficult to establish whether the account owners were the victims of political, racial or religious persecution. With racially persecuted dormant account holders, the main job was to establish a definite allegiance to the Jewish culture, which was tricky because certain names could be Jewish in one region and non-Jewish in another. This was a particularly complicated problem in Slavic nations. Intensive attempts had also been made to find the owners of the assets, but these had only been successful in two cases – one at

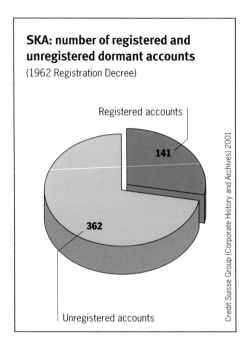

SKA: number of registered and unregistered dormant accounts

(1962 Registration Decree)

Registered accounts
141

362

Unregistered accounts

Credit Suisse Group (Corporate History and Archives) 2001

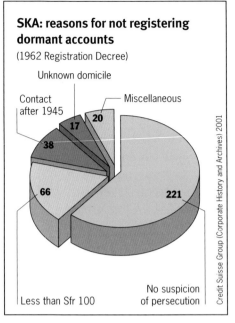

SKA: reasons for not registering dormant accounts

(1962 Registration Decree)

Unknown domicile

Contact after 1945
Miscellaneous
17
20
38
66
221

Less than Sfr 100
No suspicion of persecution

Credit Suisse Group (Corporate History and Archives) 2001

the Zurich branch and one at the Geneva branch. The legal department proposed that no customers from Communist Eastern Europe be registered. If they had not been heard from since 9 May 1945, there was reason to believe that they had been subject to political persecution, but it was also possible that they were still at large, so the banks should not put them at risk by registering their names. It was not possible in any case to correspond freely with them at that time. In the legal department's view, assets belonging to owners of unknown address should not be registered either, 'because for these people, the presumption which is necessary according to the Federal Decree cannot be made'.[84]

By 31 December 1963, the legal department had eliminated 322 cases because they did not meet the conditions laid down in the Federal Decree. The remaining 181 cases were broken down as follows: 9 people were Jews in non-Communist countries about whom research was still under way; 133 people, 99 of whom could be identified by their names as Jews, had a Communist state in Eastern Europe as their last known domicile, which was reason enough for the legal department to suggest that they not be registered; 39 cases should be registered. When the executive board decided to report owners domiciled behind the Iron Curtain, too, as stipulated in the Decree, the number of accounts registered with Bern on 28 February 1964 ultimately rose to 138. Another 3 cases were subsequently registered by the middle of June.[85]

Over and beyond the stipulations of the Federal Decree, SKA's legal department divided the cases to be registered into three categories:

SKA: registration of dormant accounts belonging to victims of the Nazi regime (1964)

	As at 28 February 1964		As at mid-June 1964 (total)	
	Number	Sfr	Number	Sfr
Category A	6	47 305	7	50 781
Category B	44	363 027	44	362 527
Category C	88	689 156	90	696 180
Total all categories	138	1 099 488	141	1 109 488

- A: High probability that the account holder had been a victim of racial, religious or political persecution.
- B: Victim status suspected owing to Jewish name and domicile in one of the countries occupied by the Axis powers to the west of the Iron Curtain.
- C: Victim status suspected owing to Jewish name and domicile in one of the countries occupied by the Axis powers behind the Iron Curtain.

In categories B and C, suspicion of persecution rested solely on the name and the domicile, whereas in category A there were concrete indications of persecution.[86] For category C assets, the danger to the potential claimants was once again emphasized. The legal department had only reported these cases 'with the greatest reluctance', since the suspicion of persecution was 'extremely weak'. It therefore urged the Claims Registry to exercise as much caution as possible when carrying out its research.[87]

On 23 June 1967, more than three years after the registration period, the Claims Registry decided that doubtful cases also fell under the Federal Decree because they still showed the characteristics required to qualify for compulsory registration, namely 'that your customers with Jewish names are [presumably] people who may have been subject to persecution pursuant to the wording of this article [Art. 1 para. 1 of the Federal Decree], and that you have not had reliable news of them since 9 May 1945'.[88]

Of the 503 cases in 1964, SKA's central accounting office did not forward 362, involving total assets of approximately Sfr 4.7 million, to the central Claims Registry in Bern.[89] The bank had decided as early as on 8 November 1963 not to report account holders with unknown domiciles.[90] The following points can be made about the two categories 'no suspicion of persecution' (221 cases) and 'domicile unknown' (17 cases):

- In about half of the 221 cases, the Jewish experts decided that the account holders' names were not Jewish.
- In a fifth of the 221 cases, one of the Jewish experts was sure or thought it possible that the name was Jewish, while at least one of the other two experts believed this to be unlikely or definitely not the case.
- In about a sixth of the 221 cases, the last domicile known to SKA was in a territory outside the influence of the 'Third Reich', for example the USA, Argentina or China.

- In about a dozen of the 221 cases, SKA decided or assumed that there was no reason to believe that the account holder had been in danger of persecution; no explanation is given for this assumption.
- Of the 17 'domicile unknown' cases, the experts came to the conclusion that about half a dozen involved Jewish, or at least presumed Jewish, names. However, because of the lack of information on domicile none of these cases were reported.
- In individual cases a Zurich or Geneva address was given, though some of these were only correspondence addresses.

The main problem was that some account holders with unknown domiciles were not reported even though one of the Jewish experts who advised the bank had declared the name concerned to be probably or definitely Jewish. Such uncertain cases were – as mentioned earlier – supposed to go to the Claims Registry.[91]

Implementation at SVB

In a memorandum about the ongoing research sent to the executive board on 9 April 1962, SVB's legal department stated that the registration criterion in the draft Federal Decree stipulating that the account holder had to be a foreigner or a stateless person, could be fulfilled. The legal department interpreted the condition that there had been no reliable contact by the customer since 9 May 1945 as meaning that the account holder had to be a victim of the Nazi regime. There was thus definitely no need to report accounts owned by people from the former sphere of influence of the 'Third Reich' who had fallen victim to a Communist regime after the war had ended. Neither did compulsory reporting extend to dormant accounts belonging to persons domiciled outside the Nazi sphere of influence. Moving on to the 'victims of racial, religious and political persecution' the legal department referred to many uncertain cases that would have to be reported to the Claims Registry.[92]

A memo from the legal department, dated 25 August 1962, stating its position on the executive board's request to produce an overview of dormant accounts and securities accounts, shows that there were still many unanswered questions associated with the planned Federal Decree. The stipulations about application and implementation were not formulated clearly enough in the legal department's view; so SVB tried to obtain further information via the FPD. However, the ministry only confirmed the known difficulties with implementation and referred the bank to the FDJP's justice section which 'had labored for 10 long years on the draft'.[93] SVB's legal department assumed that there would still be time before any Federal Decree would have to be implemented, and that there was, therefore, no urgent need to start work on any internal preparations.

After the Federal Decree had come into effect on 1 September 1963, the SVB executive board sent out a circular to all departments and branches on 4 October 1963 containing clear criteria for recording dormant accounts.[94] If there was any doubt about the cumulative fulfillment of all the criteria, the case had to be forwarded to the

**Dormant accounts at SVB:
transfers to collective accounts**[95]

In 1953, SVB's executive board decided that all assets which were owned by unknown customers, which were held in collective accounts, and which 'as far as anyone can judge' would never be paid out, should be transferred into revenue accounts.[96] This included general mandates drawn on the bank that had never been presented, drawings by other – mainly foreign – banks, where the checks concerned had not actually been presented for payment, but also postal deposits by unknown persons in favor of other unknown persons, as well as the current account assets of foreigners, especially tourists, whose addresses were 'completely unknown'. Abandoned saving and deposit books with balances of less than Sfr 1 should also be booked after ten years from collective to revenue accounts 'to cover costs'.[97] Between 1953 and 1958, SVB Bern thus made eight transfers from probable dormant accounts to a revenue account. The overall total was Sfr 35. In 1960, SVB Montreux booked the sum of Sfr 15,021 to a revenue account as 'other revenues'. This was done in compliance with an instruction issued by the internal auditors. On 26 October 1962, three (former) numbered accounts at SVB Zurich were transferred via a collective account to an 'other income' revenue account at head office in Bern. The total amount involved here was Sfr 15,459.[98] The highest amount – a total of about Sfr 1 million – was booked from a numbered account to revenue accounts by the Zurich branch between 1962 and 1992.[99]

In 1974, the executive board issued a new directive about the treatment of 'unknown customers' assets'.[100] This directive decreed that for sums under Sfr 100

a) account holders would be informed if the bank knew who they were or if they were listed in address or telephone books (if the customer did not react to this news within three months, the amount would be booked to a revenue account);

b) no research should be carried out if the account holder was 'unknown' or if the bank did not know whether he was alive or where he lived. These assets would be booked to a revenue account immediately.

This ruling was confirmed in 1977, though the threshold was raised from Sfr 100 to Sfr 1,000.[101]

All of these transfers to collective and (if necessary) revenue accounts were investigated between 1995 and 1999 as part of CSG's review of the dormant account issue.

legal department with a note highlighting the questionable criteria. All reports had to be made on the Claims Registry's official form, with a copy retained by the branch. On 29 November 1963, the executive board sent another circular, once again defining the distinction between suspicion and uncertainty. It stated that suspicion was where the client was 'an open opponent of the political regime of the time, or a Jew who lived in a territory controlled by the Nazis which was now in the West'. According to SVB, an uncertain case, by contrast, was where a customer met the registration criteria detailed in the Federal Decree of 1962, but had a domicile that now lay behind the Iron Curtain. The decision to report assets to Bern was normally made by the legal department, but in uncertain cases by the executive board. Unlike SKA, SVB did not consult external specialists. A record of expenses was to be kept for each case reported so that the bank could request compensation for the inconvenience and costs incurred as a result of implementing the Federal Decree. Legal counsels at each of the five major banks agreed that the minimum compensation payment per case should be set at Sfr 100.[102]

By the end of the internal recording procedure, the legal department had been notified of 62 dormant accounts containing assets totaling Sfr 200,000, though collective and revenue accounts were not investigated.[103] The legal department did not forward 40 of the cases to the Claims Registry. These 40 fell into four categories:

- The accounts contained less than Sfr 100, though this threshold was not observed precisely in all cases.
- The account holder's last known domicile was outside the Nazis' sphere of influence.
- Incomplete customer data (e.g. no recorded domicile).
- The assets were already dormant before 1933.

On 26 February 1964, SVB forwarded 22 reports, involving total assets of Sfr 189,204, to the Claims Registry.[104] It classified 6 of these as suspected cases, and 16 as uncertain.[105]

Implementation at Bank Leu

At Bank Leu, responsibility for finding and reporting the required information was given to the legal department at head office in Zurich. In its internal communication of 4 September 1963 to all head office departments and all branches, the legal department defined the registration criteria. Again the 'presumption of victimization' mentioned in the Federal Decree was taken to refer exclusively to victims of National Socialism, but not of Stalinism. Consequently, the legal department stated that only assets owned by the former should be reported.[106] A memorandum shows that experts could be consulted when there was uncertainty about whether a name was Jewish or not.

During its ongoing investigations, Bank Leu actively sought clients that it had not heard from for a long time. In September 1963, for example, it asked the Swiss embassy in Rome for information about a customer who had been out of contact since 1938. However, the embassy was unable to help and referred the bank to two official Italian bodies.[107] The name of the client concerned later appeared on the list made by Bank Leu on 2 February 1965, a list that also included 31 other dormant accounts that were recorded as a result of the 1962 Federal Decree but which did not meet its criteria.[108]

On 26 February 1964, the 3 cases evaluated by Bank Leu were sent with a covering letter from the central legal department to the Claims Registry. The letter explained that the judgment as to whether the people concerned could have been victims of racial or political persecution – religious persecution was not mentioned – was based solely on the names and domiciles of the clients concerned. Of the three cases submitted (total value Sfr 929) one concerned a customer from Lithuania; the bank stated that making contact with this person could cause problems for him or his descendants because he lived behind the Iron Curtain. In such a case, the bank could not accept any responsibility. Bank Leu's covering letter also stated that it reserved the right to charge a commission to cover the time spent on extended research in the archives.[109]

2.4 Treatment of registered assets

By fall 1968, 1,055 dormant accounts containing a total of approximately Sfr 10.857 million had been reported to the Claims Registry, up from the Sfr 9.471 million reported by the official closing date of 29 February 1964.[110] In a first phase run-

Dormant accounts belonging to citizens of Eastern European states

Over the course of the 1960s, Switzerland was the target of a series of diplomatic advances from Central and Eastern Europe, especially since the sum of Sfr 16,347.10 transferred to the Polish central bank's account at the SNB fell a long way short of expectations. When economic discussions were opened up during a phase of more relaxed relations, Poland registered additional claims to dormant accounts belonging to its citizens, as did Romania, Hungary, Czechoslovakia and – at least through the press – Yugoslavia.

While the Swiss Federal Council accepted that the earlier exchange of letters with Poland was binding under international law, finally leading to a payment of Sfr 463,954.55 on 15 August 1975, this was not the case with regard to the exchanges of letters with Hungary and Romania in 1950/51. Nevertheless, in the ongoing compensation negotiations with Hungary, Switzerland addressed the issue of the counterclaim and finally on 26 March 1973 promised Hungary the sum of Sfr 325,000 with no acknowledgement of legal liability. The general public did not get to hear about this because the sum was secretly offset against the Hungarian's compensation payment of Sfr 1.8 million in 1975.

As of 29 February 1964, dormant assets belonging to inhabitants of various Eastern European States – Poland and Hungary, but also Albania, Bulgaria, Czechoslovakia, the German Democratic Republic, Romania, the Soviet Union and Yugoslavia – that had been reported under the 1962 Federal Decree amounted to a total of Sfr 4,809,812.80, or 49.7% of all the assets concerned. However, on 28 February 1972 the Federal Council decided not to instigate missing persons procedures or make appeals to heirs in relation to these accounts, and instead paid the assets directly into the Heirless Assets Fund.[111]

ning from 1965 to 1970, the Registry checked to ensure that the reported assets really did fall under the Federal Decree. Based on this review, it rejected 224 reports relating to a total of Sfr 5.46 million, of which 6 had been submitted by SKA and one by SVB.[112] It then produced a list of all dormant accounts submitted by the reporting institutions and asked the guardianship office at the place where the main account was held to appoint a custodial trustee. Between 1966 and 1974 the cantonal guardianship offices established a custodial trustee for every registered account. In most cases the choice fell on the General Custodial Trustee appointed by the Federal Council on 15 July 1966, Heinz Häberlin, who had formerly been the general manager of Thurgauer Kantonalbank.[113]

The General Custodial Trustee transferred individual accounts containing less than Sfr 500 – or from 1970 less than Sfr 1,000 – directly into the Heirless Assets Fund.[114] If the Trustee thought that subsequent research would be particularly likely to locate the asset owner, even small accounts were excepted from this rule. In its report to the General Custodial Trustee, SKA said that it agreed with this procedure, though it expressed reservations about the involvement of the ICRC's International Tracing Service in Arolsen (Federal Republic of Germany) and later of the Swiss Federation of Jewish Communities (SFJC) and the Association of Swiss Jewish Refugee Relief (VSJF). Strictly speaking, the involvement of these institutions represented an infringement of banking secrecy. The bank also referred once again to the special situation of customers behind the Iron Curtain and asked that particular caution be exercised if investigations were made in such cases.[115]

Treatment of registered dormant accounts by SKA, SVB and Bank Leu (1964–1980)

	SKA	SVB	Bank Leu	Total CSG banks	Total all institutions
Reports (1964) incl. subsequent reports up to 1968	141	22	3	166	1055
Claims Registry not responsible	6	1	0	7	224
Paid into Heirless Assets Fund	95	16	3	114	699
Paid to account holders or their heirs	40	5	0	45	132

In 1967, the General Custodial Trustee sent a circular to the financial institutions reminding them that according to the SCC, guardians and custodians had to ensure that the assets entrusted to them were invested in interest bearing instruments. SKA was able to tell the Trustee that in the great majority of cases where it had not heard from customers for a long time after the war, in the customers' interests it had taken it upon itself to invest the assets held in dormant accounts and to manage these assets, primarily by buying Swiss bonds.[116] Nevertheless, the General Custodial Trustee ordered SKA to transfer all current accounts at head office to interest bearing investment accounts, and to do the same with proceeds from the sale of foreign notes and coins – except for gold coins. The Trustee's underlying concern was to ensure a conservative investment policy, meaning that dormant accounts should be transferred into watertight investments.[117]

There were three ways of submitting claims to registered assets:

- Direct inquiries to the banks: Provided a person could supply adequate proof of legal entitlement to the registered assets, the bank account would no longer qualify as dormant and the case would be struck off at the Claims Registry.
- Direct inquiries to the Claims Registry:[118] If someone instructed a legal representative (lawyer, notary) in Switzerland to submit his inquiry to the Claims Registry, this representative would first have to present the relevant power of attorney. The Claims Registry reserved the right to have this power of attorney certified by a notary or by the appropriate Swiss diplomatic representation abroad. If an inquiry matched one of the registered cases, further dealings between the claimant and the financial institution holding the assets took place via the responsible custodial trustee.[119]
- Active search by the custodial trustee: If the search was successful, the case would first be deregistered at the Claims Registry. The General Custodial Trustee would then broker contact with the bank in order to verify the claimant's identity beyond doubt. Once the bank had detailed which documents it needed, the claimant presented these to the custodial trustee. Since it was often difficult to produce original documents to verify the identity of victims of National Socialism, in many cases the General Custodial Trustee worked with sworn affidavits.[120]

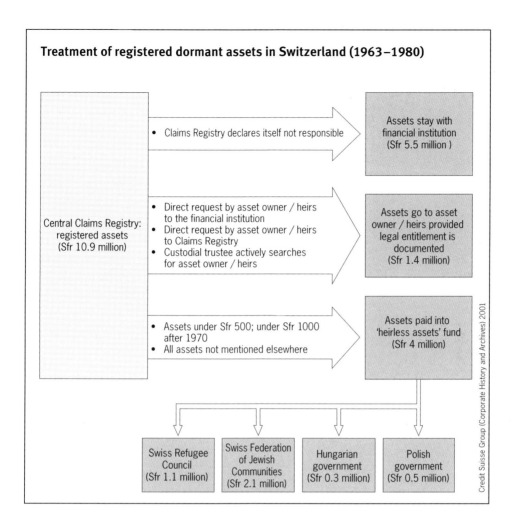

Treatment of registered dormant assets in Switzerland (1963–1980)

Central Claims Registry: registered assets (Sfr 10.9 million)

- Claims Registry declares itself not responsible

Assets stay with financial institution (Sfr 5.5 million)

- Direct request by asset owner / heirs to the financial institution
- Direct request by asset owner / heirs to Claims Registry
- Custodial trustee actively searches for asset owner / heirs

Assets go to asset owner / heirs provided legal entitlement is documented (Sfr 1.4 million)

- Assets under Sfr 500; under Sfr 1000 after 1970
- All assets not mentioned elsewhere

Assets paid into 'heirless assets' fund (Sfr 4 million)

Swiss Refugee Council (Sfr 1.1 million)

Swiss Federation of Jewish Communities (Sfr 2.1 million)

Hungarian government (Sfr 0.3 million)

Polish government (Sfr 0.5 million)

Credit Suisse Group (Corporate History and Archives) 2001

As a result of this process, Sfr 1.43 million was paid to claimants. The remaining assets – around Sfr 4 million – were transferred into the Heirless Assets Fund. On 19 February 1975, Sfr 325,000 was paid from the fund to Hungary; and on 15 August 1975, Sfr 463,955 was paid to Poland. Payments to the Polish central bank's 'N' account at the SNB also involved accounts at the CSG banks examined in this study: 17 accounts at SKA worth a total of Sfr 187,247, and one SVB account containing a balance of Sfr 1,833. This, though, was a bilateral matter between the Swiss and the Polish governments, over which the banks had no influence.[121] Two thirds of the remaining Sfr 3.18 million were transferred to the SFJC, which forwarded the money to the American Jewish Joint Distribution Committee. The rest went to the Swiss Refugee Council (SFH). On 20 August 1980, the fund was closed.[122]

3 'Dormancy' from the mid-1990s onwards

After the Heirless Assets Fund was wound up in 1980, the issue of dormant accounts was limited for almost a decade to individual inquiries made directly to the banks. Until 1989, neither the managing bodies of the banks, nor the Bankers Association, nor the Swiss authorities had very much to do with the matter at all.

Between 1989 and 1994 isolated voices on the political stage started to campaign for a legal solution.[123] On 6 December 1994, State Councilor Otto Piller submitted an ordinary question to the Federal Council, inquiring what it intended to do about 'ownerless' assets held by the Swiss banks.[124] In spring 1995, two more parliamentary actions – an ordinary question by National Councilor Jean Ziegler on 5 March and a parliamentary initiative by National Councilor Verena Grendelmeier on 25 March – called for the Federal Government to refocus on dormant assets that survived from the time of the Nazis. Ziegler and Grendelmeier said this was necessary because of inadequacies in the implementation of the 1962 Federal Decree and evidence that the banks had sometimes taken a formalistic approach to the inquiries they had received.[125] The subject was lent added urgency by a much publicized article, which was actually based on erroneous research, in the Israeli business journal *Globes* on 28 April 1995.[126] However, the Federal Council referred at this point to the efforts the banks had made at self-regulation and declared that it saw no reason for it to resort to new legislation.

In June 1995, the board of directors of the Bankers Association decided to conduct a survey of the banks represented on the board. The results were published in September of that year in the form of an interim report: there were 893 accounts and securities accounts owned by Swiss and foreign customers containing assets of more than Sfr 1,000 – all opened before 9 May 1945 and dormant since 1985 at the latest. Their total value was Sfr 40.9 million.[127] At the same time, the Bankers Association approved guidelines on how to deal with dormant accounts; these came into force on 1 January 1996.[128] From this point on the banks had to flag all dormant accounts to make inquiries and surveys easier, and had to ensure that the assets were managed in the customers' interests. In addition, a central contact point was set up at the office of the Bank Ombudsman to help with the search for dormant accounts, though there was a dispute about the size of fees that should be charged. In cases of hardship these fees could be waived.[129]

On 29 September 1995, the Bankers Association launched a more extensive survey, this time covering all of its member banks.[130] All accounts, securities accounts and safe deposit boxes opened prior to 9 May 1945 and left dormant since that time were to be recorded. The dormancy clause was later adjusted to 'since at least 1985' because many banks were not able to deliver more precise data. Finally, on 7 February 1996 only the grand total sum contained in dormant accounts owned by foreign customers was published: Sfr 38.74 million held in 775 accounts.[131] This figure met with fierce criticism from Jewish organizations, which had expected far higher sums. They thus called for an independent review of the results. On 28 March 1996, the Bankers Association finally produced an updated list – prompted in particular by a follow-up submission by SKA – of 916 customer accounts containing a total of Sfr 41.94 million.

3.1 Implementation of the Swiss Bankers Association's guidelines

Awareness of the issue within SKA

A memorandum sent by SKA's legal department on 16 January 1995 summarized the situation as follows:[132] 'The only practical experience from the 1960s was a failure. Our problem is that today we have no figures at all. But the work required and the expected results may well be completely out of proportion to one another.'

On 1 March 1995, the Swiss Sunday newspaper *Sonntags-Zeitung* asked SKA for information on 'money belonging to victims of the Nazis'. Without first making careful investigations, answering the questions posed could have been counterproductive, so SKA chose only to give a general response and to refer to the following points in particular:[133] every effort had been made to implement the Federal Decree of 1962 properly; after the Second World War many dormant bank accounts and securities accounts had been transferred to the owners' heirs or proxies; the legal department received several inquiries concerning dormant accounts every week, though after internal searches it was not normally possible to be of further assistance to applicants; it went without saying, however, that all dormant accounts were available for the legitimate owners, heirs or proxies to take over at any time; the same was true of safe deposit boxes – even if they had had to be opened, their contents were kept in separate, sealed envelopes together with an opening protocol and thus could be handed over to rightful claimants on presentation of the correct identification documents.

SKA – 1995 surveys: problems with the recording process and registration

'We are currently working on these figures. The results will not be available before the middle of October 1995.' This was SKA's response on 10 August 1995 to the Bankers Association's request for the results of the June survey. It continued as follows: 'Based on the statistical documents we have today, we believe that the overall sum will be significantly below Sfr 100 million.'[134] In personal discussions, SKA added that the dormant accounts had not been reported yet because of problems with its IT system, which had not been able to identify the accounts automatically; identification thus had to be done by hand. In fact, these IT problems meant that SKA had not started to

Towards a Federal Act on Dormant Assets

On 12 June 1995, State Councilor Otto Piller submitted the following motion:

'The Federal Council is invited to present a bill to the houses of Parliament without delay, which:

a) obliges banks and other legal entities or natural persons that manage assets, to register with a central office assets for which no legal claim of ownership has been enforced since a date to be stipulated in the Act;
b) mandates this central office to establish wherever possible who owns the assets;
c) ensures that this central office also helps the heirs of victims of the Nazis in their search for assets at the Swiss banks;
d) governs the use for public interest purposes of assets for which no rightful claimants can be found.'

At a session of the Council of States on 20 December 1995, Gian-Reto Plattner, who justified the motion in the place of its original sponsor (who had withdrawn), stated that the Bankers Association's guidelines did not yet ensure two important things: firstly, the banks were not actually obliged to report assets; secondly, assets held by lawyers and fiduciary agents were not recorded. Federal Councilor Kaspar Villiger spoke in favor of converting the motion into a postulate to be put before the Federal Council. Plattner rejected this suggestion, and the motion was not submitted to the Federal Council.

With interest newly awakened, about two dozen parliamentary actions were submitted by 1998.[135] This activity finally led to the preparation of a draft federal act on dormant accounts, which was submitted to the consultation process on 5 July 2000. According to this draft, dormant accounts should in future be reported to a Federal Government office after 10 years, and then, following publication of the details, escheat to the state after 50 years. In its response to the draft, the Bankers Association welcomed the effort to produce a legal solution, but appealed for greater recognition of the banks' efforts at self-regulation. The Federal Act on Dormant Assets is scheduled for approval in the 1999–2003 legislative period.

identify and record dormant accounts until July 1995. The advantage of this, however, was that the bank was able to adapt its methods to the specifications of the extended (second) Bankers Association survey sent to all member banks on 29 September 1995 and to the new Bankers Association guidelines.

In a first stage, a list of potential dormant accounts was produced, which covered bank accounts and securities accounts – collective accounts and safe deposit boxes were not included until 1997. In a second stage, this list was sent to all relationship managers at head office and at Swiss branches on 11 August 1995.[136] Responses were required by the beginning of 1996 at the latest; findings were entered in the bank's central customer information system (CIF). Name accounts were reported via the computer system; numbered and pseudonym accounts were registered using a form. All accounts that had been dormant for at least ten years and that were registered in this way were then frozen.

SKA informed the Bankers Association of the results of this exercise in a letter dated 3 January 1996. Commenting on the enclosed list, the bank noted that it could only say for certain about one single account that the last contact with the customer concerned took place before 9 May 1945. All the other dormant accounts had been opened before the end of the war, but it had not been possible to establish with any certainty when the contact with the customer had come to an end. All it could say for sure was that this had happened before 1985.[137] The attached list included 135 accounts worth a total of Sfr 11.713 million:

- 125 accounts belonging to foreign customers worth Sfr 11.67 million. Of these customers, 94 came from countries formerly controlled by the Axis Powers (including Japan), though some of the former Eastern Bloc countries concerned also encompassed territories that had not been under Axis control.
- 10 Swiss accounts worth a total of Sfr 42,700.

A subsequent check of the numbered and pseudonym accounts that had been reported to the Bankers Association revealed that the figures for the Basel region had not been included. As a consequence, in the revised report made on 26 February 1996 the number of accounts went up from 125 to 262. The total sum increased to Sfr 14.9 million, and the total held in foreign-owned accounts to Sfr 14.86 million.

SVB – 1995 survey: recording process and registration

The recording process used by SVB in response to the Bankers Association's survey of 29 September 1995 was largely based on the concept, criteria and execution methods employed by SKA. On 6 September, before the official letter from the Bankers Association extending the survey to all its member banks had been received, head office and branches in all regions were instructed to report all dormant accounts that had been opened prior to 9 May 1945 and which had been dormant since at least 1985. Reports had to be in by 10 October.[138] SVB investigated all accounts containing more than Sfr 10,000. Smaller balances were subject to a summary review. In general, the reports submitted from the regions were not re-checked.

The reports from the 17 regional and branch heads arrived between 6 and 24 October 1995. A total of 1,577 dormant accounts were reported containing assets calculated at approximately Sfr 14 million, though 44% of the accounts were worth less than Sfr 1,000 each. Account books that had been transferred to collective accounts were not included. SVB stated that it had not found any accounts or securities accounts that had 'been opened before 9 May 1945 and that had been dormant since then'.[139] No additional reports had to be made after the first one.[140] The subsequent recording of special cases involving dormant accounts (e.g. collective accounts), flagging of relevant accounts in the IT system and preparation of a directive all took place in cooperation with the Bank Ombudsman and in close consultation with SKA.

Bank Leu – 1995 survey: recording process and registration

Bank Leu developed its own method of recording, though the quality of the data available proved problematic. In the 1970s in particular, when customer data was entered into the new IT system, a fictional opening date was sometimes given to save time. Bank Leu was aware of this problem from the start, so it took account of all these cases when making its list of potential dormant accounts. The list was created in several stages and then sent to every relationship manager at head office and at the bank's branch offices. The investigation also covered Bank Neumünster, which had been integrated into Bank Leu. The recording process did not extend to safe deposit boxes, collective accounts, closed accounts or savings books. All accounts identified as dormant were frozen. Bank Leu's first internal directive on how to deal with dormant accounts was not, however, issued until 22 December 1995, meaning that it was not available in time to help with the implementation of the Bankers Association's survey.

In December 1995, Bank Leu reported 4 customer accounts worth Sfr 25,900 to the Bankers Association: one from Switzerland (Sfr 2,444), 2 from Germany (Sfr 16,659) and one from France (Sfr 6,797). It was unclear whether two of these accounts really had been opened before 9 May 1945. The Bankers Association's publication of 7 February 1996 included the 3 foreign accounts. Based on the relevant directive, all accounts have since been checked annually to ensure that they do not remain dormant for more than ten years.

3.2 The problem of 'dormancy' intensifies: action required on several levels

Following the presentation of survey results on 7 February 1996, the dispute between the Jewish organizations, which were disappointed with the outcome, and the Bankers Association and banks intensified. At about the same time, on 8 April, the US Senate's Finance Committee, headed by Alphonse D'Amato, announced an official investigation. The memorandum of understanding concluded between the parties on 2 May 1996 called for the foundation of the Independent Committee of Eminent Persons (ICEP), an international commission of experts made up equally of representatives of the Jewish organizations and of the Swiss banks. Under the chairmanship of Paul A. Volcker, this body was later commonly referred to as the Volcker Commission. The commercial banks' treatment of dormant assets was to be investigated by audit firms appointed by the ICEP with the consent of the Swiss Federal Banking Commission (EBK). These investigations were divided into three stages and, according to the original plan, were to be completed by the end of 1998. However, despite the efforts of about 500 auditors and numerous bank employees, delays crept in.[141]

Despite the launch of these investigations, political pressure on the commercial banks, particularly the major banks, continued to intensify. This was partly due to various hearings before the US Senate's Banking Committee and the submission to the US Federal Court of three class action lawsuits by Holocaust survivors or descendants of survivors against the Swiss major banks. The first of these class action submissions was made on 3 October 1996.[142] Strained relations were eased somewhat only on 5 February 1997 when it was announced that the three major banks CSG, SBV and SBG were paying Sfr 100 million to establish a humanitarian fund for Holocaust victims. According to the then chairman of the Credit Suisse Group board of directors, Rainer E. Gut, this fund aimed to express Switzerland's gratitude for being spared during the war, and to do so by means of a concrete commitment that would provide needy people, especially in Eastern Europe with rapid, unbureaucratic help quite separately from the issue of dormant accounts.[143] By December 2000, after the SNB had contributed a further Sfr 100 million and the Swiss private sector, especially private banks and the insurance industry, had given another Sfr 73 million, the fund, presided over by Rolf Bloch, had been able to make payments totaling Sfr 293.3 million to around 314,000 beneficiaries. The first payment to Holocaust victims came as early as 18 November 1997 when Sfr 15 million was paid to people in Riga. Payments came to an end in August 2001.[144] Jewish victims were granted about Sfr 246 million. Non-Jewish survivors – Roma/Sinti, Righteous Among the Nations, homosexuals, Jehovah's Witnesses, disabled people and victims of political persecution – received around Sfr 47 million in total.[145] The goal of providing help to Holocaust victims was thus achieved.[146]

At the end of December 1996, the Independent Commission of Experts Switzerland – Second World War (ICE) headed by Jean-François Bergier was set up as part of the implementation of the Federal Decree of 13 December 1996 on the historical and legal investigation into the fate of assets which reached Switzerland as a result of the National-Socialist regime. An ICE report on dormant accounts is due in fall 2001. The Federal Council also established a Task Force to ensure effective coordination of all the activities undertaken in the worlds of politics and business surrounding the whole issue of 'Switzerland – Second World War', appointing Ambassador Thomas Borer as its head on 25 October 1996. The Task Force was later dissolved – on 31 March 1999 – and integrated into the FDFA's historical service. This 'Switzerland – Second World War' service, headed by Minister Lukas Beglinger, operated until the end of June 2001.

In the address he was invited to give to the National Press Club in Washington on 26 June 1997, Rainer E. Gut, faced by a critical American press, called for a fair appraisal of the difficult role Switzerland had to play during the Second World War: 'We are not intent on glossing over any unpleasant aspects of our past. Nor do we wish to engage in generalized judgments of the wartime generation. All we are trying to do is to reconstruct the events of the past in as complete a manner as possible in order to achieve a just and balanced perspective.' The then chairman of the board of Credit Suisse Group was absolutely clear that: 'Where assets belonging to the victims are discovered, those assets must find their way to the victims' rightful heirs or, where no such heirs exist, to charitable causes providing help to the victims.'[147]

Publication of lists of names by the Swiss Bankers Association in 1997 and by the Swiss Federal Government in 1999

In July and October 1997, the Bankers Association, having partially lifted banking secrecy, published three lists of names of dormant account owners quite independently of the ICEP investigation – 5,570 accounts belonging to foreigners and 10,758 belonging to Swiss customers.[148] The trustee company ATAG Ernst & Young functioned as the link between banks and the people who came forward to claim assets after having seen the lists. By the end of September 2001, an international arbitration body based in Zurich, the Claims Resolution Tribunal headed by Hans-Michael Riemer,

Publication of the CSG banks' accounts in 1997

The audit firm Arthur Andersen, working on behalf of the ICEP, analyzed 792 of the dormant accounts published by SKA and SVB in July and October 1997. These were worth Sfr 23,191,970 in total.[149] Most of the assets belonged to Swiss customers (165 accounts / Sfr 1.9 million), but the largest share in volume terms was attributable to customers from France (96 / Sfr 4.17 million). Most of the other customers were from Italy (15 / Sfr 2.06 million), Germany (79 / Sfr 1.9 million), Czechoslovakia (5 / Sfr 0.88 million), Hungary (8 / Sfr 0.44 million), Austria (16 / Sfr 0.44 million), Bulgaria (5 / Sfr 0.41 million), Romania (18 / Sfr 0.4 million) and Spain (16 / Sfr 0.34 million). Two dormant accounts belonging to people with dual citizenship contained total assets of no less than Sfr 2.63 million. There were 316 unallocated accounts worth a total of Sfr 6.69 million.

Most of the accounts, namely 396, contained less than Sfr 500 – those containing less than Sfr 100 were not even listed; 33 accounts contained more than Sfr 100,000, 6 of these being worth in excess of Sfr 1 million.

had decided on more than 9,918 claims and thus on payments to victims of the Holocaust and others. All rightful claimants received the assets concerned as well as a reimbursement of any fees that had been charged; Holocaust victims were also paid a specially calculated compound interest sum. Particularly because of all the documents that had to be examined – there were usually several claims for each of the published accounts – investigating these cases took up a lot of time.[150]

Most of the claims came from the USA (20%), followed by Germany and France (12% each), Israel (9%) and Argentina (6%). The overall value of the assets included on the three lists came to about Sfr 80.2 million. 3,121 (32%) of the claims were approved and Sfr 16 million was paid to Shoah victims; Sfr 49 million was paid to other victims. The banks themselves made the decisions on the 7,368 claims to dormant accounts belonging to Swiss citizens.[151]

In January 1999, the federal authorities published a list in the *Bundesblatt* and on the Internet containing 580 names of persons relating to around 550 accounts that had been liquidated and used for humanitarian purposes as part of the Registration Decree of 1962. The approximately Sfr 3 million involved had been transferred into the Heirless Assets Fund which was later paid to the SFJC and the Swiss Central Office for Refugee Relief. According to the Federal Department of Foreign Affairs (FDFA), 'the assets mentioned especially included accounts for which no intensive search for entitled owners had occurred. These concerned assets of less than Sfr. 1,000 as well as assets of people whose domicile or nationality was unknown or whose final residence was in the then Communist countries of Eastern Europe. In the latter cases, search measures for entitled owners were not carried out, because it was feared that those affected would otherwise be subjected to hardship in their home countries.'[152]

Major banks' 1998 settlement and ICEP's 1999 final report

On 12 August 1998, the Swiss major banks and the lawyers representing the Jewish plaintiffs came to a settlement out of court. The banks undertook to pay $ 1.25 billion in installments to a 'Justice Fund', though this sum would include the dormant accounts to be paid out on the basis of the ICEP investigation (the sum for the dormant accounts has still not been paid out in full). The rest of the Swiss business world was less willing to make substantial contributions to the fund.

In spring 1999 in New York, Judge Edward Korman gave his provisional consent to the global settlement that had finally been signed by the parties on 26 January 1999, though he did not want to give his final judgment until after the ICEP's final results had been published. A worldwide campaign was launched in June of that year, which included information about how to submit claims and appeals of various types.[153]

Owing to a series of delays in the implementation of the ICEP investigation, the final report did not appear until December 1999. The main delay was caused by the difficult matching process used to identify possible or probable Holocaust victims. This involved comparing the information recorded by the banks with the so-called 'Yad Vashem Victims List' produced in Israel. This analysis of 4.1 million customer accounts from the period between 1933 and 1945 produced 53,886 accounts that could have been or probably were owned by victims of the Nazis. This figure was subsequently corrected down to 36,000 accounts, which were entered into a database.[154] ICEP recommended the publication of about 26,000 accounts that were probably related to the Holocaust. This figure was also revised downwards by 20% following a review carried out in collaboration with the banks.

The ICEP report made the following points about the behavior of the banks:

a) The auditors reported no evidence of systematic destruction of records of victim accounts, of organized discrimination against the accounts of victims of Nazi persecution, or of concerted efforts to divert the funds of victims of Nazi persecution to improper purposes.

b) There was, however, confirmed evidence of questionable and deceitful action by some individual banks in the handling of accounts, including withholding of information from Holocaust victims about their accounts, inappropriate closing of accounts, many cases of insensitivity to the efforts of heirs of victims to claim dormant or closed accounts, and a general lack of diligence – even active resistance – in response to earlier private and official inquiries about dormant accounts.[155]

Publication of the ICEP's list of names in 2001

The ICEP was dissolved in February 2000, and in March of that year the FBC approved the ICEP's request to publish a new list of possible or probable Holocaust victims, though the FBC made this conditional on the enforcement of the global settlement.[156] Once this request had been fulfilled on 16 July 2000, Special Master Judah Gribetz published a plan on 12 September 2000 for the distribution of the $ 1.25 billion from the major banks' settlement. The plan aimed to treat all classes of claimant fairly. A maximum of $ 800 million was reserved for the claims of Holocaust victims against the Swiss banks.[157] In a related action, Judge Korman was able to force Swiss industrial and service-sector companies that had maintained branches in Germany during the Nazi period to carry out further research about the possible use of slave labor, so that the claims of the workers concerned could be incorporated into the global settlement.[158] Judge Korman agreed to the distribution plan on 22 November 2000 and on 8 December appointed the former chairman of the ICEP, Paul A. Volcker, and the ICEP's legal advisor, Michael Bradfield, as Special Masters. Their task was to monitor the acceptance and examination of claims based on the list of names. The actual decisions on the claims were to be made by the same arbitrator as had worked on the Bankers Association's list of 1997, the Claims Resolution Tribunal II.[159]

Finally, on 5 February 2001, 20,825 names were published on the Internet. According to the Bankers Association, 2,600 of the accounts still contained an unspecified sum of money. Claimants had to submit their claims within six months. They could even submit a claim if their name did not actually appear on the published list, since it was possible to run a match with the database of 36,000 names, or even if necessary with all 4.1 million of the accounts audited by the ICEP. By the end of August 2001, around 31,000 people had submitted claims to the Claims Resolution Tribunal II. The actual number of claimants was still not definitive, however. Following the major banks' settlement in August 1998, Judge Korman had asked all possible claimants – including former refugees and slave laborers – to contact the Federal District Court in New York. Of the 580,000 questionnaires submitted, about 85,000 people said that their ancestors had owned assets in Switzerland. The Claims Resolution Tribunal II assumed that by the end of the registration period, there would be a total of about 50,000 claims to assess, which would have to be processed within a maximum of two years.[160]

Self-regulation by the banks – consultation on a federal act

Efforts have been made on the domestic political front in Switzerland since 1995 to regulate the treatment of dormant accounts through a piece of legislation. A bill was sent out for consultation in summer 2000, and the two houses of Switzerland's parliament are scheduled to deal with the matter during the current legislative period (1999 to 2003). The Bankers Association expressly welcomed the Swiss government's efforts to create a legislative solution; but in its official response to the draft federal act on dormant accounts at the end of September 2000, it regretted that while the draft covered a lot of details, it no longer paid sufficient regard to the advantages of self-regulation. These advantages included the ready availability of specific industry expertise, the option to differ the approach to suit the sector concerned, closeness to actual banking practice, and the ability to adapt rapidly in line with actual experiences and changing circumstances. In a spirit of sensible subsidiarity, the act should restrict itself to governing those aspects that went beyond the scope of self-regulation. The Bankers Association was particularly unhappy about the obligation that the act placed on financial intermediaries to seek contact with a customer only after eight years. It proposed that

Dormant assets in the USA, the United Kingdom and Israel[161]

Dormant assets belonging to Shoah victims are by no means a problem peculiar to Switzerland.

After the war, it would appear that the USA was home to the largest volume of dormant assets. These were treated in accordance with the principle of 'escheat'. If an account or securities account becomes dormant, it has to be reported to the authorities 5 to 10 years (depending on the state) after the last customer contact or on expiry of the last contractual period, and transferred to the government (this transfer is known as an 'escheatment'). For non-Jewish dormant accounts, the bank was obliged to search for the customer, and if no claim was forthcoming to hand over the assets to the government, though these could still be returned to a rightful claimant at a later date. In 1940/41, Jewish assets from Axis-occupied territories were frozen as enemy property and then given back to the owners after the end of the war. The plan was to transfer ownership of individually documented assets worth a maximum of $ 3 million in total to charitable organizations that would then handle any claims. But since the documentation took too much time to assemble, and in most cases was not even available any longer, it was decided in 1962 to make a lump sum payment of $ 500,000 to the Jewish Restitution Successor Organization. In the 1960s, this seemed to be the only practical solution, but it was still criticized in December 2000 by the Presidential Advisory Commission on Holocaust Assets in the United States. The Commission found fault with the lack of protection for individual people's interests, as well as with the slow treatment of claims and the inadequacy of the lump-sum payment. It recommended that a foundation be set up to help fund further investigations into dormant accounts.

In May 2000, banks in the United Kingdom published a list of persons along with details of 10,800 accounts from the Second World War that had been blocked by the government and subsequently fallen dormant. The British banks also created 'Restore UK', an agency of the British Bankers' Association, to deal with claims.

In January 2000, it was announced that there were 5,000 dormant accounts at the major Israeli banks. Another 10,000 dormant accounts were under the control of Israeli government authorities, which also managed 5,000 unclaimed real estate properties. In February 2000, the Knesset voted unanimously to establish a parliamentary commission to look into dormant accounts and state-managed unclaimed property. In April 2001, an investigation committee was mandated to search for the owners and heirs of these dormant accounts and unclaimed assets.

with event-related dormancy, banks and securities dealers should take the appropriate steps as soon as they establish that contact with a customer has been broken off. An upper time limit should only be a subsidiary stipulation, to be imposed in special cases. The Bankers Association's response also found fault with the planned obligation to publish accounts after 45 years of dormancy, but proposed a shorter deadline before assets were handed over to the state. Above all, even after the transfer – i.e. beyond the suggested 50 years – customers should still be entitled to claim their assets. It would also make sense from the point of view of costs and practicality for the Bank Ombudsman – under the supervision of the FBC – to handle the work involved, rather than setting up a new federal agency.

By the end of 2000, the Bank Ombudsman had responded to 6,700 requests for claim registration questionnaires, 3,751 of which were returned. Of these claims, 3,326 were approved; 1,886 related to the period prior to 1945, the remaining 1,440 to the post-war period. Finally, search lists provided the banks with 2,885 names for pre-1945 accounts and 1,733 names for accounts opened after the war. The search was successful in 20 cases dating from before 1945, worth a total of Sfr 10.9 million, and in 87 cases dating from after 1945, worth Sfr 11.7 million overall. Six of the pre-1945 cases, total value Sfr 6.05 million, affected CSG, as did 15 post-war cases worth Sfr 2.26 million overall. Once the 1997 name lists had been published, the Bank Ombudsman was no longer responsible for cases dating from before 1945, and so questionnaires were forwarded to ATAG Ernst & Young. In the first six months of 2001, 19 successful investigations into dormant accounts after 1945 were carried out, worth a total of Sfr 1.2 million. Of these cases, 11 – worth Sfr 0.28 million in total – affected the CSG banks.[162]

The Bankers Association's new guidelines were published in February 2000 and came into force on 1 July 2000, marking a real step-change. Based on all the experiences of the previous years, the main emphasis was now on prevention.[163] Every new customer of a Swiss bank is now given an information brochure that should help to prevent assets from falling dormant. The decisive point in the new approach is that as soon as contact breaks off with a customer, a search for the rightful claimant will be mounted using the bank's, and other, resources, though always within the parameters of banking secrecy. Only if these active measures prove fruitless is an account deemed to be dormant. Since the end of 2000, such cases have been recorded on a database managed by SAG SEGA Aktienregister AG, to which the Bank Ombudsman has access. This has made the procedure for dealing with dormant account claims much simpler. The principle that such assets have to be managed in the owners' best interests is also enshrined in the guidelines rather than being left to the individual institutions as happened before. Finally, it is recommended that the banks keep hold of key data relating to closed customer accounts indefinitely.

3.3 From passive recording to active prevention

When CS Holding was transformed into Credit Suisse Group at the beginning of 1997, a committee was set up to coordinate certain tasks that had previously been done by a variety of different departments. At the same time, the following principles were established:

- CSG believes it is absolutely essential to scientifically scrutinize the business activities during the years 1933–1945 of banks that now belong to the group.
- CSG undertakes to maintain a central overview of the surviving historical documents from all of its banks.
- CSG ensures that the 'Volcker Commission', the external audit firms and the ICE enjoy the best possible conditions for their investigative work.
- CSG believes that it is necessary not only to marshal the facts, but also to judge the conduct of those responsible at the time in context.

In preparation for the publication of the lists of names, in 1997 all dormant accounts first had to be centralized. Those with an opening date earlier than 1945 were then identified, with any uncertain cases also added to the list. In a few cases this led cus-

Results of surveys of dormant assets in Switzerland (1947–1997)

Year	Survey criteria	Total (Sfr)	SKA (Sfr)	SVB (Sfr)	Bank Leu (Sfr)
1947	Assets of victims of the Nazi regime (certain or presumed), major banks	482 000	n. a.	n. a.	n. a.
1956	Assets of victims of the Nazi regime (certain or presumed), all banks	862 410	63 300	82 920	375
1964	Assets of victims of Nazi persecution (certain or presumed), foreigners	9.47 m (additions by fall 1968: 1.39 m)	1.11 m	189 204	929
1995	All dormant accounts (opened before 1945; dormant since at least 1985). Interim results	40.90 m	11.71 m	0	25 900
1996	Assets belonging to foreigners (opened before 1945; dormant since at least 1985)	38.74 m (additions 28. 3. 1996: 3.2 m)	11.67 m (additions 26. 2. 1996: 3.2 m)	0	23 456

Year	Survey criteria	Total Swiss banks (Sfr)	Total CSG banks (Sfr)	Credit Suisse (Sfr)	Other CSG banks (Sfr)
July 1997	Assets belonging to foreigners	61.2 m	18.10 m	17.98 m	113 195
Oct. 1997	Assets belonging to Swiss	12.85 m	638 615	222 845	415 770
Oct. 1997	Assets belonging to foreigners. Additions	6.17 m	384 849	384 849	0

tomers to complain about the publication of their – apparently dormant – assets. At the same time, a team of lawyers worked with the Claims Resolution Tribunal and CSG's legal counsel to review the claims made to Swiss and foreign accounts. There were repeated difficulties owing to the fact that many of the claims were not backed up by sufficient documentation.[164] As well as the dormant accounts incorporated into the two publications, ICEP's mandate also included an investigation into accounts that had been closed, since there was a possibility that this had been done illegally. Only a thorough investigation of this matter would ensure that the reexamination of all customer accounts from the period between 1 January 1933 and 31 December 1945 was comprehensive. More than 180 CSG employees worked on this at three locations in Zurich from spring 1999. A third list of dormant accounts of possible or probable Holocaust victims that had not already been published in 1997 was posted on the Internet in February 2001.

In summer 2000, CSG issued a directive on the uniform treatment of dormant accounts, asset investigations, management of these assets, and documentation relating to accounts that had been closed.[165] The new directive covers the following main points:

- Whenever customers open accounts, preventative measures have to be taken to avoid the account falling dormant at a later date.
- In the case of accounts that are active, but for which there is no contact, an active search has to be conducted for the customers or other rightful claimants.

- If accounts fall dormant despite this active search, the assets they contain have to be managed in a uniform manner, and the relevant documents have to be archived.

The practical application of this directive has already yielded its first successes. Thanks to active internal and external searches, numerous contacts have been reestablished.

A comparison of the results of the various surveys highlights several differences between them. The sums recorded in the 1990s were much larger than those produced by earlier investigations, for example. There are a number of reasons for this:[166]

- The figures shown in the table are for the nominal sums reported.
- The criteria used to record these sums changed. In the 1990s, for example, the surveys extended over a wider range than just the dormant accounts of victims of political, racial or religious persecution by the Nazis.
- The dormant accounts registered in the 1990s had been dormant since at least 1985, so not all of them had necessarily been dormant since the end of 1945.
- The assets recorded in the 1990s had been invested to earn interest, and had thus increased in value over time.

4 Asset investigations: case studies and selected examples

4.1 The Swiss Bankers Association's practice

Prerequisites for investigation

As soon as the Second World War ended, the Bankers Association started to receive inquiries from individual heirs of Shoah victims who wanted it to investigate assets deposited by their relatives at its member banks. The board of directors of the Bankers Association issued a regulation on dormant accounts as early as on 15 March 1946 – two months before the signing of the Washington Agreement. This regulation was to remain the principle guide on the subject until 1964.

In principle, before the secretariat of the Bankers Association would forward an inquiry to its member banks, the following documents had to be presented:

- The official certificate confirming the death or disappearance of the asset owner
- The official certificate confirming that the applicant was an heir, along with the names of any other heirs
- A power of attorney if the applicant was acting on behalf of the heirs

If foreign documents were submitted, wherever possible they had to be certified by the official Swiss representation in the country from which they originated. Evidence also had to be presented to show that the deceased really had owned assets in Switzerland.[167]

Max Oetterli, at that time secretary of the Bankers Association, announced in 1952 that applicants had generally been shown cooperation. In many cases, for example, the secretariat had waived the need to see documentary evidence that would be practically impossible to find, accepting instead a credible presentation of the claim before divulging information in good faith.[168]

In a 1952 draft circular to member banks, the Bankers Association outlined its central concern. In order to 'take the wind out of the sails' of efforts to impose legal regulation, the Bankers Association was relying absolutely on the cooperation of member banks, 'and we ask you, therefore, to provide us willingly, as you have done so far, with information on request – which we will, of course, always treat with the necessary discretion. [...] We also ask that you treat direct requests on this matter to your institution with the appropriate care.'[169] According to Max Oetterli, there had been no such circular to the banks prior to 1952 because the Bankers Association did not want to give the impression that it was actively involved in locating such assets. If this impression had been given, citizens of Eastern European countries might well have been forced by their governments to write to the Bankers Association's secretariat. If the response had been positive, these people would presumably have become embroiled in a very difficult situation.[170]

Originally, the secretariat of the Bankers Association only contacted a bank during its investigations if it had been named by the claimant as possibly being the institution where the account was held.[171] In 1952, however, it was decided to collect the applications received into lists and to send these to the executive boards of all the banks, together with a request for help in all the investigations. If a positive answer was forthcoming, the Bankers Association would broker contact between the applicant and the bank.[172] Between 4 March 1957 and 21 February 1964, 17 such surveys and 4 individual inquiries were sent out, concerning around 190 parties. An existing bank account was found in 4 of these cases.[173]

The survey forms included the potential customers' last names, first names, last known addresses and in some cases also their dates of birth or professions. The banks were asked whether they held – possibly in the form of a numbered or pseudonym account – a bank account, savings book, deposit book, securities account, safe deposit box, etc., belonging to the person concerned.

Where documents had been lost during the war, in many cases the Bankers Association accepted affidavits[174], certified by a court or a notary and containing the important facts, instead. In 1960, if the search was confined to a number of banks in one or two Swiss cities, the claimant would be charged Sfr 50. A search encompassing all of Switzerland's major towns would cost Sfr 100.

By 1958, individual banks were already expressing significant reservations about this type of survey. SVB's branch in Zurich, for example, wrote as follows to the Bankers Association: 'We have noticed that there has recently been another glut of inquiries about presumed deposited assets. [...] You [the Bankers Association] are obviously trying to lump different cases together so they can be dealt with in a single investigation. However, the information is mostly so vague, and the investigation in our experience so rarely ever produces a positive result, that we have to ask ourselves whether we should continue to deal with this type of inquiry.'[175] Complaints were also made about the time involved: on 14 March 1957, SVB's branch in Zurich wrote to say that investigating a list of names at the branch and its attendant deposit counters took 11 hours, and that the Bankers Association should be cautious about accepting such inquiries.[176]

After the Federal Decree of 1962 came into force, the Bankers Association ceased its function as a central contact point for those seeking assets belonging to people who had died or disappeared during the Second World War.[177] From spring 1963, if the Bankers Association thought the matter fell under the Federal Decree, it would tell claimants to contact the Claims Registry for Assets Belonging to Missing Foreigners in Bern. If not, it would write to them to say that for technical and legal reasons it could no longer identify accounts or securities accounts by surveying its member banks. Instead it sent these claimants a list of its members and recommended that they make direct contact with the banks that they thought might be holding the assets concerned.[178]

In the mid-1980s, the Bankers Association enclosed an information sheet with its letters to claimants, advising them how to proceed with such investigations.[179] A similar information sheet followed in 1994/95.[180] Among other things, this stated that a bank was obliged to provide information on request to an individual heir about the original owner's assets, but that only the full community of heirs could be granted the power to dispose of the assets.

4.2 SKA, SVB and Bank Leu: inquiries, research and providing information

The three CSG banks SKA, SVB and Bank Leu received the first inquiries about dormant accounts shortly after the Second World War.[181] This study's examination of the research they undertook and the way they provided information was divided into the following three periods:

- Inquiries up to the Federal Decree of 1962
- Inquiries during the life of the Federal Decree 1963–1973
- Inquiries after the expiry of the Federal Decree 1974–1994

Claims made more than five years after the assets concerned were transferred to the Heirless Assets Fund lapsed in accordance with article 12 paragraph 2 of the Federal Decree of 1962. Following the expiry of the Federal Decree, i.e. after 31 August 1973, the FDJP answered inquiries about dormant accounts with a standard letter in which it brought attention to the expiry of the statutory deadline.[182]

Schweizerische Kreditanstalt

For the years between 1946 and 1962, 99 inquiries have been examined for this study. Claimants who could not identify themselves satisfactorily and who could not give any more precise details of the assets they were looking for were referred to head office, where an inquiry would be circulated among various departments. The claimant's letter would be passed from department to department and annotated with the individual departmental glosses. A large proportion of claimants – namely 44 of the 99 examined – believed that the assets they were looking for were held at SKA rather than just any bank in Switzerland. The specific SKA branch where the account had been opened was named by 10 claimants. In 92 of the 99 cases, an investigation was carried out at head office, which always included research in the general registry. In 3 cases, the investigation was extended to branches. In 2 cases searches were only undertaken in specific branches and not at head office. In 2 cases, no research was done at all. If nothing was found and insufficient identification was presented, SKA would inform the claimant of this in what has become known today as an 'Obschon' letter

Active searches for dormant assets at SKA, SVB and Bank Leu

The necessity of proving identity

Because protecting customer privacy is given such a high priority, Swiss banking secrecy is only lifted in exceptional cases stipulated by the law – in criminal proceedings, for example. Furthermore, the banks are only allowed to provide comprehensive information to the customer himself, or persons legally authorized by the customer (agents, heirs, guardians, etc.).[183]

When examining the question of how the CSG banks handled requests about assets belonging to victims of the Nazi regime, it is important to remember that the banks could not officially carry out research or provide information about the results of this research unless they could fulfill the strict conditions laid down by the Bankers Association. Documents proving that the customer had died or disappeared and that the applicant was entitled to receive information had – if he was not a Swiss citizen – to be certified by a notary and validated by the responsible Swiss representation abroad. Problems with this particular rule were most common in cases involving countries behind the Iron Curtain.[184]

Checking that these documents satisfactorily proved the claimant's identity was the responsibility of the banks' central legal departments or, in the case of SKA, the legal departments of larger branches (from 1987, for example, Basel, Geneva, Lugano).[185] With many of the requests concerning assets belonging to victims of National Socialism, entitlement could not be sufficiently proved because not all of the required documents were presented. If the claimant could prove his entitlement, SKA and SVB always researched the matter. If this research yielded no positive results, the banks produced a detailed report for the applicant and returned the documents.[186] If assets were found, these were paid out to the claimants. It could take a long time for assets to be paid out because producing all the documents was often a difficult and lengthy process, especially when the heirs of the Holocaust victims concerned lived behind the Iron Curtain. Often, the original documents simply were not available any more; so the work had to be done using death certificates issued by foreign courts declaring after the fact that people who had disappeared during the Second World War were dead as of 8 May 1945. The

banks insisted in principle that they receive an instruction from all the heirs before a payment could be made. In order to be able to make an advance payment to individual heirs despite this rule, SKA accepted letters of indemnity. The heirs receiving the payments would have to confirm that they were 'jointly and severally liable towards SKA for any losses that the bank could suffer as a result of this payment'.[187]

Case studies

In 4 documented cases, SKA carried out its own investigations. In one of these, the bank knew for certain that the customer was not a victim of National Socialism. The other 3 cases are described here. In 1946/47, SKA contacted various institutions on several occasions in an attempt to determine the fate of Mr. H. of Budapest, and in 1948 instructed a senior manager to investigate the matter locally. H. had been the manager of a mineral oil refinery. He held assets at SKA's head office and in 1930 had lodged a will with the bank for safekeeping. From 1944 onwards, his letters were retained in a customer dossier. SKA made several requests for information to the oil refinery's pensioners' association, which replied that it was dealing with the matter but that it was very difficult to carry out research at the current time. Within SKA it was decided that owing to the will, it was important to discover if Mr. H. was still alive, and if he was not, to find out who his heirs were and to whom the bank should talk about the will. The H. case was reported as part of the Bankers Association's 1956 survey, as well as in response to the Federal Decree of 1962 (a Category A case).[188] The internal sources do not allow us to reconstruct the further course of this case. At the end of the 1940s and at the beginning of the 1950s, an SKA senior manager traveled on numerous occasions to Germany in order to find the owners of dormant assets.[189] In another case, SKA Lugano contacted the ICRC in Geneva on 10 August 1949 about the fate of H. R. The ICRC immediately forwarded the bank's letter to the World Jewish Congress in London, which informed the SKA branch on 19 September 1949 that H. R. had been deported to Auschwitz on 19 August 1942.[190]

In 1973, SVB's executive board in Bern asked the FPD for help in finding out what had happened to S., a securities account holder from Lvov in Poland, or to any of his legal heirs. As a result, contact was successfully made with his son in Australia, to whom the money was paid out. The account holder himself had been deported by the Russians in 1940 and had not been heard from since.[191]

There is also evidence of similar efforts being made at Bank Leu, particularly in the files on the work done as a result of the Federal Decree of 1962. Bank Leu inquired at the Swiss embassy in Rome about a customer whose account had fallen dormant, though this research did not produce any positive results. As part of the investigations carried out when implementing the Bankers Association's 1995 survey, Bank Leu confirmed that it had not actively searched for any owners of dormant accounts since the Federal Decree of 1962.[192]

('Although' letter). On 29 August 1962, for example, SKA responded to an inquiry from M. F. regarding assets belonging to H. F.: '[...] although the documents which would prove the inheritance rights of M. F. are missing, as an exception and to avoid unnecessary inconvenience, we write to inform you that in 1944 our bank ... did not transfer any sums on the instructions of and/or in favor of Mr. H. F.'[193] In 68 of the 99 cases, SKA informed the claimant where it had conducted research, though it tended not to state specifically that it had also consulted the general registry. In 31 cases it gave no real details of where it had searched. The responses given were often vague ('no business relation with our institution' for example), or the letter would say that SKA had no commercial relationship with the person concerned. Various people were also told that depending on the case, no files or documents were available after a specific period of time (for example 10 years). In only 5 cases did SKA offer the claimants an extended search option. If foreign claimants could identify themselves satisfactorily and assets were found, the documents submitted would have to be certified by a notary and by the responsible Swiss representation in the claimant's country before a payment could be made. If, as was often the case where victims of National Socialism were involved, neither an official death certificate nor an heir's certificate could be produced, the bank would usually be satisfied with a death certificate issued by a local court (mostly stating that the person had 'died prior to 8 May 1945') and the inheritance papers. Payment was also conditional on all of the heirs identifying themselves to the bank and declaring themselves in agreement with the disposal of the assets. This caused problems especially when the heirs lived behind the Iron Curtain, but the banks insisted on the point nevertheless, so that they could be sure that assets would not have to be paid out twice. The practical solution to the problem was that the heirs appearing in person would sign a form discharging the bank from any obligations relating to claims from other heirs.

For the period between 1963 and 1973, 13 inquiries to SKA have been evaluated. In 8 of these cases, the person making the inquiry had given reasons for suspecting that the assets could be held at the bank. SKA always searched at head office and in the general registry. In 10 cases it informed the applicant where it had researched, but it did not offer a more extensive search. In other words, it proceeded as it had done during the period prior to the Federal Decree. Assets were identified in only one of the cases.

For the period between 1974 and 1994, 15 cases have been examined. In 13 of these, the people making the inquiries provided reasons for suspecting that the bank was holding the assets. SKA first carried out internal research without charging a fee. It called these searches, which included the general registry and all relevant departments at head office, 'small surveys' ('kleine Umfragen'). SKA always mentioned this search procedure in its letters of reply. In addition, an extended search at all branches in Switzerland was offered in all of these cases. Sometimes the person making the inquiry was given a list of all the branches together with a suggestion that they get in touch directly with the branches at which they thought the account might be held.

SKA's information practice: findings

Searches in SKA's general registry included all accounts held at head office as well as all name accounts and securities accounts held at branches in Switzerland. The searches also covered all numbered and pseudonym accounts at head office. Altogether, they thus accounted for 95% of all bank accounts.

In all 127 of the cases dealt with here, it is possible to tell from the registry cards whether correct information was given out or not. In all cases SKA answered the question of whether it held an account, securities account or safe deposit box at the time of the inquiry truthfully. In 28 cases there had been accounts, securities accounts or safe deposit boxes in the past, but they had been closed at some point between 1932 and 1944. However, this fact was not communicated to applicants who were not able to prove their identity satisfactorily. The information given out was correct, therefore, but incomplete and thus possibly misleading for the person receiving it: '[...] to inform you that we do not manage any accounts, securities accounts or safe deposit boxes in the name of [...].' In rather fewer cases, information such as the following was given: 'Dr. S. F. and Mrs. E. F. have not been in contact with our head office during the last five years', or 'we were not able to determine that we have managed any kind of assets in the name of Dr. S. in the last twenty years'.[194] In response to an inquiry from M. K., SKA answered on 15 June 1948 that it did not have an account in the name given. However, according to a handwritten note, there was in fact a safe deposit box, which the legal department had had blocked on 13 January 1948.[195] Finally, in some cases SKA answered that although there had been a bank account earlier, it no longer held any documentation about it dating from the period before or during the Second World War.[196]

In 1948, K. B. asked SKA for information about the account held at the bank by his father, A. B. of Vienna. He knew that this had been closed on 10 June 1939. SKA answered on 19 February 1948: '[...] that because of banking secrecy provisions, we are unable in principle to divulge information about business conducted with deceased persons during their lifetimes, even to an heir. We can possibly deviate from this principle in individual cases if all the heirs contact us and if sufficient grounds to provide such information can be asserted. This is conditional on these heirs proving their identity by means of official heirs' certificates. In addition, we need a death certificate for

Mr. A. B. [...] For your information, we can tell you that there are no assets held today at our head office in the name of Mr. A. B.'[197]

Correspondence between the SKA branch in Basel and the legal department during 1951 shows that – in accordance with general banking practice – heirs were only given information about the assets held at the bank in the deceased's name at the time of his death.[198] It was thought that providing any further information would mean infringing banking secrecy. The principles concerning the banks' obligation to provide information in inheritance cases were laid down in the Bankers Association's circular No. 87 D of 10 June 1955.[199]

The Bankers Association held further discussions about the content and scope of an heir's right to information from banks in 1966 when Zurich's Court of Appeal ordered that banks treat heirs and customers in exactly the same way when it came to providing information. The Bankers Association's legal commission set up a committee to reevaluate its previous practice.[200] The earlier circular no. 87 D was finally revised on 1 July 1974 (No. 295 D) and sent out to member banks. The rule was still that heirs should normally only be told about the assets that had been held at banks on the day of the customer's death, though as a pragmatic solution in special cases, information about the situation over the ten years preceding the customer's death could also be revealed.[201] SKA adopted this practice by 1974 at the latest. However, the first documentary evidence of this is a 1979 memorandum from the legal department that refers to this new standard procedure.[202]

Swiss Volksbank

SVB received its first inquiries about accounts possibly owned by the victims of the National Socialist regime in 1946. For the period between the end of the war and the 1962 Federal Decree, a total of 38 inquiries have been examined for this study. These were submitted either by surviving descendants and heirs or by parties they had mandated such as friends, lawyers or, in a small number of cases, diplomatic representations or Jewish organizations.[203] Family members looking for assets mostly relied on vague memories of what their deceased relatives had told them; they were thus rarely in a position to provide more information about the assets in question. Of the 38 applicants, 11 had reason to assume that the assets were being held at SVB rather than at any other bank in Switzerland. The legal department's files from 1956 – for the Zurich office – contained 9 cases in which the dependants of persecuted Jewish persons were looking for assets in Switzerland. According to the claimants, in 8 of these cases, the former owner had fallen victim to National Socialism. In one case, the owner had been able to escape via Switzerland to Spain, where he had died in 1950. In 3 of the 9 cases, the claimants were also able to say that the account was probably opened at a bank in Zurich, but more precise details were not available. In 36 cases, SVB Zurich carried out research in its general registry. This registry covered the main office itself, as well as other branches in Zurich.

Once the research had been completed, the legal office sent a standard letter in response to queries that did not provide sufficient proof of entitlement. This letter explained that banking information was normally only divulged if the person wanting the information presented written proof of entitlement (heirs' certificate and power of attorney, certified by the relevant Swiss representation abroad). If no assets had been found, SVB stated that it was making an exception in this case and confirmed that no assets were deposited under the given name. In 30 of these cases the bank also detailed the offices within the bank in which it had searched. In 4 cases no letter of reply can be found in the files today, in 4 others the bank did not say where it had searched. In 8 cases SVB offered an extended search. In cases where the person making the inquiry could present the required written proof of identity, every possible bank account was investigated with the help of internal control slips. However, the sources we have contain documentation on only 2 cases, which is why we cannot make any general comments on the bank's approach.

For the period between 1963 and 1973, 8 inquiries to SVB have been examined. In 4 cases the claimant provided reasons for supposing that assets could be held at SVB. By 1973, SVB had conducted research on at least 6, and probably all 8, of these cases; no assets were found. The bank sent out standardized replies, which pointed out that it 'often receives inquiries from people from Switzerland and abroad regarding the assets of actual or supposed clients' without being given the required evidence. The bank could not proceed without such documentary proof because it was determined to prevent any abuse. The strict formal requirements had to be met even if no assets were held at SVB. No reference was made, however, to the existence of the Claims Registry. The SVB thus deviated from its previous practice by refusing to give even negative information. In 3 cases, no reply can be found in the files. In one case, in which the claimant was able to provide more precise details about the assets concerned, the research went back no further than 1950. The bank offered to search in the archived files for a fee of Sfr 100. From 1973, SVB carried out searches in all branches in Switzerland against a fee of Sfr 200.[204]

For the period between 1974 and 1994, 27 cases have been examined. In only 4 did claimants provide grounds for their supposition that the assets in question could be at SVB. By 1994, a free survey had been carried out in individual branches in 6 cases. In the other cases, the bank offered the claimant the opportunity to pay for a search in Switzerland as a whole or in specific regions of the country. The Swiss-wide search cost Sfr 250 (1974), Sfr 500 (from 1977) or Sfr 700 (from 1986). In 6 cases the claimants were prepared to pay these fees, leading in 5 of them to a Swiss-wide survey and in one to a search of all major branches. In the case of J. K.-Z., where the claimant wrote back to say that she could not afford to pay a fee of Sfr 500, SVB proposed that it search for free at head office (Bern) and at two major branches (Zurich and Geneva for example) provided that the applicant could produce an heir's certificate. As far as we can tell, the correspondence broke off at this point.[205] In the case of A. S., though assets were found there was a problem with proving succession. SVB took an accommodating approach and accepted an affidavit from the Australian authorities in place of the death certificate and heirs' certificate.[206]

Bank Leu

No documentation on inquiries to Bank Leu from the period 1946–1962 survives, but 6 cases from the period 1963–1973 have been analyzed. In most cases the bank referred the claimant to the Claims Registry for Assets Belonging to Missing Foreigners in Bern without actually conducting any research of its own.[207] A collection of documents on the Federal Decree includes 4 standardized letters of this type. In another 2 documented cases of inquiries from outside Switzerland no such standardized letter was sent. In these cases, Bank Leu informed the inquirers that its research had proved fruitless and that they should contact the Claims Registry.

In only one case from the years between 1974 and 1994 is there any evidence that Bank Leu referred to the expired Federal Decree.

Fees charged for inquiries

The sources do not provide a complete picture of the approach taken by the three banks to charging fees. All we can do, therefore, is surmise the general trend.

SKA and SVB tended to carry out searches at head office free of charge. After about 1970, searches at Zurich branches were also carried at no cost – or so some cases at SKA would suggest. In 1947, SKA was only charging a fee of Sfr 10 for such a search. By agreement with other Swiss banks, SKA increased the fee for a search at all branches in Switzerland from Sfr 300 in the 1960s (approximately 50 branches) to Sfr 500 in the 1970s (approximately 120 branches). At the beginning of the 1980s (approximately 180 branches) the fee was Sfr 1,000, which was increased to Sfr 2,000 in around 1990 (approximately 200 branches). However, these charges were never high enough to cover actual costs. Fees at SVB were somewhat lower, but tended to follow developments at SKA.[208]

4.3 Problems with inquiries from Communist Eastern Europe

During the Cold War years, some Eastern European states tried to appropriate their citizen's assets by sending instructions to the Swiss banks that they had either forced the genuine customer to issue, or that were entirely falsified. The caution with which the banks and the Bankers Association approached such documents appears understandable, even from today's perspective. The following example illustrates the problem:

SVB managed a Swiss franc account in the name of its customer M. J., who lived in Bucharest.[209] In February 1947, SVB received a letter from her in which she ordered that no instruction issued by her in future should be accepted, unless the correspondence she sent also included a special sign. On 2 November 1948, a letter from M. J. that had been sent via SBG reached SVB. In it she asked that all of her assets be credited to the Romanian national bank's account at SBG. However, this letter did not contain the sign agreed in 1947, so SVB refused to make the payment. However, it wanted to be sure that M. J. had not simply forgotten to add the sign, so the bank wrote to her on 26 November 1948, overtly to check on her address, but covertly to check whether her subsequent letter would include the sign – the bank inserted the sign inconspicuously in pencil in the margin of its own letter. On 28 December 1949, SVB received another letter – again via SBG – apparently sent by M. J., but once again without the agreed sign. Again SVB told SBG that it was not in a position to carry out the instruction. On 13 April 1950, an unsigned letter arrived at SVB from Haifa in Israel asking the bank not to report the existence of the account to the Romanian authorities under any circumstances. Shortly thereafter, an Israeli student informed SVB that M. J. now lived in Israel. M. J. confirmed her new place of residence in a letter that reached SVB in January 1951. The Romanian National Bank wrote further letters on 26 March 1951, 9 May 1951 and finally on 6 October 1951. In September 1952, M. J. then spoke personally to SVB and explained that she had only signed the letters under duress from the Romanian central bank.

Similar incidents occurred in 1960. On 19 September 1960, SVB asked the Bankers Association for a ruling on such incidents. The Association replied that it was currently clarifying the matter with the FPD, though it also noted that in such cases SKA required the customer concerned personally to have his or her instruction certified by the responsible Swiss embassy.[210] In some cases SKA contacted the embassy locally in order to gather more information about the asset owner's situation. On 22 August 1960, the FPD wrote back and referred to a case involving Romania in which it had felt itself unable to clarify whether the person concerned had acted under duress or not. Later on, in its letter of 14 November 1960, the FPD informed the Bankers Association about the problems faced by the embassy in Bucharest. Many of the Romanians who asked the embassy to validate their payment instructions had made it clear to the embassy personnel that they were acting under pressure from the government. Nevertheless, the embassy had to validate the documents for fear of the extremely serious consequences for these people if they did not do so.[211]

Unlike the FPD, the Bankers Association thought that Swiss embassies in Eastern Bloc countries could do something to solve the problem, and that they could at any rate check the credibility of what the customers were saying. The Bankers Association also believed that it would be beneficial if one or more cases could be taken through to the Federal Supreme Court so that a ruling could be made by the highest legal authority, on which the banks could in future base their treatment of instructions received from customers in totalitarian states, and to which they could refer in the event that someone should file a claim for compensation against them. Before that, however, everything possible should be done to determine whether the payment was really what the customer wanted. On 7 November 1960, the decisions reached at a meeting between the Bankers Association, SKA, SVB, ZKB, SBG and SBV were sent to the executive boards of the member banks in a confidential circular.[212] This advised the banks not to carry out payment instructions from customers in totalitarian states if there were any indications that these instructions were signed under duress. However, the banks would have to accept that in individual cases complaints from the totalitarian governments could lead Swiss courts to order that the payments be made.

On 10 November 1960, SKA sent a strictly confidential letter to the management and administrative departments of its branches in Switzerland informing them that in recent months an increasing number of instructions had been received from clients behind the Iron Curtain, especially Romania. These instructions always requested that existing accounts be closed and the assets transferred to the account of a Romanian bank. With safe deposit boxes, an employee of the relevant embassy in Bern would normally call directly on the bank armed with a power of attorney. The assumption was that most of these instructions had been issued under duress. Unless it was possible to make personal contact with the customers in advance, therefore, carrying out the payments would leave the banks open to later claims for compensation from either the customers themselves or their heirs. The greatest caution should thus be exercised in such cases, and the legal department had to be informed immediately.[213]

As part of the implementation of the Federal Decree of 1962, SKA explained its approach to this problem in a letter dated 31 October 1968 to the guardianship office of the City of Zurich: 'As a rule we will not act in response to a written request from these countries – because most of these requests are monitored, or even forced out of the customer – but will insist that the person concerned actually be present in Switzerland.'[214] However, in a few cases, SKA did manage to make contact with customers domiciled in Eastern Europe.[215]

5 Sources

It has been difficult to identify meaningful sources at the business policy-making level relating to dormant accounts – partly because the banks' boards of directors and executive boards only rarely discussed the issue of dormant accounts, and partly because discussions that did relate to dormant accounts were not minuted. It should be noted that the Swiss banks are legally obliged to keep files for only ten years. Owing to these circumstances, it is not easy to reconstruct the decision-making processes applied by each bank in individual dormant account cases. Asset searches are better documented because the correspondence carried out by the legal departments has often been kept.

Quality of sources

Alongside the sources found in CSG's Central Corporate Archives (CCA), analysis for this study focused mainly on sources in the archives of the Swiss Bankers Association (SBA Archives), and in individual cases on those in the Swiss Federal Archives (BAR). The quality of sources for the CSG banks analyzed in this study was as follows:

- SKA: Most documents come from the legal department's files. There are only a few references in the company's directives and in the minutes of the board of directors and executive board that touch on the period immediately after the war or the time after the Federal Decree of 1962 had been implemented. Documentation on the Bankers Association's 1947 survey is also sketchy. However, there is an extensive collection of sources relating to the implementation of the 1962 Federal Decree and to the Swiss-Polish Agreement of 1949. The 'Asset investigations' chapter is based mainly on documents held by the legal department.
- SVB: The situation is the same as at SKA, except that no material is available on the implementation of the Swiss-Polish compensation agreement of 1949. The 'Asset investigations' chapter uses the general correspondence kept by the legal department of SVB's Zurich-Bahnhofstrasse branch since 1946. Since 1964, the SVB executive board in Bern has maintained an 'asset investigations' file.
- Bank Leu: In volume terms, there is little material available. The legal department's two dossiers 'Ownerless Assets' and 'Heirless Property' are important sources. There are very few references to discussions about dormant accounts in the minutes of the board of directors and the executive board. The 'Asset investigations' chapter is influenced by the fact that the legal department's general correspondence from the years between 1946 and 1964 has not survived. A collection

of documents on the 1962 Federal Decree includes some cases involving foreigners looking for assets in Switzerland. Only one such inquiry, dating from 1985, survives from the period after the Federal Decree expired. In order to find cases of successful asset searches, five boxes of files were taken at random from the 'Estates' documentation, but no such examples were found. Owing to this paucity of sources, no representative sample could be assembled.

The other sources used for this study can be commented upon as follows:

- SBA Archives, Basel: The general political analysis of the run-up to the Federal Decree of 1962 is based primarily on sources from the Bankers Association, and especially on the minutes of meetings held by its board of directors and by its legal committee. These minutes sometimes also provide an insight into the attitude of managers at the CSG banks, which is barely documented elsewhere. The Bankers Association Archives are useful for information on the various surveys conducted by the Association, as well as the political and legal discussions and analysis relating to the dormant accounts issue. The Archives also provide useful documentation for the 4th chapter on the Bankers Association's approach to asset investigations, because up to the 1962 Federal Decree, the Bankers Association responded to inquiries by conducting regular surveys of the banks.

- BAR, Bern: Sources from Switzerland's Federal Archives were used to reconstruct the discussions between the federal authorities and the Bankers Association in the post-war period, the implementation of the Swiss-Polish Agreement of 1949, and the work of the Claims Registry within the context of the Federal Decree of 1962. They were also helpful for cross-checking information from CSG's Central Corporate Archives and from the Bankers Association.

A full list of the literature used in this study is given in the bibliography at the end of this book, p. 236. A complete list of documents used can be found in the original German edition 'Zwischen Bundeshaus und Paradeplatz. Die Banken der Credit Suisse Group im Zweiten Weltkrieg' by Joseph Jung.

6 Notes

1 Memorandum of 17 July 1939. CCA.

2 Cf. AR SKA, 1936, p. 3.

3 CCA.

4 CCA.

5 Cf. regulations on payments to deposit books B, 1931. CCA.

6 CCA. On 13 June 1964, for example, the rightful claimant to an account containing Sfr 4.30 that had been booked out to the 'commissions account' on 9 April 1925 made contact. The CSG banks found that this experience of customers contacting SKA 25 or 30 years after they were last heard from was repeated following the Registration Decree of 1962.

7 Cf. memorandum of 17 July 1939. CCA.

8 Cf. circular No. 62 to the branches dated 22 May 1939; circular No. 47 to the branches dated 18 April 1940 and instruction No. 528 on the assets of unknown customers dated 3 May 1940. CCA.

9 Cf. Picard, Schweiz, p. 279.

10 DDS, Vol. 16, No. 75, p. 233, Note 2. This assurance was part of the Washington Agreement. Cf. report on the legal status of so-called 'ownerless' assets in Switzerland. CCA; Hug/Perrenoud, Assets, p. 6.

11 Cf. Picard, Schweiz, p. 284f.

12 Hug/Perrenoud, Assets, p. 57. Cf. SBA's 'Nachrichtenlose Vermögen' ('dormant accounts') chronology. CCA.

13 SKA directive W-1134 on the treatment of dormant accounts (all customer segments), 31 May 1996. CCA. SKA based its definition on the 'Richtlinien der Schweizerischen Bankiervereinigung über die Behandlung nachrichtenloser Konten, Depots und Schrankfächer bei Schweizer Banken' ('Swiss Bankers Association's guidelines on the treatment of dormant accounts, securities accounts and safe deposit boxes at Swiss banks') of 8 September 1995. CCA.

14 CSG directive W-0020 on dormant accounts, investigations into assets and documentation on closed customer accounts, 1 July 2000. CCA.

15 Cf. Girsberger, Privatrecht, p. 6.

16 Cf. ICEP, Report, Appendix R, A-116.

17 Cf. Arthur Andersen, Report, p. 79.

18 Ibid.

19 Cf. ICEP, Report, Annex 4, p. 74, Table 19; Junz, Report, A-129. ICEP assumes that 21.8% of Jews in France were killed. Helen Junz assumes 25%.

20 Cf. Statistics in www.crt.ch/frame.html (September 2001); Arthur Andersen, Report, Part J, p. 367.

21 Cf. Junz, Report, p. A-129 and A-188ff. ICEP Report, Annex 4, p. 74, table 19, states that 2.7 million Jews were killed (81.8%).

22 Cf. ICEP, Report, Appendix R, A-111, A-116, and Arthur Andersen, Report, p. 79. At Sfr 4.248 million, SKA's off-balance-sheet liabilities were not insignificant. Between 1937 and 1939 the Swiss banks' on-balance-sheet liabilities towards Polish customers fell from Sfr 19.3 to Sfr 5 million.

23 ICEP, Report, Annex 4, p. 70, table 16.

24 Cf. Hug/Perrenoud, Assets, p. 8, 10.

25 Cf. Arthur Andersen, Report, Part J, p. 367.

26 SVB circular No. 186 on 'ownerless assets', 19 September 1947. CCA.

27 Cf. minutes of the SBA board of directors, 23 April 1952. SBA archives; Hug/Perrenoud, Assets, p. 6.

The assets were blocked at that time by the SCO. The relevant decree was only revoked as part of the London Debt Agreement of 1952.

28 Cf. minutes of the LC SBA, 11 November 1947. SBA archives.

29 Cf. SBA's 'Nachrichtenlose Vermögen' chronology. CCA.

30 Cf. Picard, Schweiz, p. 280.

31 Cf. minutes of the discussions between the FPD, the SBA and the SFJC, 17 November 1952. BAR, E 4110 (A) 1973/85, Vol. 1.

32 SFJC's 'Bericht über die in der Schweiz befindlichen erblosen Vermögen der Opfer politischer, religiöser oder rassischer Verfolgung' ('Report on assets in Switzerland belonging to victims of racial, religious or political persecution'), copy of 12 December 1952, p. 3. CCA.

33 Cf. Hug/Perrenoud, Assets, p. 89; 'The Commission on Jewish Assets in Sweden at the Time of the Second World War' (final report), 1999.

34 Cf. Picard, Schweiz, p. 282.

35 Cf. 'Bericht über die in der Schweiz befindlichen erblosen Vermögen der Opfer politischer, religiöser oder rassischer Verfolgung' by the SFJC, copy of 12 December 1952. CCA; minutes of the SBA board of directors, 22 December 1952; minutes of the FDJP's negotiations with the SBA and the SFJC, 8 March 1954. BAR, E 4110 (A) 1973/85, Vol. 1.

36 Cf. Guggenheim/Schnitzer expert opinion, 31 August 1953. BAR, E 4110 (A) 1973/85, Vol. 1.

37 Cf. letter from the SFJC to Federal Councilor Feldmann, 23 July 1954. BAR, E 4110 (A) 1973/85, Vol. 1. Guggenheim, Erblose Vermögen.

38 Cf. minutes of the FDJP's negotiations with the SBA and the SFJC, 8 March 1954. BAR, E 4110 (A) 1973/85, Vol. 1.

39 Letter from the SFJC to Federal Councilor Feldmann, 23 July 1954. BAR, E 4110 (A) 1973/85, Vol. 1.

40 The SBA's arguments are detailed in the minutes of the discussions between the FPD, the SBA and the SFJC, 17 November 1952. BAR, E 4110 (A) 1973/85, Vol. 1; minutes of the SBA board of directors, 23 April 1952 and 22 December 1952. Minutes of the LC SBA, 7 May 1954. SBA archives. Cf. draft circular from the SBA to the management of its member banks on 'heirless assets', 10 November 1952. CCA; Bolla/Niederer expert opinion of May 1953. BAR, E 4110 (A) 1973/85, Vol. 1.

41 Minutes of the SBA board of directors, 23 April 1952. Cf. minutes of the LC SBA, 26 November 1951. SBA archives.

42 Cf. Bolla/Niederer expert opinion of May 1953. BAR, E 4110 (A) 1973/85, Vol. 1.

43 Bolla/Niederer expert opinion of May 1953. BAR, E 4110 (A) 1973/85, Vol. 1, p. 22, 24, 27f. – On 12 December 1952, the SBA wrote to members of its board of directors: 'Prescription of genuinely ownerless assets by the Swiss depository banks is not possible, because from the time assets that subsequently become ownerless are given to them, the banks keep these assets in their custody or in their safes as dependent holders – not as owners. Neither would such prescription be in good faith.' CCA. – 'Prescription' ('Ersitzung') is a process under Swiss law whereby ownership of chattel passes to a party that has enjoyed visible and bona fide possession of it for five years.

44 Cf. Hug/Perrenoud, Assets, p. 94f., 96ff., 100ff.

45 Cf. SBA's 'Nachrichtenlose Vermögen' chronology. CCA.

46 NZZ, 7 March 1950.

47 Cf. Hug/Perrenoud, Assets, p. 93–105.

48 For more information on the figures used in the table 'Results of the Swiss Bankers Association's surveys of Polish dormant accounts (1949–1958); payment to the Polish national bank (1960)' cf. FPD letter to SCO, 17 October 1960, and internal FPD letter of 17 October 1960. BAR, E 7160-09 1969/109, Vol. 1116; FPD letter to Minister Gygax, 14 January 1958. BAR, E 2001 (E) 1987/78, Vol. 156; folder 793: Gutgläubige Erwerbungen, Raubgut, Survey Polen III, 1949–1953. SBA archives; Erblose polnische Vermögenswerte. CCA. – No figures are given in the literature for the year 1949. Cf. the reference to 'a total sum of something over 1 million francs' in the SBA's letter of 10 February 1950 to board members, attachment to minutes of the SBA board of directors, 22 February 1950, p. 2. SBA archives. – Switzerland had initially suggested to Poland that the sum could be about Sfr 2 million. Cf.

Peter Hug, 'Verhandlungspoker um nachrichtenlose Vermögen. Schweizerisch-polnischer Briefwechsel kein Einzelfall' ('Haggling over Dormant Accounts. Swiss-Polish Exchange of Letters not a One-Off'), in: NZZ, 23 October 1996.

49 Memorandum from M. Oetterli, 'Über Sitzung mit dem EPD betr. Polen-Abkommen über erblose Vermögen vom 3.5.1955' ('On a meeting with the FPD re: Polish Agreement about heirless assets, 3 May 1955'). CCA.

50 Cf. Hug/Perrenoud, Assets, p. 3f.; SCO letter to FPD, 20 October 1960. BAR, E 7160-09 1969/109, Vol. 1116.

51 Cf. Federal Council statement to parliament on a draft federal decree about assets in Switzerland belonging to foreigners or stateless persons who had been subject to racial, religious or political persecution, 4 May 1962. BBl, 114. (1962), p. 933–944.

52 Cf. ibid.

53 Memorandum by the SKA legal department, 13 November 1967. CCA; memorandum of 7 July 1976. CCA.

54 Cf. minutes of the Bank Leu management conference, 5 June 1956; letter from the SBA to Federal Councilor Feldmann, 24 September 1956. BAR, 4110 (A) 1973/85, Vol. 1.

55 All information based on: folder on heirless assets, circular 96 D, 20 July 1956. SBA archives; SBA inquiry about dormant accounts commissioned by the FDJP, 20 July 1956. CCA.

56 SKA's response to the SBA survey 'Betr. Enquête über sog. "erblose" Vermögenswerte' ('Re: investigation into so-called "heirless" assets'), 29 August 1956. CCA.

57 Cf. folder on heirless assets, circular 96 D, 20 July 1956. SBA archives. No dormant assets were registered by Allgemeine Aargauische Ersparniskasse, Gewerbekasse Baden, Aargauische Hypothekenbank, Heusser & Cie., SBKA, Affida Verwaltungsbank or Bank Hofmann AG.

58 Cf. letter from the SBA to Federal Councilor Feldmann, 24 September 1956. BAR, 4110 (A) 1973/85, Vol. 1. Owing to this result, the FDJP, unlike the FPD, did not want to pursue the issue of special legislation any further. Cf. minutes of the LC SBA, 20 March 1958. SBA archives.

59 Letter from Fides on 19 August 1939 to Leo Gerstle. CCA.

60 Minutes of the SBA board of directors, 22 December 1952. SBA archives.

61 Cf. minutes of the SBA board of directors, 22 December 1952. SBA archives.

62 Cf. Hug/Perrenoud, Assets, p. 59f.

63 Ibid., p. 61.

64 Cf. copy of the first draft of 3 December 1957, in: minutes of the SBA board of directors, 3 December 1958. SBA archives.

65 Cf. Hug/Perrenoud, Assets, p. 62; minutes of the SBA board of directors, 18 March 1959. SBA archives. On 18 March 1959, the motion submitted by National Councilor Huber was accepted in the form of a postulate.

66 Cf. Hug/Perrenoud, Assets, p. 62.

67 Cf. ibid., p. 63f., Notes 239, 241, 243.

68 Schweizerische Handels-Zeitung, 26 July 1962.

69 Schweizerische Handels-Zeitung, 20 September 1962.

70 Cf. Hug/Perrenoud, Assets, p. 63ff.

71 Adolf Eichmann: SS Lieutenant-Colonel and head of the Jewish Affairs Department of the Reich Main Security Office in Berlin. He was able to escape unidentified from an American internment camp in 1946 and emigrate with his family to Argentina, where he was tracked down by the Israeli secret service. He was abducted to Israel and put on trial. On 11 December 1961, he was sentenced to death, and then executed in Ramleh on 31 May 1962.

72 Cf. minutes of the SBA board of directors, 6 October 1961. SBA archives; SBA to Federal Councilor Wahlen, 11 April 1959, enclosure to the letter from the SBA to members of its board of directors and legal commission, 13 April 1959. SBA archives.

73 Cf. minutes of the LC SBA, 5 February 1962. SBA archives.

74 Cf. Hug/Perrenoud, Assets, p. 65f.

75 Federal Decree on Assets in Switzerland Belonging to Foreign or Stateless Victims of Political, Racist or

Religious Persecution of 20 December 1962. Art. 3 stipulated that compulsory reporting extended to: 'a) natural persons and legal entities, trading companies and partnerships that managed, had possession of, held in custody or controlled such assets; b) official bodies that knew of such assets; c) debtors of claims owed to a person named in Art. 1.' AS 1963, Vol. 1963, p. 427–432.

76 Cf. ibid., Art. 1; Implementary Ordinance to the Federal Decree, 10 June 1963, Art. 11. AS 1963, Vol. 1963, p. 433–435.

77 SBA circular No. 3117 to member banks, 27 August 1963. CCA.

78 Cf. memorandum from SKA's legal department on 'Assets of missing foreigners', 28 November 1963. CCA, dossier 'Allgemeine Unterlagen im Zusammenhang mit der Anmeldung' ('General documents connected with registration'); Bank Leu memoranda on discussions about heirless assets, 28 November 1963 and 23 January 1964. CCA.

79 Cf. SVB circular No. 212/V-5001, 29 November 1963. CCA. The three CSG major banks, SKA, SVB and Bank Leu, generally complied with this principle. In exceptional cases SKA, for example, debited a higher amount against the registered account for additional costs incurred. The maximum amount – charged in the case concerning O. B. – came to around Sfr 300. 'Commission revenues' at SKA came to a total of Sfr 23,000 by the start of 1964. CCA.

80 Cf. Circular from SKA's legal department about assets in Switzerland belonging to missing foreigners, 11 July 1963. CCA, dossier 'Allgemeine Unterlagen im Zusammenhang mit der Anmeldung'.

81 Cf. memorandum from the SKA legal department about 'Assets of missing foreigners', 31 December 1963. CCA, dossier 'Allgemeine Unterlagen im Zusammenhang mit der Anmeldung'.

82 See documentation on 'Vermögen verschwundener Ausländer' ('Assets belonging to missing foreigners') for cases not reported to Bern. CCA.

83 On 20 December 1963, the institution in Paris stated that it was not responsible. On 16 January 1964, Yad Vashem wrote back to say that no information was available on these cases. CCA.

84 Cf. memorandum from the SKA legal department about 'Assets of missing foreigners', 31 December 1963. CCA, dossier 'Allgemeine Unterlagen im Zusammenhang mit der Anmeldung'.

85 Cf. SKA's letter to the FDJP, 28 February 1964. CCA, dossier 'Allgemeine Korrespondenz mit der Meldestelle' ('General correspondence with the Claims Registry').

86 For more information on the figures used in the table 'SKA: registration of dormant accounts belonging to victims of the Nazi regime (1964)' cf. SKA's registration of 'Assets belonging to missing foreigners'. CCA, dossier 'Allgemeine Korrespondenz mit der Meldestelle'.

87 SKA's letter to the FDJP, 28 February 1964. CCA, dossier 'Allgemeine Korrespondenz mit der Meldestelle'.

88 Claims Registry for Assets Belonging to Missing Foreigners to SKA Zurich, 23 June 1967. CCA.

89 Cf. documentation 'Vermögen verschwundener Ausländer; Nichtanmeldungen Filialen' ('Assets belonging to missing foreigners; non-registrations, branches') and documentation 'Vermögen verschwundener Ausländer; Nichtanmeldungen Hauptsitz' ('Assets belonging to missing foreigners; non-registrations, head office'). CCA.

90 Cf. minutes of the meeting of 8 November 1963 on the registration of assets belonging to missing foreigners. CCA, dossier 'Allgemeine Korrespondenz mit den SKA-Filialen' ('General correspondence with SKA branches').

91 In individual cases, however, SKA's decision not to report uncertain cases was proved correct. Cf. for example the case of J. B. CCA.

92 Cf. CCA.

93 Memorandum from SVB legal department, 25 August 1962. CCA.

94 Cf. Circular No. 178/V-5001 from the SVB executive board, 4 October 1963. CCA.

95 Cf. SVB directives of 1953, 1974 and 1977 on transfers of assets to collective and revenue accounts. CCA.

96 A revenue account is an account to which amounts are booked in the bank's favor.

97 Circular No. 54/IV-4011, 24 March 1953. CCA.

98 Arthur Andersen, Interim Report, p. 66 and Appendix B/6/3-5.

99 Cf. CCA. This case has since been resolved and the assets paid to the heirs.

100 Cf. directives Nos. 311 AJ and 230 AK, 11 June 1974. CCA.

101 Cf. directive No. 511 AQ, 19 July 1977. CCA.

102 Cf. SVB circular No. 212/V-5001, 29 November 1963. CCA.

103 Cf. CCA.

104 The 22 accounts reported by SVB comprised 7 deposit books, 10 savings books, 4 current accounts and one custody account containing gold coins. CCA.

105 Cf. memorandum from the SVB executive board, 1 November 1968. CCA; SVB executive board to the Claims Registry, 26 Feb. 1964. CCA; list of assets belonging to missing foreigners, 28 Feb. 1964. CCA.

106 Cf. Legal department announcement No. 21, 4 September 1963, on the Federal Decree of 20 December 1962. CCA.

107 Cf. memorandum, 29 November 1963, and various letters. CCA.

108 Cf. the three lists 'Vermögen rassisch, religiös oder politisch verfolgter Ausländer' ('Assets belonging to foreigners persecuted for reasons of race, religion or politics'), one list from 2 February 1965 and two undated lists. CCA.

109 Cf. letter from Bank Leu's legal department to the Claims Registry, 26 February 1964. CCA.

110 By 29 February 1964 the banks had reported Sfr 6,069,123, the SCO Sfr 2,471,900, fiduciary companies and private individuals Sfr 670,053, and insurance companies Sfr 259,805. Cf. Picard, Schweiz, p. 316.

111 The banks transferred Sfr 15,498.10, and the insurance companies Sfr 849 to the Polish central bank's 'N' account at the SNB. Cf. Hug/Perrenoud, Assets, p. 4f., 8f.

112 Cf. 'Meldung 1962' ('Registration 1962') list, 16 April 1998. CCA; 'Bank Leu 1962' list. CCA.

113 Cf. Hug/Perrenoud, Assets, p. 79ff., 91.

114 For more information on the figures used in the table 'Treatment of registered dormant accounts by SKA, SVB and Bank Leu (1964–1980)' cf. 'Meldung 1962' list, 16 April 1998. CCA; 'Bank Leu 1962' list. CCA; Hug/Perrenoud, Assets, p. 77–80.

115 Cf. CCA, dossier 'Allgemeine Korrespondenz mit dem Generalbeistand' ('General correspondence with the General Custodial Trustee').

116 Cf. circular of August 1967; SKA's letter to the General Custodial Trustee, 4 September 1967. CCA, dossier 'Allgemeine Korrespondenz mit dem Generalbeistand'. Also a table on 'Interest on SKA deposit books and investment books for foreign customers domiciled abroad' (1938–1967).

117 Cf. General Custodial Trustees letter to SKA, 10 November 1967. SKA confirmed that the requested action had been set in train in a letter to the General Custodial Trustee, 30 November 1967. CCA, dossier 'Allgemeine Korrespondenz mit dem Generalbeistand'.

118 For more information on the cooperation between the Claims Registry, the General Custodial Trustee and the guardianship authorities, cf. Picard, Schweiz, p. 302–305.

119 Cf. CCA.

120 Cf. Hug/Perrenoud, Assets, p. 80.

121 The FDFA first gave the names of the asset owners to the Polish ambassador on 17 January 1997 in the form of a list, which did not, however, contain the name of the asset custodian. The list contained the names of entitled claimants who had lived in Poland prior to 1 September 1939. FDFA Task Force to CSG, 13 May 1997. CCA.

122 Cf. Hug/Perrenoud, Assets, p. 10, 88ff.; Picard, Schweiz, p. 316ff.

123 Cf. Documentation from the Gesellschaft zur Förderung der schweizerischen Wirtschaft No. 8, 23 February 1998. CCA. For example, ex-National Councilor Andreas Gerwig and ex-Federal Councilor Kurt Furgler, acting on behalf of the Jewish Agency, tried in vain to establish a foundation into which the assets concerned could be paid.

124 Beforehand, several newspaper articles appeared in Switzerland and abroad on the subject of 'ownerless assets' at the Swiss banks, though the connection to the Second World War was not always a central point. In the 'Sonntags-Zeitung' of 11 September 1994, for example, an article by Beat Balzli said 'the banks are sitting on billions, but nobody knows about it. Tax-free black money from abroad is gathering dust in the accounts – the heirs are stumbling around in the dark.' Cf. also Weill, Milliarden-Deal, p. 18.

125 In the meantime, on 5 March 1995 Beat Balzli had written an article in the 'Sonntags-Zeitung' based on a study by Jacques Picard that had been financed by the Jewish Agency. The article 'Vermögen von Nazi-Opfern auf Schweizer Banken' ('Assets Belonging to Victims of the Nazis at Swiss Banks') referred to apparently 'serious deficiencies' in the handling of Holocaust victim's accounts. Cf. Weill, Milliarden-Deal, p. 17f.; Speich, Schweiz, p. 233ff.

126 Levin, the author, stated that in 1946 the Swiss government had undertaken to pay Sfr 285 million (95% of Sfr 300 million) for the rehabilitation of Jewish victims. Levin took this figure of Sfr 300 million – apparently to be financed from heirless assets – from an information sheet published by the Swiss Central Office for Refugee Assistance that provided an overview of the Washington Agreement of May 1946. This stated that Switzerland had undertaken to pay Sfr 250 million to settle the Nazi gold issue as a downpayment on the agreed liquidation of German assets in Switzerland. Levin extrapolated from the – erroneous sum of – Sfr 285 million, allowing for compound interest and inflation, to arrive at $ 6.4 billion, or Sfr 7.7 billion, whereas the Claims Resolution Tribunal used a factor of 10 to arrive at Sfr 2.85 billion. The mistakes made in Levin's research were detailed by Shraga Elam in his article in 'Cash' on 29 November 1996, 'Am Anfang stand die Ente' ('In the Beginning Was the Canard'). Cf. also Shraga Elam, 'Abgekartetes Spiel um Milliarden' ('Rigged Game for Billions'), Cash, 27 March 1998, which discusses a book written by Levin in Hebrew, in which he criticizes the attitude of US Jewish organizations towards the Swiss banks.

127 Of the Sfr 40.9 million, Sfr 6.8 million was attributable to clients domiciled in Eastern Europe, Sfr 6.1 million to customers in Switzerland, and Sfr 2.3 million to customers in Germany and Austria. Cf. SBA's report 'Nachrichtenlose Vermögenswerte bei Schweizer Banken' ('Dormant Accounts at Swiss Banks'), Appendix 4: interim results from the survey of 30 June 1995 on dormant accounts, documentation; SBA press release, 8 September 1995, Interim results from the survey of 30 June 1995 on dormant accounts. CCA; Beat Brenner, 'Was tun mit nachrichtenlosen Vermögen. Neue Richtlinien der Schweizerischen Bankiervereinigung' ('What to do with Dormant Accounts. New Guidelines from the Swiss Bankers Association'), in: NZZ, 13 September 1995.

128 Cf. circular No. 1193 D from the SBA, 12 September 1995, 'An die Direktionen der Mitgliedbanken: Richtlinien (Standesregeln) über die Behandlung nachrichtenloser Konti, Depots and Schrankfächer bei Schweizer Banken' ('To the management of the member banks: guidelines (code of conduct) on the treatment of dormant accounts, securities accounts and safe deposit boxes at Swiss banks'). CCA.

129 Cf. letter from the SBA to members of the board of directors' committee, 12 December 1995, re: contact office for tracing dormant accounts – fees. CCA.

130 Cf. minutes of the SBA board of directors, 28 September 1995. SBA archives.

131 Preliminary report by the SBA board of directors, 31 January 1996, minutes of the SBA board of directors 1996, SBA press conference of 7 February 1996 with commentary on dormant accounts from the period before 1945, folder 'Nachrichtenlose Vermögen' ('Dormant accounts'). SBA archives.

132 Memorandum from the legal department. CCA.

133 Cf. legal department's letter to the press office of 2 March 1995 on 'Sonntags-Zeitung's' inquiries about 'money belonging to victims of the Nazis'. CCA.

134 Cf. SKA's letter to the SBA of 10 August 1995 re: dormant accounts. CCA.

135 A total of 108 parliamentary actions on the subject of Switzerland in the Second World War had been submitted by the 2000 summer session. Cf. www.parlament.ch/poly/Framesets/D/Frame-D.htm (September 2001).
The following actions dealt with the 'dormant accounts' issue: ordinary question by Otto Piller, 'Ownerless' assets (94.1147); ordinary question by Jean Ziegler, Assets of Holocaust victims at Swiss banks (95.1021); parliamentary initiative by Verena Grendelmeier, Ownerless assets of victims of National Socialist persecution (95.407); motion by Otto Piller, Ownerless assets at Swiss banks (95.3257); ordinary question by Jean Ziegler, Jewish bank accounts. Destroyed documents (96.1018); parliamentary initiative by the National Council's Commission for Legal Affairs, Dormant accounts (96.434); postulate by the National Council's Commission for Legal Affairs (96.434) Minority Grendelmeier, Report on the treatment of individual claims to dormant Jewish assets (96.3376); ordinary question by Paul Rechsteiner, Document destruction in the Federal Police Department (96.1122); ordinary question by

Jean-Nils de Dardel, Holocaust assets. Financial gesture? (96.1145); postulate by Lili Nabholz, Dormant accounts (96.3574); interpellation by Peter Hess, Dormant accounts. Extension of investigations (96.3587); motion by Paul Rechsteiner, Dormant accounts. Compulsory reporting (96.3606); motion by Gian-Reto Plattner, Dormant accounts (96.3610); motion by the Radical Democrats, Dormant accounts; creating a fund (96.3611); motion by Jean Ziegler, Investigating committee on dormant accounts; extending the mandate (96.3680); motion by Paul Rechsteiner. Swiss financial center. Establishing an effective and credible search procedure (97.3289); motion by Paul Rechsteiner, Experiences with assets from the time of the Second World War. Legal consequences (97.3306); motion by J. Alexander Baumann, Dormant accounts at the Swiss banks. Creating civil procedural rules under federal law (97.3369); ordinary question by Paul Rechsteiner, Registration Decree. Rightful claimants from Eastern European states (97.1137); motion by Christian Grobet, Dormant accounts. Federal Council must act (97.3401); interpellation by Walter Schmied, Inadequate information to embassies, consulates and Swiss people living abroad about dormant accounts (97.3444); interpellation by the Radical Democrats, US boycott actions. Switzerland's reaction (98.3111); interpellation by Christine Beerli, US boycott actions. Switzerland's reaction (98.3116); interpellation by Liberal party, US boycott actions. Switzerland's reaction (98.3119); interpellation by Dick Marty, Boycott threats and possible concrete reprisals (98.3129); ordinary question by Didier Berberat, Agreement between UBS and World Jewish Congress. Fiscal consequences (1.10.1998) (98.1146); interpellation by Jean-Nils de Dardel, 'Global solution' and bank taxes (98.3474); interpellation by Ernst Hasler, Further requirements of the bank settlement (98.3513); ordinary question by Vreni Spoerry, Submission on dormant accounts (15 December 1998) (98.1191); motion by Werner Carobbio, Agreement between the banks and the Jewish organizations. Fiscal implications (99.3086).

136 Cf. SKA executive board's letter of 11 August 1995 to regional heads re: recording of 'dormant accounts, securities accounts and safe deposit boxes'. CCA.

137 Cf. SKA letter of 3 Jan. 1996 to the SBA re: dormant accounts at Schweizerische Kreditanstalt. CCA.

138 The accounts and securities accounts were recorded on a prepared list. As at SKA, safe deposit boxes and collective accounts were not systematically investigated until 1997, so were not included in SVB's reports, even though some regions did check safe deposit boxes, too.

139 Report 'Ergebnis der Umfrage von September/October 1995 "Nachrichtenlose Gelder"' ('Results of the September/October 1995 survey of dormant assets'), 11 December 1995. Cf. also SVB's letter to the SBA of 11 December 1995 re: dormant accounts at the Swiss banks. CCA.

140 Cf. memorandum to the president of the executive board of 4 March 1996 re: dormant accounts, SVB and Bank Leu registrations. The figures given in this memo for CS Holding's private bank group were: Bank Leu: Sfr 26,000 (4 accounts); SVB: Sfr 0. CCA.

141 Cf. information sent to employees of the CSG banks at end-December 1996 about the role of the Swiss financial center during the Second World War and Credit Suisse Group's policy. CCA.

142 Cf. www.parlament.ch/poly/Framesets/D/Frame-D.htm (September 2001). The two other class actions followed on 23 October 1996 and on 29 January 1997. – On 30 June 1998, a class action was submitted to the District Court in Washington D.C. against the SNB, accusing it of having received assets stolen by the Nazis. Cf. Nikos Tszermias, 'US-Sammelklage gegen die Nationalbank' ('US Class Action Against the National Bank'), in: NZZ, 1 July 1998. Cf. also Karl Grün, 'New York erwägt Boykott gegen Schweizer Banken' ('New York Considers Boycott Against Swiss Banks'), in: NZZ, 30 January 1997; Braillard, Fadenkreuz. On 17 August 1997, a class action was also submitted against 16 insurance companies. Cf. Nikos Tszermias, 'US-Politiker gegen europäische Versicherer' ('US Politicians Against European Insurers'), in: NZZ, 4 February 1998.

143 Cf. Federal Council's ordinance of 26 February 1997 concerning the Special Fund for Needy Victims of the Holocaust/Shoah. On the suggestion of the WJRO, three foreign Jews were chosen to sit on the seven-person fund board. Cf. www.taskforce.ch/S/S1/a2_d.htm (September 2001). On 5 March 1997, Swiss President Arnold Koller announced the government's intention to mark the 150th anniversary of the Swiss Confederation by setting up a Swiss Solidarity Foundation to reaffirm the country's tradition of humanity and solidarity. The foundation would be financed from the proceeds of revaluing the SNB's gold reserves. In the summer and autumn sessions of 2001, both houses of parliament decided

that one third of these proceeds should go to fund the Swiss state pension scheme, one third to the cantons, and one third to the solidarity fund. Swiss citizens now have to vote on this decision in a referendum. Cf. www.parlament.ch/poly/Framesets/D/Frame-D.htm (September 2001); Beat Waber, 'Dem Nationalrat ist die Solidarität kostbar' ('Solidarity is Valuable for the National Council'), in NZZ, 26 September 2001.

144 Thanks to interest of around Sfr 24 million, by the end of May 2001 a total of Sfr 297,752,838 had flowed into the fund. Approved applications accounted for a total of Sfr 293,273,313, leaving a residual sum of approximately Sfr 4.48 million. Cf. press release from the Swiss Fund for Needy Victims of the Holocaust/Shoah, 14 December 2000; 30 August 2001.

145 Funds allocated to beneficiaries as at December 2000 (number of people in brackets): Jewish victims Sfr 246,199,700 (251,844); victims of political persecution Sfr 27,461,598 (43,339); Roma/Sinti Sfr 17,726,847 (15,358); Righteous Among the Nations Sfr 3,529,969 (1,478); homosexuals, Jehovah's Witnesses, disabled people Sfr 256,991 (213). Allocated funds by region: Eastern Europe Sfr 121,522,105 (94,505); Israel Sfr 86,610,398 (124,000); North America Sfr 48,416,261 (69,554); Western Europe Sfr 34,074,202 (18,857); Australia / New Zealand Sfr 3,689,317 (3,810); Latin America/Africa Sfr 862,822 (1,506). – The Fund's final report should be published in mid-2002.

146 This is also borne out by a latter of thanks from E. C., a Jew from Kansas, USA, who wrote in June 1999: 'To whom it may concern. Thank you so much for the check of $ 502.– from the humanitarian fund set up by the Swiss banks and corporations. This money will help me pay for the special eyeglasses I have been needing so badly. I'm very grateful that I will be able to see and read much better thanks to you. Sincerely. E. C.' Information kindly supplied by Barbara Ekwall, General Secretary of the Swiss Fund for Needy Victims of the Holocaust/Shoah, 3 July 2001, 4 September 2001.

147 Jung, History of a Bank, p. 90. – Cf. www.admin.ch/cp/d/1996Oct25.145250.6782@idz.bfi. admin.ch. html (August 2001); www.taskforce.ch/Start/script.htm (September 2001); FDFA press release of 30 May 2001.

148 The details of 1,756 dormant accounts belonging to foreign customers and containing Sfr 61.2 million were published in July 1997. Information about the assets of another 3,687 foreign customers (Sfr 6.17 million) and 10,758 Swiss customers (Sfr 11.67 million) followed in October. Details of 63,621 accounts owned by Swiss customers containing sums of less than Sfr 100 (Sfr 1.18 million) were not published. The marked jump from approximately Sfr 41.94 million (March 1996) to Sfr 61.2 million (July 1997) is accounted for mainly by a revised report from SBV. Cf. Daniel Piller / Kurt Pelda, 'Entscheidender Schritt der Schweizer Banken. Kampagne zur Auffindung der Inhaber nachrichtenloser Konti' ('Swiss Banks Take Decisive Step. Campaign to Find the Owners of Dormant Accounts'), in: NZZ, 24 July 1997.

149 Arthur Andersen, Report, Part J, p. 367. – Twelve of these accounts, containing a total of about Sfr 4.6 million, were reported later on. In order to arrive at the approximate value in 1945, these figures have to be divided by 10. Arthur Andersen's figures are from July 1999. The figures delivered by ATAG Ernst & Young in August 2001 are different.

150 Cf www.dormantaccounts.ch (September 2001); www.crt.ch (September 2001).

151 Information kindly supplied by Alexander Jolles, General Secretary of the Claims Resolution Tribunal. 10 August 2001; 30 August 2001; 10 October 2001. – The total of 3,121 claims (as at August 2001) concerned 987 accounts, of which 207 were 'victim' accounts.

152 FDFA, 'Search and Compensation Procedure Established in Connection with the Registration Decree of 20 December 1962', www.taskforce.ch/G/G2/G2a/pr/981118_e.htm (September 2001).

153 Cf. www.parlament.ch/poly/Framesets/D/Frame-D.htm (September 2001); www.swissbankclaims.com (September 2001). – Edward Korman is 'chief judge of the Eastern District of New York'.

154 This included assets totaling Sfr 21.3 million at the CSG banks. In fact, the ICEP had originally considered 6.86 million accounts, but no information at all could be found for about 2.76 million of these.

155 Cf. ICEP, Report, p. 13.

156 Cf. 'Bald weitere Publikation von Holocaust-Konti' ('More Holocaust Accounts to be Published Soon'), in: NZZ, 31 March 2000.

157 Cf. 'Verteilungsplan für den Bankenvergleich' ('Distribution Plan for Bank Settlement'), in: NZZ, 13 September 2000.

158 Cf. NZZ, 18 September 2000; www.swissbankclaims.iom.int/common_docs/court_order.pdf (September 2001). On 4 April 2001, Judge Korman announced the names of the 27 Swiss companies that had registered because of the use of slave labor before 1946 and which had been included in the major banks' settlement. Originally, 37 companies had registered.

159 Cf. 'Neue Kontroverse um Holocaust-Konten' ('New Controversy about Holocaust Accounts'), in: NZZ, 20 December 2000.

160 Cf. press release 'Swiss Bankers Association publishes list of 21,000 names of account holders from the Second World War period', 5 February 2001, under: www.dormantaccounts.ch (September 2001); Schweizerische Depeschenagentur, '25 000 Meldungen zur dritten Bankenliste. Grosses Interesse an Fragebogen' ('25,000 Responses to Third Bank List. Great Interest in Questionnaire'), in: NZZ, 31 July 2001; Associated Press, '25 000 Ansprüche auf nachrichtenlose Konten. Ablauf der Eingabefrist' ('25,000 Claims to Dormant Accounts. Submission Deadline Expires'), in: NZZ, 7 August 2001. The deadline for inquiries was extended to the end of August 2001. Claims Resolution Tribunal, Introduction to the Process, under: www.crt-ii.org/_de/index.phtm (September 2001).

161 Cf. ICEP, Report, p. 128–133; 'Dormant Accounts'. Summary of the results of an SBA survey of foreign banking associations by country: status as at 26 May 1997, and Appendix 25: status as at 21 June 1995. CCA; Bronfman, Report; Eizenstat 1997; Proceedings Washington Conference.

162 A geographical analysis of the claims highlights, among other things, the way the war forced people to migrate. While most of the names claimants were looking for were Eastern European in origin (1,410 of 2,885), the relevant claim questionnaires were mainly sent from North America and Israel (758 and 416 respectively). Information kindly supplied by Stefan Peter, head of the Swiss Bank Ombudsman's contact office.

163 Cf. 'Richtlinien der Schweizerischen Bankiervereinigung über die Behandlung nachrichtenloser Konten, Depots and Schrankfächer bei Schweizer Banken' ('Swiss Bankers Association's guidelines on the treatment of dormant accounts, securities accounts and safe deposit boxes at Swiss banks') (replacing the guidelines of 8 September 1995), Basel, February 2000. www.swissbanking.org/114_d.pdf (September 2001).

164 Cf. CCA.

165 Cf. CSG directive W-0020 on dormant accounts, investigations into assets and documentation on closed-out customer accounts, 1 July 2000. CCA.

166 Cf. list of registered dormant accounts by CSG banks. CCA. – For more information on the results of the Poland surveys (1949, 1950, 1958), cf. table 'Results of the Swiss Bankers Association's survey of Polish dormant accounts (1949– 1958); payment to the Polish national bank (1960)', p. 158 of this study. The discrepancy between the two survey results of 1947 and 1949 is not explained by the available sources.

167 Cf. minutes of the SBA board of directors, 15 March 1946. SBA archives.

168 Cf. 'Interner Entwurf der SBA. Skizze über das praktische Vorgehen der SBA bei der Behandlung von Gesuchen um Nachforschung nach Vermögenswerten, deren Eigentümer während der Kriegszeit im Ausland gestorben sind' ('Internal SBA draft. Sketch of practical ways in which the SBA can handle requests for investigations into assets whose owners died abroad during the war'), 26 November 1952. CCA.

169 Draft SBA circular on 'heirless assets', 10 November 1952. CCA.

170 Cf. minutes of the LC SBA, 16 October 1952. SBA archives.

171 Cf. letter from the SBA to the members of its board of directors re: 'heirless assets', 12 Dec. 1952. CCA.

172 Cf. 'Interner Entwurf der SBA, Skizze über das praktische Vorgehen der SBVg bei der Behandlung von Gesuchen um Nachforschung nach Vermögenswerten, deren Eigentümer während der Kriegszeit im Ausland gestorben sind', 26 November 1952. CCA.

173 Cf. folder 'Avoirs en déshérence, résultats enquête, 4.3.1957 – 27.1.1960' ('Heirless assets, inquiry results, 4 March 1957 – 27 January 1960'), folder 4 November 1960 – 15 March 1963, folder July 1963 – February 1964. SBA archives.

174 An affidavit is a sworn statement in writing.

175 Letter from the SVB branch in Zurich to the SBA re: 'deposited assets', 24 May 1958. Folder 'Avoirs en déshérence, résultats enquête, 4. 3. 1957 – 27. 1. 1960'. SBA archives.

176 Cf. letter from SBV to the SBA, 14 March 1957. Folder 'Avoirs en déshérence, résultats enquête, 4. 3. 1957 – 27. 1. 1960'. SBA archives.

177 Cf. circular No. 3117 from the SBA to its member banks, 27 August 1963. CCA.

178 Cf. folder 'Avoirs en déshérence VI, cas liquidés, Januar–Juni 1963' ('Heirless assets VI, closed cases, January-June 1963'). SBA archives.

179 Cf. folder 'J 7 Erblose Vermögemenswerte in der Schweiz, März 1986 bis Oktober 1988' ('J 7 heirless assets in Switzerland, March 1986 to October 1988'). SBA archives.

180 Cf. information sheet on investigations into assets supposedly deposited at the Swiss banks by persons who have since died, 1994/95. SBA archives, circular 1193 D, 12 September 1995; CCA.

181 Arthur Andersen systematically examined the issue of asset investigations at SKA, SVB and Bank Leu. It was established that SKA received a total of 649 inquiries from Shoah victims or their heirs between 1946 and 1995. No old accounts could be identified in 70% of these cases. 14% of all inquiries connected with the Shoah resulted in the identification of assets. 16% of inquiries concerned accounts that had been closed. For SVB, Arthur Andersen discovered a total of 568 inquiries to the bank from Shoah victims or their heirs. No old accounts could be found in 96% of these cases. Assets were identified as result of 1% of inquiries connected with the Shoah. 3% of inquiries concerned accounts that had been closed. Arthur Andersen identified 24 inquiries made to Bank Leu, but did not analyze these any further. Cf. Arthur Andersen, Report, Part F, p. 279–288. In parallel with this identification of dormant accounts within the context of the ICEP process, CSG carried out the research project 'Research into the procedures used by SKA, SVB and Bank Leu to investigate assets'. The legal departments' files were systematically evaluated. About 200 representative cases were examined, divided into three periods (1946–1962, 1963–1973, 1974–1994). CCA; customer estates ex SKA, 19830835KNA00108, 19830835KNA00144, 19830835KNA00202, 19840835KNA00025, 19860835KNA00016, 19860835KNA00099, 19860835KNA00109, 19860835KNA00160, 19910835KNA00359, 19920835KNA00442, 19920835KNA00077, 19930835KNA00190, 19940835KNA00270, 19930835KNA00359, 19930835KNA00378. CCA.

182 Cf. letter from the FDJP to Bank Leu enclosing standard letter for inquiries, 17 June 1982. CCA.

183 Cf. SKA directive W-1085 re: 'Agreement on the Swiss banks' code of conduct regard to the exercise of due diligence', 31 May 1988. CCA.

184 Cf. report by CSPB's legal department on 'Handling and disposition of accounts after the war', 30 April 1998. CCA.

185 Cf. SKA directive W-1039, 3 January 1980. CCA; SKA working instruction A-1201, 11 June 1987. CCA.

186 Cf. CCA.

187 CCA. In exceptional cases SKA would also accept an affidavit from the claimant. Cf. the case of M. E. CCA.

188 Cf. CCA.

189 Journeys made by senior manager S. V. after the Second World War, memorandum of 10 June 1997. CCA.

190 Cf. CCA; recorded in 1964, but not registered. Further correspondence on this matter has not survived.

191 Cf. CCA.

192 See p. 170 of this study.

193 CCA.

194 CCA.

195 CCA. It is not clear from the sources why the safety deposit box was blocked; so it is impossible to recreate the subsequent course of the case.

196 Cf. e.g. the case of P. K. CCA.

197 CCA.

198 Cf. correspondence between SKA's Basel branch and the bank's legal department in March 1951 con-

cerning an inquiry from a Basel-based lawyer about the bank's obligation to provide information to individual heirs. CCA.

199 Cf. SKA directive No. 405, 'Instructions following the death of a client'. CCA.

200 Cf. minutes of the LC SBA, 17 March 1966. SBA archives.

201 Cf. SBA circular No. 295 D re: the banks' obligation to provide information under inheritance law. Appendix to directive No. 6, 1 July 1974. CCA.

202 Cf. SKA directive No. 6 re: the banks' obligation to provide information, 4 July 1974. CCA.

203 Cf. request concerning the VSJF's search for the assets of J. and E. F. in a letter dated 1 April 1949. CCA.

204 Cf. CCA.

205 Cf. CCA.

206 Cf. CCA.

207 It is only clear in one case that the owner was killed by the Nazis. CCA.

208 Cf. minutes of the legal department meeting of 23 May 1977 (1977/48); two minutes of the legal department meeting of 14 November 1984. Documentation 'Spesen/Gebühren' ('Fees, charges'), CSPB legal department. CCA. – In the 1960s/70s, SVB charged a fee of between Sfr 200 and Sfr 250 for an investigation into assets at all branches. In the 1980s, the cost was usually at least Sfr 500. Cf. for example the cases of P. S., L. R. or S. Z. CCA, dossiers 556, 584, 1417.

209 Cf. letters from the SVB legal department relating to the case of M. J.; similar documents at SKA. CCA.

210 Cf. letter from SVB to the SBA, 19 September 1960; letter from the SBA to SVB, 30 September 1960, re: assets belonging to Romanian citizens at Swiss banks. CCA.

211 Cf. letter from the FPD to SKA re: assets belonging to G. F. of Bucharest, 22 August 1960; letter from the FPD to the SBA re: directive No. 1410, 14 November 1960. CCA.

212 Cf. letter from the SBA to SKA, SVB, SBG, ZKB and SBV re: assets belonging to Romanian citizens at Swiss banks, 22 October 1960; circular No. 141 D from the SBA re: assets from customers and correspondents living in totalitarian states, 11 November 1960. CCA.

213 Cf. letter from the SKA executive board in Zurich to the management of branches in Switzerland re: assets belonging to clients behind the Iron Curtain, 10 November 1960. CCA.

214 SKA's letter to the City of Zurich guardianship office, 31 October 1968. CCA.

215 Cf. the A. B., I. C. and R. T. cases. CCA, dossiers 5, 23, 127; J. B. case. CCA.

Swiss banking in the Second World War

By Hans J. Mast

Contents

The author, who as a youth during the Second World War lived for a time in Vienna, tackles various aspects of wartime Swiss banking. Switzerland's role as an international financial center is often cited in an attempt to explain why Switzerland was spared invasion by the Axis Powers; supposedly the Swiss financial industry's international links and its freely convertible currency provided inestimable service to the 'Third Reich'. The following study subjects this theory in particular to close scrutiny.

1 Swiss banking at the end of the 1930s

To paraphrase the old Austrian field marshal Montecuccoli, only three things are needed for war: firstly money, secondly money, and thirdly money again. The powerful have long known that conquering and thus destroying a financial center is not, however, a good way of getting hold of money; not that this has ever prevented them from occupying such centers, as the examples of Amsterdam and Paris in the Second World War attest.

However, Switzerland's financial capabilities were so important – or so it is implied – that the 'Third Reich' wanted to keep them functioning at all costs, and so abstained from military action against the country. This theory begs the question of just how large and important the Swiss financial center was at that time. Certainly the bankers of the day, but also the authorities and politicians, described it in fulsome terms, and the country – or to be more precise, certain Swiss towns – had indeed played a role in international banking for centuries.[1] But this role had varied in importance over the course of history and had often been interrupted by severe setbacks, such as those experienced during and after the Napoleonic Wars.

In the second half of the 19th century, Switzerland still needed to import considerable amounts of capital from abroad to finance industrialization and railroad construction. It was not until after the First World War that the country developed from a capital importer into a capital exporter, thus giving its banks a foundation on which to build a highly promising international financial business. However, the first tender shoots of this upswing were blasted away again in the 1930s by the icy breath of global economic and currency crisis – and especially by the ensuing spread of currency controls – and by political tensions. As broad streams of hot money were buffeted around by the dictates of fear, Switzerland experienced alternating bouts of heavy capital inflows and equally large withdrawals of money back to other countries. The Swiss authorities were thus forced to impose stringent defensive measures, including a ban on interest payments – a restriction that was used again after the war – and an obligatory commission on foreign funds.[2] In the face of massive outflows of currency and gold abroad, exchange controls repeatedly came up for discussion, though these were always rejected as the ebb and flow of the currency situation went Switzerland's way again. When war broke out, Switzerland's financial and banking industry was thus in far from the best of health. A good indication of this is the fact that the major banks, which were heavily involved in foreign business and which at the beginning of the 1930s had

Trends in Swiss banking (1938/1945)

	Number of institutions		Number of offices		Headcount		Total assets (Sfr bn)	
	1938	1945	1938	1945	1938	1945	1938	1945
Cantonal banks	27	27	891	1 009	4 594	4 584	8.1	8.7
Major banks	7	5	195	182	9 264	8 288	4.5	5.5
Savings banks	111	119	328	358	492	671	1.6	1.8
Raiffeisen banks (credit unions)	2	2	671	819	693	869	0.4	0.7
Other banks	214	230	1 019	1 072	2 683	3 123	3.7	4.2
Total	361	383	3 104	3 440	17 726	17 535	18.3	20.9

been the most important group of banks in Switzerland, had already lost their preeminent position to the domestically oriented cantonal banks even before the war.[3]

In terms of size, too, during the first half of the 20th century, the Swiss financial industry was of secondary importance behind leading centers such as Paris, New York and, above all, London. Switzerland was undoubtedly a respected financial player in those years, but it did not develop into one of the worlds foremost banking centers until after the end of the Second World War. In the 1960s in particular, Switzerland's financial industry experienced a sharp upsurge in business. This was reflected by, among other things, the influx of foreign banks.[4] The number of non-Swiss banks operating in Switzerland increased from 57 in 1960 to 111 by 1970.[5] In the first half of the 20th century, however, the leading Swiss institutions were in no position to hold their own against the big foreign banks. Aside from the odd representative office and foreign subsidiary, SBV was the only bank in Switzerland to maintain a branch abroad – in London – prior to 1939, and this at a time when the big foreign players all had many offices around the world. At the end of the 1930s there were seven Swiss major banks, but only two of them, SBV and SKA, had total assets of more than Sfr 1 billion.[6] Meanwhile Deutsche Bank, for example, had total assets (converted into Swiss franc terms) of about Sfr 6.6 billion (1938)[7], Britain's Midland Bank had about Sfr 11.7 billion (1940), and Crédit Lyonnais around Sfr 2 billion (1939).[8] A comparison of headcounts reveals a similar picture. Whereas Deutsche Bank employed almost 20,000 before the war[9], SKA had only around 2,240 staff at that time. In the middle of the final year before war began, less than 18,000 people in total, or only about 1% of Switzerland's working population, were employed by Swiss banks.[10] In 1999, 3% of the Swiss workforce worked in banking.[11] It was not until the start of the 1960s that the Swiss banks began to build up their international networks of branches and agencies in a more concerted fashion. Until then, they had taken care of most of their foreign business from Switzerland; but by the middle of the 1990s, SKA, SBG and SBV had between them increased the number of foreign branches and representative offices from 12 (1959) to 135.[12] By making a series of acquisitions in the 1980s and even more in the 1990s, the major Swiss banks were able to improve their international competitive position quite considerably, thus rising to join the top flight of the banking world. At the start of the 1980s, the largest Swiss bank 'was around 30th in the world rankings'[13], but by the summer of 2001, both UBS and CSG were among the eleven largest financial institutions in the world measured by total assets.[14]

Prior to 1945, the Swiss financial and banking center was, comparatively speaking, of minor significance. It was very clearly structured and benefited from a population with a high propensity to save, as well as a multilingual workforce that was committed to discretion, not to mention a currency which, fully covered by gold reserves, inspired widespread confidence. But the bottom line was that in material terms, it could offer the Axis Powers little that they did not already have, and nothing that other neutral financial centers such as Stockholm or Lisbon could not also provide. There were, therefore, no financial reasons for the 'Third Reich' to refrain from marching into Switzerland.

2 The 'free' convertibility of the Swiss franc

Formally, at least, the Swiss franc may have been freely convertible – i.e. exchangeable against any other currency – throughout the whole of the Second World War, but in practical terms this general principle was full of holes. As mentioned above, from the beginning of the 1930s onwards, currency restrictions had proliferated in the shadow of the global economic crisis and the political crisis emanating from Germany. As a result, payments to other countries were subjected to control by the governments of those countries. In order to prevent these interventions from hurting Switzerland's exports too much, and in order to protect Swiss exporters and employment as best as possible, the Swiss authorities had no choice but to regulate trade with these countries by means of 'clearing agreements'. These agreements listed all the payments that could be cleared at the official exchange rate. Any outstanding balances generated by this bilateral trade could exceptionally be settled in gold or hard currency, but more normally were made good through reduced exports or additional imports, or through the granting of clearing credits. The aim of this arrangement was to put Switzerland's import activity at the service of its exports in the interests of employment policy. The overriding motto was 'Arbeit geht vor Kapital' – 'work comes before capital'.[15] Consequently, any payment for imports, or any other contractual payment from Switzerland to the trading partner, had to be made out to the SNB or the Swiss Compensation Office. The Swiss Compensation Office then used these funds to pay exporters and other beneficiaries. Swiss claims not permitted for clearing, especially capital repayments and most capital income payments, either remained blocked in the partner country or were credited to special accounts used for such purposes as tourism or capital investments. As a rule, the money in these special accounts was freely convertible, though only at rates well below the official one.

At its zenith, this dirigiste payments system encompassed more than twenty countries, which accounted for almost three-quarters of Switzerland's foreign trade by volume. Naturally, the free convertibility of the franc was suspended for most trade with these nations. Convertibility was subjected to further restrictions from April 1940 when the United States blocked the assets of continental European countries, thus placing the dollar – the last major currency of world trade – under state control. As a consequence, two months later the SNB imposed its own controls on dollar movements; more stringent restrictions now applied to private Swiss franc-dollar transactions. Of the sixty or so currencies that had been relatively freely convertible at the beginning of the 1930s, only two were now left: the Portuguese escudo and the Argentinean peso.[16]

From the middle of 1942, this narrow basis made it impossible to run a large-scale, profitable foreign exchange business. Income from the bills portfolio, under which earnings from foreign exchange transactions were shown at that time, remained at more or less the same level at all the Swiss banks from 1938 to 1945. In fact, at the major banks this income actually decreased slightly even in nominal terms from 1941; and in real terms, i.e. allowing for inflation, the fall was 42%.

In short, from Switzerland's point of view, the free convertibility of the Swiss franc was to a large extent limited to capital exports – which was not a particularly attractive option under war conditions – as well as to other payments not subject to clearing, and payments from trade with countries that did not maintain clearing agreements with Switzerland. In practice, then, free convertibility did not play a very significant role.[17]

At first glance, these observations would appear to conflict with the repeated requests made with some force by all the belligerents – the Germans and the Allies alike – for the Swiss authorities to provide them with a certain amount of 'freely convertible Swiss francs'. Such an obligation was even built in to the German-Swiss clearing agreement in the form of 'free currency reserves'. These requests from the warring nations should not, however, be seen as confirmation of the importance of franc convertibility; the belligerents' intention was rather to persuade Switzerland not to impose restrictions

Breakdown of the Swiss major banks' aggregate gross income (1938–1945)

(Sfr m)	1938	1939	1940	1941	1942	1943	1944	1945
Interest	34.7	33.8	32.9	31.5	34.5	36.0	37.5	43.1
Commissions	35.1	35.5	35.3	35.0	34.3	34.5	33.2	35.8
Bills portfolio	24.5	26.9	29.3	28.9	27.7	25.6	25.5	23.7
Securities and syndicate participation	15.4	11.0	8.2	16.0	17.5	16.7	18.7	16.7
Real estate	1.4	1.5	1.5	1.4	1.3	1.4	1.3	1.0
Miscellaneous	11.4	11.7	10.0	8.5	8.9	7.1	7.4	4.1
Gross income	122.5	120.4	117.2	121.3	124.2	121.3	123.6	124.4

SKA: breakdown of gross income (1938–1945)

(Sfr m)	1938	1939	1940	1941	1942	1943	1944	1945
Interest	9.8	9.1	9.5	10.5	11.8	12.2	11.0	11.7
Commissions	10.3	10.8	9.4	9.8	9.2	9.3	9.0	11.4
Bills account	5.5	5.9	6.0	6.4	6.2	5.9	7.0	6.6
Exchange rate differences	3.4	3.5	3.4	2.4	4.9	1.6	1.9	2.4
Securities and syndicate participation	4.0	4.1	1.8	4.1	4.2	4.3	5.4	6.4
Real estate	0.1	0.1	0.0	0.0	0.0	0.0	0.0	0.1
Miscellaneous	3.9	3.3	2.5	2.2	2.7	4.0	2.6	1.5
Gross income	37.0	36.8	32.6	35.4	39.0	37.3	36.9	40.1

SVB: breakdown of gross income (1938–1945)

(Sfr m)	1938	1939	1940	1941	1942	1943	1944	1945
Interest	7.0	7.1	6.9	6.1	6.3	6.4	6.7	7.2
Commissions	2.7	2.6	2.7	2.6	2.8	3.0	3.1	3.5
Bills portfolio	2.2	2.3	1.7	2.3	2.4	2.6	2.6	2.8
Securities	1.7	1.5	1.3	1.9	1.9	1.9	2.0	2.6
Real estate	0.6	0.7	0.8	0.7	0.6	0.6	0.5	0.4
Miscellaneous	0.9	0.9	0.7	0.7	0.8	0.6	0.8	0.3
Gross income	15.1	15.1	14.1	14.3	14.8	15.1	15.7	16.8

Bank Leu: breakdown of gross income (1938–1945)

(Sfr m)	1938	1939	1940	1941	1942	1943	1944	1945
Interest	2.0	2.2	1.9	1.8	2.1	2.1	2.1	1.7
Commissions	0.8	0.7	0.7	0.8	0.8	0.9	0.8	0.9
Bills portfolio	0.2	0.3	0.4	0.5	0.6	0.6	0.7	0.4
Securities, participations and syndicate participation	0.6	0.1	0.2	0.3	0.3	0.3	0.2	0.4
Miscellaneous	0.3	0.3	0.5	0.5	0.4	0.4	0.6	0.4
Gross income	3.9	3.6	3.7	3.9	4.2	4.3	4.4	3.8

on the use of Swiss franc credit balances as required by the clearing agreements, or to apply the SNB's restrictions on the receipt of dollars. The 'free' Swiss francs acquired in this way were only freely usable within Switzerland. Switzerland had no control over whether they really could be used for payment in other countries; this depended entirely on whether the country receiving the payments was prepared to accept the Swiss francs and convert them into its own currency.

3 The gold business

Some comments on the gold trade, a subject of heated debate in recent times, are also warranted here. Gold trading was concentrated in London until well into the post-war era. South Africa, the world's most important gold producer, and other gold-producing countries, sold their product through London. Apart from trading in gold coins, the Swiss banks had little to do with the business. Neither did they have much reason to get involved, since few of their customers – the exceptions were the jewelry and watch-making sectors – were very interested in gold, even in the first years of the war; initially the central bank was obliged by statute to keep the gold price stable at about Sfr 4,870 per kilogram.[18] There was no motive to engage in active gold speculation, especially since there were discussions in the United States at that time about reducing the official gold price.

The calm that prevailed on the gold market began to fracture, however, as the war led to increasing supply problems, inflationary pressures increased, numerous foreign currencies became progressively weaker and many countries imposed blocks on foreign assets. Gold hoarding became the norm and, as the dollar ceased to be available as an international means of payment, gold became increasingly popular as a medium for cross-border transactions. In addition, experience had shown that in German-controlled territories, a piece or two of gold pressed into the hand of a policeman or soldier at the right time could save lives and help to secure escape.

In an attempt to calm the gold market down, the Swiss authorities intervened, introducing a licensing requirement for gold trading on 7 December 1942 and setting maximum prices for the yellow metal. This more or less pushed private-sector traders out of the business, meaning that the authorities placed themselves increasingly at the center of the whole issue. Their main goal was to keep gold purchases against Swiss francs to a minimum in order to ward off inflation. In contrast with the rules for the gold standard of that time, this policy was thus essentially defensive. Accordingly, between 1939 and 1945 the SNB only purchased about Sfr 1.2 billion of gold net from the German Reichsbank, and about Sfr 2.3 billion net from the Allies.

Other elements of the SNB's policy were the sale of gold on the Swiss market and the imposition of controls on the dollar: in order to absorb domestic purchasing power, the SNB disposed of a total of approximately Sfr 546 million worth of gold in various stages on the domestic market, primarily in the form of gold coins.[19] For the same reason it limited dollar purchases at the official exchange rate to the proceeds of exports – with additional restrictions for exports of watches; it would not accept dollars from other sources, such as capital receipts or interest and dividend payments. As a result, a special free market rate developed for these dollars – known as finance dollars; this rate fell below Sfr 3, which was well under the official price at the time of about Sfr 4.30. Finance dollars only disappeared in 1949 in the face of the general shortage of dollars.[20]

4 Asset management and stock market trading

Asset management and stock market trading gave no more of a boost to the Swiss banking industry during the Second World War than did trading in gold or foreign exchange. Switzerland could not be described in any way as a safe country at that time, and most of the flight capital that did reach Switzerland through the barrier of foreign currency controls soon left the country again, along with Swiss money. The most popular ultimate destination was America. Once this money had gone overseas, most of it was lost to the Swiss banks. This was one of the main reasons why SKA decided in 1939 to set up its own securities institution in the USA: Swiss American Corporation (Swissam). This was followed one year later by a branch office, which – much like SBV's New York branch – was tailored towards commercial banking business. When the US blocking measures took effect shortly afterwards, these branches found their spheres of activity sharply restricted. But though they brought more cost than profit to their parent companies in the early years, during the 1950s they provided some of the initial impetus for the Swiss banking industry's expansion into a significant international force.

SKA's confidential documents from the time provide some insight into the development of securities business during the war years. The number of securities accounts managed by the bank between the end of 1938 and the end of 1945 hovered between about 43,000 and 46,000, while the value of the securities deposited in the accounts fell over the same period by more than Sfr 500 million to Sfr 3.9 billion.[21]

According to a list covering 1944 and 1945, which breaks down the value of securities accounts by customer domicile, about two-thirds of this sum was accounted for by customers living in Switzerland, and only about a third by foreigners, most of whom were French. The number of safety deposit boxes held at SKA fell by almost 30% over the course of the war.[22]

SKA: asset management business (1938–1945)

	1938	1939	1940	1941	1942	1943	1944	1945
Number of securities accounts	44 032	43 187	44 290	43 764	44 037	44 987	45 574	46 044
Value of securities accounts (Sfr m)	4 389.3	3 967.3	3 678.1	3 685.5	3 719.1	3 876.6	3 895.6	3 876.9
Income from account fees and asset management (Sfr m)	3.1	4.2	3.6	3.3	3.4	3.4	3.3	4.1

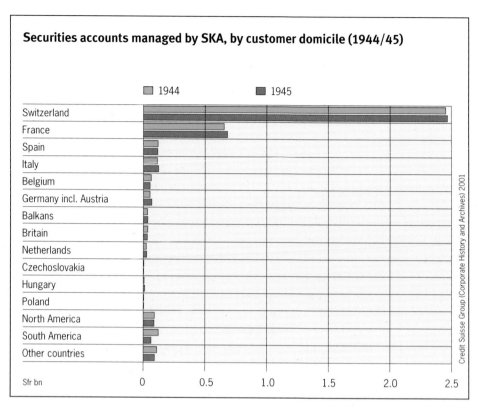

Securities accounts managed by SKA, by customer domicile (1944/45)

□ 1944   ■ 1945

Switzerland					
France					
Spain					
Italy					
Belgium					
Germany incl. Austria					
Balkans					
Britain					
Netherlands					
Czechoslovakia					
Hungary					
Poland					
North America					
South America					
Other countries					
Sfr bn	0	0.5	1.0	1.5	2.0	2.5

Credit Suisse Group (Corporate History and Archives) 2001

In order to extrapolate the picture for Switzerland as a whole from these SKA figures, we can use a formula that was commonly used in the years immediately after the Second World War. This rule of thumb stipulates that SKA's holdings of securities were between a fifth and a quarter of the overall Swiss total. The value of all securities managed by the Swiss banks during the war would thus have come to between Sfr 15.3 billion and Sfr 19.1 billion; Sfr 6.3 billion of this would have belonged to foreign customers. Even after converting these sums into modern-day equivalents, the figures we arrive at – and especially the figure for foreign holdings – are nowhere near the enormous amounts that many people talk about.[23] In order to make a comparison, we should mention that in the year 2000, banks in Switzerland managed securities worth about Sfr 3,716 billion, Sfr 2,056 billion of which was accounted for by foreign customers.[24]

Against this background, it should come as no surprise that the banks did not pay special attention at the time to assets belonging to foreign refugees – especially since they believed that these assets were being kept from direct interference by Swiss neutrality, banking secrecy and other measures used to protect foreign customers who were being persecuted for political or racial reasons. After the war, the overwhelming majority of those entitled to the assets took control of their money again; many of them found it useful that customer bank balances did not fall under a time limitation at the Swiss banks, unlike at many of their competitors in other countries. The banks subsequently found little favor with the governmental agreements made with Poland and Hungary to hand over unclaimed customer assets. One of their main concerns was that the draconian currency controls in these countries could have prevented customers from claiming what was rightfully theirs; the banks saw no reason to cut off their customers' property rights. The fact that some banks did not, however, follow the political authorities' request to report 'dormant accounts' was a regrettable mistake, especially since more and more inquiries came from customers in Eastern Europe after the fall of the Iron Curtain.

The uncertainty of the times made it difficult for investors to know which way to turn during the war, leaving them unwilling to make additional investments. Stock market turnover slumped as a consequence, despite the fact that the equity and bond markets remained firm.[25]

At the same time, the demands of the belligerent nations for affidavits hobbled the Swiss securities market. Affidavits were declarations that had to accompany foreign securities owned by Swiss investors. In order to facilitate the transfer of securities earnings to Switzerland, these affidavits were supposed to be presented to the foreign authorities as proof that the securities really were Swiss-owned rather than the property of people or companies domiciled in enemy countries. This bureaucratic system made trading even more difficult and created a considerable workload for the banks. The countless, usually very complex negotiations that the banks had to conduct with foreign states, but also with the Swiss authorities, were similarly burdensome. These ne-

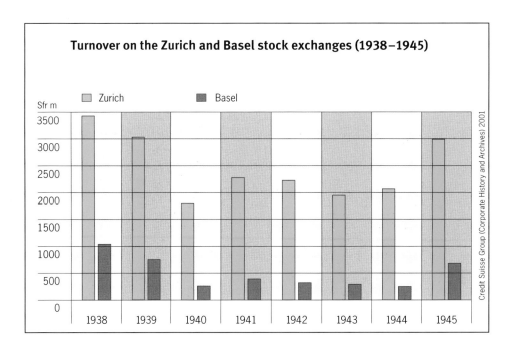

Turnover on the Zurich and Basel stock exchanges (1938–1945)

Credit Suisse Group (Corporate History and Archives) 2001

gotiations, which were conducted on behalf of the securities' owners, were aimed at protecting capital and centered on the size of, and conditions attaching to, transfers of income and capital repayments. They dealt with clearing transfers, but also payments from countries such as the United Kingdom or the United States, with which Switzerland had no clearing arrangements. It was regrettable that these negotiations all too often failed to produce the desired result, but this does not take anything away from the effort and the expense that the banks went to.

5 Business shifts

In commercial banking business, too, conditions during the war forced extensive re-structuring. This was particularly the case with foreign lending business, where the Swiss banks were very reluctant to take on new exposure without state guarantees. The Swiss government thus had to step in and act as lender for operations with foreign countries that were in the national interest. These included the 'clearing billion' – the large Swiss credit built up through trade with Germany – without which trade in goods with this partner, especially purchases of coal, would have been severely curtailed, if not brought to a complete standstill. By contrast, the banks were doing their best to reduce their outstanding exposure in other countries as far as possible. Under the constraints imposed by the war, this proved very difficult, requiring the kind of financial sacrifice that only very well funded companies could afford. Overall, the Swiss institutions reduced their assets in foreign countries by Sfr 324 million to about Sfr 1.2 billion between the end of 1938 and the end of 1944, without being able to reduce their foreign liabilities accordingly.

But even this level of disengagement proved inadequate. Immediately after the war, various banks, including two of what were then the seven major banks, collapsed under the weight of non-transferable assets and had to seek refuge with other institutions.[26] The claim that the banks were able to operate freely and profitably in the foreign arena during the war does not tally with the facts. The truth is that in all areas of international business their reverses were painful enough to take their foreign operations back to almost to pre-First World War levels. As the table below shows, with net liabilities of Sfr 170 million, the Swiss banks had become net borrowers again by the end of 1945.[27]

Swiss banks' foreign investments and liabilities (1938–1945)

(Sfr m)	1938	1939	1940	1941	1942	1943	1944	1945
Foreign investments	1493	1584	1397	1168	1061	1084	1169	1166
of which: in Germany	336	228	207	193	178	165	154	43
in the USA	306	728	697	518	445	518	573	698
Foreign liabilities	1312	1081	1051	1028	1137	1235	1220	1336
of which: in Germany	105	85	83	82	95	106	83	64
in the USA	76	59	46	44	45	60	90	138

Domestic business did not provide adequate compensation for the loss of international business. Certain sectors of the domestic Swiss economy – the government in particular – did require large amounts of finance because of the war; there was extensive lending to Swiss borrowers, and, above all, considerable issuing and placement business to be done on behalf of the Swiss government. Tellingly, 'Securities and participations' grew in 1944 to become the biggest single item after mortgages in the consolidated balance sheet of the Swiss institutions for the first time ever.

These activities were not enough, however, to sustain a real business revival. Indeed, the banks' turnover fell between 1938 and 1944 in both nominal and real (price-adjusted) terms; consolidated total assets and net profits stagnated.[28] But this overall picture is deceptive. Though business was satisfactory for the domestically oriented banks, the larger institutions, with their foreign exposure and costly infrastructure, had a hard time. This can be seen not so much from the net profits recorded – which fell by about 16% between the end of 1938 and the end of 1944, and by almost 13% between the end of 1938 and the end of 1945, a real-term reduction of 43% – as from the fact that after the war started all of the major banks cut their dividend rates, scaled back headcount, and reduced their write-downs appreciably despite the troubled times. The table below shows not only how net profits fell, but also how tax and staff costs rose. The tax burden increased more than usual during the war as a result of the two extraordinary 'war taxes' – later levied regularly as federal tax. Staff costs rose in spite of falling headcounts because wages were continuously being adjusted to inflation.[29]

Swiss banks' net profit and major items of expenditure (1938/1945)

	All banks			Major banks		
	1938 (Sfr m)	1945 (Sfr m)	Change (%)	1938 (Sfr m)	1945 (Sfr m)	Change (%)
Net profit	95.7	94.3	−1.5	25.4	22.1	−13.0
Write-downs and losses	28.9	25.0	−13.5	15.5	7.8	−49.7
Taxes and duties	21.4	27.2	27.1	7.0	10.1	44.3
Staff costs	102.1	124.4	21.9	58.5	66.5	13.7

6 Conclusion

The Second World War did not bring benefits to either the banks or to Switzerland. In contrast with that of the United States, Swiss real-term per capita national income did not rise during the war, but fell by 4%.[30] In terms of large-scale international financial business, in 1945 Switzerland found itself having to start more or less from scratch, just as it had been forced to do in 1918. Unlike many of their foreign competitors, Swiss institutions were able to enter the post-war era with their financial structures, staff and experience intact, and with the benefit of a healthy currency; but in the face of continuing currency restrictions, the banks, unlike industry, were helped little by these advantages. In the immediate post-war period, the total assets of the Swiss banking institutions, including the major banks, only increased slowly. In fact the rise was more or less in step with the expansion of Swiss national income, which underlined the fact that domestic business was far and away the most important engine of growth.[31] It was not until the 1950s that international financial flows were gradually freed up: the issue of blocked German assets in Switzerland was finally settled, cur-

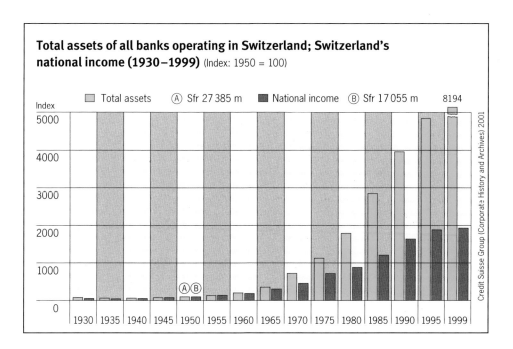

Total assets of all banks operating in Switzerland; Switzerland's national income (1930–1999) (Index: 1950 = 100)

229

rency restrictions were dismantled and colonial empires began to unwind. Only then were Swiss institutions finally able to take full advantage of the benefits conferred by their business policy. As the chart shows, growth in total assets at last became detached from growth in national income. The movement began which, despite some mistakes in domestic policy, propelled Switzerland into the upper ranks of international financial centers for the first time in its history, and which allowed the internationally active Swiss banks to move away to a certain extent from their previous very domestically oriented approach.

Hans J. Mast

Born 1920; studied law and economics; doctorates 1942 (law) and 1944 (economics); joined Credit Suisse in 1947; former Head of Economics, Public Relations and Marketing; former Senior Director and Economic Advisor to the Executive Board. Has published widely on economics, finance and banking; see p. 237 for selected works.

7 Notes

1 For more information on the development of the Swiss financial center, cf. the relevant passages in the studies of SKA and Winterthur in: Jung, History of a Bank; Jung, History of an Insurance Company. For many decades, the Swiss financial center consisted of the three main centers of Zurich, Geneva and Basel. However, especially over the course of the 20th century, Zurich grew into Switzerland's most important financial hub. Cf. Reinhardt, Finanzplatz Zürich.

2 As a result of the devaluation of the Swiss franc on 26 September 1936, there was a substantial increase especially in short-term sight deposits held at Swiss banks by foreign customers. In order to stem this tide, the banks followed the prompting of the SNB and signed a 'Gentlemen's Agreement' in November 1937, which among other things stated that no more interest would be paid on foreign-owned sight deposits denominated in Swiss francs. This agreement held until the fall of 1939. In the 1950s, a new Gentlemen's Agreement re-introduced notice periods and suspended payment of interest on foreign deposits. Cf. Jöhr, SKA, p. 384, 392. By the start of the 1930s, the major banks had already reduced or completely abolished interest on short and medium-term funds from abroad in an attempt to keep foreign capital at bay. The banks also deliberately continued to reduce the volume of deposited funds since there was nowhere for them to invest larger sums of money. Cf. Kellenberger, Kapitalexport, p. 63ff.

3 For more information on the figures used in the table 'Trends in Swiss banking (1938/1945)' cf. Schweizerisches Bankwesen 1938 and 1945. The table does not include figures for private banks or offices of foreign banks. The number of offices includes head offices, branches, agencies, deposit counters ('Depositenkassen') and collection offices ('Einnehmereien'). 'Other banks' includes the property loan banks and other local banks. The Raiffeisen banks (local cooperative credit banks) consist of the Verband schweizerischer Darlehenskassen and the Fédération vaudoise des caisses de crédit mutuel.

4 Cf. SBG, Schweizer Wirtschaft, p. 82.

5 Cf. Mast, Finanzplatz Schweiz, p. 29. Foreign banks operating in Switzerland include the branches of foreign banks as well as foreign-controlled banks.

6 The major banks were: SBV, SKA, SVB, SBG, Eidgenössische Bank, Bank Leu, Basler Handelsbank.

7 Expressed in Reichsmark, total assets for 1938 came to about RM 3.75 billion. Cf. James, Deutsche Bank, p. 318. Exchange rate: RM 1 = Sfr 1.75. Cf. Ritzmann, Statistik, p. 837.

8 As at the end of 1940 (no figures are available for 1939) Midland Bank reported total assets of £ 702 million; at Crédit Lyonnais total assets at the end of 1939 were Ffr 17.8 billion. Cf. Pohl, Handbook, p. 1226 and p. 281. Exchange rate: £ 1 = Sfr 16.64, Ffr 100 = Sfr 11.12. Cf. Ritzmann, Statistik, p. 837.

9 Cf. James, Deutsche Bank, p. 405.

10 Cf. Schweizerisches Bankwesen 1938, p. 42.

11 Cf. Schweizerisches Bankwesen 1999, p. 48. ww.snb.ch/d/publikationen/banken/text_bank.html (August 2001); Die Volkswirtschaft, 6/2001, p. B8.

12 Cf. Jung, History of a Bank, p. 167.

13 Chapuis, Schweizer Banken, p. 78.

14 Cf. The Banker, July 2001. www.thebanker.com/art1july01.htm (August 2001).

15 Cf. Frech, Clearing, p. 71.

16 The convertibility of the Swedish krone was limited by currency control measures in February 1940. In November 1939, the Portuguese escudo was pegged to the dollar at a rate of Esc 25 to $ 1, though it remained freely convertible until the end of the war. Cf. Jöhr, SKA, p. 471f.; Crettol/Halbeisen, Goldtransaktionen SNB, p. 19, Note 59.

17 For more information on the figures used in the table 'Breakdown of the Swiss major banks' aggregated gross income (1938–1945)', cf. Schweizerisches Bankwesen 1945, p. 134. Interest income derives from the difference between interest charged and interest due. – For more information on the figures used in the table 'SKA: breakdown of gross income (1938–1945)', cf. profit and loss accounts, actual figures. CCA. Commission income is the difference between commissions earned and commissions paid. The 'Miscellaneous' category includes coupons, banknotes and coins, and management fees. In 1943, Sfr 1.3 million of the 'Miscellaneous' category was accounted for by surpluses on German investments. – For more information on the figures used in the table 'SVB: breakdown of gross income (1938–1945)', cf. audit reports by Neutra Treuhand AG, Zurich. CCA. The 'Miscellaneous' category includes coupons and earnings from the foreign exchange counter. – For more information on the figures used in the table 'Bank Leu: breakdown of gross income (1938–1945)', cf. audit reports by Gesellschaft für Bankrevisionen, Basel. CCA. The 'Miscellaneous' category includes coupons (Swiss and foreign), banknotes and coins, released provisions and gold operations.

18 Cf. Crettol/Halbeisen, Goldtransaktionen SNB, p. 23, 31, 41.

19 Cf. 'Die Goldtransaktionen der Schweizerischen Nationalbank 1939–1945 – Quantitative Angaben'. Remarks by Jean-Pierre Roth, Vice-Chairman of the Governing Board of the SNB, at the press conference of 20 March 1997. www.snb.ch/publikationen/publi.html (August 2001).

20 Cf. SNB 1907–1957, p. 124ff.

21 For more information on the figures used in the table 'SKA: asset management business (1938–1945)', cf. statistics on SKA's securities accounts (parent company, branches and New York Agency). CCA; SKA profit and loss accounts, actual figures. CCA.

22 Cf. statistics on SKA's rented safe deposit boxes (parent company, branches, New York Agency). CCA.

23 The growth in the value of securities between 1938 and 2000 can be calculated – as per the consumer price index – by applying a multiplier of about 7.0. This would put the value of the securities portfolio at that time, adjusted for today's purchasing power, at about Sfr 44.1 billion. – For more information on the figures used in the chart 'Securities accounts managed by SKA, by customer domicile (1944/45)', cf. statistics folder I, results 31 December 1945, miscellaneous No. 192b. CCA.

24 Cf. Schweizerisches Bankwesen 2000, p. 49.

25 Cf. in particular the relevant chapters in the annual reports of the Swiss Bankers Association and the Schweizerische Handels- und Industrieverein (Swiss Federation of Commerce and Industry) 1938 to 1944. – For more information on the figures used in the chart 'iTurnover on the Zurich and Basel stock exchanges (1938–1945)', cf. Ritzmann, Statistik, p. 833.

26 These were Eidgenössische Bank (with SBG) and Basler Handelsbank (with SBV). Cf. Jung, History of a Bank, p. 90; Seiler, Handbuch 1, p. 603.

27 For more information on the figures used in the table 'Swiss banks' foreign investments and liabilities (1938–1945)', cf. Schweizerische Nationalbank, Volkswirtschaftliche und Statistische Abteilung (Swiss National Bank, Economic and Statistics Division): Auslandanlagen and -verpflichtungen sowie Guthaben and Verpflichtungen in ausländischer Währung der schweizerischen Banken, 1938 bis 1945, June 1946.

28 Cf. Schweizerisches Bankwesen 1938, p. 112; 1941, p. 101; 1944, p. 128, 135.

29 Adjustments for inflation pushed up salaries in the banking and insurance industry by about 40% between 1939 and 1945. Cf. Schweizerisches Bankwesen 1946, p. 55ff. – For more information on the figures used in the table 'Swiss banks' net profit and major items of expenditure (1938/1945)', cf. Schweizerisches Bankwesen 1938/1946, p. 100ff. and 148ff.

30 Between 1938 and 1942 real-term per capital income – i.e. national income after adjustment for inflation and population growth – actually fell by 11%. Cf. Jöhr, SKA, p. 462. For more information on the growth of national income between 1938 and 1945 in Switzerland, cf. Ritzmann, Statistik, p. 871.

31 For more information on the figures used in the chart 'Total assets of all banks operating in Switzerland and Switzerland's national income (1930–1999)', cf. for national income Ritzmann, Statistik, p. 871, 1930–1945; Bundesamt für Statistik (Swiss Federal Statistical Office), Nationale Buchhaltung / Volkswirtschaftliche Gesamtrechnung 1950–1999, Bern/Neuchâtel. For the total assets of all banks operating in Switzerland, cf. Ritzmann, Statistik, p. 819, 1930–1975; Schweizerisches Bankwesen 1985, p. 87, 1980–1985; 1999, p. A4, 1990–1999. The figures for 1999 national income are provisional estimates.

List of tables and charts

Abbreviations

General Abbreviations

AR	Annual report
Art.	Article
AS	Amtliche Sammlung der Bundesgesetze und Verordnungen (Switzerland's official collection of federal laws and ordinances)
BAR	Schweizerisches Bundesarchiv (Swiss Federal Archives in Bern)
BBl	Bundesblatt (the Swiss government's official organ)
BIS	Bank for International Settlements
CCA	Central Corporate Archives
ch.	Chapter
CO	Swiss Code of Obligations
CSG	Credit Suisse Group
CSPB	Credit Suisse Private Banking
CTC	Custodian Trust Company Ltd.
DDS	Diplomatische Dokumente der Schweiz (Swiss Diplomatic Documents)
Doc.	Document
EMA	Effecten-Maatschappij, Amsterdam
fasc.	fascicle
FBC	Federal Banking Commission
FDEA	Federal Department of Economic Affairs
FDFA	Federal Department of Foreign Affairs
FDJP	Federal Department of Justice and Police
Fed. Reg.	Federal Register
FDF	Federal Department of Finance
FPD	Federal Political Department
H. R. Doc.	US House of Representatives Document
H. R. Rep.	US House of Representatives Report
ICE	Independent Commission of Experts Switzerland – Second World War (Bergier Commission)
ICEP	Independent Committee of Eminent Persons (Volcker Commission); now the IAEP
IRS	US Internal Revenue Service
LC SBA	Swiss Bankers Association's legal commission
NAB	Neue Aargauer Bank
NARA	United States National Archives and Records Administration
NZZ	Neue Zürcher Zeitung
OAP	Office of Alien Property (US Department of Justice)
Ra	Rechtsabteilung (SKA's legal department)
Res.	Resolution
S. Rep.	US Senate Report
SBA	Swiss Bankers Association
SBG/UBS	Schweizerische Bankgesellschaft / Union Bank of Switzerland
SBKA	Schweizerische Bodenkredit-Anstalt
SBV/SBC	Schweizerischer Bankverein / Swiss Bank Corporation
SCC	Swiss Civil Code
SCO	Swiss Compensation Office

sec.	Section
SFH	Schweizerische Zentralstelle für Flüchtlingshilfe (Swiss Refugee Council)
SFJC	Swiss Federation of Jewish Communities
SKA	Schweizerische Kreditanstalt / Credit Suisse
SNB	Swiss National Bank
Stat.	US Statutes at Large
SVB	Schweizerische Volksbank / Swiss Volksbank
Swissam	Swiss American Corporation
USC	United States Code
VSJF	Verband Schweizerischer Jüdischer Flüchtlingshilfen (Association of Swiss Jewish Refugee Relief)
Vol.	Volume
WJRO	World Jewish Restitution Organization
ZKB	Zürcher Kantonalbank / Zurich Cantonal Bank

Currencies

Sfr	Swiss franc
RM	Reichsmark
Ffr	French franc
$	US dollar

Numbers

m	million (1,000,000)
bn	billion (1,000,000,000)

Bibliography

This bibliography includes all the works quoted in the individual studies in this English version of the book as well as other selected works. Throughout the notes given at the end of each study, the sources used are referred to in abbreviated form. For reference purposes, these abbreviated forms are also given here [in square brackets] at the end of the full form. A complete bibliography can be found in the full German edition of the book 'Zwischen Bundeshaus und Paradeplatz. Die Banken der Credit Suisse Group im Zweiten Weltkrieg' by Joseph Jung.

Literature

Albers-Schönberg Heinz, Hat die Schweiz den Krieg verlängert? Handels-, Gold- und Verkehrspolitik gegenüber Deutschland im Zweiten Weltkrieg, Zurich 1999 [Albers-Schönberg, Krieg verlängert].

Albisetti Emilio et al. (ed.), Handbuch des Geld-, Bank- und Börsenwesens der Schweiz, Thun 1999⁴ [Albisetti et al., Bankwesen].

Alk Isadore G. / Moskovitz Irving, Removal of United States Controls over Foreign-Owned Property, in: The Federal Bar Journal, October 1948, p. 3–31 [Alk/Moskovitz, Removal].

Bonjour Edgar, Geschichte der schweizerischen Neutralität. Vier Jahrhunderte eidgenössischer Aussenpolitik, 9 vols., Basel/Stuttgart 1971–1980 [Bonjour, Neutralität].

Braillard Philippe, Die Schweiz im Fadenkreuz. Jüdische Vermögen und 'Nazi-Gold' – eine Autopsie, Zurich 1999 [Braillard, Fadenkreuz].

Bundesamt für Statistik (Swiss Federal Statistical Office), Nationale Buchhaltung / Volkswirtschaftliche Gesamtrechnung 1950–1999, Bern/Neuchâtel.

Castelmur Linus von, Schweizerisch-alliierte Finanzbeziehungen im Übergang vom Zweiten Weltkrieg zum Kalten Krieg. Die deutschen Guthaben in der Schweiz zwischen Zwangsliquidierung und Freigabe (1945–1952), Zurich 1997² [Castelmur, Finanzbeziehungen].

Cattani Alfred, Hitlers Schatten über Europa. Brennpunkte der Zeitgeschichte 1933–1945, Zurich 1995 [Cattani, Schatten].

Cattani Alfred, Die schweizerische Flüchtlingspolitik 1933–1945 (Schriftenreihe Pro Libertate, No. 12), Bern 1999 [Cattani, Flüchtlingspolitik].

Chapuis Jean-Paul, Die Schweizer Banken im internationalen Vergleich, in: Halbheer Hans J. / Kilgus Ernst (ed.), Der Finanzplatz Schweiz und seine Bedeutung aus nationaler und internationaler Sicht. Festgabe zum 65. Geburtstag von Dr. Hans J. Mast (Bankwirtschaftliche Forschungen, Vol. 91), Bern/Stuttgart 1985, p. 77–87 [Chapuis, Schweizer Banken].

Codevilla Angelo M., Between the Alps and a Hard Place. Switzerland in World War II and the Rewriting of History, Washington 2000 [Codevilla, Hard Place].

Crettol Vincent / Halbeisen Patrick, Die währungspolitischen Hintergründe der Goldtransaktionen der Schweizerischen Nationalbank im Zweiten Weltkrieg, Zurich 1999 [Crettol/ Halbeisen, Goldtransaktionen SNB].

Durrer Marco, Die schweizerisch-amerikanischen Finanzbeziehungen im Zweiten Weltkrieg. Von der Blockierung der schweizerischen Guthaben in den USA über die 'Safehaven'-Politik zum Washingtoner Abkommen (1941–1946), Bern/Stuttgart 1984 [Durrer, Finanzbeziehungen].

Fisch Jörg, 'Der Kriegsverlängerer'. Ein Porträt der neuesten helvetischen Erfindung, in: NZZ, 8 July 1997 [Fisch, Kriegsverlängerer].

Girsberger Daniel, Das internationale Privatrecht der nachrichtenlosen Vermögen in der Schweiz (Bibliothek zur Zeitschrift für schweizerisches Recht, Beiheft 23), Basel /Frankfurt am Main 1997 [Girsberger, Privatrecht].

Goodman Carl F., United States Government Foreign Property Controls, in: Georgetown Law Journal, 52/1964, p. 767ff. [Goodman, Foreign Property Controls].

Guggenheim Paul, Die erblosen Vermögen in der Schweiz und das Völkerrecht, in: Schweizerischer Israelitischer Gemeindebund 1904–1954. Festschrift zum 50jährigen Bestehen, Zurich 1954, p. 107–120 [Guggenheim, Erblose Vermögen].

Halbrook Stephen P., Target Switzerland. Swiss Armed Neutrality in World War II, Rockville Center NY 1998 [Halbrook, Target Switzerland].

Hofer Walther / Reginbogin Herbert R., Hitler, der Westen und die Schweiz 1936–1945, Zurich 2001 [Hofer / Reginbogin, Hitler].

James Harold, Die Deutsche Bank und die Diktatur 1933–1945, in: Gall Lothar et al., Die Deutsche Bank 1870–1995, Munich 1995, p. 315–408 [James, Deutsche Bank].

Jöhr Walter Adolf, Schweizerische Kreditanstalt 1856–1956, Zurich 1956 [Jöhr, SKA].

Jung Joseph, Winterthur. The History of an Insurance Company, Zurich 2001 [Jung, History of an Insurance Company].

Jung Joseph, From Schweizerische Kreditanstalt to Credit Suisse Group. The History of a Bank, Zurich 2000 [Jung, History of a Bank].

Kellenberger Eduard, Theorie und Praxis des schweizerischen Geld-, Bank- und Börsenwesens seit Ausbruch des Weltkrieges (1914–1939), fasc. 3: Kapitalexport und Zahlungsbilanz; Vol. II: Im Konjunkturzyklus der dreissiger Jahre, Bern 1942 [Kellenberger, Kapitalexport].

Lambelet Jean-Christian, Kritische Würdigung des Bergier-Berichts 'Die Schweiz und die Flüchtlinge zur Zeit des Nationalsozialismus', in: Schweizer Monatshefte, 3/2000, p. 7–15 [Lambelet, Kritische Würdigung].

Lambelet Jean-Christian, Le mobbing d'un petit pays. Onze thèses sur la Suisse pendant la Deuxième Guerre mondiale, Lausanne 1999 [Lambelet, Mobbing].

Littauer Rudolph M., Defrosting of Foreign Funds, in: World Trade Law Journal, 1/1946, p. 163ff. [Littauer, Defrosting].

Mast Hans J., Finanzplatz Schweiz – Fluch oder Segen? (Schriftenreihe der Schweizerischen Kreditanstalt, fasc. 42), Zurich 1977 [Mast, Finanzplatz Schweiz].

Mast Hans J., Das schweizerische Bankwesen (Schriftenreihe der Schweizerischen Kreditanstalt, fasc. 27), Zurich 1977.

Mast Hans J., The Swiss Banking Industry (Credit Suisse Special Publications, Vol. 51), Zurich 1978.

Picard Jacques, Die Schweiz und die Vermögen verschwundener Nazi-Opfer. Die Vermögen rassisch, religiös und politisch Verfolgter in der Schweiz und ihre Ablösung von 1946 bis 1973, in: Studien und Quellen, 22/1996 [Picard, Schweiz].

Pohl Manfred (ed.), Handbook on the History of European Banks, Frankfurt am Main 1994 [Pohl, Handbook].

Reeves William H., Displaced Corporations in War Time – Switzerland's Answer, in: The Business Lawyer, November 1958, p. 205–213 [Reeves, Displaced Corporations].

Reeves William H., Private Foreign Capital and United States Policy: Is Confiscation of Enemy Assets in the National Interest?, in: Virginia Law Review, December 1954, p. 1ff. [Reeves, Capital].

Reeves William H., The Control of Foreign Funds by the United States Treasury, in: Duke Law Journal, Winter-Spring issue 1945, p. 17–60 [Reeves, Control].

Reinhardt Eberhard, Die Entwicklung Zürichs zum Finanzplatz. Separatabdruck aus: Schweizerische Zeitschrift für Kaufmännisches Bildungswesen, 1953 [Reinhardt, Finanzplatz Zürich].

Ritzmann-Blickenstorfer Heiner (ed.), Historische Statistik der Schweiz, Zurich 1996 [Ritzmann, Statistik].

Schiemann Catherine, Neutralität in Krieg und Frieden. Die Aussenpolitik der Vereinigten Staaten gegenüber der Schweiz 1941–1949. Eine diplomatiegeschichtliche Untersuchung, Zurich 1991 [Schiemann, Neutralität].

Schweizerische Bankgesellschaft (publ.), Die Schweizer Wirtschaft 1946–1986. Daten, Fakten, Analysen, Zurich 1987 [SBG, Schweizer Wirtschaft].

Schweizerische Nationalbank (publ.), Das schweizerische Bankwesen im Jahre 1930ff. Mitteilungen des Statistischen Bureaus der Schweizerischen Nationalbank (from 1996: Die Banken in der Schweiz), Zurich 1931ff. [Schweizerisches Bankwesen …].

Schweizerische Nationalbank 1907–1957, Zurich 1957 [SNB 1907–1957].

Schweizerische Nationalbank, Volkswirtschaftliche und Statistische Abteilung: Auslandanlagen und -verpflichtungen sowie Guthaben und Verpflichtungen in ausländischer Währung der schweizerischen Banken, 1938 bis 1945, June 1946.

Seiler Franz, 'Hotelsanierung', in: Handbuch der schweizerischen Volkswirtschaft, herausgegeben von der Schweizerischen Gesellschaft für Statistik und Volkswirtschaft, Bern 1939, Vol. 1, p. 601–604 [Seiler, Handbuch].

Speich Sebastian et al., Die Schweiz am Pranger. Banken, Bosse und die Nazis, Vienna 1997 [Speich, Schweiz].

Trepp Gian, Der Finanzplatz Schweiz im 2. Weltkrieg. Was wussten und tolerierten die Alliierten?, Zurich 1997 [Trepp, Finanzplatz].

Vogler Robert Urs, Das Bankgeheimnis – seine Genese im politisch-wirtschaftlichen Umfeld, in: Schweizer Monatshefte, 3/2000, p. 37–43 [Vogler, Bankgeheimnis].

Wagner Meir, The Righteous of Switzerland. Heroes of the Holocaust, Hoboken NJ 2001 [Wagner, Righteous].

Weill Pierre, Der Milliarden-Deal. Holocaust-Gelder – wie sich die Schweizer Banken freikauften, Zurich 1999 [Weill, Milliarden-Deal].

Winzeler Christoph / Beutter Friedrich, Das Bankkundengeheimnis, Bern 2001 [Winzeler/Beutter, Bankgeheimnis].

Studies and reports

Arthur Andersen, Report to IAEP on the Credit Suisse Group (Final Draft), 12 July 1999 [Arthur Andersen, Report].

Arthur Andersen, Interim Report on Phase 2. Forensic Accounting Investigation, 18 June 1998 [Arthur Andersen, Interim Report].

Plunder and Restitution: The U.S. and Holocaust Victims' Assets. Report to the President of the Presidential Advisory Commission on Holocaust Assets in the United States, Washington 2000 [Bronfman Report].

Eizenstat Stuart E. (ed.), U.S. and Allied Efforts to Recover and Restore Gold and Other Assets Stolen or Hidden by Germany During World War II. Preliminary Study prepared by William Z. Slany, Washington 1997 [Eizenstat 1997].

Frech Stefan, Clearing. Der Zahlungsverkehr der Schweiz mit den Achsenmächten (Veröffentlichungen …, Vol. 3), Zurich 2001 [Frech, Clearing].

Hug Peter / Perrenoud Marc, Assets in Switzerland of Victims of Nazism and the Compensation Agreements with East Bloc Countries. Report on Historical Investigations, Commissioned by the Swiss Federal Government, Federal Department for Foreign Affairs, Task Force, 29 October 1996 (Federal Archive dossier 4), Bern 1996 [Hug/Perrenoud, Assets].

Independent Committee of Eminent Persons, Report on Dormant Accounts of Victims of Nazi Persecution in Swiss Banks, 1999 [ICEP, Report].

Junz Helen B., Report on the Pre-War Wealth Position of the Jewish Population in Nazi-Occupied Countries, Germany, and Austria, in: Independent Committee of Eminent Persons, Report on Dormant Accounts of Victims of Nazi Persecution in Swiss Banks, 1999, appendix S, p. A-127–A-206 [Junz, Report].

Independent Commission of Experts Switzerland – Second World War: Switzerland, National Socialism, and the Second World War. Final Report, Zurich, 2002.

Newspapers and magazines

The Banker, Bund, The Business Lawyer, Duke Law Journal, Federal Bar Journal, Georgetown Law Journal, Kurier, Neue Zürcher Zeitung (NZZ), Virginia Law Review, Voix ouvrière, Die Volkswirtschaft, World Trade Law Journal.

Acknowledgements

The original impetus behind this academic reassessment of Credit Suisse Group's history came in 1996 from Rainer E. Gut, Chairman of the Board of Directors of Credit Suisse Group (1983–2000). The mandate subsequently issued by the Executive Board of the then Schweizerische Kreditanstalt (Credit Suisse) was twofold: to view and sort the bank's archived documents and thus create new, professionally organized Central Corporate Archives; to review the history of the bank in the Second World War and then the history of SKA as a whole.

In the wake of the complete restructuring that followed shortly afterwards, this mandate was extended to the new Credit Suisse Group. The first results of the ensuing research were published in 2000 ('From Schweizerische Kreditanstalt to Credit Suisse Group. The History of a Bank', NZZ Publishing). Lukas Mühlemann, Chairman of the Board of Directors (since 2000) and Chief Executive Officer (since 1997) of Credit Suisse Group, made the publication of this volume and the original German edition possible. I would like to take this opportunity to first thank both Rainer E. Gut and Lukas Mühlemann for their continued support and for allowing the freedom without which proper research would not be possible. Please see the orginal edition ('Zwischen Bundeshaus und Paradeplatz. Die Banken der Credit Suisse Group im Zweiten Weltkrieg. Studien und Materialien') for a list of all the people who contributed to the production of this work by discussing specific topics in more detail and providing valuable information and insights. The original edition also lists all the archives, libraries and documentation units that kindly made material available.

Thanks to Dr. Hans J. Mast for agreeing to write a study of Swiss banking during the Second World War. Many thanks also to Dr. Werner de Capitani, Dr. Alfred Schaufelberger and Philip Hess for their invaluable advice.

Special thanks go to the current and former employees of Credit Suisse Group's Corporate History and Archives department.

The studies, articles and documentation relating to Credit Suisse Group are the product of wide-ranging research and systematic assessment of sources. The various stages of this work and the production of the basic texts were carried out by research teams whose personnel changed over the years. The names of all the people involved can also be found in the original German edition of this book. The following people, to whom I am very grateful, worked on the main sections translated for this English edition:

Swiss-American financial relations: Dr. Helen Oplatka-Steinlin (November 1996 to December 1998), Martin Trachsler (October 1997 to May 2001), Nicole Schenker.
Dormant accounts: Peter Allemann (March 1998 to May 2000), Andreas Schiendorfer (January 1999 to September 2001), Dr. Ulrich Vonrufs (April 1998 to September 2000).

I would also like to thank V. Elizabeth Powell for her work on the translations, Edgar Haberthür for his meticulous proofreading, Roger Turin for producing the charts, and Heinz Egli, NZZ Publishing, for all his help.

Finally, I am very grateful to James Knight for translating these texts into English.

Joseph Jung